D0884990

Other Books Sponsored
by the American Institute of Planners

Environment for Man: The Next Fifty Years
Environment and Change: The Next Fifty Years

Environment and Policy

The Next Fifty Years

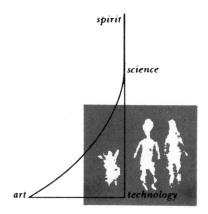

Based on papers commissioned for the American Institute of Planners'
two-year consultation, Part II: The Washington Conference, October 1-6,
1967

ENVIRONMENT AND POLICY

THE NEXT FIFTY YEARS

Commissioned and Edited by
WILLIAM R. EWALD, JR., AIP
on behalf of the
American Institute of Planners'
Fiftieth Year Consultation

INDIANA UNIVERSITY PRESS

Bloomington & London

SECOND PRINTING 1970

Copyright © 1968 by Indiana University Press

All rights reserved

Published in Canada by Fitzhenry & Whiteside Limited, Scarborough, Ontario

Library of Congress catalog card number: 68-27344

Manufactured in the United States of America

253-12265-1 cl   253-12266-X pa

Contents

Preface

The title of this consultation commemorating the Fiftieth Anniversary of the American Institute of Planners, THE NEXT FIFTY YEARS, was chosen deliberately. Like the old reprobate who said "Regardless of my past, my future is unspotted," we make bold a hope that this commemoration will make a significant turning point in directing the growth and well-being of our American urbanization.

Despite some fifty years of intensive planning endeavor, we face today an urban crisis of formidable character. The large city, or metropolitan community, is one of the most complex of man's creations. Full control of its character and growth is yet to be achieved. As planners, we can give form and shape to the community, both small and large;

but we have learned that great social and economic problems can soon distort, even destroy, the best of plans.

Our problem today, the urban crisis, calls for most complete coordination of all those forces that produce the modern city. Planning and building the most complete transportation system will not eliminate blighted districts and slums. Complete and comprehensive housing reform and control, by itself, will not produce an efficient and attractive city. More is needed. This more is what we have failed to discover.

Let us hope that this consultation will sharpen our understanding, clarify our objectives, and will inspire the leadership required to meet the challenge of this urban crisis.

It is generally assumed that our urban population will double in the next thirty to forty years. It is also assumed that most of this enormous added population will find accommodation within our 250 or so metropolitan cities. Does this really make sense—and especially so when we consider our failure to solve our present problems of slums, of air and water pollution, of traffic congestion, not to mention others?

While we have great technological ability with which to deal with some of these problems, can we truly solve them all—and at what cost?

We did not consciously plan this great concentration of population. Should we blindly continue to follow such an obvious policy of laissez-faire or has the time not come when we should consider a deliberate planned policy of a more rational pattern of population distribution? In the long run it should involve far less cost, produce greatly superior urban environment, and result in much greater human satisfaction.

The American Institute of Planners and our cosponsors have gone to great length to bring together the expertise that is needed to think through with us the creation of a proper urban environment for our ever burgeoning population. It is hoped that we can examine, resolve, and help to stimulate action on four things: the plans to be made, the steps to be taken in their implementation, creation of the widest possible public understanding, and the leadership required. These cannot be achieved without prodigious effort. As planners, must we not provide the required initiative at this most crucial stage of the development of the American city?

In this preface I would like to acknowledge on behalf of all of the members of the American Institute of Planners the tremendous debt that we owe the sponsoring groups. Without their great assistance in both moral encouragement and substantial backing, it would be quite impossible to conduct such a Fiftieth Anniversary consultation; and so we thank particularly all of those groups—corporate, public, citizens', and religious—which have done so much during the past several years to make it possible.

Benefactors:
 American Institute of Planners
  and all chapters of the Institute
 The Ford Foundation
 Rockefeller Brothers Fund
 University of California
 U.S. Department of Housing
  and Urban Development
 U.S. Public Health Service

Patrons:
 Central Hudson Gas & Electric Corporation
 Edison Electric Institute
 Episcopal Church
 General Electric Company
 International Business Machines
 Lutheran Churches of America
 Maryland-National Capital Park and
  Planning Commission
 A. W. Mellon Educational and Charitable Trust
 Methodist Church
 National Council of Churches
 National Science Foundation
 Shell Oil Company
 United Presbyterian Church
 University of Notre Dame
 Urban America, Inc.

Organizations which gave other valuable assistance:
 American Academy of Arts and Sciences
 American Academy of Political and Social Sciences
 American Institute of Architects
 American Society of Civil Engineers
 American Society of Landscape Architects
 American Society of Planning Officials
 Building Research Institute
 Committee for Economic Development
 Hudson Institute
 Indiana University Press

Kaiser Aluminum and Chemical Corporation
National Association of Housing and Redevelopment Officials
The Rand Corporation
Science Information Exchange
Smithsonian Institution
Society for Applied Anthropology
Society for the Psychological Study of Social Issues
Stanford Research Institute
Trans-action Magazine
U.S. Department of Housing and Urban Development
U.S. Public Health Service
World Futurist Society
Xerox Corporation

Individuals who made a special personal effort to finance the consultation:

A. D. Asbury
Harland Bartholomew
D. S. Bennett
T. Ledyard Blakeman
Isadore Candeub
Frederick P. Clark
Malcolm H. Dill
W. C. Dutton
William R. Ewald, Jr.
Irving G. Ewen
William E. Finley
Donald B. Gutoff
Stephen A. Kaufman
Barnaby C. Keeney
Philip M. Klutznick
Peter A. Larson
Aaron Levine
Harold M. Lewis

C. David Loeks
Howard K. Menhinick
Martin Meyerson
Louis B. Muhly
Perry L. Norton
Robert M. O'Donnell
Paul Oppermann
Lawrence M. Orton
Russell H. Riley
Glenn A. Rick
W. G. Roeseler
George H. Smeath
Marvin R. Springer
Alan M. Voorhees
Donald H. Wolbrink
Robert N. Young
S. B. Zisman

HARLAND BARTHOLOMEW, Chairman
Fiftieth Anniversary Committee
American Institute of Planners

Environment and Policy

The Next Fifty Years

William R. Ewald, Jr.
Development Consultant, Washington, D.C.

*Consultant to the AIP Project on the Next Fifty Years
and Program Chairman of Part II—The Washington Conference*

Introduction

The papers collected here were commissioned for Part II of the American Institute of Planners' two-year examination into THE NEXT FIFTY YEARS/ 1967–2017, The Future Environment of a Democracy.

Part I culminated in Portland, Oregon, in August, 1966. It attempted to handle such questions as: If we had the technology and the economy —both said to be imminent—what kind of environment would we build? What could environment contribute to a "good" day? The Institute's multidisciplinary conference that year, Optimum Environment—with Man as the Measure, began an effort to organize thinking in those terms.

Breaking new ground, the Portland conference examined the physiological, psychological, and sociological impacts of the physical environment. It raised the basic question: how do we turn from an environment

3

designed by expedience, based on tolerable minimums, to understanding and seeking the optimum environment? From the searchings made in the papers presented in Portland, it was clear that science is not prepared to define either "optimum" or "environment," nor has it measured Man in his own terms. Further, it was evident that the values by which we might establish priorities to research the optimum environment are not yet understood. (See *Environment for Man: The Next Fifty Years,* Indiana University Press, 1967).

In Part II—The Washington Conference, October, 1967, AIP was host to an effort that strove: (1) to explore for the philosophy and values we as people choose as guides into THE NEXT FIFTY YEARS; (2) to understand the pending rates of change in the development of technology and our society in these fast-moving times; (3) to begin a nationwide discussion of the policies and programs we must consider if we truly understand our values and the pending rates of change and intend to build a truly human environment in THE NEXT FIFTY YEARS.

This book is built around the policy-program resource papers of thirteen of the fourteen authors commissioned for the Washington Conference.* To assist these authors Committees of Correspondence were established. An outstanding member of the American Institute of Planners served as chairman, but full responsibility for the proposals was the individual author's, not that of his advisory committee or of the Institute. To further assure the objectivity of this policy-program investigation, critiques were commissioned for each paper, totally independent of the Committees of Correspondence. The title, Committees of Correspondence, was selected to link this effort concerned with the tyranny of the environment with the Committees of Correspondence of Samuel Adams' days, concerned with the tyranny of a king.

Another group of papers commissioned for the Washington Conference articulates the philosophy needed to cause a creative development of our environment. (See *Environment and Change: The Next Fifty Years,* Indiana University Press, 1968). They examine the need to look further ahead in these fast-moving times than we are used to doing. They define as art, spirit, science, and technology the empirical and nonempirical forces at work in creating the environment. The history of our evolving planning institutions and urban life (conceived in administrative, political, physical, social, and economic terms) is investigated, and study made of the impacts from technology, the new

---

* The fourteenth paper is included in the other conference volume, *Environment and Change: The Next Fifty Years* (Bloomington: Indiana University Press, 1968).

scale of life and new rates of change. There evolves in these papers a growing comprehension of the need to develop systems to order this complex mix of components.

Further, philosophic statements concerning the future role of the individual and society were developed. What values do we believe we want to enhance? What preparations for change are needed for society and for the individual? What is the desired relation of society, the individual, and human institutions? Finally, the predominantly national focus was widened to put the conference in the real context of the future—youth, technology, and the world community. In sum, the book *Environment and Change: The Next Fifty Years* is a statement of philosophy, values, and forces of change.

It can be seen the Washington Conference taken as a whole dealt with moral and philosophical issues. Yet it attempted to bring this level of abstraction down to "stream of time" specifics with applicable recommendations. That was the primary responsibility of the authors and the Committees of Correspondence—the papers of this book. These statements are intended to make explicit enough for national discussion the issues which the basically short-term oriented institutions of our society need to learn how to consider.

Each author in preparing his statement of policies and programs for the next fifty years was asked to state:
1. Steps to be taken by 1970, 1980, 2000, and 2020;
2. Implications at world, U.S., multistate region, state, multicounty region, and local scales;
3. The professional disciplines needed.
It was not expected that each paper would give equal emphasis to all points. It is difficult, if not impossible, for example, to imagine the professional manpower required to build an undefined future. It is an effort that nevertheless was made.

The stream-of-time perspective was deliberately included in the charge to each author to foreclose any leaping to unchallengeable recommendations concerning what should be done *beginning* fifty years from now. It also was intended to avoid short-term expedients that did not have the seeds of the future in them.

Each author was provided a basic set of projections of population, GNP, etc., through 2017, especially prepared by the Hudson Institute. Each author also received statements of the consultation's purpose, a "stand-in" philosophy statement, and a special bibliography and research service organized for them by the consultation core staff. It was expected that authors would choose different levels of detail, or emphasize requirements of a particular location or time. By asking that all papers cover the same basic points, all starting from a common base, it was felt a more useful product would result.

It is perhaps necessary to say that the policy and program recommendations sought for each of these thirteen areas of great importance in American life were sought for the entire nation, the rural areas—both prospering and impoverished—and the small towns, as well as for the totally urbanized life we are told to expect. The wilderness and the open beach and the spaciousness of our land are a part of our national psyche whether we all use them or not. We did not intend that these papers focus exclusively on the great metropolitan regions of the future, though we expected emphasis there.

Perhaps it should be repeated here that it is the creative development of the individual and his development of his society that is our concern. The so-called pragmatic nuts-and-bolts, short-term view was considered static and nonproductive for the purposes of this work. A definition of pragmatic by the AIP consultation would include something that works in the future.

Preceding each commissioned paper in this book there is reproduced the original charge as made to the author. These charges were not considered to be either absolutely restrictive or absolutely complete. They were indicative. Complete freedom was assured within the ground rules of the points to be covered by every paper. It was understood that the mission of each paper was to make explicit statements of policy and program with cost implications where possible. The President's Commission on National Goals, "Goals for Americans"; the Rockefeller Reports, "Prospects for America" and "The Pursuit of Excellence, Education, and the Future of America"; and other studies supplied to the authors and committees were recognized as the base on which to build. It was hoped to move on from there. Some papers were expected to have more policy than program in them and vice versa.

To test the soundness and validity of these papers, and to assure the objectivity of purpose of the consultation, two independent critiques of each were commissioned. The critiques follow each paper. Committee comments are sometimes included as notes to a paper. A special paper by the Surgeon General has also been included in this book.

Selection of the papers to be given at the 1967 conference was determined after a special meeting of the AIP executive committee in Montreal, late in May, 1967. Even those selected were necessarily summarized in their final presentation at the conference.

Here then, available intact for the first time, are the commissioned papers and their critiques for policy-program recommendations to the American Institute of Planners' Fiftieth Year Conference, THE NEXT FIFTY YEARS—The Future Environment of a Democracy.

PART I

The Urgent
and the Important

Minority Groups: Development of the Individual

This paper was commissioned to deal with the current flagrant abuse of minorities, but with a difference. It is proposed that the obvious destruction of identity and mental health in minority groups (especially those in poverty under the present social welfare system), can be considered as a forewarning for *all* minorities of the society, should our society become mass or strict-majority oriented. How, with this example before us, do we establish means to assure that the development of the environment over the next fifty years is also a development of the individual—with the latter given the priority? What are the impacts of what we do now to minorities? How can we work on this?

Must an urban society give up freedom to achieve personal safety?

The question of job opportunities, civil peace, good housing, good use of leisure time, and the motivation for retraining in a technological society may or may not be a question of participation in society's basic decisions. How is this to be considered?

Author: Bayard Rustin, Executive Director, A. Philip Randolph Institute
Chairman: Paul Davidoff, Associate AIP, Director, Graduate Division, Urban Planning Program, Hunter College
Committee: Tom Kahn, Executive Director, League for Industrial Democracy; John Kenneth Galbraith, Harvard University; Gerhard Colm, Chief Economist, National Planning Association; Elizabeth Wickenden, Technical Consultant, National Social Welfare Assembly; Albert Mayer, AIP, Architect; Leslie W. Dunbar, Executive Director, The Field Foundation; Herbert Gans, Center for Urban Education; Leon H. Keyserling, Economist; Walter Thabit, AIP, Planning Consultant

Bayard Rustin

Executive Director
A. Philip Randolph Institute

Minority Groups:
Development of the Individual

It would appear that the public morality in America at the present time is being dominated, to an alarming degree, by a concern with technological and corporate priorities. This concern, quite naturally, ignores the problems and aspirations of the ordinary individual, particularly the individual who is not equipped either by spiritual inclination or technical training to participate in the processes and values by which these priorities are pursued. A humane culture as we have imagined it and dreamed of it in America, and which at certain periods of our history has appeared possible, seems today to be on the verge of being sacrificed to the special exigencies of the marketplace: That is to say, as the new technological and organizational obsession spreads, the possibility of our creating an engaged social conscience recedes further and further into the background, leaving more and more people, particularly our minorities, stranded and neglected in a deepening mire of social and economic problems.

This, I must concede, is in some ways a familiar process. The roots of the crisis in which the individual life now finds itself are deep in the processes that for a long time have been at work in the cultural and economic history of the West: We have been victims not only of faulty planning, but also, in crucial respects, of no humane planning at all. As Michael Harrington remarks in *The Accidental Century*:

> History, after all, has always been stumbling into new social systems. The industrial revolution and the capitalist economy were neither anticipated nor planned. The English in the 17th century thought that their upheaval was over theology, the French of the eighteenth that theirs was over philosophy. In retrospect, each event had more to do with the rise of a business civilization than with either God or man. . . . This accidental revolution is the sweeping and unprecedented technological transformation of the Western environment which has been, and is being, carried out in a casual way. In it, this technology is essentially under private control and used for private purposes; this situation is justified in the name of a conservative ideology; and the byproduct is a historical change which would have staggered the imagination of any nineteenth century visionary. In following their individual aims, industrialists blundered into a social revolution. There is indeed an invisible hand in all of this. Only it is shaping an unstable new world rather than Adam Smith's middle-class harmony.[1]

If it is true, as seems probable, that more and more of our cities will be the homes of the very poor and the very rich, that generations of poor will breed more generations of poor, that crime and mental disorder will increase, and that the gap between the very rich and the very poor will increase, then there can be no doubt in the minds of those who retain a belief in a humane future that one of our higher social priorities in the coming decades must be the development of an environment of conditions compatible with, or dedicated to, the restoration of the dignity of the individual, particularly those who have been most grievously victimized. That dignity cannot be achieved unless man is able to control his environment, rather than having his environment control him, as happens today. To cite Michael Harrington again: "The hope for the survival and fulfillment of the Western concept of man demands that the accidental revolution be made conscious and democratic."[2]

In preparing ourselves for this task, and in seeking to enlist the cooperation and support of some of the major institutions in our society, one of the efforts we will have to make is to demand of people more than private expressions of their commitment, which, as we well know, have never been in short supply in America. We have seen on many occasions that while many Americans have been ready to confess personal anguish and declare personal morality, they have nevertheless been quite prepared to go along with business as usual. They have, in other words, been far less ready to mobilize these personal concerns—assuming them to be sincere—into any concerted social action to bring about necessary social change. This must be deeply troubling, because the problems we are in, and the greater problems we face, are not going to be solved by token individual concern, but by relating commitment to practical action in behalf of social and economic change, and also by the institution of conscious and democratic planning.

There are many examples in our history of people who declared their personal commitment, but who remained hesitant to place themselves in the service of causes to bring about broad social change. Let me cite two of these examples. One night, one of our founding fathers had a frightening dream. He dreamed that he saw America being torn asunder by slavery. On waking, he inserted into his will a provision for the manumitting of his slaves upon his death. But like Pilate of old, who had found no fault whatever with the accused, all that great American did was to wash his personal hands of a great moral issue. What he ought to have done was to have followed the full moral implications of his dream and put the full weight of his power and prestige behind measures in the Congress of the land to abolish the brutal institution of slavery. Instead, several decades later, when that founding father had, we suppose, won a place for his private conscience in heaven, the nation was indeed being torn asunder by one of the bloodiest civil wars in human history.

In a more recent example, during the summer of 1966, Martin Luther King, Jr., was stoned and spat upon in Chicago while helping Negroes to fight segregation, one of the continuing legacies of slavery. Many people, confessing themselves of liberal sympathies, claimed that they were shocked by the treatment received by Dr. King. They referred to King's attackers as bigots, racists, and old Nazis. Yet the truth of the matter is that none of these people, proud as they claimed to be of their liberalism, cared to involve themselves deeply in efforts to bring about the kind of social and economic change in Chicago that would have made the demonstrations which King led unnecessary, or, since they were necessary, that would have made it possible for him to exercise his democratic right free of the threat of such ugly reprisals.

Therefore, I repeat: to do the things that need to be done to restore decency and concern to the problems and aspirations of the individual, some way must be found to mobilize personal commitment and personal morality into an affirmative surge of national action and will.

At the heart of this problem—the dehumanization, demoralization, and exclusion of the individual from the prevailing concerns of our society— is the problem of our minorities. And increasingly today the heart of our minority problem is being located in the urban centers of our nation. None of us—even those who are least interested in solutions—can have escaped the sense of fear and frustration that is building up in our cities, perhaps toward an explosion whose effects we might not be able to control. And none of us can deny that this situation is being brought about by the gradual diminution of social morality and social concern for the value of the individual. As minorities are driven to the cities in search of a better life, those in a position to help them fulfill these aspirations shrink from them to the greener suburbs, leaving behind growing reservoirs of helplessness and misery.

This is by no means an excessive estimate. An objective profile of what the cities will look like in the year 1980, or even 2000, gives no less cause for concern. In a paper written for the Center for the Study of Democratic Institutions, Victor Palmieri, president of the Janss Corporation, states:

> Within the next two decades—probably by 1980—the core area of almost every major metropolitan city of the United States will be a racial—predominantly black—island. This is not a speculation. It is already very largely a fact in Washington, Chicago, and New York City. It is rapidly becoming a fact in Detroit, Philadelphia, and Los Angeles. Three established factors—the rate of population growth among minority groups (almost three times that of the white population in the City of Los Angeles); the increasing income level and mobility of middle class white families; and the resulting domino effect on racially impacted school districts—will maintain the velocity of the trend and virtually guarantee its ultimate outcome. . . . This, then, is the city of the future—the very near future. A black island spreading like a giant ink blot over the heart of a metropolis which is bankrupt financially and paralyzed politically.[3]

One doesn't even have to wait for tomorrow. The situation as it presently exists in the cities is frightening enough. Heads of minority families are demoralized by the lack of the kind of employment that would enable them to support their families in dignity and decency. Crime and drug addiction increase as young men and women cast about to find a way out of the pressures of their situation. The transportation system is inadequate. We do not have schools that take into account the lives and backgrounds of the minorities nor the need to prepare them to play a profitable or meaningful part in the technological revolution. We do not have housing that minorities feel is decent enough for them to live in. There is a shortage of the kind of work that can create in them a feeling of self-respect. The air is being poisoned. The rivers are contaminated. The slums grow, and the conditions in them become more intolerable every day.

It is in the face of this situation that white majorities become fearful of their mental and economic security and the minorities become more and more frustrated. The privileged majorities either retreat into pockets of resistance or flee to the suburbs, a flight, incidentally, which the government has been subsidizing for years now by the building of new highways and the establishment of suburban housing. While the white majority has been able to find these outlets for their fear, there has been no outlet for minority frustration except in rioting. The cycle seems so vicious that I am convinced that this whole problem—the problem of our minorities and of our cities—grows out of one source, and that is fundamental social immorality in our society; the failure or unwillingness to establish humane priorities; the absence of a major public commitment to eradicate poverty and slums.

Of course, it would be a mistake to believe that these conditions penalize only the ethnic minorities. Studies such as Michael Harrington's *The Other America* show that the white poor in some of the cities and in certain rural areas of America are every bit as deprived and demoralized as are the black and other minority poor. What is interesting and startling in this regard is that the white poor remain relatively quiescent, due no doubt to the fact that there are forces at work in the society which inhibit them from forming a common front with other minorities to find common remedies for their common problems. No one minority segment can, in the present circumstances of American economic life, lift themselves up by their own bootstraps; and therefore there can only be the most limited gains from the lonely struggle being waged by the black poor, the Puerto Ricans, and the Mexican Americans. The reason for their lonely struggle is not that blacks and other ethnic minorities are any more convinced of the need for social change than are poor whites, but that the poor whites are convinced, from their belief in some of the racial assumptions of the society, that they are superior to Negroes and other minorities. This is another instance of what I mean by saying that the plight of the poor and other minorities is the result of moral, social, and economic contradictions in our society.

For a general overview of the factors at work against the American worker, black and white alike, I will quote again from the *Accidental Century* and then from the AFL-CIO. Harrington writes:

> Between 1909 and 1962, American industry increased the worker's output by 2.4 percent a year. But then, this five-decade trend conceals a most significant shift. From 1909 to 1947, the productivity gain was only 2 percent a year. But between 1958 and 1963, productivity per man-hour went up 3.1 percent a year. And it was, of course, in this period of accelerated productivity growth in the fifties and early sixties that automation and cybernation began to emerge as an important factor in the American economy.
>
> Translate these gross quantities into some of their significant details. In 1964, ten men could produce as many automobile motor blocks as 400 men in 1954; two workers could make a thousand radios a day, a job that required 200 a few years before; 14 operators were tending the glass-blowing machines that manufactured 90 percent of all the glass bulbs in the United States of America. During the fifties, Bell Telephone increased its volume by 50 percent and its work force by only 10 percent.
>
> This same trend also illumines an economic paradox: the coexistence, in the late fifties and early sixties, of prosperity and chronic unemployment. More unskilled and semiskilled jobs in private manufacture were destroyed than created, and joblessness persisted at over 5 percent of the work force despite the prosperity (this 5-percent figure is an understatement; it does not count those driven out of the labor market, possibly a million and a half workers, nor the underemployed; a "true" estimate of involuntary idleness would be in the neighborhood of 9 percent). At the same time, the machines were the source of enormous profit, and thus there was a deformed "prosperity," benign for corporations, malignant for millions of workers.[4]

And a resolution at the twenty-fourth meeting of the AFL-CIO executive council, August, 1966, pointed out:

> Profits have skyrocketed—moving up far out of line with wage and salaries. The result has been increased living costs that have washed out much of the value of workers' wage gains. In the past year, the buying power of most workers' take-home pay has hardly advanced at all.
> • Corporate profits soared 52 percent before taxes, and 67 percent after payment of taxes.
> • Dividend payments to stockholders rose 43 percent.

- Weekly take-home pay of factory workers increased only 21 percent and, in terms of buying power, merely 13 percent.
- Total wages, salary and fringe benefits of all employees in the entire economy increased only 33 percent—reflecting increased employment, as well as gains in wages and salaries. This trend continues in 1966, with wages and salaries lagging behind the sharp rise of profits and dividends.[5]

I myself wrote in the November, 1966, issue of *Federationist* magazine that a vicious cycle was being set in motion:

Failing to deal with the social and economic roadblocks to equality, we stoke the fire of frustration in the ghetto; violent riots and cries of "black power" in turn feed a white backlash which makes constructive solutions to the problems of blacks and whites more difficult. Finally, backlash only confirms Negro isolationists in their hostility toward white America. We are today at the crossroads. Within the next 50 years, if the cycle of fear and frustration is not broken, if the just economic demands of the labor movement are not coupled with the democratic aspirations of the Negro people, and if men of goodwill do not join in the fight for programs such as the Freedom Budget for all Americans, which would end poverty within the next ten years in this country, then we may very well be propelled into a racial nightmare. And not only the ethnic minorities will benefit from the Freedom Budget; 75 percent of the poor are white. All of us are affected by the persistence of poverty—in the conditions of our neighborhoods and schools, in our tax rates and public services, in the quality of our lives.[6]

Areas of Minority Problems

The excluded and victimized minorities are composed basically of three groups: (1) those who, through no fault of their own, cannot find work; (2) those who work but do not make enough money to live decently; and (3) those who are physically and psychologically incapable of working, or who, because they are too young or too old to work, are not provided for. And finally, to identify a feature that touches upon all three groups, these minorities are primarily people who, because of their race, their color, or their creed, are deemed to be unequal to the others. Therefore, any solution of the problem of our minorities, of their morale and identity, must deal in one way or another with all of the above conditions.

Let us look at some of the specific areas of minority problems, how they developed, how we can attack them, and, in attacking them, how we can restore individual dignity to the lives of our minorities.

The Ghetto

Many of the proposals which have been made to improve the ghetto seem to center around the need to renovate them and make them more habitable. I find myself in basic disagreement with this approach. The problem of the ghetto cannot be solved with scotch tape, string, and paste. It is a problem which needs to be attacked radically, which is to say, at the roots. Therefore, rather than attempt to improve the ghetto, what we need to do is tear it down, physically and spiritually. We ought to make it possible for many people who up until now have been forced to live there to move out into new towns and communities and neighborhoods; we ought to make it possible for some to make a voluntary decision to remain there; and we ought to make it possible for others who are now living outside to move in without fear of feeling degraded. Let us not forget the fundamental nature of the ghetto: no amount of repairing can remove from it the stigma of what the society says it is—a reservation in which to keep people whom the larger society does not care to associate with and whose problems it has no interest in dealing with.[7]

The people who are most overcome by the spirit of the ghetto are the young people, those bursting with optimism, hope, and a sense of possibility, but who are forced to make a truce with the reality that there is nowhere outside for them to go. The result is that they turn in on themselves and on their own neighbors with self-destructive frustration and violence. We cannot afford to preserve, in any form, an environment that breeds such bitterness, such despair. Arthur Dunmeyer, a young man from Harlem, in his testimony before the Ribicoff Committee in Washington, expressed as graphically as I have ever heard what it means for a young man to deal with himself and his sense of possibilities from within the confines of the ghetto. He said:

> They tell you, "Look, if you do something wrong you are going to be put in the hole." You are in jail in the hole or out of the hole. You are in jail in the street or behind bars. It is the same thing, a matter of existing, and this thing of feeling like a person regardless of if it is illegal or not.[8]

The mental health of young Negroes in the ghetto is therefore essentially the mental health of someone who is actually in prison, and if we are going to liberate hundreds and thousands of young, pent up, frustrated minds into the optimism and open air of the American dream, then we have got to abolish the institution of the ghetto, not refurbish it. Ghettos have no place in the spirit which for centuries we have been told is the spirit of America.

Ralph Ellison, in his testimony before the same Ribicoff Committee, suggested a new morality for our cities that I believe is identical with the climate that needs to be created in place of the one that presently hangs over the ghetto.

> Well, I think that one of the things that we can do about the city is to look at it, to try to see it, not merely as an instrumentality for making money, but a place for allowing the individual to achieve his highest promise. And with that in mind, you would try to construct a city or reconstruct a city in ways which would encourage a more gracious sense of human possibility. You would teach, if at all possible, the immigrants, whether they are black or white or brown, that there is certain knowledge which one must have in order to live in the city without adding too much discomfort to his neighbors.[9]

The Negro Family

The social psychology of the Negro family is one that is relevant not only to life in the ghetto, but also to the life of any low-income Negro community in general. And the source of this psychology is to be found in the traditional and systematic exclusion of the Negro man from employment opportunities that would enable him to bear his full responsibility in the home as man, husband, and father. There are few fathers in American social science literature who have been studied as thoroughly and as closely as the Negro father and, yet, there is no father for whom so little has been done. In 1940, Edward Bakke described the tragedy in which a jobless father finds himself:

> The jobless father is no longer a provider, credit runs out, the woman is forced into the labor force. Then, if relief becomes a necessity, the woman is even more of the focal point—and the welfare investigator is often a woman, too. The father is dependent, the children bewildered, the stability of the family is threatened and often shattered.[10]

This description is of the plight of a white unemployed family, which indicates that the problem of being an adequate provider and maintaining an image as man and father is not one that is peculiar to the Negro father. Here, more recently, is a description of the mental disposition and social situation of the Negro father vis-à-vis his wife and family:

> The common feature of paternal care in the lower class is its frequent absence. . . . For many reasons . . . the father is a lesser figure in the household. The fathers frequently oscillate between two poles: they are either seclusive, taciturn, violent, punitive, and without interest in the

children, or they are submissive to the mother. Often, they are irresponsible or alcoholic. . . . Nevertheless, kind, benevolent, and provident
fathers do appear in this group. Here again, this occurs mostly when
the father can achieve economic security and, with the assumption of
full masculine prerogatives, is enabled to express more positive behavior
toward his children.[11]

What has happened in America is that the post-Emancipation labor
market denied many Negroes the opportunity to become "economic
fathers"—the breadwinning heads of stable families—just as the laws of
slavery had denied them the juridical right to marriage and children.
Therefore, we find today that 35 percent of all Negro children live in
broken homes; 25 percent of Negro women who have been married are
divorced or separated; 14 percent of all Negro children are receiving
Aid to Families of Dependent Children.

There is only one answer to this problem, and it is not to give impoverished black families lectures on the virtues of middle-class living. The
answer is to give the men jobs, provide every able-bodied man a job,
and provide the opportunity for them to avail themselves of decent
housing and decent schools. As Dorothy Height, president of the National Council of Negro Women, remarked, "If the Negro woman has a
major underlying concern, it is the status of the Negro man and his
position in the community and his need for feeling himself an important
person, free and able to make his contribution in the whole society in
order that it may strengthen his home."

Minority Poverty and Joblessness

The white immigrant waves of the nineteenth and early twentieth
centuries faced ethnic and religious prejudice but they were never confronted, as today's ethnic minorities are, with an organized system of
race hatred with its own laws and myths and stereotypes, its own
economy. Those of the older generations of the white poor who fought
their way out of poverty could thus assimilate into American life as soon
as they acquired money, education, mastery of the language, and so
forth. Also, the older white immigrant came into an economy which
could put grade school dropouts to work. The minorities who are struggling today are faced with an entirely different problem; they must
compete not only within race prejudice but also against machines.

Moreover, the unemployed rates today are much higher for some
groups than they were even during the worst years of the Depression. As
James McGregor Burns points out, 20 percent of the working population

was then unemployed. Today, a U.S. Department of Labor study estimates that in the 12 largest areas unemployment rates between 14- and 19-year-olds range from 18.4 percent in Washington, D.C., to 36 percent in Philadelphia, with the rate running about 30 percent in seven areas. The rate for nonwhite girls is somewhat higher than for boys (over 40 percent in Philadelphia and St. Louis).[12]

I believe, therefore, that in the same way the society provided the old immigrants with opportunities to lift themselves and play a meaningful role in the American social and economic order, so also it is obliged to find a way to provide today's minorities with the opportunity and potential to lift and save themselves. And, in keeping with our present circumstances, any program which is conceived to help our minorities out of their present plight must include, first and foremost, a program for full and fair employment, i.e., federally guaranteed jobs for all those—whether members of minority groups or not—who are eligible or can be made eligible for employment in the production of goods and services in the public sector. Gerhard Colm of the National Planning Association is correct when he suggests that such a program of full employment per se will not solve all the problems of poverty, and especially not the racial problems, but it would contribute substantially to the solution and would create the best conditions for attacking the residual problems.[13] Second, the program must include a two-dollar minimum wage; and, third, a guaranteed annual income for those too old, too young, or too sick to work.

We need federally financed public works programs for the creation of the necessary physical institutions—more schools, more hospitals, more roads, more clinics, more psychiatric facilities, more libraries. Not only should the poor benefit from the increased services of these physical facilities, they should also participate in building them—acquiring skills while being paid. This is especially important if we are going to convince young minority group members to take advantage of training or retraining programs. One cannot train young people in a vacuum and expect to win their seriousness, their hope, or their cooperation; in other words, one must show them that the jobs exist for which they are being trained, and that they can work on those jobs even while they are being trained.

Part of any program for full employment is the need for a "redefinition of work." This is necessary to make up for the inroads which automation has made into areas traditionally served by human labor. That is to say, we must redefine work around those kinds of effort which the technological revolution cannot affect. What are some of these? They involve creating a whole new hierarchy of nonprofessional workers to help the professional perform some of the functions he now performs.

Elizabeth Wickenden, Consultant to the National Social Welfare Assembly, describes those functions very well:

> Creative play with young children, visiting home-makers service for the ill or the motherless home, work with older people, masculine leadership for adolescent boys, the interpretation of family planning to overburdened mothers, neighborhood organizations—to name just a few of the present sub-professional jobs—are possibilities.[14]

Jack Conway correctly points out that by creating "decent jobs, a whole host of public and private services will be improved and the entire population will benefit. In short, the public wants improved services and education, health, recreation, police protection, housing and other public and private services."[15]

There must be creation of new opportunities for human services. Academic study should be redefined as work bought and paid for. Many functions which are performed today by underprivileged people but which do not have the stamp of prestige should be redefined as prestigious labor and be paid for at dignified wages. All of this, of course, must be part of a grand plan to solve poverty and to create new motivations and liberate new energies by which minorities can achieve a new sense of belonging and a new sense of identity in American life.

I would make the two-dollar minimum wage the next major priority. That alone could do as much as the entire poverty program in terms of helping people rehabilitate themselves through their own lucrative labor.

James Farmer, James Forman, Dorothy Height, Dr. Martin Luther King, Jr., A. Philip Randolph, Roy Wilkins, and I all testified to this need before the General Sub-Committee on Labor of the House Committee on Education and Labor on June 29, 1965. We said:

> We believe that minimum wage protection must be extended to one of the most cruelly used groups in the land, those people who work long hard hours at back-breaking or menial jobs and who are nevertheless poor. . . . If the country faces up to this problem it will do more than grant justice to a particular minority. It will take a giant step towards the solution of the problems that affect all of us, black and white. . . . This nation can take an important step in remedying part of the injustice that has been done to the Negro. It can simultaneously better the situation of an even greater number of whites. We have the opportunity, in short, to achieve an integrated social justice.[16]

Even the passage of a two-dollar minimum wage is modest. It guarantees an income of $4160 for a year's work, and that is roughly $2000 less than what the government has computed to be a "modest but adequate" urban family budget. We should not be satisfied until every American family has at least that "modest but adequate" income. For now, however, an increase of the minimum wage to $2.00 is a responsible and reasonable step in the right direction.

Here, I would like to discuss the most common argument against extending wage coverage and against raising the minimum wage itself to $2.00. Rising labor costs in unskilled and semiskilled work, it is said, provide an incentive to employers to mechanize or even to automate. The results will be the elimination of precisely those marginal jobs which now provide at least an employment opportunity for unskilled Negroes, young people, and others who are not qualified to compete in the modern economy. There is some truth in this argument. If Congress simply amends the Fair Labor Standards Act and lets it go at that, then the result could be negative. That is why we cannot regard minimum wage as a panacea. That is why my proposals make sense only within the framework of a national commitment to generate new jobs.

I would then add a guaranteed annual income. But let us consider a few figures. As recently as March 3, 1967, Joseph Alsop wrote in his syndicated newspaper column:

> At present, a million American families with 3,200,000 children are living on welfare. In addition, another 3,600,000 American families with 11,800,000 children, though not caught in the welfare trap, are subsisting in grinding poverty that mocks and dishonors our national affluence.

To this, I would add a recent observation by Walter Reuther, President of the United Auto Workers:

> Measured by our resources, we are doing less to provide our older citizens with security and dignity than any other industrial country in the world.

Now, obviously, we need a bold social and economic innovation to end the pathetic dependence of so many millions of our citizens on the caprice of welfare agencies, and I would suggest that the innovation ought to be a guaranteed annual income for those who are too old, too young, or too sick to work; or mothers of families who cannot or should not work.

I do not believe that the way to deal with man is to deal with him only as an economic person. In this society, one's spiritual judgment of himself has to be related to his role in the production of goods and services. He is someone because he does something which society puts value upon; and, therefore, while I am for a guaranteed income for the categories I have described, I am for a guaranteed wage, not income, for others. We cannot keep on handing out checks like leaflets. A man needs to feel that the check he gets is a wage for services to the society and, given the nature of our Western values, I do not believe that he can feel dignity and humanity by simply having checks given to him periodically.

Education

For more than twenty years, the quantitative and qualitative shortages of classrooms in our public schools have been accumulating. Instead of remedying these adequately, we have tended to reduce the estimates of shortages. We need, for many years to come, a construction program of more than a hundred thousand public classrooms a year. This would require outlays of several billions of dollars. Allied with this we need a hundred thousand new teachers per year in the public schools. Regarding higher education, it has been estimated that there are now at least 200,000 young people who are ready for college but lack the means; the figure is probably much higher, and this problem is acute among young Negroes and other minorities. The number will increase because of the very high birth rates during the early postwar years and continuing improvement in secondary education. Comparing 1975 with 1963, the number of students who should be enrolled in schools of higher learning should approximately double. Under existing programs, neither the facilities nor the personnel will be available to meet these needs.

Any new and progressive education program for the future must include in its priorities the provision of the above needed facilities as well as plans to upgrade and improve the climate of learning in our schools and most urgently in our ghetto schools; motivate minority group youth; reinforce in them a respect for their own past and history; prepare them to share in the benefits of the technological revolution; destroy all forms of segregation; and create in them a sense of unlimited possibilities in the present and future processes of the society. Above all, with respect to excluded minorities, the society ought to address itself to the following question posed by Irving Howe:

What then is to happen to these millions of young people for whom the society has less and less need, who are kept penned up in schools simply because no one knows what else to do with them, and whom the dominant values they have absorbed from the social air keep from grasping the true ends of education?[17]

Housing

(On the question of housing, particularly as it concerns our minorities, I will quote directly from *"The Freedom Budget for All Americans,"*[18] which embodies my thinking on the subject, and with the preparation and writing of which I was associated. The *Freedom Budget* states:) "The removal of the slum ghetto which now infects our cities, and of substandard housing in other areas as well, is the top specialized priority. . . . It is an 'end' priority because slum-living is an ultimate evil in itself, both a cause and a by-product of poverty, and perhaps the main factor in what has been called the 'self-perpetuating' nature of poverty. And it is a 'means' priority, because rapid expansion of home construction, with other outlays which it would spark, can perhaps contribute about half of the 22 to 27 million new jobs we need by 1975.

"Although there is no decisive single test of what constitutes unsatisfactory housing, the 1960 census described as 'seriously deficient' about 9.3 million housing units in the U.S., or about one-sixth of the total. Allowing for what appears to be some understatement, at least one fifth of all our people were ill-housed when this Census was taken. The bad housing is occupied predominantly by the poor. According to the Census, less than 21 percent of all owner-occupied housing in metropolitan areas was unsound. But in the case of occupancy by families with incomes under $3,000, about 60 percent of the former type of housing and about 34 percent of the latter type was unsound. And among consumer units with incomes under $2,000, it appears that at least 4 out of 5 lived in unsound housing.

"The poor in the main are not getting decent housing because it is not 'profitable' to provide it for them. Even with the protection of Government insurance through the Federal Housing Administration, far less than one percent of the new single-family homes are purchased by those with incomes under $4,000. The production of new rental housing for the poor on a 'profitable' basis has been even more negligible. And the provision of new housing for the higher income groups does not enable decent housing to be 'handed down' to the poor in any substantial volume. The proof positive of this is the amount of substandard housing still in use, and its highly unsatisfactory rate of reduction in recent years. . . . Although our urban renewal efforts have been grossly inadequate, the re-housing of slum dwellers has lagged even further. In consequence, many slum dwellers have been crowded into other slums, where they pay even higher rents because of the shortages thus created. In a more commendable effort, massive projects to re-house the poor should be built first and, after they move, the slums they have left should be torn down. . . . Making our cities decent places in which to live would reduce the outflow of the affluent to the suburbs. It would at least slow down the process whereby we are now rapidly becoming two Americas—with the poor forming increasing proportions of those living in the cities, while others move out. And with the affluent and influential forming a reasonable proportion of the total city population, the cities would have both the means and the will to finance adequately the popular services which are now being starved—with this starvation aggravating the very poverty which it reflects. . . .

"The replacement of slum ghettoes with new housing for their occupants at an adequate pace would not only make other aspects of urban renewal acceptable, but also augment them greatly. Development of community facilities and public improvements of all types would follow in the wake of the needed housing effort. More would be spent for every commodity which enters into housing and every other urban construction, and for furnishings and equipment within the structures. An annual average of almost 700,000 more housing starts during 1966–75 than in 1965, or 7 million more for the decade, coupled with extensive rehabilitation and related community improvements, would entail for the decade as a whole about 230 billion dollars more direct investment than would result from maintenance of the 1965 level of housing and related activity. Considering the multiplier effects, the increased spending due to this program over the decade might aggregate 450 to 560 billion dollars and create 45 to 65 million man-years of employment, or 4.5 to 6.5 million on an average annual basis."

Participation of Minorities in Social Change

The foregoing are some of the basic areas in which minorities have suffered in the past, and are still suffering, but in which they should be protected from suffering in the future. And, as I suggested earlier, the creation of a more humane future—a more humane twenty-first century—

for these people requires a commitment in social morality such as we have not had in any previous period of our history.

I should like to say a word about one or two of the possible ways in which the minorities themselves can help to generate or set in motion the sweeping social changes that the coming decades demand. Without going into the Freedom Budget,[19] I must say I believe the programs it puts forward represent the most urgent demand for economic change in the lives of the poor in America, and provide a rallying point around which millions of America's poor and excluded can mount a massive campaign in behalf of their own future.

This brings me to the point I really want to make: the need for organization and coalition. As stated earlier, the only elements among the minorities that are in any significant motion are the Negroes and Spanish-American minorities. This is a serious problem because these groups do not have sufficient political power to deal with any of the stubborn economic problems in the society. The only way in which these problems can be dealt with is through the creation of a political coalition made up of Jews, Catholics, Protestants, the labor movement, liberals, the students, intellectuals, civil rights workers, and other minority groups. And I believe one of the key partners in this coalition has to be the labor movement, particularly because it has been the most successful voluntary organization for the abolition of poverty in American history.

Elizabeth Wickenden points out that "such a coalition will become effective when there is a wide-spreading network of mutual interest. This involves a very delicate balance of what is particular to one group and what is the common interest of many groups. . . . More members of the majority need to recognize their own interests are jeopardized by an excluded submerged minority, not through fear but through real understanding."[20]

The economic challenge that now faces minority groups gives the labor movement an opportunity to face up to a new and profound challenge. Almost half of the heads of poor families work hard and long—yet they are still poor. Some of them are denied coverage under the nation's collective bargaining policies—especially Mexican-American farm workers—others lack Social Security, some work at sub-poverty wages, and many work in unorganized shops. Therefore, I believe the labor movement's program for increasing the minimum wage and extending its coverage can constitute a major step forward for the working poor. I also believe that the labor movement must bring its unique skills—

organization and collective bargaining—to the unorganized poor. Some trade unionists have already suggested that strong, stable internationals and locals should "adopt" organizing campaigns among workers who are so poor that they cannot pay the cost of organizing themselves, at least at the outset. Others have indicated that union organizing experience can make a major contribution to help organize the poor for "maximum feasible participation" in the war against poverty.

While I have no doubt about the value of maximum feasible participation in solving problems of poverty, or any other problems, I would like to add that we ought to look at maximum feasible participation as broadly and realistically as possible. More than anything else, it should represent from here on one of the vital features of the grass-roots relationship to the political institutions of the society. In other words, I am all in favor of maximum participation if it means participating as fully as possible in the political decisions of the entire society. Finally, in whatever way one interprets maximum feasible participation, it should not relieve political parties and other social institutions of their obligation to act with courage, commitment, and responsibility in solving people's problems. That is, maximum participation of the people in the solution of their problems should not be an excuse for the traditional political institutions to shirk their own responsibilities to seek and propose remedies for the ills of the people.

All this takes me back to the need for coalition—a coalition of effort, a coalition of conscience, a coalition of social morality, and a coalition of concern. I have no crystal ball, I have no way of knowing whether the new century that we create in America will be the one that ought in all justness to be created. But I do know that at the present moment we can ask no less. I do know that it will be a tragedy if we cannot find social answers to the problems created by the progress of technology and automation. Therefore we ought to fight for what is right, now. And in doing so we have to work to weld behind us a broad coalition of morality, now. If we reject the possibility of this kind of coalition, or if we despair that it will ever come about, then we are rejecting and despairing of the only viable democratic alternative that is available. We cannot look any longer to third political parties. No third political party could do what Catholics, Protestants, Jews, intellectuals, students, civil rights workers, labor organizations, Puerto Ricans, Mexican-Americans, and other minorities did for the passage of civil rights bills, voting rights bills, public accommodations bills, and the March on Washington. If we cannot build that force again, this time around economic and social priorities for the excluded members of our society, then we are on our way to a social cataclysm that we will not be able to control except perhaps by tyranny.

Coalition Politics

One last word. To effectively regulate the human environment for the next fifty years, two factors are essential: (1) deliberate planning and (2) a strong coalition of force to compel the national government to embark upon that planning.

In *Beyond the Welfare State*, Gunnar Myrdal writes:

> There is in all planning, even if it were ever so earthily rooted in comprehensive studies of fact, an element of belief in reason as an independent force in history and in the freedom of choice by which man can change reality according to his design and so turn the course of future development. In essence, planning is an exercise in a nondeterministic conception of history. . . .[21]

Albert Mayer interprets this statement as a cry to move "forward boldly and resolutely." I agree with him entirely. As I think about the necessity for coalition, however, I am forced to recognize that there is no definitive blueprint for its achievement. I do believe, though, that the conditions and the elements exist around which we can begin resolutely to try to bring about such a coalition.

Already the labor movement, the civil rights movement, and many liberals have agreed on a series of ideas, many of them put forth in the Freedom Budget, for all Americans. While I do not believe the Freedom Budget, as it stands, represents the end of our fight for social progress, I think that if we can agree on the goals and strategies it puts forward it can mobilize us into action and ultimately into social and economic change.

Undoubtedly there will be differences among those of us who represent the basic hope for coalition politics. Some of us will make mistakes, and some will even backslide. But these differences will be inherent in our commitment to democratic methods and democratic discussion.

One thing stands out clearly, however, and that is that the problems that face us are of immediate concern to every one of these groups. Every one of these groups is concerned with the fact that 5 percent of the families in the country still get as much as 20 percent of the total income and that the lowest 20 percent gets only 5 percent.[22] Everyone is concerned that there must be a redistribution of wealth and an increase in democratic and social equality. No one of these groups can by itself achieve the remedies for these situations.

One way of bringing about this coalition is to weld it from within the Democratic Party where all the groups are now represented. This means organizing as a strong counterforce to the Dixiecrat-Republican coalition that stymies the progressive programs of the Democratic party. This means that we must support Southern Negroes in their efforts to defeat Dixiecrat candidates for Congress. It means, ultimately, working within all the state Democratic parties to make sure that candidates—from dog catcher to senator—are people committed to creating a climate within the national party that will represent its natural majority.

Those of us who are planners must not let a given "demonstration city" or a new town or urban renewal project divert us from the massive changes that must be made in the society. The Freedom Budget for all Americans is only a skeleton. It needs flesh on its bones. That flesh will be provided by local people, by city planners, by educators, and by professionals.

In closing, I quote again from Michael Harrington's *Accidental Century*:

> America has for some time been engaged in the wrong argument. It has been debating as to whether or not the future should be collective and social, and ignoring the fact that the present is already becoming so. The real issue is not whether, but how, this future will arrive—unwittingly or consciously chosen. If the new society imposes itself upon a people who do not notice a revolution, the moment will constitute the decadence of the Western ideal. . . . Either Western man is going to choose a new society—or a new society will choose, and abolish, him.[23]

Notes

1. Michael Harrington, *The Accidental Century* (New York: Macmillan, 1965), p. 16.

2. Ibid., p. 42.

3. Bernard Weissbourd, *Segregation, Subsidies and Megalopolis* (Santa Barbara, Calif.: Fund for the Republic, Inc., 1964).

4. Harrington, p. 245.

5. *Proceedings of the AFL-CIO Executive Council*, August, 1966.

6. Bayard Rustin, "Civil Rights at the Crossroads," *Federationist* (Washington, D.C.: AFL-CIO), November, 1966.

7. For a description of positive practices, case studies of successful projects in a number of cities, as well as a broad outline for a program for planning and developing integrated cities, see Albert Mayer's *The Urgent Future* (New York: McGraw-Hill, 1967).

8. Arthur Dunmeyer, "Testimony Before the Ribicoff Sub-Committee on Executive Reorganization," *New Leader*, September 26, 1966.

9. Ralph Ellison, "The Crisis of Optimism," *The City in Crisis* (New York: A. Philip Randolph Educational Fund, 1967).

10. Edward Bakke, *Citizens Without Work: A Study of the Effects of Unemployment on the Workers' Social Relations* (New Haven: Yale University Press, 1940).

11. Dr. Abram Kardiner and Dr. Lionel Ovesey, *The Mark of Oppression* (Cleveland: World, 1962), pp. 347 ff.

12. "A Sharper Look at Unemployment in U.S. Cities and Slums" (Washington, D.C.: U.S. Department of Labor, 1967).

13. Gerhard Colm, May 25, 1967.

14. Elizabeth Wickenden, June, 1967.

15. For a more detailed and complete study of the New Careers concept, see *New Careers for the Poor*, by Frank Riessman and Arthur Pearl, and a pamphlet on the same subject published by the A. Philip Randolph Educational Fund, and written by Frank Riessman; with an introduction by Michael Harrington.

16. Testimony reprinted by the A. Philip Randolph Institute (New York: 1965).

17. Irving Howe, "Introduction," *Urban School Crisis* (New York: League for Industrial Democracy, 1966).

18. A. Philip Randolph Institute (New York: 1966), pp. 44 ff.

19. In October, 1966, the A. Philip Randolph Institute detailed a $100 billion federal "Freedom Budget" as a master plan to eradicate poverty in the next ten years. The Institute has set up local committees in Philadelphia, Pittsburgh, and Sacramento in an effort to rally local support behind the Freedom Budget and to develop economic plans for metropolitan areas. The Budget has strategic importance; it is, of course, a prime example of the type of economic planning this paper would advocate—one that sets priorities and establishes a timetable while measuring resources. The budget provides a meeting ground for civil rights leaders to discuss strategy and tactics. It is neither an abstract demand nor a one-issue document and provides the opportunity for labor, liberal, religious, and other white supporters of the civil rights movement to ally themselves with the civil rights movement in an ongoing project, rather than just during periods of crisis or mass demonstrations. It gives an opportunity to students, who have become disillusioned with social and economic conditions, to join the civil rights movement, because it provides work opportunities for those who are academically oriented as well as those who are activist oriented. The budget is particularly important at the grass-roots level. It removes the intercommunity squabble for money and adds a programmatic and ideological rallying point, while helping local people relate their demands to the national economy.

20. Wickenden.

21. Gunnar Myrdal, *Beyond the Welfare State* (New Haven: Yale University Press, 1960).

22. Mayer.

23. Harrington, p. 275.

Comments on

Rustin

RICHARD HENRY LUECKE
Urban Training Center, Chicago

When Bayard Rustin writes briefly on a problem which has engaged him for an entire generation, the chief danger is that what he says will seem shorthand to the rest of us. My comments merely point to certain considerations which seem too lightly touched, which seem to call for further analysis, or which appear to require more clearly enumerated proposals than Mr. Rustin has given us in these pages. They are the comments of one who has learned much from this master theorist and strategist, as has everyone else in my generation, including some who at present profess to disagree with him.

American society has been led in the past and is being led precipitously at present, Mr. Rustin argues, by technological happenings, priorities, even obsessions. This sort of progress leaves further and further behind minority groups who never got in the game or are, by reason of race, mostly excluded from the game. The resulting split constitutes a moral question for the society, which needs, Rustin says, to remember individual or human values, to harness individual moral commitments to corporate social projects, and to take conscious and democratic control of events. There can be little question that Mr. Rustin has outlined the chief issue on the social agenda for the next fifty years.

I will leave the economic logistics of Mr. Rustin's argument to critics more equipped to deal with them, though I suspect some of their comments will parallel my own by calling for additional emphasis on economic development emanating not only from the private sector but from community actions themselves. Following are three observations bearing on more specifically "moral" elements in Mr. Rustin's discussion.

1. If we are "to deal with the flagrant abuse of minorities, but with a difference," namely, that this abuse "can be considered a forewarning for *all* minorities of the society should our society become mass or strict-majority oriented," then the problem we have conceived is even broader than that of admitting disinherited groups to a larger share of the goods of a technological society. It includes also the organizational tasks of providing for individual and cultural diversities in such a society. The "forewarning," ultimately, is to everyone alive—though the comfortable are less likely to admit the threat.

This suggests that there may be certain qualities or gifts in minority groups which deserve to be preserved, and that something may be gained by actually listening to such groups—which seems a first "morality," in any case. Capacities for sustained face-to-face relationships, present enjoyment, leisure activities, for generalized "cool" as distinct from specialized "hot" functions, are sometimes listed as residual strengths among the poor. The Appalachian who grinds to a stop in the city with a guitar strapped to his back, who prefers to work three days a week for wages, three on family projects, and one on the weekly hootenany, has a lot to learn about technological and corporate facts of life if he is not to be exploited indefinitely by day labor enterprises. But he may also have something to teach about diversified values and styles which might somehow become incorporated in a new environment. It may be possible to learn from the ills of the poor something about a more general illness, as Aarne Siraala suggests in *The Voice of Illness*.

Considerations of this sort might indicate an enlarged role for local polities in developing urban environments—even, and especially, in the event of large scale programs for the poor.

2. There are in Mr. Rustin's argument certain pivotal, ethically laden phrases which serve as middle terms between the conditions he describes and the policies he proposes. What we are to remember in the face of technological and corporate changes, are "the dignity of the individual" or "the value of the individual," and this should enable us to seek "a humane culture" or "a more humane future." But surely the meaning of these conceptions is exactly our question. Qualities of human life in community need to be unpacked or unfolded if they are actually to move us between facts and programs. What seems needed, for all its special complexities, is work in "societal ethics" which keeps one eye on more empirical social sciences and the other on political decisions, but which remembers Mr. Rustin's insistence that there is no simple movement from the former to the latter.

The persistent danger, of course, is that moral imputation will ignore factual information—in which case our analysis will serve only to heat issues where light was needed to focus them. No doubt there has been some racial malice and immorality in the "flight to the suburbs," as Mr. Rustin avers. But a historian of the city like Richard Wade, who is no enemy of civil rights or of the city, liberally documents an initiation and explosion of mobility exactly commensurate with the development of transportation devices, and finds the movement out of early "stable" ethnic neighborhoods quite commensurate with that out of urban neighborhoods at present. This is in its own way helps to explain the failure of a variety of measures in communities with ghettos (including "motivational training"), since their residents have never been allowed the one motivation which has served the rest of American society. Martin Luther King's goals in Chicago *might* remain unachieved, as Mr. Rustin agrees, for lack of involvement by "liberals." Yet it seems quite possible that the elites of Chicago are in favor of "open housing," and that what is chiefly needed, if that is the goal, is actual move-ins by people willing to accept the struggle. Local actions for limited gains are not infrequently sacrificed to longer-range goals requiring national publicity and discussion. Those are tactical decisions, to be argued with the people for whom they are made. Charges of "immorality" on such occasions serve to obfuscate the discussion of those choices, and do not sufficiently signal the programs to be undertaken on every side.

3. In advocating a new coalition of blacks, poor whites, labor, "new class," students, and others who are to work on and then through the Democratic party, Rustin cautions against grass-roots organizations which neglect this national focus. To this we might add a caution from the other side. Large scale politics are not immediately useful to members of minority groups or to the poor in gaining redress for the kind of abuses they daily suffer. Elections seem a circuitous route for treating open wounds; the difference between candidates

in most elections seems an indifferent matter to the poor. The systems on which the poor are dependent are remote. Court actions are expensive or delayed. Many grievances of pressing importance to the poor are not actually negotiable through normal channels.

In addition to the new "national action and will" for which Bayard Rustin calls, and on the way to it, we will probably have to give painstaking and expert attention to "local action and will." The agenda for the next fifty years almost certainly includes the manifold tasks of forming many new polities or new "political spaces" having differing scales of responsibility—from those of neighborhood to those of international scope. Not least important for "minorities" will be local and client polities sufficient to gain a measure of response from metropolitan and federal systems, to contend for local enterprises and services, and to make room for specially chosen goods and values within their own environment.

GEORGE SCHERMER
Consultant in Human Relations

Mr. Rustin's paper was written before the fire this time had burst with full fury in Newark, Detroit, and several dozen other cities in the nation. In the light of what happened during the summer of 1967, one might say that Mr. Rustin understated the problem. However, that would be unfair to him. Of course, Mr. Rustin and many others have known that this rage was upon us and that the explosions could occur at any time. But no responsible person, such as Mr. Rustin, would have declared its inevitability. To have done so would have been the equivalent of shouting "fire" in a crowded theater. It was always essential that the language used to forewarn the American people could not and would not be interpreted as the cry of a madman.

The predictions now have become facts. It is not possible to tell whether the convulsions will bring us to our senses in time or whether they are no more than the beginning of disaster to come.

There are those who say that the riots and destruction are beneficial—that they will prompt America at last to take the steps, to remedy the wrongs, to initiate the programs necessary to build the good society. I cannot concur. I will not applaud war on the sophistry that after the war there will be peace or at least a cessation of hostilities. The rioting is a madness born of sheer meaninglessness and desolation. Rioting is not an instrument of social change but a terrifying symbol of social failure. It confirms Mr. Rustin's warning that the social conscience of America has receded so far that more and more people have been left "stranded and neglected in a deepening mire of social and economic problems."

I am aware that Mr. Rustin did not choose the topic of his paper. Fortunately, he has chosen to focus upon the problems of minorities from a moral, political, and economic point of view. Fortunately also, he does not pose a dichotomy between issues of morality and economics and politics. A truly democratic society with clearly defined moral values and goals would use politics and economics as instruments of social policy. Insofar as a society is less than democratic or is confused about its values, economics and politics become the shapers as well as the instruments of policy.

If this is to be the age of man and if the environment is to be hospitable to man, we must somehow provide for two-way communication between the minorities, the disadvantaged, and the poor on the one hand, and those who are shaping the environment on the other. Such questions as the following are as yet unanswered:

1. How are those people who are so completely alienated from society to develop an identification with and a sense of self-investment in their physical and social environment?

2. How are we to find and develop a common ground of communication, understanding, and aspiration among all our people—including both those who are "in" and those who feel cast out?

3. How, in terms of concerted community, social, and political action do we get from where we are today to where we might like to be five, ten, and twenty years from now?

If we cannot answer these questions soon, the next fifty years will prove to have been as accidental as Michael Harrington's *Century.* Mr. Rustin provides some of the ingredients that are missing. He proposes a program that is oriented both to long-range goals and to immediate objectives and strategy.

As one of the architects of the "Freedom Budget," he has been able to draw upon it for the principal elements which he presents in his paper. I think that for the type and length of his presentation he develops his points concerning jobs, minimum wage and income well enough. I applaud his concern for a "redefinition of work," the expansion of job opportunities, a minimum wage covering all jobs, and the psychological importance of useful and meaningful occupation.

Unfortunately, the paper becomes hurried and trite in the sections pertaining to education and housing. Education is treated in two paragraphs, neither of which contributes anything profound or new. On that subject, however, I find myself confronted with a comparable dilemma—education, is too broad and complex a subject to be dealt with in a few paragraphs. Mr. Rustin devotes more space to housing, but his contribution does not match the calibre of the balance of his work. His estimates of housing needs are conservative, but that is not the issue here. What is disappointing is that he does not relate his proposals for increased housing production to his earlier expressions of concern for the role of the male in the subculture of poor and disadvantaged

Negroes. Home building on a large scale will mean more jobs and that in itself will be important to Negroes. But there must be planning, a system that will enhance the role of the Negro male in the building and the improvement of his physical and social environment.

Shelter is more than walls, roofs, and mechanical gadgetry. In planning and developing new housing or in rehabilitating neighborhoods, an entire living environment is created. No matter how perfectly the plan is laid out on the drawing boards or how solidly the structures are built, they will remain sterile and meaningless unless those who live in them have invested something of themselves in their creation.

This is not to say that each man must have had the experience of building his own hut for his family. Some of the most stable neighborhoods consist of old structures that have been made over and adapted many times. However, the people who are there have contributed something of themselves to the neighborhood.

I shall not attempt to supply a blueprint here. I am aware that most "self-help" housing ventures have floundered. We get more houses built when government underwrites the ventures and private contractors supply the initiative and the management. But it is my conviction that we must incorporate the ingredient of personal involvement and participation in an appropriate measure if there is to be identification on the part of the individual in his physical environment and his community.

Mr. Rustin is at his best when he moves into the arena of political action. Here the idealist and the political realist are welded into one. He has steadfastly resisted the emotional appeal of romanticized racism and the heroics of would-be martyrs. If there is to be a revolution it must have power, and black power is not enough. There must be a coalition built upon both the desperate needs of the minorities and the moral commitment of liberals in the churches and synagogues, the labor unions and the political parties. He is not sanguine, but he dares not consider any alternative.

To his closing paragraphs I say "Amen" without reservation. But intellectual approbation will not be enough. The coalition he describes had tremendous appeal and power a few years ago but barely exists today. To rebuild it to effective strength demands the utmost in commitment, courage, and active participation. This is not a time for ivory-tower objectivity, even among planners. All must play the role of responsible citizens and all must accept the risks of active commitment to the principles we believe in.

Education for a Full Life

This paper was commissioned to look into education as the great future engager of man's mind and his time throughout his lifetime—for all men. The need for relearning as well as initial learning—of deepening understanding for personal satisfaction and development as well as for occupational reasons— of preschool as well as in-school education, all of these are the concern of this paper.

For economic, social, and physical demands of living, a lifetime of being educated, if fully taken into account, would revolutionize our community environment. How far can (or should) technology go in this education and training? What sort of education should be planned, and for whom? When and where should this education occur? What are the implications for the environment?

How are teachers to be educated? Should we develop curriculi concerned with mastering the next fifty years at all levels of schooling? How does the pursuit of excellence in peacetime become equated with courage needed in war? How can a healthy excitement for life be stimulated by continuing education for a full life?

Author: Robert M. Hutchins, President, Center for the Study of Democratic Institutions

Chairman: Martin Meyerson, AIP, President, State University of New York at Buffalo

Committee: Arthur Singer, President, Educational Services, Inc.; Gilbert F. White (Past President, Haverford College), Geography Department, University of Chicago; Jacqueline Grennan, President, Webster College; Fred Hechinger, Education Editor, *The New York Times*; Theodore R. Sizer, Dean, Graduate School of Education, Harvard University; Harold Howe, U.S. Commissioner of Education; James P. Dixon, President, Antioch College; Eugene Groves, President, U.S. National Student Association; Alan Pifer, Acting President, Carnegie Corporation of New York

Robert M. Hutchins

President, Center for the Study of Democratic Institutions

Education for a Full Life

Education for a full life is now possible, and has long been so in the rich countries of the world. If such education is not offered in these countries to everybody for his whole life, it is not because these countries have not the resources to finance such a program, but because they do not yet accept the definition of education that such a program implies.

An educational system is a political phenomenon. Every educational system reflects the aims of the state that supports it. When education is taken seriously, it is thought of as an instrument by which the political community may reach its goals.

Education is now taken seriously everywhere. Individuals are convinced that they need it, or at least the formal indicia of it, in order to get ahead in life. States regard it as an indispensable means of attaining power and prosperity.

These attitutdes are new, dating on a world scale from the end of the last war. In the United States it can hardly be said that education was taken seriously before that date.

As late as 1917, education beyond the barest minimum was regarded in this country as something largely irrelevant to the needs and interests of the great majority of the people. It was of course required for those few who were destined for the learned professions; and it was a way in which the children of the rich could enjoy bright college years before they settled down to the solemn business of getting richer.

European countries took education more seriously, but only in a limited sense. In those countries education was adjusted to one's station in life. Working-class children were thought to need little or none.

In the United States research was not valued, because the connection between science and technology was not clearly understood. Yankee ingenuity specialized in taking scientific ideas from other countries and making profitable applications of them. It has often been said that every idea that went into the atomic bomb came from Europe. A university president forty years ago had no harder job than raising money for the support of research. Neither government nor industry was interested. What money there was came from the big foundations.

Education and research began to be taken seriously in the United States only when they seemed to be the path to prosperity and power. President Lyndon B. Johnson in 1965 urged businessmen to support expenditures for education on the grounds that they were a good investment. He pointed out that a college graduate would earn on the average $300,000 more in his lifetime than a man who had stopped with the eighth grade. President John F. Kennedy made education a weapon in the Cold War. He said, "This nation is committed to greater advancement in economic growth, and recent research has shown that one of the most beneficial of all such investments is education, accounting for some forty percent of the nation's growth and productivity in recent years. In the new age of science and space, improved education is essential to give meaning to our national purpose and power. It requires skilled manpower and brainpower to match the power of totalitarian discipline. It requires a scientific effort which demonstrates the superiority of freedom."

Since every state wants to be as strong and rich as it can, educational systems are now supported because of the general conviction that they will help individuals and nations reach these goals. Industrial and industrializing countries are primarily concerned with training in "marketable skills" or meeting assumed manpower requirements or producing the scientists and technicians they believe they need in order to become as strong and rich as they can be.

But this is not interest in education for a full life. It is in fact the opposite. It is an education for a very limited life, if not an empty one. I believe that within the next fifty years this conception of education will be abandoned, if only because it will gradually become clear that the aims implicit in it cannot be achieved.

An educational system that aims at manpower rather than manhood has to have some rational understanding of the manpower requirements it purports to serve. Then it has to have some reasonable assurance that it can match supply with demand. No country has as yet been able to accomplish these results. Even where the same authorities control demand and supply, as in the Soviet Union, the effort to put the two together has resulted in nothing but frustration.

The difficulties of combining production training and education in the Soviet Union reached such a point that in 1958 a member of the Academy of Pedagogical Sciences, N. Versilin, spoke as follows: "First and foremost, we cannot resolve the problem of labor training without considering the necessity of improving general education; to reconcile the two is extremely difficult. Secondly a contradiction arises in connection with the student's freedom of choice of his vocational occupation and the selection of students by their aptitude, ability, and interest. Children who live on Zelenina Street in Leningrad must attend public school No. 44, and consequently these students must take their production training in the rope factory. Thus, place of residence decides the fate in vocational specialization of students in this school. Fortunately or unfortunately, the rope factory cannot employ all the graduates of this school, and the vocational trades specialty which the students have acquired cannot be used because there are only a few rope factories. A year ago the Baltic Machine Works required metal workers and milling machine operators, and this year it needs welders and assembly workers. What should the vocational orientation of the school be in this case? The increased emphasis on vocational subjects has already considerably reduced the quality of general education. All attempts to combine education with production training in industrial enterprises have had negative effects . . . ; after all, why should a student study for two years a trade which he could learn in a three- to six-months apprenticeship course anyway?"

The situation is worse in countries that have plans but that do not exercise the same kind of control that is possible in the Soviet Union. In France, for example, every attempt to harmonize manpower requirements and student enrollments has failed.

Two of the most striking characteristics of American society are the mobility of the population and the rapidity of technological change. In countries exhibiting these characteristics it is self-evident that an education designed to teach a boy or girl how to do something that is now being done at a particular place is almost certain to be a waste of time. It may be even worse: it may be an actual handicap to the student when he comes to apply the skill that his instructors have mistakenly taught him. It is now commonly said that a boy graduating from high school may expect to have three different kinds of jobs during his life. How can we tell what skill we are to teach him? How do we know what skill will be marketable when he tries to sell it? As the rate of technological change is accelerated, it will become clear that almost by necessity training for a job will have to be given on the job or immediately beforehand. Education takes time, and job requirements can change in no time at all.

All countries are now convinced that what they need is more scientists and engineers. Some forecasts seem to intimate that in twenty-five years there will be more scientists and engineers than people. Though the training of those who are needed may have to be more specialized and rarefied than in the past, there is no reliable evidence that the number will increase. At the height of the technical revolution in the United States, many engineers are out of work. One hears that the developing countries require scientists and engineers in limitless quantities, but Greece, India, and Egypt are exporters of highly trained manpower of precisely the kind they are said to need.

Computers can now program computers. Computers can do the job of industrial designers. Those who formulate educational policy in terms of increasing national power and prosperity through the production of large numbers of scientists and engineers might be better advised to direct their attention to the quality rather than the quantity of the product.

Those interested in national power and prosperity often assume that the industrial labor force will require, to operate industry and to gain a livelihood, a relatively large amount of scientific and technical education.

In fact, the most important single cause for the new interest in education after the Second World War was a belief that a new scientific and technical age had opened in which nations and individuals, if they were to flourish, or even to survive, would have to have much more education, and particularly much more of a scientific and technical kind. Can increased scientific and technical training, for the purpose of earning a living and manning the industrial system, supply "marketable skills?"

Beyond the scientists, engineers, and skilled repairmen, the workers in automated industry will require *for their work* no education whatever. For their work they will not even need to know how to read, write, or figure. The ordinary worker in the industry of the future will have to be able to see whether a red light is burning or hear whether a whistle is blowing. Illiterate Spanish women are now supervising automatic bakeries in West Germany. They ride back and forth on bicycles in front of the ovens. When the warning signal goes on, they report to a repairman. Since they cannot speak German, they do so by pressing a button.

The idea that education in some way leads to a brighter economic future for the individual is fostered by the undoubted fact that higher and higher educational requirements for the same job tend to appear as more and more of the population reaches a higher stage of education. The certificates, diplomas, and degrees demanded do not reflect any changes in the skill or intellectual power demanded of the applicant. They reflect rather the larger supply of applicants with certificates, diplomas, and degrees. A job for which elementary education was once regarded as adequate may come to require a Ph.D., and will do so if the number of Ph.D.'s available becomes large enough.

In periods of slack employment the educational system has a tendency to become a personnel system for business. The same phenomenon has appeared all over the world. If the time comes at which the same proportion of the population of the United States graduates from college as now graduates from high school, jobs that now require a high school diploma will demand a college degree. As the premium for education falls, the market for the educated widens. If an employer has a choice between a man who has had a lot of schooling and one who has had little, he is likely to choose the one who has had a lot, not because the more educated man is better qualified, but because this is an easy way to sort out applicants. This may show that it is advantageous, statistically, to an applicant to have the largest possible number of the highest possible certificates, diplomas, and degrees. It of course shows nothing whatever about the advantage to a country or an industrial system of educating the young with a view to national prosperity and power.

The notion that education should be directed to economic growth may rest on a confusion of causes and effects. When we look at the whole panorama of nations, we are likely to conclude, with C. Arnold Anderson, that the quantity of formal education has only a moderate statistical association with economic development. He suggests that incomes predict primary school enrollments better than enrollments predict incomes. He adds that levels of schooling often seem to be rather byproducts of development than sources of it. He points out that Czarist Russia was a high income country in comparison with most of the underdeveloped world today and that it enjoyed rapid gains in production. Yet the census of 1897 reported that only 44 percent of the age thirty to thirty-nine males were able to read.

There is undoubtedly a high correlation between the number of years a population has spent in school and per capita gross national product. We cannot positively say whether the years in school have resulted in the high GNP or whether the high GNP has resulted in the years in school.

As gross national product grows, education is likely to grow with it. But this is not necessarily so. It has not been so in Brazil. That country has one of the fastest growing economies in the world, yet its educational level is lower, in proportion to the population, than it was before its economic expansion began.

Affluence, automation, democracy, and a high rate of technological change have been with us for a very short time. These characteristics of a modern industrial society both enable and require us to undertake education for a full life. Since we cannot assume that our successors on this planet will be irrational, we must suppose that they will notice the shortcomings of limited, partial education for a limited, partial life. They will then seek to transform their educational systems to prepare for a full life for all.

It must be admitted that this is an uncharted area. The effort to educate everybody has never been made. Education in the West, beyond the merest minimum that is necessary to prevent the individual from becoming a danger to or a drag on society, has traditionally been designed for the elite. Naturally enough, the education of rulers was limited to those who were destined to rule. The others were shunted off into the labor market or into some kind of training for some kind of useful work.

It was never supposed that a country would be wealthy enough to educate everybody; it could not afford the financial outlay, and it could not do without the labor of those who would be spending their time in school instead of in work. The idea of educating everybody to the limit of his capacities in his own and in the public interest scarcely crossed anybody's mind.

Educational institutions were organized for the benefit of those who were prepared to take advantage of them. These were in general the children of the wealthier classes. Their vocabulary, background, interests, and prospects determined the methods, content, and aims of education.

The style of the secondary school and the university meant that the child from a working class home or from the slums entered a different world when he went to school. In highly exceptional cases he could adjust himself to it and conquer it. In the ordinary case, however, he could not hope to succeed. Frustration and failure were the result.

Even today the children of the wealthier classes have a tremendous advantage in school. Everywhere in the world the school is an institution that favors children that come from "good homes." This is as true in the socialist countries as it is in the "capitalist" West.

In the advanced industrial countries the unemployment of youth is becoming a serious problem. In all countries vocational training looks like a more and more doubtful enterprise. The two normal exits from the school appear to be closing. We are therefore faced with the necessity of trying to educate young people whom we have never had to take very seriously before.

In view of what we have learned about the importance of the earliest years of life, and in view of what we know about the influence of the environment, efforts will doubtless be made to remove children from "bad homes" in bad environments and put them in crèches, kindergartens, nursery schools, and boarding schools. The best school cannot accomplish much as long as the child remains in a bad neighborhood. It is too much to hope that the school can win a single-handed triumph over all the other forces in the culture. Even in a highly pluralistic society, the educational system is more likely to be a reflection of the culture than a cause of it. In this country, where education is controlled by fifty different states and operated through thousands of different school boards and boards of regents and trustees, the tone, content, and aims of education are strikingly uniform, so much so that we can say there is an American educational system.

The ultimate solution of the problem of bad homes and bad neighborhoods is of course to make them good. The schools can do very little about that. All they can do is to try to minimize the effects of such homes and such neighborhoods.

This will mean a tremendous change in the attitude of the schools toward their pupils. Heretofore those who came from the alien subculture of poverty were looked upon as stupid and got rid of as soon as possible. Now they will have to be given vast quantities of special attention in order to compensate for the handicaps under which they labor. The attempt will at last have to be made to offer them, as well as their more fortunate contemporaries, education for a full life.

This education will have to be the same for everybody. Since the slum child is to be one of the rulers of our country, he must be educated for this role. Since we cannot tell what he will work at, or whether he will work at all, he too will have to be helped to learn how to become human by using his mind.

We may call the education he will have to have "liberal." This is the education appropriate to a free man in a free society. This is education for a full life. It goes without saying that we do not know how to give this education to everybody; it is not altogether certain that we know what it is. Perhaps the greatest educational task of the future is to find out what liberal education is and how it may be made available to all. Although there may be many paths to liberal education, it can have only one purpose and that purpose provides the test of any methods that are proposed. An educational program that aims at technical proficiency is partial and illiberal. The aim of liberal education is to acquire understanding and a means to further understanding.

In the next fifty years radical changes in the organization, financing, and administration of educational institutions seem certain to take place. The aim will be lifelong learning. The object of schooling will be to equip the student with the means and motivations for continuing his education throughout his life. Under these circumstances no teacher will ever imagine that he must teach his students something about everything that they will encounter in their later careers. Since liberal education will be regarded as the central purpose of the schools, it will be possible to eliminate those parts of the curriculum which have nothing to do with this purpose and which have attached themselves to the course of study because there was no standard by which they could be excluded. A six-year elementary school, a three-year high school, and a three-year college should suffice to give everybody a basic, liberal education. Only those students interested in and qualified for independent study should go on to the university.

The multiversity does not appear to be a viable institution. There is nothing to hold it together, and something that is not held together is likely to fall apart. An institution cannot operate indefinitely at cross-purposes, and of these the multiversity has an abundance. There is no way of successfully combining the care of the young, vocational certification, and scholarly research.

The multiversity's task is complicated because it has no criteria of judging what it is asked to do. As a usual rule, it will do whatever it is asked to do, provided the money is available. The American multiversity has been taken over by the commercial, political, and military establishment, because these are the elements in our society that have the money. An institution that accepts large grants for other people's purposes must of course substitute those purposes for its own.

I do not say that the purposes of the commercial, political, and military establishment are illegitimate. I merely say that the university, as I conceive it, is not a good place in which to carry them out. Institutes, training schools, and research programs of various kinds might be committed to these purposes, leaving the university free for its unique task.

We may perhaps discover what that task is by asking what the university could do that nobody else could do. The university could be a center of independent thought and criticism. It could put everything in its place, both the place it is in now and that which it ought to occupy. It could draw the circle of knowledge by seeing everything in relation to everything else. It could be a beacon to our society, and through it to the world. Interdisciplinary studies would be the essence of such an intellectual community. Such a community ought to be small enough so that the members of it could have some understanding of one another's work. If it were small enough, its affairs could be conducted by its members, and the class of professional administrators could be abolished. The board of trustees or the board of regents would be a critical body the purpose of which would be to offer disinterested and friendly comment upon the work of the university. The community would be bound to consider these opinions, but would be free to reject them.

In such a community the old problem of research versus teaching would be solved because there would be no difference between them. The students would be junior partners in the intellectual enterprise.

Such a university will, I believe, replace the multiversity within the next fifty years, not merely because the multiversity will be found to be unworkable, but also because we shall come to realize that what we need most of all is wisdom, and that wisdom comes through understanding. The brilliant short-run achievement of specialized investigations cannot blind us to the fact that the byproducts of this type of scholarship, usually unforeseen, have brought us to the point where if we are not blown up we shall be suffocated or run over. We know everything except how to make democracy work and what to do with ourselves. We know everything except what is most important for us to know.

Two factors are likely to shift the financing and control of education from the town, county, and state governments to the national government. The first is that education is now becoming a major preoccupation of the central governments of all countries. The shift in the United States in the last ten years has been dramatic, and everything indicates that federal support will increase decade by decade. The second factor that is likely to intensify the tendency toward centralization is the high mobility of the population. When, as in the United States, 15 million families move every year, it is difficult to maintain the notion that education is a local matter. The entire country has an interest in the quantity and quality of education available in every part of it.

Vast sums of money will be required for education; they will be beyond the capacity of local and state governments.

These expenditures will be largely for the purpose of re-equipping the schools. We are on the verge of a technological revolution in education. It may go so far as to dissolve the institutions we have known or to make them largely unrecognizable.

We can form some idea of the possibilities if we imagine a learning center in every home. Its basic elements might be a telephone, a television set, and a console. Teachers might go from house to house like visiting nurses. The bulk of the instruction and the examinations would be handled by computers.

At present the cost of this equipment is such that it would be highly uneconomical to install it in every home. It is now being placed at central points in colleges and universities, where it is available to students in much the same way as books in a central library. As the equipment becomes cheaper, it will be possible to increase the number of points at which it is available. This will diminish the importance of any one point by making it unnecessary to go there. When the number of points reaches its ultimate limit, a computer in every home, it will in principle be unnecessary to leave home in order to get an education.

Or at least to get the education the computer and its connections will supply. In principle the computer will eventually be able to supply any kind of education that is desired. But I am afraid we may come to desire the kind of education that is easiest for the computer to provide. In fact we desire that kind of education already. When Americans think of education, they think of information and training. Machines can do a better job of this kind than people. They are quicker and more reliable. The criteria of speed and efficiency are standards to which we are devoted, which we have applied wherever we can, and to which education as we have known it has been highly resistant. We shall now have the opportunity at last to apply our favorite standards to mechanized, electronic education. We shall have the enthusiastic support of the large, rich, and powerful commercial organizations that are interested in selling their equipment to educational institutions.

The danger then is that the technology of education will in effect determine its methods and its aims, though in principle there is no reason why this should be so. Forebodings in this regard are justified by the fact that mankind has so far been unable to control technology, so much so that in some quarters it is referred to as autonomous.

Mass education is a repellent term. It involves a contradiction. A mass can be trained or informed, but it cannot be educated. Education involves helping individuals to become human by learning to use their minds.

The safest course will be to turn over to the machines the task of training and informing, thus relieving teachers for the work of education.

The technological revolution in education seems certain to disperse educational facilities and thus assist not merely the progress of universal education but also of universal, lifelong learning. We already understand what Margaret Mead has called the most vivid truth of the new age, that no one will live all his life in the world in which he was born, and no one will die in the world in which he worked in his maturity. We are prepared to act on the supposition that continuous retraining is necessary throughout a worker's life. We are also prepared to believe that everybody is going to have more and more free time. Life cannot be full if this free time is empty. Nor does it seem possible that human beings can be permanently satisfied with the usual ways in which they now spend their free time. The human appetite for recreation is probably not insatiable.

The reduction of labor for subsistence to the vanishing point will have to bring with it, if we are not to go mad, a reorientation of Western man, who has looked upon work as the principal, characteristic, human activity. Unless work can be redefined, this view will have to be abandoned.

If it is abandoned, what will take its place?

At present, I am sure, most men in the West would receive the news that there might be no work, or very little, for them to do with consternation. Their alarm would not be diminished if a guaranteed annual income were promised them. Their difficulty would be not that they could not live, but that they could not imagine how they would get through the day.

Sir Julian Huxley has talked of a fulfillment society. This is one, I suppose, in which everybody leads a full life. Can men believe they are living full lives if they are not working for a living or to enlarge their material possessions?

Can we look forward to a learning society? This would be one in which men aimed to learn how to live a full life, how to achieve fulfillment. The contribution of educational institutions, or of any educational system, no matter how organized, might best be defined as intellectual. The task of education would be to help people learn how to be human, to lead a full life, and to achieve fulfillment by helping them learn how to use their minds.

Additional Comment

ROBERT M. HUTCHINS

It is obvious that school should be as joyful as possible. It can never be as joyful as Leonard and Poppy imagine, for certain aspects of learning, as Aristotle said, are accompanied by pain. It can seldom, if ever, be a pleasure to learn French irregular verbs.

I think it is outrageous to propose the kind of chaos in a field that deserves serious attention that Leonard and Poppy have in mind. If there are educational institutions, they must have a purpose, and it must be something beyond offering anybody whatever he would like to do.

It is absurd to propose the abolition of compulsory education. This would simply mean that those who need it most did not get it. It would also mean that children would once more be at the mercy of their families. Compulsory public education is a victory of the community over domestic greed.

In Belgium, in 1869, a serious move to prevent children of under eleven years of age being employed in factories was defeated on the argument that it was better to have them working in conditions that could be rigorously controlled than to have them mercilessly exploited at home.

The main object of the commissioned paper was to show that though we have the conditions that would permit education for a full life, we have not got and are not proposing to get it. The reason is that we do not want it. We believe that the aim of education is economic success, national power, and "upward social mobility." As long as we cherish this illusion, we shall not have education for a full life.

It is indispensable to get rid of this illusion. The extent of it is indicated by all public statements on education and by the naive enthusiasm with which they are received.

There is no way to get rid of a widespread and deepseated illusion except by showing clearly and repeatedly that it is one.

Until the illusion is got rid of, additional expenditures, additional gadgets, additional buildings, and additional staff will merely make our prospects worse; we shall simply have more means of achieving the wrong ends. Teaching machines, television of all kinds, films, etc., will not help us to escape the illusion; they simply give us more effective ways of spreading and deepening it. The same is true of educational reorganization.

If we can escape the illusion, then in the light of our new understanding, we can decide what to do. If we accept the idea of the learning society—how many of us do?—then we can ask what steps can be taken to bring it about. New technical devices, new programs, new methods, and new types of institutions can then be used to help us reach our new goal.

The attack should be made simultaneously all along the line. In view of what we have learned about the earliest years of life, we shall have to consider the importance of crèches and nursery schools. In view of what we know about the effects of the environment, we shall have to consider boarding schools for the least privileged rather than for the most privileged members of the society.

To take seriously the idea of liberal education for all means that we must put forth a tremendous effort to find out what liberal education is. It cannot be what we customarily suppose: it cannot be simply what goes on in colleges that call themselves colleges of liberal arts. Still less can it be 120 semester hours of miscellaneous material passed with an average grade of 60 or better on the basis of course examinations given by the teachers who have taught the courses. Technology may help us reach everybody; we can reach them with a liberal education only if we know what it is. Technology does not tell us what it is or, by itself, interest us in finding out. Since the technology will enable us to do anything we want to, we shall have to decide to what extent educational institutions are to exist, what they should be like, and to what extent instruction and investigation should be conducted on their premises.

In seeking to answer these questions, it does not seem to me helpful to identify education with life. Everything that happens to a man is in one sense part of his education. But I take it for granted that there will always be educational institutions and that they have some special responsibility. This must at least be something beyond offering the citizen the chance to do under their auspices whatever he likes on the ground that whatever he likes will be educational.

By a process of elimination too long to go into here, I reach the conclusion that the special obligation of educational institutions is to protect and develop those human interests and activities which have some identifiable intellectual content. Educational institutions should not relieve other institutions of their responsibilities. If they make the attempt to do so, they will disintegrate. I would predict a dim future for an educational institution that attempted to fill the role of the church, the family, the YMCA, the Boy Scouts, or the apprenticeship program. In all these institutions, learning—some of it very important—takes place. But none of these institutions can be expected to protect and develop our intellectual heritage.

The acceptance of this notion of the special obligation of educational institutions would have drastic effects upon American schools, colleges, and universities. Institutions that set out to safeguard and expand the life of the mind would be required to abandon irrelevant activities. For example, such a popular irrelevancy as intercollegiate athletics would have to go, even though learning of a sort undoubtedly takes place in and through it. The effects on institutions of adult education would be equally serious: their primary responsibility would be to offer adults of all ages the continuous opportunity to lead, however intermittently, the life of the mind.

I say nothing here against other institutions with other objects. I am in favor of all kinds of things that I do not regard as educational. I am in favor of sports, refresher courses, and technical schools. I am in favor of the church, the family, the YMCA, and the Boy Scouts. I am in favor of life. But I see nothing to be gained and much to be lost by failing to distinguish among these activities and institutions. It is a philosophical truism that we must distinguish in order to unite.

Comments on

Hutchins

GEORGE B. LEONARD
West Coast Editorial Manager, Look *Magazine*

JOHN POPPY
Senior Editor, Look *Magazine*

We certainly agree with Dr. Hutchins that the old vocational model of "education" is already anachronistic and must be abandoned. Training just for marketable skills is, as he says, "limited, partial education for a limited, partial life." Any of us with a hopeful view of the future will applaud his predictions for educational technology—home learning centers, computers doing elementary training and informing, the ultimate reshaping of the whole institution of "schools"—as a sign that his instinct for the positive is still keen. Yet, considering the boldness of Dr. Hutchins' innovations at the University of Chicago in the 1930's and '40's, we have to confess ourselves dismayed by the tone of this paper.

Repeatedly, Dr. Hutchins tells us how badly things were done in the past; repeatedly, he leads up to a point at which he could break through to the future, to programs for action, to ways of transcending past errors; repeatedly, he frustrates us by pulling back. One example: After spending half his paper saying what *won't* work, he declares that "affluence, automation, democracy and a high rate of technological change . . . both enable and require us to undertake education for a full life . . . ; our successors . . . will then seek to transform their educational systems to prepare for a full life for all." At last, we think, he is going to blow off all the pressure built up in the first half, define the full life, and suggest some ways to transform both life and learning. But instead we get a sidestep into the past.

Not only does Dr. Hutchins seem unable to nerve himself for specific proposals; from beginning to end, he offers a definition of education that seems, in light of recent developments, pitifully narrow. "The contribution of educational institutions, or of any educational system, no matter how organized, might best be defined as intellectual." Where does that leave the emotions, the autonomic systems, the body senses, the interpersonal skills—all the areas that formal Western education has neglected in favor of the verbal-rational intellect? Strict intellectual behavior was developed most highly in the West as a way of fragmenting the world for a fast pay-off, to enable us to control matter and energy, to organize and govern ever-larger social entities such as colonial empires, to wage efficient war—not necessarily to help individuals live full lives or become fully human. From what Dr. Hutchins says, we are led to expect education in the future to be more of the same. His implication that the full life depends entirely on more use of *mind* is, we submit, the Academic Heresy.

We need an expanded view of education. It must include schools and some aspects of formal training, of course; but if we are serious about reaching for the full life, it must go beyond. It must take into account man's ancient dream—that every human being uses only a fraction of his abilities, that there must be some way for everyone to achieve far more of what is his to achieve, not just mentally, but sensually and even mystically. It must draw on the knowledge that science has at last turned its attention to the central questions of human capabilities. Looking deep into the brain, experimenters are finding unsuspected wave forms so subtle and complex as to suggest that, for all practical purposes, the human creative capacity is infinite. Looking afresh into human action, researchers are finding new ways for ordinary people to achieve what appear to be miracles of feeling and doing.

Let us say at this point that the needs are so clear, the opportunities in this consultation so great, that we find it impossible to bear Dr. Hutchins' evasions politely. Despite limited space, we want to make some proposals of the sort he could have made:

1. By the year 2000, the present system of educational priorities, giving most money, attention, and status to the upper grades, will be overturned. Critics from Rickover to Conant to Hutchins have concentrated on the high school and college years because the results of inadequate schooling show most dramatically there; but it is now clear that in any effort to reach individuals, the effect will be more effective and lasting, the younger they are. Long before 2000, top graduate students in education and the behavioral sciences will vie for positions in the grades from pre-kindergarten through second grade. There, pay, prestige, possibility for exciting research, and opportunity for service will be unequaled.

2. The first job of the educational establishment will be to demonstrate to every student that all learning is *joyful*. Watch a baby explore his world; you will see that "education" is not just working algebra problems or listening to lectures on Greek history. It is doing anything that changes you. The baby receives his own changes ecstatically; by 2020 we will realize that solving an elegant mathematical problem and making love are only different classes in

the same order of things, sharing common ecstasy. Advanced learning will no longer be self-conscious and painful; it will be like pursuing a pretty girl.

3. The next job will be to help very young children learn the culture's commonly agreed-upon knowledge and skills (spelling, reading, figuring) not only in an easy, joyful, efficient way, but *in a way that helps them learn that such knowledge is tentative*. Learning how to "break set," to assimilate new perceptions, will be part of any curriculum. Even with our present crude techniques—using programs and computers—the commonly agreed-upon stuff can be learned individually in, conservatively, one-third the tradition time. By 1970, demonstration schools could be set up to explore ways to teach the basic skills by the end of the first grade.

4. Then what? The remaining years of childhood and adolescence can be devoted to exploration and to flexible, powerful, individualized learning activities—not just in traditional subjects, but in many new areas having to do with aspects of human functioning that are presently neglected. Much of what will be studied by 2000 A.D. does not even have a commonly accepted name today. An increased population engaged primarily in human-service work will make it necessary for people to handle more and more intense, brief contacts with each other; they will practice encounters, non-verbal communication, empathy, extra-sensory perception, and other skills now regarded as far-out. Already, Dr. Joe Kamiya at the University of California Medical Center in San Francisco has explored a simple way of teaching people to control their brain waves, using an EEG machine and a simple computer; this suggests that nothing, even teleportation, is too far-fetched for us at least to consider.

5. By 1980, the traditional one-teacher-to-thirty-students presentation system will no longer exist. There will be no exams as we now know them, and no regular, fifty-minute class periods. "Teaching"—the authoritarian mode of handing down information a student must accept—will be dead by 2000 (some would say much sooner). The job of the educator will be to act as a *facilitator*—one who creates a rich, responsive environment that will elicit the most learning and change from the student.

6. It follows that compulsory education must be abolished. Not only will totally voluntary school attendance help retain the joy that compulsion now squashes, but educators will have to make their material relevant to the needs of the students, or they won't get any students.

7. Education for the full life will involve the full community. It will not be restricted to schools, classrooms, and courses. Today, most real learning takes place outside classrooms. An obvious step is to admit that the total environment *is* part of a person's educational experience, whether we like it or not, and go on to use it systematically (instead of separating school and "bad homes and bad neighborhoods" as Dr. Hutchins would have us continue to do.) Get the children out of the classroom into the offices, libraries, courts,

parks, factories, shops, and studios of the community; put them on a super-sonic flight for field trips abroad; it won't cost any more money in the long run than alienation, delinquency, unemployment, and war do already.

8. Knock down the walls between university and community. By 1980, the universities could have a new function: Higher education would not stand apart from life, but would be the chief substance, the very center of existence, the communication-work-recreation center of each community. The demarca-tion between "student" and "non-student" will blur and finally fade away; by 2020, every member of every community can be, to one degree or another, a member of the university.

In this space we have managed to give only the sketchiest outline of what could be a thorough list of proposals supported by existing data. But our function is not to do Dr. Hutchins' job for him; we hope that we have given some indications of why we feel disappointed by his paper and by the frag-mented view of "education" that he—along with most members of the aca-demic establishment—offers.

If we persist in seeing schools as separate from the rest of the community —as having to "win a single-handed triumph over all the other forces in the culture," in Dr. Hutchins' words—we might as well admit that they will fail to do anything but contribute to our ultimate destruction. If the universities, in a world that is changing as rapidly as ours, limit themselves to the "intellect" and stay committed to some "unique task," they will fail.

Much of what Dr. Hutchins says against "vocational" education can be said against his own definition: it is suffocatingly restrictive. It is unsuited for the needs of the future. It won't work.

HOMER D. BABBIDGE, JR.
President, University of Connecticut

Mr. Hutchins is predicting a revolution in the American attitude toward education. He believes that within the next fifty years we will abandon our present view, which he describes as manpower-oriented, and that "liberal education will be regarded as the central purpose of the schools." Clearly, if this prediction is sound, there are a lot of changes in store for American education.

But one must ask whether this is a realistic prediction or a fond hope. Mr. Hutchins has long been admired for his advocacy of liberal education, and it may just be that "the wish is father to the thought."

Many features of his essay indicate that Mr. Hutchins regards himself as a realist. He says flatly that "an educational system is a political phenomenon," that education is "an instrument by which the political community may reach its goals," and that "it is too much to hope that the school can win a single-handed triumph over all the other forces in the culture." Education in this context is clearly an expression of society, an enterprise largely—if not exclusively—shaped by outside forces. And Mr. Hutchins does not assume that this will change; he seems to be saying that education will continue to be a function of social, economic, and political forces.

But Mr. Hutchins believes that society as a whole will come to realize that we are not using education wisely for society's own purposes. He predicts a kind of great awakening to the realization that our system is (a) not doing for us what we thought it was doing, and (b) not equal to changing social needs. Hutchins doubts that manpower training can be successfully related to manpower needs, and questions whether education really contributes to economic growth. And he makes clear that he regards present-day education as totally unequal to the needs of a leisured society, which he views as a certain consequence of technological change.

How realistic is it to assume that the American people will come to share Mr. Hutchins' views? Certainly it is dangerous to underestimate the enormity of the shift in thinking that would be required. The author himself says, "The American multiversity has been taken over by the commercial, political, and military establishment, because these are the elements in our society that have the money." Pretty clearly, the money is on the side of present-day education, with all its manpower and economic-growth assumptions.

Mr. Hutchins projects an educational system consisting of a six-year elementary school, a three-year high school, and a three-year college, with "only those students interested in and qualified for independent study" going beyond this to the university. How realistic is this in the light of economic and social forces than can now be discerned? The Secretary of Labor has recently proposed fourteen years of compulsory schooling, not so much for educational reasons, as to keep more people out of the labor market. In the face of such forces, is it reasonable to predict a twelve-year system?

I raise these questions only because Mr. Hutchins seems to take the position that what is needed in education will come about only as controlling political and social agencies perceive that need. Even assuming the validity of Hutchins' prescription of what *ought* to be, the question remains whether it is *likely* to be. Petitioners for change have some responsibility to assess the feasibility of the changes proposed.

Some of Mr. Hutchins' forecasts seem certain. It is almost self-evident that something like "life-time learning" is in store, that the pressures to employ technology in education (abetted by "powerful commercial organizations") are heightening, and that we can look forward to greater federal financing of education. But there are some improbable predictions here, too. The vision of a university free of external pressures, rid of administrators, and subject only to the "disinterested and friendly comment" of its Trustees is a candidate for this category. And I think it unlikely a school system devoted entirely to the liberal arts—and "the same for everybody"—is in prospect.

Mr. Hutchins is properly concerned that our scientific and technical development may outrun our ability to manage this development, and the consequences of such lack of control are chilling, as he describes them. His faith that broad-scale liberal education can give us the means to "make democracy work" and to know "what is most important for us to know" is impressive. Whether this is a fond hope or not, no nation can afford to disregard his charge "to find out what liberal education is and how it may be made available to all."

Health Services in a Land of Plenty

This paper was commissioned to weigh our choices for the good life, to examine the costs and rewards of physical and mental health for all people of all ages. At which point is man's ability to adapt to his man-made environment too costly in human health terms? Can we afford good health for all? Which priority should there be for research? What are the great innovations to be made? What institutional changes will be required? Does health for all mean bureaucracy for all? Is that a price we *have* to pay? Are the aged to exist or live, and how? How can public health practices catch up to the foreseeable needs? What sort of deliberate genetic control do we want or need?

Author: Odin W. Anderson, Professor and Research Director, Center for Health Administration Studies, University of Chicago

Chairman: Jerome W. Lubin, AIP, Chief, California Health Information for Planning Service

Committee: James P. Dixon, President, Antioch College; James C. McGilvray, Medical Secretary, World Council of Churches; Herman Somers, Woodrow Wilson School of Public and International Affairs, Princeton University; Arthur Weissman, Director of Medical Economics, Kaiser Foundation Health Plan, Inc.; Jack R. Ewalt, Department of Psychiatry, Harvard Medical School; William H. Stewart, Surgeon General of the United States; Ray E. Brown, Director, Graduate Program in Hospital Administration, Duke University Medical Center; W. Benson Harer; John M. Weir, Director, The Rockefeller Foundation

Odin W. Anderson

Professor and Associate Director
Center for Health Administration Studies
University of Chicago

Health Services in a Land of Plenty

This essay is an attempt to assess the future development of our health services system. If public policy objectives are to assure the population of relatively equal access to preventive, curative, rehabilitative, and custodial services, we are faced with basic philosophic and pragmatic questions that I should like to pose and attempt to answer in a context of facts and personal assumptions stemming from experience. Hence, this is not so much a prediction of what will take place as it is a statement concerning the nature of the process and the social and political methodology needed to attain desired objectives. It is also a statement of guidelines on emphasis and some estimates of expenditures, facilities, and personnel.

Ends and means are reciprocals, and the ambitious ends envisioned here perforce affect and limit the range of means. I subscribe to the premise that this country has potential resources to come within reasonable approximation of equal access for all to the desired range of services, and without competing unduly for resources required by other enterprises such as the construction of highways, the improvement of education, going to the moon, reducing poverty, or maintaining a military establishment. Since I assume that scarcity in the usual pre-1930 and pre-Keynesian sense no longer exists, this premise naturally influences my observations and generalizations. A health service system in such a context will be relatively loose and expansive. I am sure some observers will regard my concept as wasteful and inefficient. I feel, however, that there is need for a great deal of room in which to maneuver, particularly to facilitate humaneness in such matters as the mitigation of waiting time for patients and the reduction of pressures on physicians and others who provide care. If affluence has any advantages, it seems that one of them should be a health service system based on generous proportions.

From the foregoing, then, flows my quite emphatic assumption that—to attain our objectives—we can and should allocate considerably more resources to the health services system than we now do, from both the public and private sectors of the economy, in order to maintain and accelerate the impressive gains of the past. The public policy should be pervaded by a sense of expansiveness in order to fill out our developing health services, an enterprise in which it has been inordinately difficult, so far, to establish criteria of performance other than of a very gross nature. I would stress organizational patterns secondarily because the relative abundance or scarcity of personnel and facilities directly influences the methods of delivering services. I would prefer to experiment with methods of delivery in a context of abundance rather than scarcity. If abundance is not manifest, then, of course, my proposed plan of action fails, and I must rearrange my thinking to adjust to scarcity. This would probably be a much simpler task, because solutions in a context of scarcity seem to be self-evident. This is perhaps why there is a tendency among many in the health field today to approach problems primarily in terms of shortages, deficits, and gaps in the health services establishment.

Personal Values: Refractions from Facts and Events

Since policy flows from the value system of a particular society and of every observer, I feel a need to state mine. It is a truism that each of us sees objects, events, and facts through a system of values more or less predictable. Thus, a Marxist's view of society will be very different from that of a Christian mystic. In the American context we share many common values regarding political rights, but diverge in degree regarding the role of government, and, in this context, its responsibilities for the provision of health services. The social scientist, in order to gain perspective, must be able to detach himself from the social environment to a high degree, an ability that should grow with training and practice although it is never totally attainable. This does not mean that social scientists have no personal values but should mean that they are able to identify values in terms of explicit means and ends and that they can make clear the consequences of alternative means of attaining certain social ends.

A premise of the social scientist is that all social systems function according to a central value system which gives a society meaning to its participants. Cultures vary widely. Some are incapable of developing an industrial type of society, given the value-premises industrialized societies live by, even though resources may be available. Others, like our own, develop into full-scale industrial systems because of a desire to manipulate the natural resources in the interests of comfort and aggrandizement. Important byproducts of our scientific and industrial development are the health services whereby we attempt to lengthen the life span, prevent and cure disease, and reduce pain. Other means of reaching for these goals are improved housing, nutrition, and education, but health services are the most direct means.

We take it for granted that the development of an extensive and high quality health service is virtually an end in itself. Hence, we believe that one of the marks of a humane and good society is reasonably equal access to health services for all people regardless of ability to pay and, to some degree, even regardless of residence, as in sparsely populated areas. This value has come to be considered a basic human right, beyond dispute in principle, in the same sense that a person has a right to be free of bodily harm from others as he walks on the street. Such "rights" are not 100 percent achievable, but their single most important aspect is that the values they represent are omnipresent motivations.

The public policy debate is over means, not ends. Health services have become a social enterprise essentially removed from the free market method of allocating goods and services. Our pervasive value orientation, therefore, focuses on the needs of the population rather than on demand and the problems of supply, although it is evident that we have not succeeded in keeping up with demand. It follows that subsidizing those who are unable to pay the going prices of health services is a vital part of public policy. Once we accept this policy, the debate over means remains within definable limits. It becomes inadmissible then to argue, for example, that if a person is too poor to afford a lifesaving health measure he should die. By definition there are no unworthy patients. Only the means vary. The end is constant.

For life to be worthwhile I believe we must subscribe to dogmas such as the inviolability of the person, the dignity of man, and equal opportunity for "life, liberty, and the pursuit of happiness." A most specific dogma is equal access to health services regardless of income, although it must be recognized that such an objective, among others, is only approximately attainable. Equal access, like "absolute" health or a universally accepted definition of "happiness," outruns human capacity. We must live only partially fulfilled because absolute equality of access to health services is, in practice, impossible, even though it is an acknowledged goal for which we should constantly strive. I entertain essentially unattainable objectives in order to lash myself to struggle for them, but I am not blind to reality. In the same way, we must be realistic with respect to availability of personnel, quality or quantity of care, facilities, finances, and degree of acceptance by the health professions and by the public. Hence, I have come to regard methods of attaining essentially utopian objectives as a process rather than as an "only" or "best" way. Living, too, is a process. And it is perhaps just as well. We would not be content for long with attainable absolutes.

There is no "best" method because each method of providing health services has inherent advantages and disadvantages. Each depends upon what is regarded as the best composite of advantages in time and place, hence is viable and never static. We have to work, then, toward a balance of conflicting desires through bargaining, the net result being totally satisfying to no one, but partially satisfying to nearly all. Various types of bargaining characterize our social and political system. I believe that this system results in the greatest net freedom of action for most people and most interest groups.

Much as I feel constrained by the early training and current objective circumstances that limit my freedom, I am not a fatalist nor a complete determinist. However, I assume a very thin, and therefore most important, margin (perhaps as little as 5 percent) of indeterminism wherein novelty and creativity have some play. Because I regard these forces and circumstances as impersonal, I do not need to subscribe to a devil (or angel) theory of human behavior, though at times I have wished for that human luxury.

All the foregoing, I feel, has relevance to what we can reasonably expect of nurses and physicians in delivering optimum service day after day in various contexts. One environment may be more conducive to "tender loving care" than another, a fact to be lived with. Only compulsive idealists and geniuses claim to transcend their daily environments; hence a system of delivering health services must be geared to what can be reasonably expected of rank and file personnel who can be recruited and trained with such available resources and standards as can be mustered and instilled with a degree of intelligent reciprocity from the public. Methods of delivery must have some relationship to the tolerance levels of personnel and patients. Such tolerance levels are difficult to determine; again, therefore, at the risk of belaboring the point, I foresee a health system which is generously proportioned.

As for planning, a process which is by its very nature future-oriented, I believe there are severe limitations on the extent to which we can "invent the future." At the same time, there must be bold, but tentative thrusts into the world of tomorrow to provide us with a sense of direction, even though it is necessary that we modify pace and details of specific programs toward a comprehensive goal, i.e., equalizing access to preventive, curative, rehabilitative, and custodial services. Some social endeavors lend themselves to relatively more detailed planning than others. Results depend on the planners' ability to determine and measure variables. Hence, it would seem that a network of highways—with such variable components as miles, cement, application of the laws of eminent domain, speed of traffic, and cost—can be more easily planned than a health service system in which the input, and particularly the output, variables are by comparison elusive, and exceedingly unstable over time—disease patterns, for example, or new preventive and therapeutic measures, or a host of other factors. Then there are variations within the health system. Medical schools, to cite but one example, need to be projected at least ten years ahead for completion in order to realize an appropriate output of professional manpower; yet other human components of the health team, such as ward orderlies, call for much shorter projections as a result of lesser training needs. Each element requires relatively long or short periods for feedback, and thus, we must live tentatively and uncertainly. We must acknowledge a constant state of tension between the past and the emerging future, knowing that never will there be a static or perfect solution. Inherently, there are no absolute solutions and no totally adequate health service because there are scarcely any scientifically derived criteria. If such criteria were developed, then planning would become easier. Under present circumstances we must rely largely on best judgment, a tenuous basis for public policy formulations when experts disagree in good faith.

Components of a Health Service System

It is apparently useful to regard all groupings of human beings and organizations as systems that may be dissected by operations research and the computer. Actually, the factor analysis concept is old in sociology and in the physical and natural sciences; it does, therefore, seem to have useful applications for health services. The systems analysis approach is, in fact, now being considered and will be a severe test of the level of sophistication of systems analysts.

The literature characteristically sets up health services as a conglomerate of seemingly disparate parts. At best an "ideal" model is visualized; at worst, a simple classification of objects and functions is presented. Generally, the interrelationships of the various components and the essentially dynamic nature of the system do not emerge. Hence the plethora of concepts and principles of medical care administration provide no convenient levers with which to grasp some comprehension of the functioning of a health services system in a particular social and political environment. There seems to be no concept of alternative approaches in various contexts and with regard for their consequences. Somehow there is always implicit an ideal model wherein it is projected that all patients are wise, physicians and nurses all dedicated, and money in plentiful supply. Obviously, such an elaborate fantasy is of little value for realistic current appraisals or for future planning. I shall therefore attempt a theory of a health services system on the basis of our knowledge today and possible transformations for tomorrow.

I shall assume that the health services endeavor can be treated as a totality and that it lends itself to the kind of analysis applicable to other large human endeavors such as the military establishment, the automobile industry, or the educational system. The health services system encompasses a range of personnel, facilities, and central human problems of disease, disability, and death. Industrially developed countries have built an elaborate health services edifice based on the scientific and medical discoveries of the last hundred years or so. It can be shown that the health services represent a more or less closed system with a hierarchy of personnel who are recruited and trained and rewarded in certain ways. It can be shown that patients enter and exit at certain portals and that they are sorted, managed, and "disposed of" in various ways. From country to country in the Western world there are variations, from a central core of similarity, of such key elements as the types of facilities and personnel, sources of funds, portals of entry and exit for patients.

In the United States the self-evident service units and organizational structure include the physician; the general hospital; clinics; the nurse; auxiliary or paramedical personnel; the pharmacist and pharmacies; nursing and convalescent homes; home care programs; and goods such as hearing aids, braces, crutches, wheelchairs, and other devices associated with maintaining the maximum functioning of the body. Then there are various methods of finance—general taxation, insurance, direct pay from patients, and so on.

A parallel structure is observable in dentistry, which is more or less separate from the services that are the concern of physicians. Another parallel structure which for social-historical reasons and also for reasons of therapeutic methods and milieus exists as an entity is the complex of mental hospitals and psychiatric services in psychiatrists' offices. In the past decade or so there has been an increasing but slow fusion of the health services for so-called somatic disease and mental disease, exemplified in large part by the establishment of psychiatric units in general hospitals for short-term assessment and treatment. Further, there has been the development of community mental health clinics for patients living at home. Finally, another large segment or system within the health services establishment is the official public health department supported by federal, state, and local funds and charged mainly with sanitary environmental control, communicable disease control, preventive services for mothers and children, and health education. Sometimes official health agencies are also charged with medical programs for the indigent, programs for special diseases such as cancer, and the disbursement at the state level of Hill-Burton hospital construction funds. Finally, another segment that cannot be ignored in terms of its effect on health and on legitimized health services is that of practitioners such as chiropractors, naturopaths, and faith healers.

In the main, tax funds support the services for special groups such as veterans, for maternal and child care, for those with communicable diseases, for long-term care of the mentally ill and the tubercular, and for health services for those with low incomes. Recently, the segment of the population 65 years of age and over has been added, financed by a payroll tax through the Social Security system. Federal funds assist in the capital financing of voluntary and public hospitals, in grants for medical research, training grants for researchers, nurses, and public health workers, and in loans for medical students. The total expenditures for all health and related activities in 1966 exceeded $40 billion or about $200 per person. The split between the public and private expenditures is roughly 25 percent and 75 percent, respectively. The health services system in this country resides, therefore, largely in the private sector, which provides and pays for the great bulk of services for acute and somatic diseases.

There are many interrelationships between the private and public sectors of American society, but government is largely a buyer of services from the private sector, a rather classic pattern for filling governmental needs ranging from missiles to medical care. As a prominent example, ownership of the great bulk of hospital facilities resides in the private sector in voluntary institutions, as does ownership or rental of offices by physicians, dentists, and pharmacists. Voluntary hospitals are increasingly regarded as a quasi-public resource, however. Physicians, dentists, and pharmacists are still, in effect, private entrepreneurs with professional constraints, a role ambivalence which is presumed to cause many strains.

I have mentioned that about 75 percent of the funds for health services comes from private sources. Within the private sector approximately one-third of all funds comes from private insurance agencies, which have been a steadily growing influence. Within insurance a large proportion of premium or subscription cost is paid by employers through payroll deductions and as a result of collective bargaining with organized labor. Thus, the ownership, financing, and operation of the health services system in the United States is diffused, with a wide dispersion of sources of funds and decision-making units. The system is essentially pluralistic with the various sectors negotiating with and accommodating to one another.

The various components of services—hospitals, physicians, pharmacists, dentists, etc.—are relatively autonomous units that maintain an implicit and continuous contractual relationship with one another. Physicians negotiate for privileges to admit patients to a hospital; physicians refer patients to one another; prescriptions written by physicians are filled at pharmacies; and, therefore, with few exceptions, the gatekeeper of this system is the physician. The patient enters the system via the general practitioner, the obstetrician, ophthalmologist, otolaryngologist, psychiatrist, pediatrician, or internist. He is much less likely to enter through referral by the other specialties. The system is an "open" one, and the bulk of the medical care in this country is provided within and among its components. The patient may go to a solo-practitioner or a physician in group practice. He may join a fee-for-service and free choice type of health insurance plan utilizing the prevailing system, or join a closed group-practice prepayment system if there is one in his area. At first glance the structure seems very complex, and some knowledge is required if patients are to use the system well. It is regarded as highly desirable, although the principle continues to be debated, that a person have a stable relationship with a personal physician who will marshal other medical resources in the community on the patient's behalf as they are needed. Those who favor a "rational" system play down the concept of a personal physician; those who are less concerned with a rational system are likely to emphasize the merits of a personal physician for everyone.

The health services are presently utilized a great deal. Use has doubled and tripled for hospital and physicians' services respectively during the past thirty years. Today there are about 130 hospital admissions per 1000 population, five physician visits per person per year, and 60 surgical operations per 1000 population. This means that annually there are over 25 million hospital admissions, 1 billion physician visits and 12 million surgical operations. At least 130 million people see a physician at least once in a given year. About 80 million people see a dentist at least once. By any standard, then, the health service enterprise is enormous and touches the lives of the great majority of the population. It is regarded as expensive, although so far it absorbs only 6 percent of the gross national product and 6 percent of annual family income. The latter is highly variable according to income level and use. Despite the impressiveness of use statistics, however, and a gratifying increase in utilization of services, especially in recent decades, there are many criticisms of the prevailing system as described.

Past and Current Disease Patterns

In any time and place a combination of circumstances and factors generates certain disease and death patterns and methods of coping with disease and death within the life cycle. The biological, social, and cultural factors are so interrelated that life styles affect health levels both favorably and detrimentally, regardless of the ignorance and poverty or knowledge and affluence of particular countries. There is a rough but nonetheless real relationship between disease and death patterns and certain social and technological conditions. Looking back at the history of Europe during the past thousand years, we can see five patterns of disease. These are not exclusive in any one period, of course, but can serve as outstanding features distinguishing the different centuries in terms of primary health problems. The traceable stages of disease are as follows:

1. *Leprosy and plague.* These diseases seem to have characterized the period between 1000 and 1500 A.D., although Europe was then ravaged by outbreaks of many other diseases as well.

2. *Louse-borne diseases and syphilis.* Toward the end of the fifteenth century, diseases carried by lice became increasingly widespread. From that time until the second half of the nineteenth century, the louse pursued a triumphant course, and typhus fever and other louse-borne diseases became the dreaded companions of wars and famines. As cotton and soap won over wool and dirt, typhus virtually disappeared from western Europe. Syphilis also characterized the period from the sixteenth to the eighteenth century but became gradually less virulent and prevalent.

3. *Gastrointestinal diseases.* During the nineteenth century in Europe the major health problems of communities were diseases spread through the gastrointestinal tract. Those that had the greatest impact were cholera and typhoid fever, closely linked to the urban expansion which followed the industrial revolution. The lack of environmental sanitation permitted gastrointestinal excretions to spread freely and transmit disease. Toward the end of the century these diseases began to decline as cities benefited from proper sewage disposal and the purifying of water and milk.

4. *Tuberculosis and the communicable diseases of childhood.* The impact on European populations of nineteenth century developments in sanitation, microbiology, and nutrition did not become grossly evident until the latter part of the century. Reductions in the adult death rate prior to the introduction of immunization and better hygiene came about apparently as a result of general improvements in living conditions, particularly the stabilization of the annual food supply. During the late nineteenth century and continuing into the twentieth century, a number of diseases of the respiratory tract which had been leading causes of death began to decline, for example, tuberculosis. Concurrently, beginning in most countries about 1880, the communicable diseases of childhood gradually declined as causes of death, and progress

in combating them accelerated during the twentieth century as a result of immunization and more effective therapies.

5. *Cardiovascular-renal diseases, malignant neoplasms, and accidents.* With the twentieth century decline in morbidity and mortality from gastrointestinal and respiratory diseases, particularly among children and young adults, many more individuals now survive into the age groups associated with such non-communicable diseases as cancer, arthritis, and cardiovascular and renal diseases. In fact, reductions in deaths from all other causes have exposed accidents as the third cause of death today.

Perhaps increasing concern with conditions such as asthma, peptic ulcers, ulcerative colitis, and others that are less specific symptomatically —the psychosomatic diseases—characterizes the present period. We have been becoming increasingly aware of psychosomatic disorders as causes of illness and ill-being, and it is felt that a positive approach to health services must deal with these qualitative aspects of life. Indeed, it can be said that when a nation can report that heart disease is the leading cause of death and that there is increasing concern with psychosomatic diseases, a high level of health and health consciousness has been achieved in terms of current knowledge. Disease and illness are never eliminated, but patterns change, and, as a consequence, so do perceptions of goals.

Evaluation of the Current Structure and Functioning of the Health Services

The health services systems of all industrialized countries are experiencing tremendous strain because of increasing specialization, concomitant rising costs, growing demand, and changing morbidity patterns. The intensity of the strain varies only in degree; its cause seems to be embodied in two major factors. (1) With the trend toward specialization and consequently greater complexity, increasingly more formal organization is apparently necessary. (2) The system geared to acute and short-term episodes of illness is besieged by the increasing prevalence of long-term illness, thus straining the facilities and procedures designed primarily for short-term care. The system is required to develop facilities and personnel for long-term care from a tradition of short-term and acute care patterns. This is not easy and may even be impossible given the desire for standards, because personnel are much more interested in patients with short and acute episodes of illness than those with long, drawn-out illnesses who are likely to be elderly.

Compounding these problems is an inherent inability to define an adequate health service. The health services system of a country faces essentially the same fundamental difficulties as its military establishment in determining what are adequate facilities, personnel, and finances. Both are charged with utopian goals—maximum health or maximum military security for all. Health services systems or military systems are the ultimate expressions of social policy arrived at partly by accretion and partly by directed planning (and in my opinion, mostly by accretion) in relation to ends that inherently have no logical limits set by objective criteria.

Underlying the two causes of strain on the health services system mentioned earlier, it would seem that there are two fundamental characteristics that condition the operation of the entire structure and underlie the many frustrations and discomfitures in social and administrative policy. These two exceedingly elastic elements in the core of the health services system make discussions of a range of alternatives very difficult. One is the variability of the perception of illness and what people do about illness; and the other is the necessary discretionary judgment and responsibility (together with the authority) that is required of physicians, the chief gate-keepers of the system. These crucial elements are usually ignored or overlooked. I would like to believe that if they were recognized and acknowledged, the endless and frenetic debates over such issues as adequacy, proper and improper use of services, and high costs of services would cease and we could advance to a level of discussion concerned with a range of alternatives. Hence, again, my reason for emphasis on generous proportions to allow these two elements maximum play. Both force an uncomfortable degree of necessary flexibility on the range of methods of delivering services if the total system is to be responsive to the needs of patients and of physicians.

Use of services and price have gone up in all countries, and all countries complain about relative shortages of various types of personnel. These problems will persist. Consequently, there is a great deal of indeterminacy in the range and amount of personnel and services—not to mention expenditures—that can be justified in the interest of a good health service. The current expenditure for health services, comprising 6 percent of the gross national product, could conceivably be tripled, in other words increased to $120 billion or $600 per person per year, if the public policy were adopted to allocate our resources to cure, ameliorate, and prevent illness, and to rehabilitate all people who could benefit from the tremendous technology and knowhow we have today. Rather than embark on such a course, we develop an over-concern for "efficiency," that is, for running a tight system with waiting lists, high occupancy rates, and other personal inconveniences. This is paradoxical. With all of our affluence and technology we choose restriction instead of a public policy directed to a "loose," convenient, and humane system. A loose system would be considered expensive and presumably wasteful even in an economy with the largest discretionary income in the history of the world and an income that is growing.

I suggest that the current seemingly conglomerate and unwieldy structure of the health services system has an intrinsic ability to change, an ability that flows out of the bargaining and challenge and response activities of the various groups at interest, government included. It seems to me that this ability is the source of initiative and motivation among all of the interest groups, as long as there is a shared consensus on ends. This is in keeping with my understanding of the American temperament. The system is characterized by inducements and persuasion rather than directives and force, although a judicious mix of the two kinds of interrelationship is always present in negotiations.

I emphasize increases in finance in order to assure concomitant increases in personnel and facilities to keep pace with the needs of our growing population and even to exceed them. I emphasize quantity, given the prevailing minimum standards; reorganization of services is a subsidiary, although an important, issue. Our resources and our medical pluralism can enable continuing demonstration of a range of methods of delivering services. These methods already exist in this country; they have been virtually inhibited in other countries with centralized financing and direction. I argue that the several methods should be free to develop as far as they are inherently able without artificial supports or constraints of legislation and without arbitrary controls on quantity and quality from any source. We can afford this pluralism and looseness. There is no best method, and this country need not be stifled by a single pattern.

The whole field of computer technology is in a trial and testing stage in relation to its use in medical diagnosis and therapy. The extent to which computers can someday replace or supplement the services of nurses and physicians is unknown. My own intuition is to doubt the general application of computer technology, contrary to the belief of many. It would seem, however, that mass physical examinations can be facilitated along the lines of some demonstrations now taking place that apparently are efficient and relatively inexpensive. It would also seem that computers can assist immeasurably in diagnosis and consequently better therapy. Such technology should be conceived of as helpful to the physician and not as a replacement for him.

Many suggestions are currently being made for increasing the type of supporting personnel for physicians so that "routine" work can be delegated. This concept is hardly new and has been variously considered since modern medicine was established at the turn of the century. What may be new is the concept that in certain episodes of illness the physician should be the last rather than first person to see the patient in a spectrum of individuals responsible for care. It is also held that the physician should be shielded from the possibly trivial blandishments of patients who are not satisfied with seeing only auxiliary personnel. There is danger here that teamwork can become a protection for the physician from his patient rather than providing protection for the one who is ill. The medical fortresses are emerging with moats of auxiliary personnel and office receptionists. I believe we are bedazzled by the organizational model of modern industry, which is product-oriented, and are uncritically applying many of its management principles to the delivery of health services, which are service-oriented and personal. While recognizing the growth of specialization and the need for teamwork, I believe that emphasis should be placed on giving the patient direct access to the physician rather than on minimizing that access. The difference in emphasis, however, results in different teamwork structures. I grant that so valuable a resource as a physician should be used efficiently in order to stretch the short supply, but I would rather see a very serious emphasis on training more physicians than on bolstering the medical profession with multiple ranks of auxiliary personnel. I regard the issue as mainly a social engineering problem. There are many more qualified applicants to medical schools than there are openings for students in medical schools. An eventual increase of 25 to 50 percent over the current supply, and in relation to population, would be salutary for medical care in this country.

Finally, I feel that the benefit structures of health insurance need to be expanded to eliminate the economic catastrophes to families of people with high-cost episodes of illness. There has been steady improvement in benefits for many years, but the uninsured or uncovered portion of medical expense is still too large. This is not to argue for first dollar payment and "comprehensive" coverage, which are in my mind essentially administrative issues relating to cost and volume controls, but to urge that health insurance approximate the near total reimbursement of high-cost episodes.

I would not wish to see the sources of payment and the providers of service in a tight contractual bind (necessitated by the pure service benefit type of insurance) because the providers of service, particularly hospitals, would have too little room in which to maneuver and maintain financial soundness. Other areas of the health economy must likewise remain flexible, although the medical profession needs increasingly to set up and follow fee norms so that physicians' fees can be reasonably predicted over time. Also, a larger supply of physicians would increase the bargaining power of the big buyers of service and the general public. Certainly it would be likely to ease recruitment of physicians into salaried group practice units. I stress the need to permit the providers of service, the public, and the big buyers of service room in which to negotiate since all three parties must find an equilibrium for the benefit of the total structure. Until recently, the providers of service called the tune in terms of price and methods of delivery. Now the big buyers are beginning to call the tune. But no group should remain in a dominant position indefinitely to dictate to the others. This principle is the essence of our social and political system. Centralization of finance, controls over cost and volume of services, as well as controls over personnel and facilities do not encourage looseness and abundance. While this may seem to be a rather dogmatic assertion, I believe it can be supported by experience. It has great implications for planning the health services establishment.

Current Mortality and Morbidity Patterns and Potentials for Change

For the first time in the history of mankind, a reduction in mortality from the leading cause of death is up to the individual assisted by the health services and the social system. It is no longer simply a function of relatively simple social controls such as the provision of pure water or vaccine to entire communities. The leading cause of death, heart disease and its related disorders, is also a great cause of disability, although to an increasing extent, many of the deaths and much of the morbidity stem from unhealthy habits, which, if changed, would result in fewer deaths and less disability. Apparently, knowledge in itself is not a sufficient motivating force. And perhaps we have much to learn about what can be more effective. In the meanwhile, in a society which prides itself on the freedom of the individual, I suppose people should be permitted "to dig their graves with their teeth" or to die gradually from cigarette smoking, even if they do so with full knowledge. We are ethically bound, simultaneously, to repair the results no matter how they are caused by providing expensive personnel and technology as expressions of social compassion.

In prevention and treatment it seems that we are running out of specifics unless, for example, it is found that there is a specific cure for cancer. But all of the other prevailing ills such as arthritis, heart disease, diseases which seem to be of metabolic origin, and mental diseases of neurological origin or tied to social stress need a great deal of management and patience. As the number of diseases that can be handled in terms of specifics decreases even further—and the remaining margin is small—we are increasingly faced with the management of long-term chronic diseases associated with survival and wear and tear. Certain disabilities may respond in varying degree to deliberate rehabilitation measures; others can only be palliated and managed. Increasingly, we must teach people how to live gracefully with inevitable disabilities. In many instances we may also have to learn to view death with dignity and fortitude as a benevolent aspect of our destiny rather than to resort compulsively to kidney, heart, and other organ transplantations with their concomitant stresses on medical personnel, facilities, and society in general.

If present trends continue, society may find itself accommodating a growing number of ill people who will tyrannize the well with their constant needs for batteries for heart pacemakers, for example, or cans of regularly delivered oxygen, or dialysis equipment that can be used in the home. The public policy implications are frightening to contemplate, but it seems that this type of medicated survival (as distinct from medicated comfort for the arthritic, for example) is theoretically possible on a large scale. We have not yet developed the ethical and institutional structure to deal with such horrendous policy decisions, nor do I have any easy suggestions. Yet, such developments are the inevitable end products of a highly technical, research-oriented society.

The future pattern of disease is quite unpredictable, but optimism for the immediate future is unfounded and not very helpful. Our modern environment is new in the history of mankind, and it is impossible to foretell what the new ecological relationships will mean to human health. We are told that there is continuous genetic pollution of the human bloodstream, as it were, which can result in a debilitated population. But some authorities, perhaps as well qualified, say this is not so. We are discovering that the social system itself generates disease and that only by changing the social system and human behavior patterns quite drastically can we hope to reduce the incidence of certain diseases. In certain instances, however, new social controls and a radical change in habits are seemingly worse than the presence of disease. Highly restrictive patterns may, in fact, be even less desirable than some diseases and may usher in fresh symptoms unheard of in the past. Heart disease and overeating or syphilis and promiscuity may be ineluctibly associated; however, their prevention is not as simple as one might hope. Changes in human behavior are not easily come by, and rarely do they follow a prescribed course.

The Matrix of Future Alternatives

As I review the development of the health services structure in Western countries since the advent of modern medicine, beginning with the latter part of the nineteenth century, I am struck by its seeming spontaneity and leisureliness. Various groups of private citizens founded and financed hospitals; the practitioners of medicine were already recognized and accepted and began to make arrangements with the hospitals. In this country initiative by the private sector preceded action by the public sector; and the private sector continues to be the leader in health services development and innovation, aided and abetted and prodded by public forces. The services for low-income families were and continue to be a subsidiary aspect of the total system.

In Great Britain the private sector also assumed leadership through its famous voluntary hospitals, but with charity as central to the system rather than subsidiary. In Sweden, the public sector assumed leadership, as was also true with a few exceptions everywhere on the continent. The forms taken by various health services systems seemed to be conditioned by needs as interpreted by the health professions in dialogue with those who had money, whether private or public. Later, payment mechanisms to finance the daily operations of the systems were grafted on to the organizational forms that had evolved more or less by the spontaneous interplay of forces and interests. Voluntary health insurance agencies simply accepted the prevailing structure of the health services. In Great Britain, the National Health Service through its centralized financing embraced the prevailing organizational form and "rationalized" it into hospital service regions of some sort, filled out the hospital staffing structure, and used the currently existing hospitals. The same happened elsewhere in Europe.

Even so brief a review shows, particularly in this country, that developments have been predominantly local; that initiative has been local. The federal government has entered the picture to support and nurture this form of creativeness, the Hill-Burton Hospital Survey and Construction Act being a prime example. Now the intent within the health field seems to be to fuse local initiative and central guidance. I use the word guidance rather than control because there is as yet little central control. As long as local areas retain their prerogative to participate in the federal largesse or to turn it down, as in the case of Title XIX of Medicare, control cannot be considered centralized. Another example is seen in the decentralized administration of payments to the providers of services under Title XVIII of the same act. The federal government, then, must remain in a negotiating capacity with the private health sector, unless it elects to build its own facilities—a most unlikely event.

Our tremendous and imposing and capable health services structure is now entering a period characterized by such planning jargon as coordination, integration, cooperation, cost-benefit analysis, and cost, volume, and quality controls. The many relatively autonomous units are now nudging each other at every turn, and hospital planning councils have sprung up in many major cities. The agencies that administered the Hill-Burton Hospital Survey and Construction Act are turning more toward a deliberate overall planning function than they envisioned at the inception of the law. Now we are hoping to fuse the creativity of local initiative and pride (which presumably are diminishing in the face of more central financing, guidance, and possibly control) with regional plans in order to eliminate overlapping of facilities and personnel and to assure a more even distribution of expensive and complicated medical hardware. Undoubtedly, this development was inevitable, and now we face the problem of "planned" spontaneity, initiative, guidance, and control.

The United States Public Health Service, the National Institutes of Health, and the Social Security Administration have been exceedingly salutary forces in challenging the health services establishment to put forth its best efforts and to accelerate its pace. I believe there is a constant need for a balancing of power, finance, and interest, and such balancing is certainly still characteristic of the current system. The federal government will continue to buy most of the health services it needs to fulfill its programs and provide them only in exceptional instances; the federal government will subsidize research as well as conduct much research under its own auspices. The federal government is a salutary force as long as the private sector I have described meets it head-on. It is salutary because the health services establishment needs a goad in addition to the pressure which can come from patients only. Until now the private health establishment has determined the structure, range, and location of services, and the form of capital funding and daily maintenance, as well as the forms of health insurance. It is then in exceedingly good shape to debate the questions of methodology with a powerful force, the federal government, the official custodian of the general welfare. Like all power centers, the federal government needs to be watched and balanced, as do also the health insurance agencies and all of the professional health associations. This is the nature of pluralism.

I believe there is a consensus that the currently developing structure provides a matrix for innovation, efficiency, creativity, and quality, and for maximum freedom for individual groups to maneuver toward constant improvement and the highest degree of excellence of which they are capable. The prevailing public policy assumption seems to be one of "beefing up" the system rather than changing it in substance. However, changes in the system will emerge from the negotiating and bargaining process rather than through preconceived blueprints. The current heart disease, cancer, and stroke program exemplifies this policy.

The chief disadvantage of this system—in terms of the felt urgency of the medical problems around us—is that it is unable to move very fast; and even when the system does move, the final resolutions to problems seem often to be far from ideal because the interests of many groups must be accommodated. It seems that the only way to move fast, at least to achieve short range goals, is to delegate authority to a central body; the various groups involved then subordinate their own immediate interests for the larger whole in order to attain specific objectives. I believe this is the central dilemma in formulating public policy for the health field currently and for the long-range future.

Instead of the relatively deliberate and, to many, maddeningly slow development of the health services to serve fully current and future needs, it seems to me that we may be gearing ourselves to a protracted series of crash programs under the umbrella of an overall public policy of extreme urgency. To a certain extent this may indeed be necessary if the many perplexing medical problems facing us are going to be solved adequately and quickly. We must marshal the resources of the country in a semi-military, although democratic, manner to keep pace with, if not to exceed, the growth of the population and the endless proliferation of medical discoveries and technology. We need to be backed by much more money than is now being spent to increase and spread the health resources of the country, and to fill out the range of services and goods necessary for full-scale prevention, rehabilitation, and management of many intractable diseases.

This prescription has serious implications for our usual way of solving problems, but I see no other way to attain the very high objectives we seem to have set for ourselves, and I suggest a semi-crash method to attain them, although I fear the consequences. For some time to come the main stimulus will be the federal government. The questions we must face, then, are difficult: Are the means worthy of the end? Can we catalyze the forces within our social and health system to meet a constant state of urgency or semi-urgency? Or shall we settle for lesser objectives, or fewer objectives, or work more slowly and carefully for the long haul? At the very least we probably can settle for something between our current evolutionary and pragmatic approach and one of faster pace and bolder innovations. It seems to me that the latter would bring the risk of wrecking the existing structure and its variants, a structure I believe to be fundamentally sound in terms of what I consider the possible and in terms of promise for continuing innovations in delivery of service.

Recommendations Dictated by the Objectives and Circumstances

My recommendations for the present and future are dictated by the public policy objective in this country that all people should have relatively equal access to high quality health services of all types needed for the prevention, diagnosis, and treatment of illness; for rehabilitation, and for the management of long-term illnesses. The emphasis is on prevention when possible, cure if prevention fails or is not possible, rehabilitation when indicated, and management and custodial care when everything else has been done with the maximum cooperation of the health services system and the public.

Although this is a very lofty objective, I assume that as individuals and as a social system we are capable of doing more than we believe is possible and at a faster pace than deemed endurable. I am, therefore, not necessarily assuming that it is possible to carry out these recommendations to their fullest, but I am assuming we have not yet tested our system completely to determine how near the stated goals we can get. Perhaps the fundamental test is to see how long we can sustain the level of intense activity and pressure necessary to attain these objectives. War, hurricanes, and similar emergencies seem to bring out the heroic (or demonic) qualities in man, but after each challenge we lapse into less intense daily routines. A health or social system cannot be incandescent constantly. But this is a matter of judgment, and we probably do not yet know to what extent we can improve our performance and still live a tolerable daily life with manageable personal stress created by the strain to attain our objectives.

I must then assume that we need to engage in at least a semi-crash kind of planning and development for health services during the next ten years to keep pace with, or better still, to outpace the social, economic, and medical forces swirling about us. Perhaps thereafter we can assume flying altitude, so to speak. In a rough order of importance, the following are the factors that will condition our activities:

1. Population increase and both absolute and relative increases in the aged.

2. Absolute and relative increase in long-term illness, and particularly of patients who are unable to help themselves in their most elementary needs.

3. Environmental pollution, especially air and concomitant respiratory illnesses.

4. Increasing urbanization and concurrently increasing social and technical complexity.

5. Increasing division of labor and concurrently increasing specialization in medicine and continuing fragmentation.

6. Unabated developments in medical technology, particularly in body repair and organ transplantation.

7. Increasing labor market alternatives that will lessen the relative attractiveness of helping services, particularly services requiring direct body care and serving of patients. Some types of such services cannot be bought in terms of caring for long-term patients with dignity. Only the dregs of the labor market seem to be available now and in the future. The truly dedicated element is dwindling.

It would seem self-evident that the most pervasive force is the continuing increase in population. Current estimates are:

1965	195,000,000
1970	209,000,000
1980	240,000,000
2000	320,000,000
2020	420,000,000

At this very moment we are passing the 200 million mark. There will be an average annual increase of 3 million people from now until 1980, 4 million from 1980 to 2000, and 5 million from 2000 to 2020. Concurrently, it is predicted that the gross national product will double, quadruple, and so on, as will disposable personal income. Hence, as the economic pie gets bigger, a constant percentage allocation for health services will result in more money; if the percentage allocated for health increases, as seems likely, even greater financial resources will become available. Obviously, the civilian labor force will increase more or less in relation to the total population, from 78 million in 1965, 83 million in 1970, 100 million in 1980, 140 million in 2000, and 180 million in 2020. The hours of work per worker will decrease, but I assume this cannot be true for managerial, professional, and related personnel. They will continue to work long hours to keep the system functioning. The others can presumably and metaphorically go fishing, or assist in their off-hours in manning the tremendous helping service establishment that will be necessary to care for long-term illnesses.

I have been asked to estimate needed health personnel, facilities, and money for the present, and for 1970, 1980, 2000, and 2020. I would like to indicate at least the direction the health field should take and the general style in which the "planning" should be conducted. However, a detailed table showing growth by stages is given in Appendix A.

As I have already indicated, I believe that the main style of planning should be one of expansiveness, erring on the side of generosity rather than scarcity. Basically, I believe that this is "realistic" because our economy is expanding, with resulting increases in social and personal discretionary incomes; our disease problems are becoming more serious because of increases in chronic illness associated with survival into the upper age groups, and because we are increasingly able through such measures as organ transplantation to sustain the lives of the disabled, handicapped, and physically dependent. Moreover, our standards of needs are changing in accord with our expanding standard of living and our broadening perceptions of health. Finally, integral to all the foregoing, are the questions of prevention of illness, rehabilitation, and the wide range of activities that fall within the purview of mental health. To these ends, there are some who believe that the medical schools should assume a larger service function for the community, as is now envisioned by the heart disease, cancer, and stroke program. But the schools have to look to their main functions of training and research with, in my view, priority on training. It is possible that the residents in various medical specialties could be used to advantage in staffing health centers for the poor or in other community functions, but I certainly do not see this resource as very substantial unless there is an increase in the number of students in medicine.[1]

At worst, then, we can assume only a life saving and emergency type of service and allow our health services system to fall back to half of the facilities and personnel we have today simply by not increasing their number and by maintaining current absolute ratios. However, if we are going to follow the trends and wishes of our implicit public policy, we must increase the ratio of the health resources to population for the next fifty years, and greatly increase the facilities and personnel, now in dangerously short supply, that are associated with long-term illness.

The simplest and the most simple-minded approach would be to assume a constant ratio of current facilities, personnel, and finance to population and use this as the rock-bottom base for the next fifty years. I would plead for nothing less, certainly, and seriously work for a relative increase in personnel and finance, plus additional types of facilities and personnel including nursing homes, rehabilitation services, physiotherapists, nurses' aides, various types of psychiatric personnel, and home care services. Our policy makers in and out of government need to be sensitized to a philosophy of expansion and they should not be presented with neat stacks of figures other than as illustrations of what should be done. It is less than candid, and unprofessional, to promise tidiness.

On another important aspect, there is a pervasive conventional wisdom that reorganization, efficiency expertise, good cost accounting and other managerial devices will enable the system to perform at a much higher level of efficiency than it does currently. This "wisdom" assumes that it is possible to provide care for many more patients at a higher level of quality—in other words, that there is considerable slack in the present system. As a member of a university faculty engaged in research in the social, economic, and administrative aspects of the health services and in the training of future administrators, I certainly subscribe to the belief that the health services system can benefit from the strengthening of the managerial corps and managerial concepts. Tremendous resources are at stake that require the attention of a managerial elite. It is my observation, however, that the emerging managerial elite and the elite of the recent past do not understand the applicability to a health service system of the managerial techniques and concepts characteristic of modern industry. I refer here to the administration of professionals, patients, and a social system, and not to the cut and dried bookkeeping and hotel aspects of the system. The latter can certainly benefit by tidy administration with respect to billing, food service, management of non-professional personnel and so on. I would hope, however, that we are moving in the direction of management concepts that are peculiar to the health services system and that are more analogous to concepts familiar to universities and research organizations than to industry. Sophisticated managerial theory reflects a growing realization that there is a range of managerial styles related to types of enterprise. This is relatively new to the health field. Hence, I tend to fear the premature and naive application of managerial concepts appropriate in industry to health services. If this were not so, there would be no need for the programs in hospital and medical administration that have proliferated during the past twenty years.

I quite simply make the judgment that there is not much slack in the present system, particularly if we wish to accomplish the goals envisioned. Nor do we know the consequences of what it would mean to the system if we tried to take up the slack, rationalized delivery sufficiently to ration resources, set tight priorities, and established queues for so-called non-urgent conditions. I refer to currently popular suggestions of weekend surgery in order to utilize surgical resources seven days a week; utilization review committees; and other suggestions which essentially represent a tinkering approach to slow the pace of rising cost. I would not suggest a directed, drastic, and long-range reorganization of methods of delivering services either, other than what can emerge from the bargaining process between providers of services and big buyers.

I do not see any inherent reason, for example, why industry and organized labor could not bring about changes in the delivery of services if they really desired them. I do not believe that the force of law should be used to dictate methods of delivery; changes should result from bargaining over different methods of delivery. The methodology of change I suggest probably seems untidy and irrational given today's planning propensities, but in view of my skepticism regarding our ability to spell out who should get what, when, and where for how much, I can only suggest the bargaining process and an insistence on an abundant supply of health personnel and facilities. Government should be the principal stimulus for personnel and facilities, and the private sector can deliver the services as ingeniously as constraining conditions permit.

Unless we think and act in expansive terms, our approach to the health services and their delivery will be like fighting a cheap war.

In this arena of relatively equal power centers, who watches over the public interest? The federal government, particularly with its vast taxing power and its increasingly sophisticated bureaucracy, should be the constant and goading presence in the health field. Also, various groups with direct consumer interests such as labor unions and church organizations can establish the medical equivalent of the ombudsman to assist the average citizen to cope with the medical establishment. The government should remain essentially a buyer of services and a stimulus to increasing their supply. It should not be an owner of services.

In a viable pluralistic system, leadership may emerge at any time from any segment of society. The evolution of our health services is replete with examples of shifting stimuli, of challenge and response. One has but to recall Blue Cross and the concept of prepayment in the thirties; delayed response by Blue Shield in the early forties; even further delayed response, but eventually a tremendous surge of activity by private insurance companies after 1945, and especially their innovation of major medical coverage; and the establishment of group-practice prepayment plans in the latter thirties and during the forties. All of these now historic movements occurred in the private sector of the health field and in large part were reactions to the imminence of universal compulsory health insurance from 1939 to 1952. The private sector blunted the drive for compulsory coverage and drove the movement in 1965 into legislation covering those 65 years of age and over in the sweeping act known as Medicare. Until that year the American Medical Association seemed to consider bargaining in the American political arena beneath its dignity. But Medicare forced it into a bargaining stance and greatly weakened the traditional AMA appeals to "private enterprise." Today, federal legislation is pushing the private sector to more serious consideration of how it will meet a complex of problems. It should be remembered that the federal government is the representative of the collective majority. It is the ultimate expression of our national policy and power within which the various groups at interest work out their destiny in relation to the public interest.

If we assume constant ratios to population, we will need to produce annually the following numbers of health personnel and facilities and, in addition, many new categories of personnel now emerging (for example, physiotherapists, inhalation therapists, and cytotechnologists) and perhaps new ones not yet known or dreamed of (see appendix for additional detail):

1. Currently there are 287,000 physicians in practice. By 1980 we will need to graduate 11,000 a year in order to maintain a constant ratio of physicians to population. We are currently graduating 7,400 physicians a year, although the number is increasing. In the future there will also be an indeterminate number of physicians from foreign countries, but as a matter of public policy we should probably not gear our supply to this source. By 2020 we will need to produce 19,000 physicians to keep up with projected population growth.

2. Currently there are 100,000 dentists in practice. By 1980 we will need to graduate 3,900 dentists a year to maintain a constant ratio of dentists to population. We are currently graduating 3,000 dentists. Perhaps more extensive fluoridation will reduce the need for a constant ratio.

3. Currently there are 532,000 registered and active nurses (and 316,000 inactive ones). We will need to graduate about 65,000 nurses a year by 1980 to sustain the high attrition and to keep up with the increase in population. Currently we are graduating 35,000 nurses. There is the possibility of activating many inactive nurses. There is also the question of nurses' aides and similar auxiliary personnel which are increasing.

4. Currently there are 100,000 registered pharmacists. By 1980 we will need to graduate 6,000 a year to maintain the present ratio of pharmacists to population. We are graduating 3,000. I believe, however, that we could sustain a decrease by having fewer pharmacies (drug stores) that are staffed by full-time pharmacists.

5. Currently there are 740,000 general hospital beds. To maintain the present bed-population ratio we will have to add only 11,000 beds per year by 1980. According to current trends, we are actually adding 20,000 beds. We can, therefore, diminish the rate of increase, a trend that is probably taking place already. The current consensus in the health field seems to support a constant ratio, but not an increasing one. Long-term facilities are now to be increased.

6. Currently there are 685,000 mental hospital beds. We would need to add 10,000 beds a year by 1980 to keep pace with population growth. We can probably allow this figure to drop because of increasing outpatient care of the mentally ill. We are, in fact, experiencing a net loss in beds for care of the mentally ill.

7. Currently there are 37,000 tuberculosis hospital beds. We can allow this figure to decrease on the strength of past trends in incidence of tuberculosis and the decline in use of tuberculosis hospitals for treatment. There is in fact a net loss of beds in these hospitals.

8. Currently there are 400,000 beds in nursing homes and similar facilities. Considerable expansion is indicated here, as well as improvement in existing facilities. Estimates of needs for any type of facility and personnel are at best guesswork, but for nursing homes we can only assume that there should probably be a ratio of 3 beds per 1000 population. The current ratio is about 2 per 1000. Accordingly, there should be an immediate increase to 600,000 beds. By 1980 there should be a total of 720,000 beds or a ratio of 3 beds per 1000 population in our extended care facilities.

It is not my intent that these estimates be precise. They do provide an opportunity for projections on the basis of alternative assumptions of more, less, or the same numbers of personnel and facilities. To engage in gross estimates is better, it seems to me, than not to attempt any projection, as long as there is basic agreement on trends and direction.

The American Institute of Planners also asked that I make parallel estimates for regions of the United States. In these, I was also asked to take into account urban-rural differentials and, finally, to consider this country in relation to world needs over the next fifty years. However, I do not believe it is practical or valuable to make such estimates; I can only assume, on a regional basis, variants of plus or minus the national estimates. I have been impressed with the similarities of expenditure, facilities, and personnel patterns among states and regions. The rank order and patterns of expenditures and use by types of service will doubtlessly remain much the same and will vary mainly in degree. As for world obligations, I can only say that if we are able to produce personnel in abundance, they should be funnelled through our various foreign policy programs to assist other countries. The "brain drain" to the United States from other countries is manifestly ridiculous, but I do not advocate legislation to stop the entry of foreign professionals to the United States. On the other hand, we should not conduct recruitment campaigns in other countries. We should admit those who come on their initiative without organized or official inducement.

In these projections of facilities and personnel, I have dealt mainly with conventional types. There will be new types of professional and technical specialization, and specialized types of personnel for simple custodial care. The entire health services system will be strengthened by an increasing number and range of managerial personnel with recourse to economists, behavioral scientists, computer technologists, and other specialists in an increasingly managerial society.[2] There will necessarily be a great increase in the production of information in order that personnel may comprehend and operate the health system. There should be little excuse for managerial failures due to lack of necessary information. Such information can be provided by the research and development divisions of the health services, hospital planning councils, and routine indicators increasingly produced by the professional associations, operating agencies, and governmental reporting services.

I repeat that I offer no blueprint of methods for delivering services. I prefer to see various methods of delivery and finance in this country develop as a result of the bargaining process. Government, perforce, has to bargain because it does not, in substance, own the facilities nor hire the personnel. Government again, perforce, needs to make choices of economical and efficient ways to buy the services for which it has been given responsibility, in other words for providing for the various segments of society that have become its charge.

Is it possible to approximate these goals in the general style which I am suggesting? Well, apparently with little effort we increased national total health expenditures from about $3 billion in 1929[3] to $43 billion in 1966, 37 years later—almost a fifteen-fold increase—and per capita yearly expenditure for medical care from about $25 to $200—an eight-fold increase. The facilities and personnel during those years remained relatively constant in relation to population, and the health services system was able to absorb a doubling of use. It is unlikely that the same ratio of resources to population can absorb much of an increase in use in the future unless resources are at least kept constant. However, it is desirable that resources be increased, particularly with the development of new types of facilities and personnel. Since I subscribe to the concept that a patient should see a physician first during a disease episode rather than last, I do not feel that reorganization of physicians' services could be of much assistance in economizing on physician manpower. I find it mysterious that some would presume to increase physician productivity by decreasing the time physicians spend with their patients.

There will be proportionate shifts among the sources of funds. As long as the various levels of government do not enlarge their responsibilities to include the general population now cared for through voluntary health insurance, it seems reasonable and likely that the governmental share of the health dollar may rise from the current 25 percent to 45 percent. Medicare alone is likely to increase the governmental share to, say, 30 or 35 percent. In fact, if Medicare and the other government programs now in effect are to be carried out with even minimum adequacy, the government proportion must be increased. Within the private sector, the voluntary insurance portion will also increase and, it would seem, eventually become the source of 80 percent of non-governmental expenditures for health services. This portion is subject to a great deal of negotiation between the providers and the big buyers of service, and will continue to constitute the most dynamic portion of the health services enterprise, assuming that the framework of the present system is not radically changed.

If we are not willing or able to carry out the foregoing recommendations, we are likely to regress to an essentially emergency care type of system, dazzling as it may be, for crises such as heart failure, lung cancer, and organ transplantation. End-product activities rather than prevention, rehabilitation, and management of long-term illness will be the keynote. As a nation we love the dramatic and the visible; the painstaking, long-range activities tax our patience quickly. The arthritic and the mentally ill can suffer in silence while the heart surgery patient makes front page news, is whisked away by helicopter, and provides *Life* with color photos of virtuoso surgical performances. The question is: does this concept of health services suit our appetite for the dramatic or our true health needs?

It might well be asked if the tremendous direct expenditures for services (indirect expenditures being loss of income and productivity as a result of illness or death) could not be reduced considerably by preventive measures, early diagnosis, and rehabilitation. In answer to this question, it has become fashionable to apply cost-benefit analyses to the health field. A recent and well-designed study showed that the direct annual cost of illness in 1963 was $34 billion and the indirect cost, $24 billion, a total of $58 billion. The study report showed cost classifications by disease and by age, and quick estimates could then be made of how much money might be "saved" if specific diseases were cured early enough or eliminated altogether. However, no estimates have been made of how much might be "saved" if current know-how were applied optimally. It is unlikely that the overall social cost would be reduced appreciably, if at all, for in order to optimize the application of health services, we would have to spend or invest more money than we now do, not less. Moreover, the eventual "return" on the investment would be—is —very difficult to calculate, and patients would have to seek care earlier and more frequently than they do now, a form of behavior not known to result in economies, at least not necessarily. I feel that it is inappropriate to apply cost-benefit analysis to a health service because the primary public policy interest should be aimed at alleviating pain and suffering and reducing the number of premature deaths. A *cost* analysis, then, is appropriate for determining what is entailed, and not a *cost-benefit* analysis. The "benefit" aspect of a cost-benefit analysis is meaningless in economic terms if my premise is accepted, and irrelevant in a society which regards the individual as inviolable. Cost-benefit analysis may be appropriate for countries that may be described as developing, particularly in the setting of long-term priorities. But in as highly developed and affluent a society as ours priorities need not be set on the basis of cost-benefit. The overriding purpose of a health system should be humanitarian; if it is not, we must be prepared to assume the risk of separating "worthy" patients from the "unworthy," and "interesting" patients from the "uninteresting." If cost-benefit analysis had been used to set priorities, Medicare would never have been passed. There is a place for cost *effectiveness* analysis, however, providing good measurements of effectiveness exist. Unfortunately, they do not at present. We need, therefore, to work toward measures of effectiveness and to include as crucial components of effectiveness the attitudes of patients and health personnel. "Effectiveness" tends today to be defined in narrow economic terms and masquerades in algebra.

We pride ourselves on our pragmatism, and mistakenly assume that we are able to set social objectives without the benefit of fixed doctrines. We do have fixed doctrines, however, as expressed in our liberal and democratic dogma, that all individuals stand equal before the law, that all individuals should be able to fulfill themselves to the extent of their capacities, that all individuals should have equal access to health services. Our methodology is pragmatic, not our utopian objectives, and we can draw on the resources and organizational genius of the nation in a pluralistic society to carry out those objectives. This is why I am reluctant to impose specificity onto my projections for facilities, personnel, and money. My emphasis is on the methodology of bargaining for an activity which has no logical limits. The setting is our expanding economy.

In essence, I believe that the nature of the current thrust of the federal government is congenial to the American social, economic, and political system. Measures such as the program for heart disease, cancer, stroke, and related diseases, the public law to stimulate comprehensive health planning, and Titles XVIII and XIX of Medicare are challenging the private sector in a manner in which it could not possibly challenge itself. If the challenge of Title XIX can result in an acceleration of the usually sluggish medical programs for those with low incomes, if Title XVIII can be restrained to assist those 65 years of age and over (or those receiving Social Security disability pensions), the private sector of the health services system can continue to improve health insurance benefits, aided and abetted by government for bricks and mortar and the training of personnel in increasing numbers. Eventually government may become the chief source of income for the daily delivery of services and for facilities and personnel in the total system. A single source of income will tend to freeze whatever pattern of delivery of services exists at the time. It seems reasonable to predict, however, that if government does become the chief source of funds, the private sector will still be a relatively influential force because of the apparent propensity of the American middle class (families with annual incomes of $10,000 or more, currently comprising 20 percent of the population and due to become larger) to make choices. It may well be that a governmental health insurance system could focus exclusively on those with low incomes and the private sector (including private insurance) represent those with higher incomes, and, accordingly, the mainstream of American medicine. In a dynamic health service system it would seem salutary that an uneasy equilibrium continue to exist between the private and public sectors without implying that these sectors be clear-cut. The many interrelationships and dimensions create an unmatchable vitality.

The extent to which we can continue to wind up our social system like a steel spring without at the same time living in a constant state of seeming crisis in order to care for sick people and to delay death remains to be seen and tested. In our society the choices can be made quite consciously through an explicit public policy. Individual choices within the system will continue to center on spending money and effort to achieve one objective or another. But the constant balancing of group interests and individual needs represents a continuum and goes on indefinitely.

Appendix A

Projections of manpower and hospital bed needs
1965 to 1970, 1980, 2000, and 2020

1965 population—200 million

Medical resource	Current rate per 1,000 population	Number needed at current rate	Attrition per year[a]	Total number to be added to stay even with current rate	To be added per year	Total graduates required[b] this year
MD's (active)	1.44	287,000	5,740			
Dentists (active)	.49	97,500	1,950			
RN's (active)	2.66	532,118	21,285			
Pharmacists (active)	.50	100,000	4,000			
General hospital beds	3.71	741,292	—			
Mental hospital beds	3.43	685,175	—			
TB hospital beds	.18	37,196	—			
Nursing home beds	2.00	400,000	—			

1970 population—209 million

Medical resource	Current rate per 1,000 population	Number needed at current rate	Attrition per year[a]	Total number to be added to stay even with current rate	To be added per year	Total graduates required[b] this year
MD's (active)	1.44	300,960	6,019	13,960	2,792	8,811
Dentists (active)	.49	102,410	2,048	4,910	982	3,030
RN's (active)	2.66	555,940	22,238	23,822	4,764	54,004[c]
Pharmacists (active)	.50	104,500	4,180	4,500	900	5,080
General hospital beds	3.71	775,390	—	34,098	6,819	6,819
Mental hospital beds	3.43	716,870	—	31,695	6,339	6,339
TB hospital beds	.18	37,620	—	424	85	85
Nursing home beds						
at current rate	2.00	418,000	—	18,000	3,600	3,600
at optimal rate	3.00	627,000	—	227,000	45,400	45,400

1980 population—240 million

Medical resource	Current rate per 1,000 population	Number needed at current rate	Attrition per year[a]	Total number to be added to stay even with current rate	To be added per year	Total graduates required[b] this year
MD's (active)	1.44	345,600	6,912	44,640	4,464	11,376
Dentists (active)	.49	117,600	2,352	15,190	1,519	3,871

1980 population—240 million (*Continued*)

Medical resource	Current rate per 1,000 population	Number needed at current rate	Attrition per year[a]	Total number to be added to stay even with current rate	To be added per year	Total graduates required[b] this year
RN's (active)	2.66	638,400	25,536	82,460	8,246	67,564 [c]
Pharmacists (active)	.50	120,000	4,800	15,500	1,550	6,350
General hospital beds	3.71	890,400	–	115,010	11,501	11,501
Mental hospital beds	3.43	823,200	–	106,330	10,633	10,633
TB hospital beds	.18	43,200	–	5,580	558	558
Nursing home beds						
at current rate	2.00	480,000	–	62,000	6,200	6,200
at optimal rate	3.00	720,000	–	320,000[d]	21,333	21,333

2000 population—320 million

Medical resource	Current rate per 1,000 population	Number needed at current rate	Attrition per year[a]	Total number to be added to stay even with current rate	To be added per year	Total graduates required[b] this year
MD's (active)	1.44	460,800	9,216	115,200	5,750	14,966
Dentists (active)	.49	156,800	3,136	39,200	1,960	5,096
RN's (active)	2.66	851,200	34,048	212,800	10,640	89,356[c]
Pharmacists (active)	.50	160,000	6,400	40,000	2,000	8,400
General hospital beds	3.71	1,187,200	–	296,800	14,800	14,800
Mental hospital beds	3.43	1,097,600	–	274,400	13,700	13,700
TB hospital beds	.18	57,600	–	14,400	700	700
Nursing home beds						
at current rate	2.00	640,000	–	160,000	8,000	8,000
at optimal rate	3.00	960,000	–	560,000[d]	16,000	16,000

2020 population—420 million

Medical resource	Current rate per 1,000 population	Number needed at current rate	Attrition per year[a]	Total number to be added to stay even with current rate	To be added per year	Total graduates required[b] this year
MD's (active)	1.44	604,800	12,096	144,000	7,200	19,296
Dentists (active)	.49	205,800	4,116	49,000	2,450	6,566
RN's (active)	2.66	1,117,200	44,688	266,000	13,300	115,976[c]
Pharmacists (active)	.50	210,000	8,400	50,000	2,500	10,900
General hospital beds	3.71	1,558,200	–	371,000	18,500	18,500
Mental hospital beds	3.43	1,440,600	–	343,000	17,150	17,150
TB hospital beds	.18	75,600	–	18,000	900	900
Nursing home beds						
at current rate	2.00	840,000	–	200,000	10,000	10,000
at optimal rate	3.00	1,260,000	–	860,000[d]	15,000	15,000

a. Attrition rates are figured as follows:

MD's and dentists: 2 percent per year, based on unpublished studies and educated guesses by the American Medical Association and American Dental Association.

Pharmacists: 4 percent per year, based on a study done by the Illinois Pharmaceutical Association. Rates for pharmacists are higher than those for MD's and dentists because registered pharmacists sometimes go into other lines of work while this is quite rare for MD's and dentists.

RN's: The only good data available on current attrition is that half of the current graduates are inactive within one year of graduation. Attrition is arbitrarily placed at 4 per cent in addition to the large loss from the graduating class.

Hospitals and nursing homes: attrition is assumed to be minimal.

b. This is the sum of losses through attrition which must be made up plus the number needed to stay even with population growth.

c. This is double the number of graduates needed in order to allow for the high attrition rate of new graduates.

d. Based on 1965.

Sources: Physicians: American Medical Association; Dentists: American Dental Association; Nurses: Illinois League for Nursing; Pharmacists: Illinois Pharmaceutical Association; Hospitals: American Hospital Association (JAHA Guide Issue, August, 1966); Nursing Homes: U.S. Department of Health, Education, and Welfare (Characteristics of Nursing Homes, 1961).

Appendix B

Projection of percentages of expenditures for all health and health related goods and services by source of funds for selected years, from 1965 to 2020, United States

			Private		
Year	Percent of GNP	Federal, state and local governments	Direct pay by patients	Voluntary insurance	Other
1965	6%	25%	45%	25%	5%
1970	7	30	33	33	4
1980	9	45	11	42	2
2000	9	45	11	42	2
2020	9	45	11	42	2

Note: The percentage of the total labor force related to health services, professional and non-professional, should increase from the current 5 percent to 6 percent in 1970, and 10 percent by 1980 and thereafter. This is in line with the increasing orientation of our economy to the service industries. The health services will always be very labor intensive.

Notes

1. The thought is not for the poor in health centers but for the community around the hospital.

2. It has been suggested that I include consideration of environmental health personnel such as are needed in air and water pollution control. Certainly there should be some linkage with the health system through the official public health departments. I simply do not feel competent to deal with this essentially engineering problem, but I do wish to indicate that it requires serious attention. Unless it is solved, personal health services may become relatively useless.

3. Expenditures dropped to $2 billion in 1933, however, during the early stages of the Depression, a natural consequence although contrary to public trends.

Committee of Correspondence: Notes

Jack R. Ewalt, M.D.

(See page 65.) The federal government has joined private and state resources in subsidizing community mental health centers. New grants for construction and for staffing in the initial years are available on a matching formula basis. These centers will provide part-time care (day hospital and night hospital) as envisioned on page 65, but also in-patient service, out-patient service, rehabilitation service, and emergency service to all age groups and all diagnostic categories. It is anticipated that these community-based centers will be able to care for all but long-term mental patients requiring permanent hospitalization.

(See page 69.) Perhaps we are now in the sixth era—the era of concern over well-being. Much health effort is now directed toward the positive aspects of health, i.e., a stimulating, satisfying existence with attention to diet, exercise, environmental and personal safety, and the constructive use of leisure time.

(See pages 84-85.) We are experiencing a net drop in the number of patients hospitalized for long-term mental illness on any day. This is in part due to better care of the patients in the mental hospitals and in part due to the fact that large numbers of patients are now being cared for in community general hospitals, and an ever increasing number in the newly established community mental health centers. Long-term hospital beds will not need expansion at the rate heretofore described except places for retarded children who are so severely retarded that they require 24-hour nursing care. The construction of the in-patient portions of community mental health centers, however, will probably need to proceed at about the rate described in Item 6. Many of the centers will be part of the community general hospitals. It is estimated that approximately 2,000 community mental health centers are needed to provide adequate coverage of the population. If 2,000 such centers are added over the next ten years and if they average 40 beds each (some will be larger and some will be smaller) a figure of 8,000 to 10,000 additional beds per year is approximately correct.

Paul J. Sanazaro, M.D.

(See page 65.) It is my prediction that the greatest advances in health services research will stem from advances in behavioral science and the understanding they generate of the social determinants of disease and of non-utilization of preventive and remedial measures now available. The trap to avoid is the assumption that continued expansion of the health service system as presently constituted will continue to yield commensurate benefits. It is more than likely that the result will be an even wider chasm between what can be done and what is done by professionals and patients alike.

(See pages 82-83.) Two legitimate domains of directed medical care require more concerted planning, delineation, and organization. Both are subsystems which should be built with a clearly determined obsolescence so that neither will at great public cost outlive its social purpose. The first subsystem is for the delivery of quality medical care to that large population of Americans who cannot or do not utilize available services, largely because of social, economic, and cultural factors. Prepackaged comprehensive care must be brought to these millions of people, but must also be discontinued as the barriers to care are removed and utilization of the private system does, in fact, occur. The second subsystem is for the provision of the very expensive technology (in machines, men, and medicines) which private sources cannot provide equitably across our nation for all citizens. As successive discoveries eliminate the need for these (e.g., massive radiation units almost predictably will be supplanted), the public administrative machinery that brought these into being must not be allowed to propagate itself in the absence of a clearly defined national need for successor technologic complexes.

By dissecting out these two major strands of legitimate government subsidy and treating them openhandedly, we reduce a growing hazard: the continued blurring of public and private responsibility for improving the medical care required in order to fulfill our expressed commitment to the physical and mental well-being of all citizens.

(See page 86.) The health services system has attained the economic size and technologic complexity which invoke national planning and public subsidy for continued orderly growth and development. A clear decision is called for. Either the present bargaining on the basis of individual interests will continue to determine the nature of the interaction between government and the multiple private sectors, or a viable nationally representative organization must be created through which to channel and focus the public and professional concerns that must be advanced in all health service bargaining with the government.

Comments on

Anderson

HERMAN M. SOMERS
Woodrow Wilson School of Public and International Affairs
Princeton University

I fully agree with Dr. Anderson's plea for a generously proportioned health system and that this will call for large inputs of additional resources in the future. However, he appears to believe that "efficiency" standards are contrary to that objective. This seems to derive from his noneconomic use of the term which suggests to him "running a tight system of waiting lists, high occupancy rates, and other personal inconveniences."

Efficiency means maximizing productivity, or high output relative to input. Productivity includes quality. Quality includes the morale and satisfacton of the consumer. Waiting lists and personal inconveniences, therefore, detract from efficiency.

Dr. Anderson assumes there is very little slack in the current organization of health services. I believe the evidence is contrary. He appears to say that a "loose" system tends to promote quality. I know of no evidence to support that view. Those of us who argue for greater efficiency do so in the belief that it is conducive to improved quality, even when efficiency does not represent a money saving.

Group practice, for example, probably does not deliver care more cheaply than solo practice, but it is more efficient in that it is conducive to better care and makes more effective use of medical manpower. Preventive medicine does not appear to reduce costs. It is efficient because it appears to result in better health.

In terms of long-range planning it appears improbable that we can achieve the generously proportioned health system that Dr. Anderson and I agree is necessary, without more effective use of resources, particularly manpower.

In the light of competing urgencies, we must contemplate skilled manpower as a scarce resource for a long time ahead. Cost-benefit and cost-efficiency concerns are not necessarily devices to save money. They can be important means for determining the most effective use of given resources and for making more informed choices among alternative ways of organizing our resources. I do not believe the present system has sufficient automatic regulators giving it inherent capacity to maximize effectiveness. Planning and purposeful action are required.

In short, concern for efficiency is not at odds with Dr. Anderson's objective of a generously proportioned system. It is more likely to contribute to the goal by making it more practicable and attainable.

ARTHUR WEISSMAN
Director, Medical Economics
Kaiser Foundation Health Plan, Inc.

I, too, favor a flexible medical care environment in which alternative methods of delivery of health care services should coexist. Yet there is serious doubt whether we in the medical care field will be permitted the luxury of building the "abundance" Dr. Anderson seeks without better justification and rationale than the simplistic arguments that (1) we live in an affluent society, and (2) we have shortages of medical care personnel and facilities which are being aggravated by our expanding population. The increasing pressure for more effective organization of health care services will give this facet of our problem equal if not greater importance than that of achieving abundance of health care personnel and facilities. Furthermore, a more effective organization of health care services and delivery system could be the best guarantee of sufficient resource allocation to permit a generously proportioned health care system.

In a given community with eight general hospitals and a population which can be effectively served by two cardiac surgery teams, the existence of six cardiac teams would truly represent abundance. It also represents a situation in which the thinning out of the experience for each team would militate against optimal skill. Although trite, it appears to need repeating that more does not necessarily mean better in medical care. The literature documenting unnecessary surgery is clearly a case in point. From the experience of our medical groups in recruiting physicians we would question whether more general surgeons are needed and whether more in this category correlates positively with good medical care.

Just as the equation more = better must be rejected, the equation less = better must also be rejected. This latter equation still may be offered as a justification for medical care for the indigent in our country. I mention this because a great gulf separates Dr. Anderson's conception of a broad consensus favoring the utopian objectives of adequate medical care for all our people and the actual behavior of decision makers in our states and local communities who are clearly not tuned in to this consensus. A review of Title XIX programs in actual operation would, I believe, support this contention.

Dr. Anderson identifies major changes in the next fifty years in population size and composition and in patterns of morbidity. He also identifies major shifts in the requirements for medical care—shifts toward greater and greater need for services for chronically ill who require some form of custodial, domiciliary, or substitute home care. He recognizes that great changes can be expected in medical technology. He is, however, most reluctant to anti-cipate or suggest change in the organization and delivery of health care services. In fact, change in these aspects of the medical care scene is dis-missed with derision when he refers to "tinkering" with delivery systems. If I did not know Dr. Anderson I would believe that he had—with eyes focused on the rear view mirror—deliberately backed himself into the status quo corner.

There is another type of appraisal. Dr. Anderson is saying that he does not contemplate substantial change in the organization and delivery of health care in the next fifty years. He is challenging the advocates of change to make explicit the reasons for change and the desirability of specific forms of change. Moreover, he does not want us to get bogged down with issues which slow down the drive toward his primary target of abundance, i.e., a loose fitting, generously proportioned system.

He is unimpressed with the efforts to date in health services planning, in cost-benefit analysis, in the contributions to direct patient care of computer-ization of functions, and in the organization of health care services. He views these efforts in much the same way that we frequently view campaign prom-ises before an election. Although I agree with his lively skepticism, we need to press for commitment through effective demonstration to show that these efforts are not empty promises. We need demonstrations of patterns for ef-fective use of resources, and we need serious discussion of alternatives avail-able to us in establishing and revising these patterns.

Dr. Anderson needles us with other challenges. He expects us to behave in mountain goat fashion—to leap from one health care system crisis to another in our unsuccessful effort to reach and maintain as yet unquantified levels of health care personnel and facilities. Again it seems to me that if we develop mechanisms for the assumption of responsibility for developing rationale sys-tems for organizing and delivering health care services, we will in time reduce the need for the crisis approach to this problem. We should not toss in the sponge at this time. We must not assume that the health care system has to be either exclusively free-wheeling, or exclusively controlled from centralized sources.

LEONA BAUMGARTNER
Visiting Professor of Social Medicine
Harvard Medical School

Each individual, as Dr. Anderson wisely points outs, approaches a problem from his own particular set of values and so, as he attempts to predict what the future holds, each has his own crystal ball. Trained in the laboratories of the fairly exact science of immunology and in medicine but with years of experience as a physician and health administrator, my crystal ball inevitably holds somewhat different pictures from that of the skilled social scientist, Dr. Anderson. What is similar or dissimilar in our views of the future of health services in this country?

I agree with three main points made by Dr. Anderson.

First, the concept of "looseness" in which the health system, if it can be dignified by this term, is likely to develop. In the past, we have accepted a laissez-faire posture in almost all its developments. Just one example, hospitals are not built necessarily where they are needed but may be built where land is given or is cheaper, built as a monument to a public figure, a donor, or to foster the political ambitions of an individual, or located for other reasons not related to the need of the area for a hospital. We are not a nation given to long-range planning, or plans on a large scale. In fact, planning has only recently lost its unsavory quality when used in the governmental arena. Health planning is a new practice, and health planners have only recently begun being trained. We are a pragmatic people. We try out new ideas; we rise to emergencies—but we also "let nature take her course" and "muddle through" many a crisis.

The situation in health affairs today is such that a more aggressive approach is certainly needed if the public is to gain from the postwar explosion of scientific and technological knowledge. The sophisticated techniques for prevention, diagnosis, and treatment of disease which that explosion has produced are being imposed on a health care system ill-equipped to absorb them and ill-adapted to change. The time for change is here.

Second, I also agree there is no best way to reorganize the system, and even if there were, it obviously could not be quickly imposed on or substituted for the present one. Changes will come through trying out a wide variety of approaches—but, hopefully, with some sense of urgency—the "semi-crash" programs Dr. Anderson mentions. In the cancer, heart, and stroke programs there may already be a beginning.

The innovations generated locally with local initiative but with some central or regional guidance seem most likely to produce socially useful solutions. Our past experience gives a good example. The crippled children's programs supported by the federal Children's Bureau allowed for a variety of programs which took into account local interests, needs, and resources. But the central group supplied technical assistance, set standards, and otherwise helped the local community to develop new health services with a better quality of service than had previously existed. One of the tragedies of Medicaid and Medicare is that this noble example was overlooked.

It would seem wise in developing new approaches not to be utopian and strive for an ideal set-up but to gear the experiments to what may reasonably be expected to be viable. There have been enough demonstrations that prove health services are better if richly supported and manned by superior people! What is needed are different workable models which use more effectively what is available or can readily be made available. Dr. Anderson, I take it, agrees with this approach, although his emphasis on planned experiments is less than mine. In my opinion, he has not sufficiently emphasized the necessity and the opportunity for evaluating these different approaches. To be sure, measures of the adequacy of health care are almost totally lacking today. There is no reason why they should not be developed and used. The study and evaluation of the health service system in this country needs now to receive major emphasis in universities and research institutions, as well as by top administrators of the services themselves.

Third, I agree on the need for allocation of more resources to the health sector. To the several factors pushing in this direction, more emphasis might have been laid on the rising expectations of the people as to what modern medicine can produce for them. The miracles of wonder drugs, open-heart surgery, artificial kidneys or limbs, and the disappearance of polio and measles epidemics are all widely publicized through magazines, radio, and television. The people expect new wonders every week—and they want immediate access to them. Health as a human right for every citizen, regardless of his ability to pay for it, is now a political issue to which the Congress has responded, and probably will continue to respond if public demand is maintained. This may lead to the big buyer (i.e., government) laying down more restrictions, but it probably means, too, that greater allocation of resources in this affluent society will go to the health sector. Dr. Anderson's description of that sector might well have noted, in addition to the points he made, that the health business is already the third largest in the country measured in terms of money spent and people employed. Only agriculture and construction surpass it. He also did not mention the school health services, which constitute a real problem. With the new federal school-aid legislation these services are expanding. Begun at a time when the nature of health problems were those of filth and contagious diseases, they need critical reevaluation now that these conditions are largely conquered. As often organized, the school health services constitute one of the least efficient of our health services. They are so deeply entrenched, however, both in practice and even in legislation, that change is difficult. As such, they are a good example of why our system will change slowly.

There are some points I would add to Dr. Anderson's paper. I feel he has greatly underestimated the ability of science and technology to come up with new solutions. There may well be specifics for various types of arthritis, heart and mental disease, as well as vastly improved ways of handling the handicapped and chronically ill. There have been developments in nonmedical fields of management, communication, et cetera. Potential improvements of the health care system can be expected through the appropriate application of these techniques. In other words, science and technology in the next few decades may come up with solutions for some of today's problems—even though in themselves they may create new ones.

I also believe the ethical problems of what Dr. Anderson so aptly calls "medicated survival" (through transplantation of artificial organs and other techniques) demand more attention than he has given them. These are problems the health professions cannot face alone. Fortunately, in a few places, lawyers, theologians, philosophers, economists, historians, and others are beginning to think through some of the implications of these scientific developments. The current dialogue on experiments on humans is often the chief focus of these discussions, but hopefully such groups will expand their discussions and continue to contribute to the solution of these problems jointly from many disciplines and backgrounds. To change moral and ethical codes takes time. Nothing less seems likely to be useful in this area of health care, and the problems are already upon us. *137589*

Dr. Anderson also trains the spotlight rather more on physicians than many others in the field might. The increasing specialization which has arisen out of greater knowledge has given rise to the disappearance of the family physician or general practitioner, and the increases in the numbers and kinds of medical specialists. It continues to do so. Organ replacement specialists are already here. The same force is also adding specialists other than physicians. It would seem likely that these allied health professionals will be of far more importance in the future than indicated in Dr. Anderson's paper. He has called for many more physicians but has dodged the important question of what they are being trained for. He seems enamored of the idea that patients will want to be seen and that physicians should "see patients first." Experience does not necessarily prove this point to be valid. For many years in New Zealand specially trained "nurses" took almost total medical care of infants, with pediatricians seeing only a few referred patients. Millions of American men and women of the United States Navy have seen the Navy Corpsman first without complaint or detriment to their medical care. Recently, a carefully controlled experiment at the University of Kansas Medical School has shown that public health nurses with additional training can give routine pediatric care to children. They use pediatricians as consultants. They overdiagnosed only 5 percent of the cases—i.e., they were a little more cautious than physicians. They secured more complete histories from the mothers, who apparently felt freer to talk to them. When offered a choice later on, many mothers chose to stay with the nurse. Progress in the manpower field would seem more likely if we could break away from looking at the doctor and his traditional way of working and study the whole health job to be done. The total job can then be "de-skilled," i.e., broken up into its component parts according to the skill needed to do that part. The work to be done by persons with different skills and training is then clear. This approach has worked in other industries. Why not in the health industry? Care should be taken to allow workers to move from one level to another without penalties. In today's health scheme this is seldom possible. A greater mobility of personnel upward and more careful simultaneous analyses of the many jobs to be done in the health services could help solve the problem of shortages of physicians and nurses. The task cannot be done by any one group.

The healthy skepticism of those who believe that a cost *benefit* analysis holds the magic secret for dealing with current economic and manpower problems in the health field is refreshing—as is the idea that a cost *effectiveness* approach must be more vigorously applied. I would put somewhat more emphasis on organizational patterns, for the methods of delivering services influence the need for personnel and facilities, just as Dr. Anderson points out the latter influence the former.

There is also less in Dr. Anderson's paper of the importance of prevention than seems indicated. The great gains made in increasing life expectancy and in controlling infectious diseases in the past half-century have been associated to only a limited extent with the delivery of more or better personal health services by private practitioners of medicine. They have come through efforts to prevent diseases, to eliminate the causes in the environment, to protect the individual from acquiring disease. More recently there is emphasis as well on earlier diagnosis to prevent later disability. As the nature of the ills to which man succumbs inevitably continues to change, the search for the primary causes and their elimination, so far as is possible, remains a most important aspect of health services. The recognition at birth of congenital malformations, for example, is an increasingly important aspect of orthopedic care. Treatment then will prevent adult crippling. Man-made hazards to health in air, water, surroundings, multiply as man's ability to manipulate his environment grows. To acquire a balance that is favorable to the health of the population as well as to their enjoyment of the comforts that come through the rapidly expanding new technologies is a major problem. These developments all demand an emphasis on prevention that is not spelled out in Dr. Anderson's paper.

It is good to have mention in the paper's second paragraph of facilitating "humanness." This may be a reason behind Dr. Anderson's wish to have the patient see the doctor first. But for that the doctor and all the other members of the "team" must have the time, the sensitivity, and will to re-humanize the practice of medicine. The trick is to get the new science and technology efficiently and widely applied with the same personal touch which is attributed to the family doctor and which other large personal service industries in our American culture have learned how to provide.

DONALD C. RIEDEL

Associate Professor of Public Health, Dept. of Epidemiology and Public Health
Yale School of Medicine

The enormous complexity of our health services system and some of the many strains and constraints on it have been well outlined by Professor Anderson. There can be little quarrel with the assertion that health planning, either short-term or long-term, is difficult, that our theoretical framework is deficient, and that our techniques for analysis are in many ways primitive.

Health is assumed to be a basic human right, and the development of a high quality, accessible health service system to be the means for attainment of this goal. As pointed out, public policy debate centers around the methods appropriate for the development of the system, and not the goal.

Because of the great difficulty in foreseeing future configurations of need (i.e., morbidity and disability), demand, and effective demand, and because of the dearth of yardsticks by which to gauge the effectiveness of the components of the health service system, individually or in concert, Professor Anderson suggests adherence to a "relatively loose" system and the allocation of proportionately more resources to "maintain and accelerate the impressive gains of the past." Individual groups should be assured maximum latitude to "maneuver" toward improvement. Under such an arrangement, changes in the system will "emerge from the negotiating and bargaining process rather than by preconceived blueprints." Thus, progress would emanate from a series of (hopefully) interrelated thrusts and parries by providers, consumer groups, financing agencies, and planning agencies.

It can be argued that in the future there will be a decreasing probability of pumping proportionately more monies into the health services system to make it "looser" than it is at the present. The demands for "efficiency" and "effectiveness" are becoming more persistent and better articulated. In fact, the "abundance" specified by Professor Anderson as the basis for his thesis might very well be short-lived without meaningful program evaluation in all sectors of the health services enterprise.

Reliance on the "bargaining" process assumes that the individuals or agencies involved have rational and accurate assessments of alternative courses of action, that is, the ability to weigh the direct and indirect costs of programs vis-à-vis the anticipated benefits. Furthermore, the influence of "big business" and "big labor" as goads usually operates through the payment mechanism, an imperfect arrangement at best.

Experimentation with new forms of delivery of health services and the accompanying payment mechanisms would create the frame of reference necessary for sound decision-making. If this cannot be accomplished within the confines of an existing program, then purposive experimental programs with the appropriate manipulative techniques must be conducted outside the "natural" system. The results of such experimental programs in delivery should help to develop, or at least identify the elements of, the criteria for adequate health services Professor Anderson specified as essential for successful planning. Evaluation under experimental conditions is not the same as "tinkering."

Professor Anderson is quite correct in pointing out the importance of perception of illness on the part of the (prospective) patient and the necessary discretionary judgment of the physician as factors conditioning the operation of the health services structure. One might disagree, however, with the assumption that they should be given maximum play because there is a certain amount of variability inherent in them. Knowledge of the direction and degree of influence of *determinants* of variation could serve as the basis for programs of planning and/or action. For example, effective programs of health education, built upon studies of the factors determining perception of illness, should in fact reduce the hiatus between "true" need for health care, "recognized" need, and demand. Residual variation in perception could conceivably be accommodated in the planning process.

Similarly, we have the capacity to gain better knowledge of the judgment process on the part of the physician. Various studies have demonstrated the feasibility of establishing professional criteria for the "need" for health services, appropriate use of diagnostic and therapeutic services and facilities, and patient management. The first large-scale study in this area was conducted over thirty years ago, under the sponsorship of the Committee on the Costs of Medical Care. Recent advances in techniques of medical audit and utilization review now make it possible to establish standards that could very well be used in the planning process.

With estimates of need derived from professional criteria and a delineation of alternative mechanisms of prevention, treatment, and rehabilitation, it would be possible to critically review problem areas which are the keystone to the health services structure. For example: What steps are necessary to meet "true" need for health care? Which can be compromised? At what levels should the planning process be directed? Who should participate in the planning? What are the measures of program success?

This reviewer had hoped Professor Anderson would address himself to some of these questions, specifying the implications of alternative answers. One can question the usefulness of projections of needed personnel (even at minimum levels) based on the current professional/population ratios.

William H. Stewart

Surgeon General, Public Health Service
U.S. Department of Health, Education, and Welfare

Health—The Next Fifty Years

Fifty years ago we were engaged in fighting the war to end wars, a war that would, among other things, make the world safe for democracy. Crumbling, along with many of the cities of Europe, was the cool Victorian certainty that everything was evolving for the best. Man was not as sure in 1917 as he had been in 1910 that science, guided by enlightened hands, would shape a world of eternal abundance and order.

Looking backward with the divine clarity of hindsight, we can now read some of the handwriting that was then on the wall. Listening with all the static screened out, we can hear a few authentic voices of prophecy coming at us across the years.

One was the voice of Albert Einstein who, twelve years before had written an equation that put new dimensions of potential for self-improvement or self-immolation into man's hands. Another was the voice of Pablo Picasso who was turning from the artistic glorification of the individual human being to the presentation of man as form and fragment.

Symbolically at least, it is possible to derive much of what has happened over the past half century from these two sources. Einstein overturned man's vision of the external world around him. Picasso turned man's vision of himself inside out. Today we find fragmented, formalized man the uneasy master of overwhelming science and technology.

And so we come together in 1967 to view the next half century. It is most appropriate that we do so, and I am impressed by the company assembled. I hope, though, that we shall be listening not only to ourselves and to each other. I very much doubt that a similar group, had it been assembled in 1917, would have included the right voices. I have parallel doubts about us. The trouble with us is that we have prospered by the present and are probably, therefore, shackled to it. We may well be akin to the Roman sage of the fourth century, described by Lewis Mumford, who confidently predicted an endless proliferation of good public baths and better public roads while the Visigoths were gathering at the gates.

Whose are the authentic voices? Do they come from those who are doing the planning, or from those who are being planned at?

What, for example, are the op artists, the beat poets, the flower children trying to tell us? What can we learn from them, or from the fact of their existence?

Obviously a considerable portion of the youth of this country feels an estrangement from our society. These kids have opted out. Basically, I think they are disenchanted with impersonal institutions, with super-human technology—with what appears to them to be the irrelevance of our society to humanity and human values.

We can call them immature and wish they would wash. But we can't ignore their expression of a deep hurt. They are suffering a wound that calls for treatment. That treatment somehow must be built into our thinking about the next fifty years.

Meanwhile another group clamors still more loudly for our attention—the dispossessed in our urban ghettos and in the rural wastelands. What are the rioters trying to tell us? What should we be learning from them and from others like them who suffer in silence?

The root of their malady is painfully clear. While the majority of our society reaps the benefits of technology, they are reaping nothing but frustration. In the midst of incredible productivity, they are jobless. In the midst of abundance, they are wanting. In the midst of health, they are sick.

This vast disparity occurs in a negative social environment which is self-sustaining and self-perpetuating. Lack of jobs, lack of education, lack of access to the rudiments of health combine to harden the stratification of society. The pressures of fragmentation which weigh upon all of us weigh heaviest on the poor. This severe illness of our society demands immediate medical attention. In fact, equity of opportunity must be established as a prerequisite to all other treatment.

Neither the disenchanted nor the dispossessed is a new phenomenon. Both have been with us always. In years and centuries gone by, they have been dealt with largely by lamentations and platitudes—which is to say that they have not been dealt with at all. Or they have been suppressed and contained—which passes the problem on to the future in intensified form.

The exciting thing—the new phenomenon—at this moment is that they can be dealt with if we decide to do so. Professor Jerome Frank has said it this way:

> In the past, men could shrug their shoulders in the face of most of the evils of life because they were powerless to prevent them. . . . Now there is no one to blame but ourselves. Nothing is any longer inevitable. Since everything can be accomplished, everything must be deliberately chosen. It is in human power for the first time to achieve a level of human welfare exceeding our wildest imaginings or to commit race suicide, slowly or rapidly. The choice rests only with us.[1]

Each of us views this awesome choice through his own special lens— mine is the lens of health, someone else's is the lens of education, and so on. My objective for the year 2017 is the healthy man; another might be the educated man. I think we are looking at the same fellow—the integral man. Moreover, it is clear that the health system and the educational system and a great many other systems are going to have to work together to produce him, and that all these systems will have to change substantially if this healthy, educated man is to be typical of his time.

What is this healthy man toward which we aspire?

First, he is as free of disease and disability and the imminence of premature death as medical science of the twenty-first century can make him. Projecting the pace of recent progress across the next five decades, he should be in pretty good shape. He should look forward with confidence to a longer lifespan than we do today. He should be free of the presence or threat of most of the communicable diseases. He should have at his disposal a remarkable battery of curative and rehabilitative skills when chronic illness threatens to limit his activities. He, or at least his children, should be comparatively free of the menace of congenital defects.

Second, he lives in an environment that is free of specific, preventable hazard to his health. He is not compelled to place his life or health in jeopardy as a condition of his employment, or as a condition of urban living.

In short, he is the beneficiary of excellent medical care—preventive, curative and restorative—and of environmental health protection. But this is only the beginning, not the end of the story.

For the truly healthy individual is not simply un-sick. He is not merely an aggregate of undiseased organs existing in sterilized and de-carcinogenated surroundings.

Rather he is not only strong but conscious of his powers and eager to use them. His environment is not just protective but positively conducive to productive and stimulating living. The healthy human being of the year 2017 is equipped for self-fullfillment physically, emotionally, and socially.

How do we get there from here? Obviously no amount of adjustment in the health system alone can take us there. But there are a number of changes within the health system that will move us in that direction.

In my view, the fundamental and revolutionary change needed in the health system is to reorient it to the human being. The individual person should be the center around which the health service system revolves. His total state of health should be its measure of success or failure. This radically different orientation would rid us of a great many prevalent absurdities typified by the classic statement, "The surgery was a success but the patient died."

The fact is that we in medicine are suffering from fragmentation of the human being just as society is suffering from fragmentation of the body politic. With the application of science to medicine has come specialization. With increasing technology has come depersonalization. As a result, we seem to have greater concern for a specific gene or lobe than for the human being it belongs to. Within the medical microcosm the ultimate object of the enterprise—the person—is lost in a swarm of preoccupations with the technique, with the professional subgroup, with the efficiency of the facility, and so on.

This, I submit, is a very special irony in medicine, which has the most humanitarian purpose of all the disciplines stemming from science. How can health possibly be seen as irrelevant to people? In this situation, the physician must heal his own art.

Historically, across the long span of the centuries back to Hippocrates, the practice of medicine consisted largely of an unequal struggle to prolong life and reduce misery. The struggle was unequal because available knowledge was unsystematic and tools were rudimentary at best. The doctor almost always lost. The good doctor was "good" because, lacking the ability to cure a specific ill, he gave "care" to the whole patient and made him feel better, temporarily at least. He was a skillful, an artistic comforter.

Then, beginning in the late eighteenth century and continuing into the twentieth came a period when the tide of the long battle began to turn, not so much by curing diseases as by keeping them from happening to large groups of people. Some of these gains were external to medicine —a general rise in living standards and levels of acceptance brought better nutrition and cleaner surroundings for most of the people. We learned how to treat public water supplies. We learned how to immunize against some diseases. In most of these instances society was the patient and the individual benefited as a member of the community.

Now for the past few decades, and especially since World War II, we have been in a third historical period—the therapeutic age. Primacy has been given to diagnosis, treatment, and cure—through the "wonder drugs," "wonder surgery," and other applications of biomedical science and technology. During this same period we have also made important advances in medical rehabilitation. The accent has been on the specific disease or disability, the focus on the diseased organ or tissue.

This surge of emphasis on the therapeutic aspects of medicine will undoubtedly continue for a while as technology is further exploited. But this further exploitation will demand further specialization of professional performance, and it contains the seeds of further fragmentation of the individual. It will also result in further depersonalization of the circumstances of health service unless we take positive steps to counteract this tendency.

The shift that must take place over the next half century is the emergence, once again, of the individual as the central purpose of medical science. This will place a much higher priority on prevention—not only of disability and death but of deviations from the norm that interfere with individual fulfillment. It will, in fact, alter and enlarge upon the traditional concept of prevention—which is essentially a negative concept—into a concept of health maintenance and health advancement.

The traditional concept of prevention has been to create conditions in which disease and premature death will not happen. The concept I am looking toward in the twenty-first century is to create conditions in which the healthy individual, as we have envisioned him, *will* happen and will be the norm.

Such a transition will involve new health strategies on a large scale. All of these strategies entail picking up the pieces of our fragmented present and putting them together as an integrated whole. We are concerned with the body and mind of every individual and with the social and physical environment in which these many individuals will be living.

As a first step we shall need to overcome our tunnel vision of death prevention as the primary object of health endeavor. We need to be concerned with not only the number but also the quality of man's years.

Part of this process will require a new economic orientation. We shall be shifting from today's sickness insurance to genuine health insurance. We shall be building incentives into the system for prevention, for maintenance of optimum health, for serving the individual rather than his diseased parts. These incentives will need to be apparent to both the provider and the consumer of health services.

A major strategy for immediate implementation will be a massive emphasis on and investment in developing health systems that meet the needs of today's dispossessed. Our goal of the healthy individual must apply to all our people—no lesser aspiration would be conceivable today. Yet for great numbers of the poor the wonder cures of our therapeutic age and even the basic preventive measures of fifty years ago are still out of reach. This imbalance must be redressed before we can hope to soar higher toward 2017.

We shall have to devise and put into practice new systems of organizing health services, including the facilities and institutions that provide them. Heretofore, the hospital—the great citadel of cure—has been considered the heart of the system. But if we envision a system which emphasizes health protection and advancement, admission to the hospital will be an admission of failure. The hospital will be the place of last resort—essential but no longer dominant. Rather we shall need to invest heavily in ways of getting preventive and health maintenance services out where the people live—related to home and school and workplace. We need to build flexibility into both the structure and the operation of health care facilities. In planning such facilities we need to consider first of all the people to be served, and the patterns of flow of community life.

Perhaps most important of all, we shall have to reorient our education of health professionals to the new goal of optimum health. If their highest object is service to the healthy individual, they will need an understanding in depth of society and the humanities. Only thus will the technical specializations, built on top of this base, be fully useful. To accomplish this transition, we shall have to start quickly. For medical education is a long-time process; it must chart a course that intersects the trajectory of practice a full decade in the future.

Our strategy of environmental health must begin, but not end, with removal of specific hazard. The first step is to understand that the environment is the habitat of man. We need to appreciate both the potential and the limitations of our air, land, and water, and relate these to satisfying living. While we are worrying about pollution we need also to worry about noise and light, stress and speed, and their impact on the healthy man. We need to build new partnerships, based on new incentives, among governmental bodies in many fields at many levels and between these and the full range of private enterprise.

For it is very clear that no single element of society can bring the healthy man into being. To accomplish all or part of this great transition, medicine and the health disciplines will have to develop new working interrelationships with virtually all of the other fields of knowledge that impinge upon the human being and help to bring out the best in him. Health, broadly conceived, must be a determinant in housing and city planning, for example, just as spatial patterns of living must be among the determinants of health programs. Happily, the beginnings of these interlocks are becoming visible in broader concepts of planning that are being applied to problems of the city and to problems of health.

I am convinced that realizing this vision will be well within our technical capability by the year 2017. Whether it is within our societal capability remains to be seen. I think we must try.

All the planning we do must be polarized toward the goal of human fulfillment—the integral man. However sophisticated the apparatus of our planning process may be, it must ultimately be accountable to the individual human being for the critical choices. And these choices must always be evaluated against a yardstick of human values.

Given this goal, this accountability, and this measure, we shall proceed ahead on those courses of action which promise to advance the quality of living. That which is irrelevant to this purpose will be subordinated or cast aside. We shall have no time in these fifty years for irrelevancy.

Note

1. Jerome Frank: "Galloping Technology—A New Social Disease," cited in Don Fabun, *The Dynamics of Change* (New York: Prentice-Hall, 1967).

The Problems and Promise of Leisure

This paper was commissioned to explore the re-creation of the individual. What this means is the highest possible employment of leisure, as suits the individual. The need for privacy and reflection and more than muscle exercise is in mind here.

There is controversy today only over the rate at which more leisure will become available. There is doubt that we have very much leisure today (if all household chores, commuting, etc., are taken into account). But there is little doubt that there will be a lot of leisure in the foreseeable future, for certain sectors of society.

What psychological impact can this new leisure be expected to have on the overstressed professional or the under-occupied, semiskilled worker whenever in the next fifty years the predicted leisure comes? What impact will this have on the environment? Do all individuals dare reflection? Is it positively not good for some? How can leisure develop real meanings in our society?

Author: Sebastian de Grazia, The Eagleton Institute of Politics, Rutgers—The State University

Chairman: Perry L. Norton, AIP, Professor of Planning, Graduate School of Public Administration, New York University

Committee: Gibson Winter, Professor of Social Ethics, Divinity School, University of Chicago; Warren Ost, Director, Commission on Leisure and Recreation, National Council of Churches; Dennis Gabor, Department of Electrical Engineering, Imperial College of Science and Technology, England; Gordon K. Douglas, Chairman, Department of Economics, Pomona College; Edward D. Lindaman, Manager, Interdivisional Projects, Apollo Program, North American Aviation, Inc.; Wayne R. Williams, Eckbo, Dean, Austin and Williams Architects; John Wagner, Director, Interreligious Committee of Los Angeles, Regional Goals Project

V

Sebastian de Grazia

The Eagleton Institute of Politics
Rutgers—The State University

The Problems and Promise of Leisure

The otter is playful,
the beaver industrious.
Which leads the better life?
Ti-tzu

Introduction

Over the past fifty or one hundred years the "idleness problem" has
been supplanted by the "leisure problem." Though people once excori-
ated idleness and today laud leisure, the problem is one and the same—
the problem of free time. Moreover the problem is not the existence
of too little free time but the threat of too much. Medically speaking,
in Karl Marx's day a problem of too little free time did exist. Today
no labor union would claim that its workers needed more free time
for their health's sake. If anything, the thing they, but more particularly
ministers, physicians, and psychiatrists fear, is the effect on their health
of free time in too large a dose, the effect, that is, on people's mental
health or on the social health of the community.

112

Most Americans when they use the word *leisure* have free time in mind. The confusion in usage is of recent origin. It dates from the rise of the commodity mentality. In selling products for use in free time, advertisers have wished to associate their goods with the ethical connotations of leisure. More recently others, like social workers, psychiatrists, priests and ministers, worried about free time spent solely along commercial guidelines, have tried to add a self- or social-improvement twist to free time, again by calling it *leisure.* Now it has reached a new stage where, as the whole economy trembles at the slightest threat of unemployment, the word leisure is being groomed for impending, forced free time.

There is another question, the question of real leisure. Here the difficulty is not of too much but of too little. And the penalty for lack of leisure is not the unhealthy individual or a disturbed community, but an uncreative, unlovely country.

Free Time: More, Less, or the Same

To begin, will there be more free time for Americans in the future? Theoretically, yes. Projections have been made of how much free time there will be in coming decades. Similarly, calculations can be made as to whom the increase will go and as to whether some classes of the population will be favored above others. The work week is to get shorter by about an hour and a half each decade. By the year 2000, the overall average of hours worked is to be 31 per week or 1600 hours per year. It may go down as far as 21 per week (1100 per year). In the year 2020, on-the-job hours are to average about 26 per week, or 1370 per year, or (as above) as low as 16 hours per week, or 870 hours per year. With such figures at hand, it is not surprising that many wonder what people are going to do with their time.

Regarding who will have this free time, it seems that workers in all industries, be they manufacturing, trade, mining, construction, will benefit equally. Since the population will be both aging and growing younger,[1] those over 65 will not benefit (presumably they are today already out of the labor force), while those at work under 25 will reap the harvest of shorter work weeks. Women, though, are to have less free time, since many more of them are to take jobs in 2000 (43 percent as against a participation rate of 37 percent in 1964),[2] unless one calculates by the usual labor statistics, in which case women have no free time at home but acquire it, paradoxically, when they are counted as working women.

Breakdowns on amounts of free time for the managerial and official classes have received less attention from these projectors for 2000 and 2020, but by the logic of extrapolation alone they will still be working the longest hours.[3] In 1960 they put in on the job an average of ten or twelve hours more than other categories of workers and an on-and-off the job total of over sixty business hours per week.

Studies have also been made of the impact that future expanses of time will have on the physical environment, focusing on how much money and acreage should be set aside for parks, woods and wilds, for roads leading to them, and for saving them all from congestion. Generally, the conclusion a reader might easily draw from them is that the demand for recreational space is as inexhaustible as the money and acreage are not; and that all roads lead to congestion.

In tabular form the figures given above on the future work week and year appear as follows:

Length of Average Work Week and Work Year in Non-Agricultural Industries 1960 and Projected to 2020 (in hours)

Year	Work week	Work year
1960[a]	38	2,002
1970[b]	37	1,924
1980[b]	35	1,846
2000[c]	32	1,600
2020[d]	26	1,370

Sources:
a. Sebastian de Grazia, *Of Time, Work, and Leisure* (New York: Twentieth Century Fund, 1962), Table I, p. 441.
b. Adjusted from 1976 figure given in Table B-25, *Outdoor Resources Recreation Review Commission, Projections to the Years 1976 and 2000; Economic Growth, Population, Labor Force and Leisure, and Transportation.* ORRRC Study Report 23 (Washington, D.C.: U.S. Government Printing Office, 1962), p. 71.
c. Mark Wehle and Gus Weiss, *II Economic Projections* (Croton-on-Hudson, N.Y.: Hudson Institute, 1966, mimeographed draft), pp. 62-63, 85-88.
d. Mark Wehle and Gus Weiss, *Supplementary Projections for 1965-2020* (Croton-on-Hudson, N.Y.: Hudson Institute, 1967, mimeographed draft), p. 3.

Now that I have put together this little table, my advice to the reader is not to bet on it heavily.

An Aside on Projections

We cannot expect the projections of the work week to tell us much of how much free time people will have in the future. First, the figures refer to regular time on the job, taking no account of overtime or moonlighting. Second, they include part-time workers, who should not be considered in calculating the length of the regular worker's work week. Third, they take no account of the increase in work-related factors, in particular the journey to work which has lengthened in time as the work week shortened. Indeed, the decrease in the official work week's length is better explained as the result of the worker's need to find time to get to work and back home than of his craving for leisure. None of these nor other pertinent factors are taken account of in the statistics used in typical projections.

The Outdoor Resources Recreation Review Commission based its prognostications of leisure on the Bureau of Labor Statistics, U.S. Department of Labor, report of June 14, 1961, and the Hudson Institute followed suit. The figures were carefully compiled and the projections properly described. Unfortunately the concepts employed to arrive at what the ORRRC entitled "leisure" were essentially the average work week and the GNP. These concepts, however convenient they may be, were designed for different uses. Thus statisticians concerned with measuring the length of the work week sought a figure which, when multiplied by average employment, would yield total man hours worked. This, in turn, when multiplied by estimated output per man hour would yield an estimate of our gross national product. For their purpose an average work week that reflects the hours of all employed persons—full- and part-time workers, men and women—is the appropriate figure. For measuring the amount of time on the job and the amount of time away from the job in the context of free time, however, an entirely different statistical measure is necessary. The more appropriate figure is the length of the work week of the average American male who works full time—that is, today, at least 35 hours a week.

Projections cannot be separated from the figures they are launched from.

Today's Time

One must bear in mind that readings into the future of free time, which have been tried ever since the industrial revolution, have been scandalously wrong. The problems of more time, how and by whom it will be enjoyed, cannot be separated from people's thoughts, hopes, fears, and goals. Recent forecasting has generally credited Americans with a simplistic psychology in which they appear as craving more free time, no matter what. A scrutiny of the available evidence reveals that they have not taken more free time, do not appear to wish more (though it be available to them), and do not seem likely to change in this respect over the next decade or two. The American full-time male worker puts in an average of nearly eight hours a day, six days a week.[4] Contrary to what is widely believed, he has taken his gains in productivity not in the coin of free time but in coin of the realm.[5] He has no more time free of work than men have had elsewhere when not caught in times of crisis or rough transition.

Technology and free time have sides to them that oppose each other. An age that breeds technology must be one that is beguiled by and desirous of material things and therefore must buy or somehow acquire them, to do which it must use up the time any one machine or device may save. Any primitive tribe enjoys more free time than a resident of the United States today. It is doubtful that any civilization ever had as little free time as we do. The commodity mentality, fascinated by the made and purchasable thing, holds the American worker in a vise of working overtime to buy time-saving devices and "leisure goods."

The Future: Forced Free Time

Perhaps, independent of what people desire, there are forces coming into being that will propel them toward more time off the job. We have indicated already that increased time and distance between home and job have influenced the demand for more time off the job. In the future, automation, a larger population among which to spread available work, and a rising GNP with which to buy time may lead to increased free time. This may not be the case, however, so long as consumption continues to spiral upward.

An upward and onward spiral is just what the forecasters forecast. I shall not assemble another little table here but merely recall that forecasters see automation marching through business, government, and industry, population mounting lustily, and the graphic peak of the GNP at 2020 disappearing in a roseate cloud. If income doubles, let us say, and expenditures double too, it is hard to see how free time can increase. The worker will be working full-time and overtime as today to spend on what he wants to have. But statistics show that he has more free time today than ever before in history, do they not? No, they do not. They show that the American worker cannot be working any harder than he is now. He has in effect no time for free time.

A Second Aside on Projections

Another unfortunate aspect of present statistical practice is that by using concepts for a purpose different from the original, work not embraced by those concepts is left out of calculation. A persistent example of such use of the GNP in free time and leisure estimates is the case of women. Without apparent contradiction, projectors can speak of an increase in female labor force participation rate, in family incomes, in GNP, in the proportion of consumption expenditures, and of course of additional leisure.[6]

If your wife comes over to do my housework and I pay her for it, while mine goes over to do yours and you pay her, the work done is approximately the same as before but the GNP increases by two new wages. (This suggests that if a country, especially an underdeveloped one, wishes to shoot its GNP skyward, almost double, it should get its housewives to take in each other's laundry.) Should, instead, my wife go out to work, we may hire someone to do the housework she previously did (if any), or she or I or both of us may work at it ourselves overtime, or we can neglect the housework (and children, perhaps) and let house and home deteriorate. The last case is the only one that does not belie the GNP figure. In the first case, there are two GNP-productive persons where there were none before, and in the second case there is overtime going on that, because it is unpaid, remains outside the GNP and unaccounted for in calculations of the shorter work week.

We seem to refuse to recognize in figures that one person if he or she works needs another to tend to him or her, their house and their progeny. Perhaps our standards of personal care are too high. If so, we should admit that we may be lowering them.

Forced Free Time (continued)

If consumption keeps pace with production, then, there should be no increase in free time or general unemployment. Yet some of the factors just mentioned may lead to unemployment. Apparently automation, many fear, cannot spread jobs as widely as industrial economy has hitherto been able to do, because the skills it requires demand an above-average intelligence.[7] If this be true (and much of the rest of this paper is based on this possibility) unemployment may be in the offing. But will it necessarily? Instead of calling it unemployment, why not call it free time? Workers may not be asking for more free time, but let us cut down their work year without cutting down their pay, let us call this time off the job, "leisure," and, lo!, unemployment has disappeared.

Politically this is a triumph. Where before the economic system could be charged with failure, now it can be and is already heralded as the great provider of undreamed of leisure. "Undreamed of" is correct. The kinship of unemployment and free time, when both have elements of unwillingness in them, deserves close attention. Workers will take this "leisure," but today they do not ask for it. On the other hand they did not ask to be caught in the swamp of commodities either; yet today they find themselves there, waist-deep. It may all be a question of the proper psychological preparation.

Preparing for the Future

From one view the future is being adequately anticipated. Business, government, and industry are selling the future as an age of riches and leisure for everyone. There are some, however, who sense that all is not right, that workers are being faced with more time off the job while having no desire to take it. If workers had a desire for more free time, would they not have some idea of what they want to do with it? This is where the stubborn thought reaches in: "the problem of leisure" is not the problem of not enough but of too much free time. On reviewing the arguments pro and con made by various groups—labor and business in their more thoughtful moments, the medical profession and clergy, welfare workers and educators—one can hardly come away without feeling that free time is a threat and a problem rather than the gateway to an exciting age of leisure.[8]

The doubts these voices raise demand a reconsideration of the impact of more time on the individual. By and large the solution they talk most about is not to cut free time down—for that seems to them impossible—but to provide the worker with ways of filling his future empty time. The foreseers of riches and leisure promise the worker all sorts of intriguing new equipment and facilities for sports, travel, comfort and entertainment—at a flick of the finger.

Personally I am weary of reading such predictions of the future. Their fascination with devices and products is incredibly naive. Can they really believe the stuff they put out? Yes, they can. They are testimony to the strength of the technological religion, which in the midst of so much disillusion, conserves its grand illusion, that a great industrial-scientific day is still a-borning. In 2020, reads one projection, our standard of living will be three to seven times higher than that of 1965 and in tune with this increase will be the increase in leisure time.[9] I ask, will we be able to stand it?

The more apprehensive writers do not look to the cornucopia of commodities to fill men's time. For this reason they place more of their faith in government and non-profit institutions. They recommend programs for churches and synagogues, universities, housing authorities, settlement houses, clubs and neighborhood circles. The lion's share goes to the government, but not merely to the central government. A state government should have a Deparment of Leisure with architects, planners, statisticians, engineers, demographers, and social scientists, while subordinate leisure agencies should include psychologists, sportsmen, naturalists, and hobbyists. Also, each city of, say, 75,000 or more inhabitants, should boast a municipal Department of Leisure. Preparation for leisure would begin no later than high school.

These writers are right to be concerned, but the institutions they propose lack underpinnings. The preparation they would give are in things like aesthetic appreciation, social ease, prowess in games, sightseeing, outdoor life, nature study, skill in hobbies. They may also include preparation in "intellectual growth," but here they reveal a most serious weakness. The only philosophy they have to bank on is that exalting the fullest development of the individual's potentialities. What kind of clue does this give them except to let the individual be an individual, to let him develop his potentialities by himself? If you are going to tell him how to fill his empty time, you will be pushing him along the old road of self-betterment dearly loved by the nineteenth century. On the whole, however, that century kept the government off to one side. The present proposals may end by recommending that state legislatures enforce local standards, that departments of leisure should never try to give people what they want, for most people do not know what they want and should be encouraged or compelled to learn to like things they dislike.[10]

The difficulty is even greater than such writers believe. They think It involves complexity and the possibility of undemocratic compulsion. This would be true were it a simple task like sewage disposal or air pollution, both of which are problems amenable to a rational plan, an organized attack, and an efficient system of execution. Free time cannot easily be handled this way. The word "free" in free time refers to uncommitted or unobligated time. If there is any constraint at all, the freeness vanishes.

The specter is that of an economic system constraining workers not to work. To solve the problem of filling the time then emptied, the system applies the same method it applied successfully to work—rationality, organization, and efficiency. Except that this time the method will not work. Preparing for the future in this way will bring trouble.

For all the fun that is poked at the gospel of work today, it has been a crucial part of American belief. As such it served and still serves to make sense and give meaning to existence. But it is weakening. All the nice talk itself of free time and leisure is a detraction. Writers jeer at the conformity and methodicalness work requires. Their painting a future workless world as a utopia is almost the last straw.

If the economic system is producing unemployment that it must justify as free time, it must yet produce a substitute for the work ethic. What is there to substitute for it? It is useless simply to recommend that men get the same satisfaction from leisure that they get from work. A hard worker used to be an object of esteem. Is he today? Work used to be, and still is, good for you, a remedy for pain, loneliness, the death of a dear one, a disappointment in love, doubts about the purpose of life. Steady methodical work built a great and powerful and prosperous nation. Can leisure do the same?

Religiously, politically, economically, militarily, and mentally it is still thought better to work than to do what you please. The men who go to work in the morning and come home at night are still the pillars of the nation. If these pillars tumble, the country has lost an important part of its cohesion.

To sum up, free time today does not exist in any great quantity. Projections based on the conviction that an extraordinary amount is being enjoyed are in error. Yet free time can be had in the future and in large quantities. It has already been available for a long time but few wished to take it or felt they could afford to. To get them to take it or wish for it, the worker-consumer pattern has to be broken. The "consumer" part of the dualism is not deep. It is a recently acquired belief, post-Depression, to be exact. The "worker" part of the pattern is a longer, ingrained tradition. It may take decades yet to break. Certainly it will not go at the speed projected, but the process may have already begun.

What may shatter the work ethic like Humpty Dumpty will be the need to conceal latent unemployment. One way already in evidence is to call it free time. But since it is not wanted, it is not free but forced free time. The constraint is hidden.

Disaffection

There is another place in which unemployment even today may be inaccurately assessed—in universal college education. Here the young are removed from the labor force for four or five years. When accompanied by a military draft prospect for those not making the grade at school, college becomes for many not a choice but an extension of compulsory education. This may be hidden unemployment too, and not all the young are taken in by it. Possibly for this reason disaffection with the work ethic is appearing most dramatically today among youth.

Among the young there is a vocal minority whose antipathy to work is more ideological than the bum's or the philosophic hobo's once was. Their doctrines include an antipathy to technology and science as well, and to what is sometimes called the Establishment, namely all those in positions of influence in the political, military, industrial, and scientific world. To talk to these persons of a higher standard of living, mounting GNP, the American way of life, larger incomes, more free time, and the cornucopia of commodities reaps nothing but scorn. They no longer worship these gods. What they want in exchange is not clear but what they reject is easy to see—the world prophesied by the projections we have been studying.[11]

Disaffection will not remain restricted to youth. Deprived of a sense of purpose, with the old gods gone and without new ones, other people will fall into a hedonistic attitude toward life, wherein all they can justify is to get what they can out of pleasure. Historically this is at times accompanied but typically followed by some form of religious revival. Until then there is reason to fear, as some do, that more free time, forced free time, will bring on the restless tick of boredom, idleness, immorality, and increased personal violence.

As more and more free time is forced on adults, disaffection will spread. If the cause is identified as automation and its preference for higher intelligence, non-automated jobs may increase, as it is thought, in the categories of trade and services[12] but they will carry the stigma of stupidity. Men will prefer not to work rather than to accept them. Those who do accept will increasingly come to be a politically inferior class composed of women, immigrants, imported aliens, and humanoids.[13]

There may then be three classes: (1) an elite that works on top policy, administrative or manufacturing tasks with automated accoutrements, or in the arts and communication—writing, filming, designing, etc.; (2) a free time citizenry accepting its dole status but disenchanted and even rebellious; and (3) those of inferior political status who will perform the unpopular trades and services.

There are other alternatives of course, but this one reveals that a whole future world is possible on which today's statistical projections have little bearing.

Should it continue, the process of disaffection will spread most rapidly in the cities. Projections for free time in the future indicate that regional fluctuation in the length of the work week or work year will be small.[14] This may be so but its significance will have a regional difference nonetheless.

One may look on the capital area of the United States as a megalopolis, the urbanized region extending from Boston to Washington.[15] Eventually it may arc over to Chicago. The rest of the country, including climatic resorts like Florida and California, can be regarded as the provinces. From these areas, for decades to come, there will appear in the cities of the capital persons as yet relatively untouched by the disillusion of forced free time. The flow of provincials may provide a breathing spell of stability for the rest of the country, a time in which solutions to the problem of hidden unemployment, forced free time, and disaffection will have to be found.

There should be lots of time free for thinking up a solution, but a problem of such magnitude requires a creative solution. Free time can bring more recreation and an appetite for spectacles, but genius or creativity—that is doubtful. Free time leads to recreation; it is leisure that bears directly on creation.

The Rhetoric of Leisure

For those concerned with the sanity of the individual or the integration of the country, it is natural to worry about too much free time. As we have seen, the problem does not exist at present but well may in the future. Furthermore, it is more serious than anyone thought. Advertisers sell wares within the worker-and-his-job pattern. Social workers may feel that other leadership is necessary besides that of commercialism, but at least it is some guidance. The threat to come is that the worker model which up to now has supported the industrial system will bite the grime and grease, leaving no heirs. In the ideological vacuum, there will be those who will look back on advertising and think nostalgically of the good old days. The advertiser was bound by some standards, slight reeds though they may then have seemed.

Now leisure is a state of being, of being free of everyday necessity. Distinct from free time, it requires freedom from time and work—not hourly, daily, or monthly freedom, but freedom from the necessity to work, preferably over a lifetime. By contrast the present American free time is one-half of a pendulum—jobtime/free time. First you work, then you rest and recreate yourself.

Leisure has no particular activities. Men in a leisure condition may do anything; much of what they do may seem to an outsider suspiciously like work. It is modern usage to refer to such activity as work. Creative work ought not to be called work at all. Not having anything to do, these men do something. Often they may turn to religious ritual, music, wining and dining, friends and poetry, and notably to the play of ideas and theory; in short, to the theoretical life, to contemplation.

With the lack in America of a strong tradition of leisure, it is not surprising that we must ask, "What can leisure do for us?" The benefits are the benefits of cultivating the free mind. If persons have been brought up with a liberal education and have no need to work at anything except what they choose, they enjoy a freedom that lays the conditions for the greatest objectivity (for example in science), the greatest beauty (for example in art), and the greatest creativeness (for example in politics). Leisure is the mother of philosophy, said Hobbes. If such are its benefits, and we need them sorely, can we increase leisure?

To increase leisure is difficult. It is not contained, as is free time, by time (off work) and space (for recreation). To increase free time it is usually enough to send a man, any man, home early from work. For his recreation it is usually enough to give him some space to play in. How to provide leisure?

All steps that can be taken by the government through legislation and institutions, by business organizations, schools, and churches, steps that have a limited value even for free time have much less value for leisure. There are traces of the leisure ideal in some recent attempts by government and universities to provide in centers and institutes a creative setting, for scientists in particular. These efforts and others can help only inasmuch as they diffuse an appreciative climate, through teaching and example. Much more than this cannot be done directly.

There are two important limits to face. First, not everyone has the temperament for leisure. According to the Encyclical *Rerum Novarum*, all mankind would be capable of enjoying leisure were it not for the Fall.[16] For most people, leisure lacks sufficient guidance and sense of purpose; the leisure life is too hard. Those who have the toughness or psychological security for it are not many. Second, since leisure will have nothing to do with work (except that freely chosen, which then by definition should not be called work), it involves having means of support. In modern terms this means that whoever is to lead a life of leisure should have some form of economic independence.

The objectives in creating more leisure should be these: to allow the greatest number of those who have the temperament for it to develop to their fullest extent; to allow them to secure the means of existence without work; and to create an atmosphere more friendly than hostile in which they may live their kind of life.

A number of the developments we have been discussing do affect these objectives. A liberal education is almost a sine qua non for the growth of the leisure temperament. Universal education today may soon see to it that all will have a college education. On the negative side, however, the education is not being freely chosen; military service is the alternative. Education, moreover, has declined in quality and will continue to because of the great numbers of students in compulsory attendance and the nursery school climate of the college as a place to put grown-up children while the adults go to work.

Also, forced free time will not have to expand much to reach a net separation of income from work. Recent proposals for a guaranteed annual wage or salary intimate the separation already. Should this happen, the wherewithal for a life of leisure will be there for all who think they have the temperament. Many will try; many will drop out; among the survivors the right few will be found.

The last-mentioned prerequisite, an atmosphere friendly to leisure, may be brought about by the increase in free time whether forced or not. If both parts of the worker-consumer model break down, if more free time is not only forced upon men but in time also sought and taken, the accompanying change in attitude may well be receptive to true leisure. A more relaxed pace to life may bring about a more favorable view of the whole ideal, as well as more reflection, more refinement, and less ambitious political, military, and economic projects. Play in man's free time is a taste of leisure. In turn the ideal and practice of leisure create standards for the enjoyment of free time. Indeed without leisure the outlook for the resolution of the problems of hidden unemployment and forced free time seems desperate: hedonism, disintegration of social and political ties, crises of law and order, a cynical and callous foreign policy.

There are other developments that may influence the future attitude toward leisure, such as population growth, urbanization, increased prosperity and commercialism, and military events. Population growth and metropolitan concentration do not in themselves prohibit leisure. Traditions related to the leisure ideal in China, India, and England amply support this proposition. As for urban versus rural environment, the stimulus for the very ideals of civility and leisure has come from cities. Prosperity and the business and commercial spirit (to be distinguished from the work gospel and industrial materialism) are not inimical to leisure, as instances from ancient Greece and the Renaissance indicate. Instead the martial or expansionist temper or the desperate defensive position of a nation may be the most harmful influence, for it pits leisure against patriotism. Yet even this hypothesis needs qualification.

The use of professional forces or of mercenaries poses less of a problem than does the drafting of militia. Minor or border wars combined with imperialism, accompanying high spending, climate of experimentation, lack of fear of real danger to the nation, devil-may-care mood of soldiery on leave—these may be compatible with, possibly even conducive to, a favorable view of leisure. Costly, desperate wars, last-ditch defensive wars, though, may stamp out its slightest expression.

Leisure for the few, free time for the many: that is what appears to be coming. A not unpleasant prospect spoiled only by the introduction in free time of the adjective "forced."

The United States and the World

All over the globe one encounters the modern attitude to free time. A worldwide change in vocabulary has occurred. The word *leisure* is in the air. Governments now have to promise it, or write it into their constitutions. The United States is partly responsible for furthering this development, especially of late, through its serving as the model for many other of the world's countries. The usual invidious statistical comparisons are made, as misleading as ever, to show how the United States is far advanced in the shorter work week, which then is automatically equated with leisure.[17] Now, although even in Europe as in the United States itself this linguistic change is as recent as the twentieth century, it is important. By turning things upside-down, turning idleness with its contrast to work into leisure, it reveals itself as a revolution.

As long as the United States is militarily dominant, other countries and peoples will measure the success of their economy and government by the length of the work week. Their goal will be to compare with the United States, to acquire and use the technology that brings on such riches and leisure. Migration to the United States will continue, the service occupations will be open for foreigners, and many will come for these relatively well paid but lowly esteemed jobs. There may also be opportunity for the managerial and professional classes; they will come to this country for the riches or prestige they hope to command; of leisure or free time they will have little. Migration of these latter groups has recently been brought to official attention and unofficially dubbed "the brain drain."

Policy and planning must be forearmed. The crisis, if it is to come, will occur before these next fifty years are up. It will be the crisis of disbanding a labor force that is no longer needed, of changing men's faith in work to a faith in what we can see today only dimly as a life of non-work. By 2020—the date is just remote enough—a path may be cut toward the leisurely life. The concern thereafter may merely be to keep the path well trodden.

Final Aside on Projections

Planning, to be planning, must have some control over the elements in its plans. Projections assure no such control. Moreover, the planner who bases his work on projections is condemned to make only small plans. I have earlier criticized available projections for their incompleteness and irrelevance. They also keep the planner from setting out and building a world closer to his heart. Projections are based on old, not new, conceptions. They lead the planner by the nose up the trajectories of graphs—with their old notions of standard of living, GNP, population trends, natural resources— and when he gets there, he finds himself in a new and brighter toyland where even the lethal toys have been removed. Most projections do not permit the threat of war to distract their calculations, or of revolt or economic disaster, all perfectly possible too, in the next fifty years.[18] Having eliminated the disturbing factors— population explosion is merely another big figure, automation's preference for brains seems not worthy of consideration, consumption demand is inexhaustible—the world they finish with at the tops of their curves is a brightly lit, incessantly euphoric toyland. Extrapolation gives them the old world, only more so, a dismal world capable of winning the enthusiasm of only the old guard.

Much better is it for the planner to paint a world out from his mind or to seek it in a place so remote in time and place it seems like a new world. Methodologically he would be on just as sure or just as shaky ground. The qualifications all reputable projectors make reveal their uncertainties, incompleteness, and subjectivity. They speak of their "naive" projections or methodology, their resort to a "judgment alternative"; they acknowledge that "projections of future population are admittedly fictitious. No one can actually predict future population and anyone who claims he can is either a fool or a charlatan."[19] Certainly for everyone who says we shall soon be walking on each other's heads, there is another who confidently asserts that population will begin to level off in the next generation.[20] If we are going to be fictitious, we may as well extend our range of approaches.

Now unless there is global war or economic catastrophe the future holds great cities in its hands. With the present layout of American cities, the lack of recreational facilities for everyday use, and the infatuation with the great outdoors, how will the city-dweller fare with more time on his hands? Clearly the city has to be turned into a place for him to live in and enjoy, rather than a place to escape from to restore his senses. In questions of physical environment, the city must get top priority. But how to plan for it? I suggest that it is not enough to trace projections slavishly. One must drop everything and think about it, dream about it, talk about it, study it, write about it—objectively. This one can do in leisure.

Failing that, I suggest choosing the most beautiful city in the world as a model. Which is it? Venice, of course. Yet we must remember that Marco Polo, himself a Venetian, said there was a better one. In the closing years of the thirteenth century he described it for our guidance and inspiration.

> At the end of three days you reach the
> noble and magnificent city of Kinsai
> (Hangchow), a name that signifies "The
> Celestial City." This name merits
> from its preeminence, among all
> others in the world, in point of
> grandeur and beauty, as well as from
> its many charms, which might lead
> an inhabitant to imagine himself in
> paradise. . . . Marco Polo happened to
> be in Kinsai at the time of the annual
> report to his Majesty's commissioners
> of the revenue and number of inhabitants,
> and he learned that there were 160 tomans
> of fireplaces [that is, of families
> dwelling under the same roof]; and as a
> toman is ten thousand, it follows that
> the whole city must have contained
> 1,600,000 families. . . .[21]

Notes

1. Mark Wehle and Gus Weiss, *II Economic Projections* (Croton-on-Hudson, N.Y.: Hudson Institute, 1966; mimeographed draft), p. 83.

2. Ibid., p. 84.

3. For projection to 1976 of the work week in hours of this category, see *Outdoor Resources Recreation Review Commission Study Report 23* (Washington, D.C.: U.S. Government Printing Office, 1962), p. 59.

4. See S. de Grazia, *Of Time, Work, and Leisure* (New York: Twentieth Century Fund, 1962), p. 69 and passim. For recent data from time budgets see Survey Research Center, *Summary of United States Time Use Survey* (Ann Arbor, Mich.: Institute for Social Research, 1966; mimeographed.)

5. See S. de Grazia, *Of Time, Work, and Leisure,* p. 143.

6. See Wehle and Weiss, *Economic Projections,* pp. 84-88.

7. On the fear of unemployment as a result of automation, see for example, T.J. Gordon and Olaf Helmer, *Report on a Long-Range Forecasting Study* (Santa Monica, Calif.: The Rand Corporation, Sept., 1964, mimeographed), pp. 20, 44. On automation and intelligence see "The Future of the Stupid," by Sir George Thompson in his *The Foreseeable Future* (New York: The Viking Press, Inc., 1955), and Leon Bagrit, "A Nation of Computer-Keepers?" in *The World in 1984,* ed. Nigel Calder (Baltimore: Pelican Books, 1965), II, pp. 128-32.

8. For these arguments see S. de Grazia, *Of Time, Work, and Leisure,* pp. 268-76.

9. Mark Wehle and Gus Weiss, *Supplementary Projections for 1965–2020* (Croton-on-Hudson, N.Y.: Hudson Institute, 1966, mimeographed), p. 4.

10. For an example of systematic proposals, see James C. Charlesworth, "A Comprehensive Plan for the Wise Use of Leisure," and Paul G. Douglass and Robert W. Crawford, "Implementation of a Plan for the Wise Use of Leisure," both articles in *Annals of the American Academy of Political and Social Science,* Monograph 4 (April, 1964), pp. 30-46, 47-69. On the role of government and industry in free time activities, see S. de Grazia, *Of Time, Work, and Leisure,* pp. 357-60.

11. The writings of Paul Goodman often touch on youthful alienation. See his "The Empty Society," *Commentary,* Nov., 1966, pp. 53-60, and *Growing Up Absurd* (New York: Random House, 1960.)

12. See, for example, Figure 26 in Wehle and Weiss, *Economic Projections,* p. 51.

13. On menial tasks of politically inferior women and aliens, see Barbara Wooton, "Winners and Losers in the Rat Race" in Calder, *The World in 1984,* II, pp. 132-35, and for the political status of humanoids, H.D. Lasswell, "The Political Science of Science," *American Political Science Review,* L (Dec., 1956), p. 976.

14. See Table B-20, *ORRRC Study Report 23,* p. 68.

15. See Jean Gottman, *Megalopolis,* (New York: Twentieth Century Fund, 1960) and Jerome P. Pickard, "Future Growth of Major U.S. Regions," *Urban Land,* XXVI (Feb., 1967), pp. 3-10.

16. "Even if man had never fallen from the state of innocence, he would not have been wholly idle; but the labor which would have been his free choice in that case, and his delight, became compulsory by his sin, and a painful expiation of it." Pope Leo XIII, Encyclical "Rerum Novarum," May 15, 1891.

17. A comparative table of U.S. and European weekly working hours from 1850 to 1950 can be found in W.S. and E.S. Woytinsky, *World Population and Production: Trends and Outlook* (New York: Twentieth Century Fund, 1953), p. 367.

18. See for example, Wehle and Weiss, *Economic Projections,* p. 1. On war, compare Bureau of Labor Statistics, *Projections 1970: Interindustry Relationships, Potential Demand, Employment* (Washington, D.C.: U.S. Department of Labor, 1966), pp. 118-19;

for forecasting of war, upheaval, and unemployment, compare Gordon and Helmer, *Long-Range Forecasting*.

19. The quotations are respectively from Wehle and Weiss, *Economic Projections*, title page and p. 82; *ORRRC Study Report 23*, p. 7 and passim; and Phillip M. Hauser, *Population Perspectives* (New Brunswick, N.J.: Rutgers University Press, 1960), p. 168.

20. For leveling-off forecasts, see Gordon and Helmer, *Long-Range Forecasting*, pp. 15-20, 43.

21. Marco Polo, *The Travels of Marco Polo* (New York: New American Library, 1961), pp. 209, 220.

Comments on

de Grazia

THOMAS P. F. HOVING
Metropolitan Museum of Art

If I were to give the gist of Dr. de Grazia's essay, "The Problems and Promise of Leisure," I would say that it is the warning about a revolution. It is a clarion to awaken us to economic and sociological revolution involving production, unemployment, and creativity based upon a project of concept of job—non-job deficiencies. For this reason, the essay is illuminating, exciting, and not at all specious. The trouble is that few will heed the warning or the call.

Dr. de Grazia does well in introducing clarity into the muddle of words relating to non-work activities; namely, free time, forced free time, and leisure. Free time is what we have off the job. Forced free time, on the other hand, is a decidedly sinister euphemism for unemployment. Naive thinking on the part of Dr. de Grazia, one might say, but if so, it is the naïveté that comes with thought and wisdom. Leisure, according to the author, is a state of freedom from everyday necessity to enable the strong and gifted to think creatively. All lead to distinct problems and all have their penalties.

The promise of forced free time is no promise at all, but a sort of frenetic misery made up of hedonism, the disintegration of moral, social, religious and political ties, the breakdown of law and order and an even greater cynicism and callousness in our foreign policy. The promise of real leisure (for those who can stand it intellectually and psychologically) is that it will give the creative mind the full opportunity to solve the impending "promise" of a plethora of forced free time.

In sum Dr. de Grazia is giving clear warning that in our next fifty years we may be faced with a revolution of our entire work—non-work balance, and that we will have a lot more unemployment and that we may tend to call it free time instead of what it really is, and that although greater opportunities for leisure may exist, the atmosphere in America will probably be even more dull and unfriendly to the cultivation of true leisure than it is at present. And nobody is thinking about this.

When it comes to suggesting solutions for the problems of too much forced free time and too little opportunity for true leisure, Dr. de Grazia bows out. To his credit, however, it must be added that his role lies far more in isolating and defining the problems than in solving them. He is right in emphasizing that those millions who may be unemployed in the future (or, more accurately, oppressed in a state of forced free time) must be prepared by educational means for their bittersweet condition. Just what this educational process might be is not hinted at. Dr. de Grazia observes that thought and planning must start at once so that free time, in its projected abundance, will not lead to the consuming tendencies of boredom, idleness, immorality, and increased personal violence. Fine. But he only alludes to the fact that it is up to the central government to invent, manufacture, and put into operation the complicated machinery that may hopefully grind out solutions. This is perhaps debatable, although few would deny that only through the rigorous leadership of the federal government will the needed meeting of minds from the public, business, and labor sectors come about. No such imaginative leadership appears to be in the offing.

In formulating how the promise of true leisure can be brought to fruition, Dr. de Grazia is only slightly more explicit. First, broad receptivity to leisure must be engendered. A tradition for leisure must be built up in the United States. And, second, economic independence must be available for those who can, owing to their temperaments and psychological make-up, stand a state of creative leisure. In one respect, I believe Dr. de Grazia is wrong about creating leisure. He states that although there are traces of the leisure ideal in recent attempts by government and universities to provide a creative setting, more in this line cannot be done directly. In my opinion much more needs to be done. Good grief, much more! Tangible results will spring forth only from active work to enhance the creative atmosphere. For this, too, we need leadership in the federal sphere. To my mind, none is in the offing.

The great value of Dr. de Grazia's essay is that it is one of the first to define clearly the triad of social elements that will make up the troubles in the next revolution; namely, too much free time, a forced free time, and too little leisure, and one of the earliest warnings of the dire consequences of a tripartite society; namely, division into factions of the elite intelligent, the drone of forced free time status, and the menial. The ironic point is that if the definitions are not studied and the call for a receptive attitude for true leisure time goes unheeded, our society is headed for destruction. And you just know that no one will listen. You know it.

But every nation and government has its time, whether one wholly dedicated to defense or semi-conquest or drying up of the mind and spirit like Sparta, or one dedicated to the growth and cultivation of the spirit of humanism, like Athens. The sole consolation is that the one retains, even in isolated and ruined physical memory, a universal promise and the other is an oblivion on a hot, dusty plain.

GEORGE CANDILIS
Architect, Paris

In "The Problems and Promise of Leisure," Sebastian de Grazia begins with an analysis of the very schematic statistical provisions which are based, above all, on the relation between the GNP and the necessary work hours. Progressively he frees himself from the simple view: leisure equals utilization of free time and comes to demonstrate, more and more, the actual part that leisure is called to play in the future.

Starting from the interrelationship, work–future development–GNP–leisure, he comes to a master demonstration of the complexity of the problem, its importance, and the necessity to establish a new attitude, a really new conscience in all the fields of life: political, economical, and, finally, urban. He concludes: "With the present layout of American cities, the lack of recreational facilities for everyday use, and the infatuation with the great outdoors, how will the city dweller fare with more time on his hands? Clearly the city has to be turned into a place for him to inhabit and enjoy, rather than a place to escape from to restore his senses. In questions of physical environment, the city must get top priority. But how to plan for it? I suggest that it is not enough to trace projections slavishly. One must drop everything and think about it, dream about it, talk about it, study it, write about it."

The vision of those cities which will incite to leisure, future Venices or Kinshais of Marco Polo, is quite an ingenious simplification of the future. The urban problem forms a whole. It begins at home, goes on in the street, in the district, in the city, in the region, in the whole country. It has its deep complexity, too.

As for me, I prefer to get still freer from today's perspectives and look toward the future in order that, during these next fifty years, a policy, or rather a moral attitude, be confirmed and prepare men for the new life of the twenty-first century civilization. "So, for a hundred years, leisure has been born, grown up, and valorized. It is now in full expansion. It is not a secondary product of the present civilization but a central one. Could the world have entered already the *civilization of leisure?*" (Joffre Dumazedier).

If we admit that leisure of multitude, of the biggest number, is in the process of becoming a critical phenomenon of the contemporary civilization, we have to analyze and put forward the apparent or hidden relations which exist between leisure and the different activities of everyday life, and above everything else, we have to clarify its actual significance, its contents, its different aspects, and the predominant and increasing part that it is called to take in our society.

An a priori definition of leisure is quite dangerous and inopportune. Its significance in modern society suffers a deep transformation under our eyes. The analysis of leisure in the whole complexity of its structure brings us to examine it through its various fundamental aspects: leisure–free time, leisure–free activity, leisure–frame of mind.

Leisure–free time: the overly simple formula of the "three–eight," eight hours for work, eight hours for sleep, eight hours for leisure, gives place to a not-so-simple definition of the manner in which each person occupies free time. Effectively, the definition of leisure–free time is linked to the relation, leisure–activity, and, as leisure is the consequence of free time, leisure activities are free too, isolated from those considered necessary and obligatory. Leisure–free time and leisure–activity complement each other in a more abstract notion: leisure–frame of mind which needs a new mental, social, political, economical, and military attitude of thinking and living—a new culture.

A common denominator can be found in those three viewpoints of leisure, time, activity, frame of mind: that is, leisure equals liberty of choice. Consciously or not, men choose and orient their leisure in order to find again a physical and psychical balance, deteriorated by the sustained effects which result from the obligatory activities of everyday life, of their work, of the confusion and tiredness born from the excessive densification of their urban surroundings. In that way, leisure comes to be a biologic repairer based on the harmony between two rhythms: rhythm of life and rhythm of leisure.

Leisure assumes three very important functions, relaxation, entertainment, development. Relaxation: in order to deliver men from tiredness; leisure of rest, silence, *farniente*, leisure to be occupied without definite aim, without imperative target. Entertainment: in order to deliver men from boredom; leisure of escape, strangeness, change and search where imagination can be given free rein. Development: in order to deliver men from automatism of thought and conventionalism of everyday actions; leisure for the culture of the body and the soul, blooming of personality. These three functions are interdependent; they coexist at variable degrees, in all situations, and for all human beings.

It is not possible to isolate the problem of leisure from the concept of the set of man's life. Leisures come out permanently, are overlapped with the other activities, and, under determined conditions, dominate them. The everyday–urban leisure must be an integral part of the conception of the city itself and become more and more a determinant component of its structure. The weekly–suburban leisure rhythms the relation between town and country and creates the balance of occupation and utilization of earth. The seasonal–regional leisure, "the holiday," closely determined by climatic and geographic data, becomes increasingly a predominant component for the planning of the territory.

This permanent, unending, diversified, and increasing presence of leisure in the life of men impregnates and changes the very conception of the art of building and implies the predominance of equipment in future realizations. This new optic brings new forms of human groups, new relations of those groups among each other, new conceptions of life, and it requires, above everything else, a new moral attitude.

PART II

The Contribution of Urban Form, Transportation, and Housing to a New Standard of Life

The Possible City

This paper was commissioned to examine those critical decisions which can make the greatest contribution to the creation of a vital, inspiring, human environment in our cities. It is concerned with physical and aesthetic forms insofar as they contribute to and serve the needs of human urban life.

Are there policies to be determined to assure a great concentration and access to variety in our communities, utilizing technology to the fullest appropriate extent? Can we locally set community performance standards? The scale of community this paper is concerned with ranges from community in the cluster-of-houses sense, to the community of the nation and the consideration of national policies for the placement and evolution of cities in the future. The question of scale is itself of vital importance.

It is expected that a reworking of the metropolitan region will dominate this paper although entirely new cities, new major metropolitan centers, and nurtured growth points are all part of it.

The question of standard of life versus a product-oriented standard of living is in mind. This paper is urged to give particular attention to open space from the scale of little neighborhood plazas to vast open spaces that could provide a "dramatic edge" to the city.

Controlling transport and communication to provide the desired impact on urban form is a different way of considering technological impacts from leaving it to this technology to decide "for itself" its application over the next fifty years.

Author: Kevin Lynch, AIP, Professor of City Planning, Massachusetts Institute of Technology

Chairman: Stanley B. Tankel, AIP, Planning Director, Regional Plan Association, New York

Committee: Anthony Downs, Senior Vice President and Treasurer, Real Estate Research Corporation; Howard Moody, Judson Memorial Church, New York; Rai Y. Okamoto, Okamoto/Liskamm, San Francisco; Boris Pushkarev, Chief Planner, Regional Plan Association, New York; Lowdon Wingo, Resources for the Future, Inc.; Hans Blumenfeld, AIP, Consultant, Toronto.

Kevin Lynch

Professor of City Planning
Massachusetts Institute of Technology

The Possible City

The issue for the future city is how it affects the growing of human beings. If we knew better, we might add: and the survival and development of other living organisms. But our knowledge and our ethics are still too limited for that. Growth occurs (or fails) within a spatial pattern of activities and spaces, and that pattern plays a role in the growing. There are various world futures which we can imagine: Does any of them include a city suited for growth? Can we make that possible city a probable one?

Social changes cause environmental problems—congestion, discomfort, obsolescence, pollution, abandonment, overload—and in return environment frustrates change. The changes themselves are disturbing. Landmarks are swept away, associations dissolve, we lose our roots in particular places, our values waver. We may be poisoning the world with our technology; and so we fear our power as well as delight in it. The changes occur unevenly: groups are exploited or left behind; in a relative sense they become poorer, their ways of life more archaic and despised. They are excluded from the common opportunities. The bitter contrast of the ghetto will become more visible as advantaged groups gain mobility.

So we hope to make environments which accept change, and also to manage that change so that it occurs in the areas of need, and does not degrade the living community. Environment might be used to decrease deprivation and segregation, rather than to sharpen it. It might create more intricate ecologies. Indeed we might learn, not simply to accept change, but to see its possibilities and delights.

Our fear of change is accompanied by a fear of powerlessness, the loss of meaningful participation and control. The individual makes only marginal alterations in the system in which he lives. Perhaps there were never more than rare periods in history when the individual had any autonomy, but we feel that he should have, and does not now. Fears of impersonal control are evoked by recent advances in biology, in psychology, in information systems. People are aware of the extent to which their lives are already manipulated. Alienation and loss of purpose are talked about; they also exist. The increase of leisure and material production threatens to exaggerate those feelings by detaching men from the work that has been their central purposeful activity.

Environment can counteract this loss. Surroundings can be designed to be open and responsive to the user; they can encourage him to learn and to become involved; they can be a vehicle for autonomy and local decision, an object of creation and purposeful absorption. Technology might increase individual option and control, rather than decrease it. None of this will of itself solve these dilemmas, and yet it can countervail.

Our possible city must therefore have certain characteristics: adaptability coupled with a sense of past and future continuity; equalization of opportunity; a diversity of species, habitats, and ways of life. It must be open and responsive, experimental and engaging. These are crucial qualities for the future. However general, they direct attention to particular possibilities. But these possibilities will not come of themselves. Our cities become more rigid, segregated, and unresponsive. Are there chances to move in an opposite direction?

For the future, I assume a steady growth of the world population, and, in the developed countries at least, rising incomes and expectations. I hope for an increase in international cooperation, and a flow of resources to reduce international and intranational inequalities. I do not hope for radical political shifts in this country, although they will occur elsewhere in the world, but for increased public intervention and investment in city development. I expect a continuance of the current restraints on how cities grow: a diversity of users, a dispersion and conflict of decision, institutional and environmental inertia. I hope for some shift in the attitudes of people toward each other: a greater mutual tolerance, concern and delight, a desire to see human potentialities realized. We might even progress from a human-centered ethic to one which values the whole interdependent living community, to an attitude which welcomes diversity, both human and non-human. Quixotic, perhaps, but possible; a development in which the city could play a role.

The Edge of the Metropolis

We can expect the metropolis to be the normal environment of the future: the realized desire of those seeking space, better services, congenial neighbors, and a home of their own. Present estimates are that 80 percent of our population will be living in such regions by the year 2000, and that the largest of these metropolises will coalesce into four giant megalopolitan regions—on the Atlantic seaboard, along the lower Great Lakes (these two may even grow together into a single belt), in Florida, and in California—four regions containing 60 percent of the U.S. population on 7½ percent of its land. The horror of critics is unjustified: This is a superior environment by past standards. It doesn't "eat up" land, nor will it cause the end of civilization. It frees large areas of the country for rural and recreational uses. The apparent threat of extended urbanization can in fact be turned to our great advantage— can be but may not be. The metropolis has serious problems. Social groups are increasingly segregated in space. There is a lack of diversity and a lack of identity. If you have no car, you are stranded. There are no concentrated centers. But none of these difficulties is inherent in the metropolitan form.

If you ask anyone to imagine a city of 50,000 square miles, 600 miles long (as the Californian megalopolis is projected to be), he feels desperate because he imagines a mechanical enlargement of the present city. But one need not feel lost in a region, simply because it is encompassing. Setting limits is only one way of structuring. Such a region could be a very diverse place, it could be clean and open, the quality of its life could be pleasant and challenging. It could be a homeland, a beloved landscape. We cling to the notion of the rural-urban dichotomy —small cities in a rural hinterland, a world with an outside and an inside. That world is fading before our eyes. The sense of being at home depends neither on size, nor on traditional form, but on an active relation between men and their landscape, a landscape which they made and which speaks to them. How can we achieve this in such vast areas?

Guiding the development of these great regions will be a staggering task, considering our difficulties in managing the growth of much smaller and less complex areas. Even by 1975, we can expect new construction to double the present rates. The sheer quantity of new environment, which will be most striking at the fringe but also substantial in the city interiors, is an opportunity and a threat. There will be a growing body of used environment, which must be continually adapted and maintained, or painfully rebuilt, while attending to a great diversity in user wants and needs. If anything, this diversity appears to be increasing. No central agency can direct the details of this process.

The most effective opportunities for environmental quality are at the point of development. One such opportunity is at the edge of the metropolis, where public (or mixed public and private) authorities might assemble and plan large chunks of undeveloped land for diverse urban uses, which would then be transferred to private and public development agencies for actual construction. These would not be "new towns" in the old sense. The authorities would work with the normal urbanizing process, much as several large private land developers are doing today, but on a far more comprehensive scale. The private developer works under severe limitations of market and political control, yet his product is the environment of the future.

Here at the growing edge our evolving ideas for clusters of mixed low density housing, for the maintenance of ecological balance, for intense diversified centers or continuous open spaces, for new modes of transport or the control of climate, light, and sound, could most easily be put into practice. Any existing social, or built, or natural identities could be preserved. The authority could create a sense of place by specifying particular environmental characters to be built into various zones. The region would become a mosaic of distinctive and well-fitted districts, a human landscape built from the beginning. No one is building it today. All large developing areas at the metropolitan fringe should pass through the hands of capable public authorities, but not through a single central authority. It should be a public responsibility to see that an adequate supply of land for development is constantly available throughout the metropolitan region, that it is well planned, well serviced, and free of speculative surcharge.

This public power must only be used if it will reduce the growing segregation of our population by race and class. Rather than straining to entice the middle class to return to the central city they have left behind, we should make it possible for others to move out to the suburbs that they would like to reach. This will be a long effort, contending with resistance from the suburbs and fear on the part of the movers. It will require concerted action on jobs, housing, and transport—a massive resettlement. It will mean the construction of substantial quantities of new housing within the reach of lower income groups. Technology promises future reductions in building costs, and we should press to realize those promises. Until they are realized, the construction of housing must be subsidized. We must create development agencies which can take on those resettlement tasks, in the newly organizing areas, but also in scattered locations throughout the inner and outer zones. They will necessarily be engaged in the provision of social services, the improvement of transportation, and the distribution of employment, as well as in building houses. Grants to local authorities to pay for the additional services required must accompany these movements, to make them politically palatable. "Sister" relations between inner and outer districts, with exchanges of services and visitors, might precede permanent population movements. It may be unrealistic (even undesirable) to hope for a fine-grained mix of social groups, but we must destroy the one-color school district and the single-class town. We are already building the future metropolis. If we refuse to intervene decisively, that future is an even suburbia and a frayed interior. It will have its amenities. It will have its costs—not least being a denial of growth to a sizeable number of people. And it will be a splendid opportunity gone by.

The System of Centers

Strenuous efforts are being made to "save the downtown" as a last vestige of concentrated urbanity. Indeed there is something lost, if we should no longer have places of intense activity, of diverse services and opportune encounters. The outward dispersion of high intensity activities to widely scattered sites deprives us of social and visual meeting points, as well as of the opportunity to live close to the action or to enjoy a rich array of supporting facilities. But to maintain a single center as the dominant focus of employment and services is to swim against the flood. As far as it is successful, it will preserve commuter congestion and the ghetto.

We have a better opportunity: to channel high density housing; services such as health, education, shopping, culture, and entertainment and concentrated and interlinked employment, such as offices and business services into a galaxy of metropolitan centers, each large enough to provide substantial diversity and to support a local transit system, provided with structures linked at many levels, pedestrian carriers, and climate control. To the extent that these centers had a special character of activity and form, they could stand for differentiated areas of the region, and might encourage social interactions over a broader geographic base, less tied to class and race.

In and near these centers people might live who, by choice or necessity, wished to be close to work and services. The centers might also serve as points of reception for families escaping from the central ghetto. Centers could be built out of older incomplete foci, or encouraged to coalesce in the regions of new growth. Their range of activity and their physical character could be guided in a way which would be impractical over larger areas. Building or rebuilding the important focal points is another crucial development task which might be undertaken by public authority. There are significant advances to be made in the design and maintenance of such intensive locales.

Change and Renovation

Activities that occupy the older areas are constantly changing, and we have burned our fingers in trying to manage that change. Even the oldest areas are rarely completely abandoned, but become specialized for other activities, often more diverse than the original ones. The contrast of activity and setting can be quite evocative. If we do anything here, it should be to facilitate these shifts in use, to assist in the gradual specialization and decrease in density of the central areas. The danger lies in the attempt to cling to the present—to save the downtown, for example, or to congeal our problems by rebuilding at higher densities. We must encourage the central areas to open out, to become the locus for particular uses and institutions, the residence of people with special tastes, or attractive vacation areas in which open space and intense urban activity are closely mingled. Some concentrations of high density housing will persist, particularly at the core, but we can expect to see apartment living widely distributed throughout the metropolitan region.

Areas of particular historic interest or environmental character should of course be conserved, but they occupy a small fraction of the land. The central ghettos might be transformed, not only into centers of political power and social reconstruction, but also into settings of prestige, the symbolic centers of cultures newly visible in our society. As a prerequisite for unlocking this process of change, its costs must be openly accounted for and justly allocated. The burden now falls on deprived and powerless people.

One promising avenue for dealing with the existing city is the search for underused space and time, and its readaptation for a desired activity. We can explore the use of streets as play areas, or the possibilities for using roof tops, empty stores, abandoned buildings, waste lots, odd bits of land, or the large areas presently sterilized by such mono-cultures as parking lots, expressways, railroad yards, and airports. We may find room for new modes of transit, additional housing, schools, or special recreation.

Another strategy is to find ingenious ways of adapting or reconditioning the existing environment with a minimum of disturbance to existing users. Rehabilitation techniques have not yet proved very promising, except where the degree of improvement desired is small, or where it has been done piecemeal by the user-owner, employing his own labor and capital, and making a fit to his own particular desires. New techniques which aided this latter process—packaged amenities which are easy to insert; tools, power, and materials for use by the individual; training and guidance in rebuilding—would all be useful. Technical services and information must be made available directly to the user of environment, particularly to those who presently have no voice in political and developmental decisions.

Perhaps we can organize a rebuilding and maintenance industry, and begin to conserve our still-useful environmental stock in a more systematic and efficient way. Renewal-and-rehabilitation has traditionally focused its attention on the oldest parts of the central city. The problem for the future is the conservation and improvement of what are now the new suburbs. Surely there are ways in which sophisticated technology could be employed in such essential tasks as the cleaning or refacing of outdoor surfaces, the modification of noise and climate, routine housekeeping, the prevention of fire, the removal of waste, the provision of local communal services or the insertion of small gardens or micro-recreation facilities. It is just this kind of environmental renewal that can provide jobs for many of the lowest skilled or racially excluded workers. Maintenance technology should be designed to make use of such men, and then to train them in more complex skills.

We will always be concerned with the problem of obsolescence. Technology and styles of life will shift in the near future at least as rapidly as they have done in the near past. One reasonable response is to make sure that any new environment is highly adaptable, able to accommodate new functions at low economic or social cost. We know very little about how to do this. We can only make vague guesses: building at low density, providing growth room or surplus capacity; providing a high capability for circulation and communication; separating functions and structures that are likely to change from those likely to be permanent; using temporary or movable structures (only if we are later able to control their disposal, however); establishing a neutral grid to regulate locations and connections; setting up a monitoring system which will call for adaptation at the first signals of change. We have much to do to develop and test these ideas. The urgency and permanence of the problem would make full-scale research worthwhile. For example, we would like to be able to specify levels of adaptability as performance standards for new construction.

Mobility and change add novelty and adventure to living, but exact an emotional price. The sense of continuity with the past, the feeling of "home," of belonging and commitment, has some relation to geographical fixity. Change must be made psychologically tolerable. One may be trained to live in a changing place and with changing social relationships. One may shift his point of reference from a small spatial community to a larger unit (a metropolis, a nation), or to a stable but spatially shifting social unit (the traditional solution of the nomad), or to a stable set of connections with persons who are dispersed and shifting in space, or even to a symbolic home occasionally visited (a function that summer cottages may be taking on for some of our mobile middle class).

In any case, environmental form must take account of these stresses: providing clear orientation for the newcomer, with a proportion of familiar stereotypes; clarifying the image at larger and larger scales, so that the individual may feel that he is only moving about within his permanent "home"; providing symbolic landmarks of continuity with the past; making change legible in itself. Behavior changes rapidly; physical form may be used symbolically to stabilize it and give it continuity, as well as to support it functionally. By expressing what shifts are going on, how they arose out of the recent past and are likely to continue into the near future, the environment can help us to live with change, and even to enjoy it.

It will also be necessary to establish and protect areas of little change, of archaic ways of life, for those who do not choose to follow the common pattern. Tenure of a second home in a stable setting may make change elsewhere more acceptable. In a shifting world, one must know how to forget and how to remember, how to conserve and how to dispose of environment. The problems of change and mobility will be fundamental ones for the future city. They tempt us with new possibilities as well.

Design for Mobility

Mobility, access and communication are indeed the essential qualities of an urbanized region—its reason for being. Cities can be most simply described as being dense networks of communication, and the movement of persons is the critical process. Thus the system of movement is strategic for the quality of the future environment. We are spending large sums on highway systems, and are encountering increasing resistance from those who are dissatisfied with highway performance. Despite troubles of parking and congestion—he can go from door to door at will, over very large territories and in a short time—the car owner is far more mobile than he ever has been. If the car kills, if it pollutes the air and occupies big space, it also confers a new personal freedom. So we become more and more dependent on a single mode of transport, although many cannot use the car because they are too young, too old, too disabled, or too poor to own one.

One of the most efficient ways of enhancing the adaptability of an environment (and to improve the chances and choices of its citizens) is to increase the accessibility within it, so that activities can easily shift from one location to another, or as easily shift their linkages, for example, so that workers can move from job to job without moving their home, or vice versa. Good accessibility is a psychological as well as a physical fact. Fast transport is not enough; people must also feel free to enter, and the location of activities and the system of access must be perceptually legible. To increase the level of accessibility will be to continue an historic trend which is freeing more and more persons from the tight bonds of place, and increasing their scope for action. The future difficulty will not be how to prevent traffic jams (which should ameliorate as urbanization disperses and flow patterns become omni-directional), but how to prevent relative disadvantages from increasing: children locked into suburbs, low-paid workers tied to scarce jobs, old people shut in golden age corrals. Public policy should increase the access for all groups to a wider and wider area. We should have a free transit system, operating over extensive regions. The evolving new communications services should be brought to everyone, via accessible local terminals.

Rather than dream about a return to "efficient" mass transit, we should build a diversified system of small-unit, flexible transport which caters to all groups: safe vehicles in which children can roam or that are suitable for the infirm, programmed mini-buses that will work in low density areas, special carriers for high density centers, recreational vehicles, or those that challenge the user by requiring skilled control. The automobile need not be abolished, but modified and regulated to prevent pollution, increase safety, or decrease noise, congestion, and the preemption of valuable space. The routes themselves can be diversified: direct lines for people in a hurry, slow leisurely tours for pleasure, challenging routes to test your skill, safe easy ways for children or the elderly: motor ways, bus tracks, bicycle paths, horse trails, moving belts, waterways, footpaths. Innovation in vehicle and channel design should be a public function.

We can expect the mobility of population to increase both in frequency and in range. People will be on the move for better jobs, but also for better climate and environment. Distant vacations, pilgrimages, temporary and seasonal communities will be commonplace. Environmental quality will become more important for the economic survival of a place, and places will be liable to receive sudden shifts in load. The Easter mobs on the beaches of Ft. Lauderdale, or the influx to the Sunset Strip in Los Angeles, are signs of the future. Adaptability and the rapid organization of environment will be crucial. We must be able to shift services, personnel, and equipment, even to employ mobile settlements. These pose new problems of design, which should now be under study. As a simple example, we are presently unable to deal with the design of the trailer park, even though it is by now a common residential environment.

Travelling is traditionally considered an unfortunate necessity, a "waste of time" to be minimized. Yet recreational travel is widespread, and ordinary routes could easily be designed to make travelling a delight, and not just a necessity. The sequence of open spaces, motions, visible activities, lights, planting, textures, views, could all be managed to the pleasure of the moving observer. Views can pick out the principal elements of a city region, its most interesting activities, its history, geology, and fauna. Highways might move through giant sculptures.

Our existing arterials, unpleasant and illegible as they are, are with us for another generation or more. They can be improved with the same techniques. At little additional cost, the metropolis may be endowed with a network of scenic corridors. Air travel is a more resistant problem, since present technology is directed toward anesthetizing the experience. Even here, there may be ways to exploit the act of flight.

Our roads have a single purpose, and are driven heedlessly through the landscape. We could use rights-of-way for many other purposes than circulation, for housing, for example, or for recreation or commerce. Roads can be designed to enhance their flanking areas to make space for local facilities. They could be an integral part of the landscape, rather than a scar. Roads are the observation platforms of a city, the prime means by which people organize large regions, making them psychologically as well as physically accessible. The design and development of the entire movement system, including its vehicles, its associated facilities, and its multipurpose rights-of-way, is one of the great environmental opportunities: it touches on vital interests; its construction is a customary public function; it is an object of great interest for many citizens; it reflects and makes possible a new way of life; it offers unexpected possibilities of form.

An Open Environment

It is crucial for our purpose that the future environment be an "open" one—which the individual can easily penetrate, and in which he can act by his own choice. Development of the individual has been an historic role of the city, but it has never been articulated as a conscious goal of environmental policy. The growth of leisure, the economic demands for high skill, the danger of leaving a section of our population behind in helpless ignorance combine to make this humane ideal an urgent social requirement. An education is gained in many ways, not least via the city itself.

The provision of a new kind of open space would be one strategic and yet tolerable way of building an educative city. Here also there is a tradition of government action, although I am not speaking just of the spaces colored green on official maps, but of the areas which are open to the freely chosen and spontaneous activity of city people. I include vacant lots, sandbanks, and open dumps, as well as parks, woods, and beaches. I do not mean tennis courts or baseball diamonds, which, however desirable, are designed for standardized activities, but the uncommitted complement to the system of committed uses which make up an urban region—the ambiguous places of ill-defined ownership and function. There are many possible kinds: pits, mazes, raceways, heaths, woods, thickets, canyons, beaches, allotments and do-it-yourself cabins, rooftops, hobby yards, caves, marshes, canals, dirt piles, junk yards, aerial runways, undersea gardens, ruined buildings. The zones between contrasting regions are of particular value, because of their ambiguity, flux, and range of choice: shore lines, quiet gardens in city centers, the edge of woods, the meeting of salt and fresh waters. This kind of open space may even be within doors: in barn-like buildings where people can organize various activities at temporary stands.

Space of this kind extends the individual's range of choice, and allows him to pursue his purposes directly, without elaborate prior planning or community constraint. Since social investment is low, he has a chance to demonstrate mastery and to participate actively in a way usually denied him in the protected and expensive, committed environment. Here he can act at his own pace and in his own style. Open space is a place of stimulus release, withdrawal and privacy, in contrast to the intense and meaning-loaded communications which confront him elsewhere. Modern information techniques threaten to submerge our privacy and individual autonomy. In a preferred environment, one can deny communications, as well as seek them—one can protest, even rebel. The guerillas of the future will need a base of operation.

This kind of open space is a place for the try-out of new roles without too serious a risk. It permits the user to learn in a dialogue of action and response. It corresponds to our desire for an autonomous, creative environment. I am not speaking simply of places for "fun," but of places where people may develop commitments and run risks of their own choosing, where they may invent their work and their play, learn to care about things and people, and to exert the effort that care demands.

Open space is also a means whereby other species may be preserved and observed in their appropriate habitat. It is crucial for maintaining water resources, and for moderating climate. Widespread areas of low economic commitment, particularly if they are planned to follow distinct natural divisions, will ensure a diverse set of ecological communities. Open space is of obvious service in preserving future flexibility, and it should be public policy to maintain such a land reserve.

For all these reasons, the acquisition and development of a set of uncommitted spaces throughout the urbanized region is a strategic action. As our metropolitan regions expand, we should reserve an extensive web of them. In the older areas, now lean of public ground, there are a variety of lands that can be turned to this use. Our cities might take on a porous texture, embracing open and rural uses, so that the boundary of city and country is erased, and the urban region becomes a complete human environment. Many of these spaces might be in public hands, but much of it could be private, given suitable easements, agreements, or public incentives. They need not be of great size, but should be ubiquitous, highly accessible. Many of them could be based on land presently discarded and unused. Some of them might be only in temporary open-space use, between clearance and recommitment, being part of a continuously maintained land reserve inventory. While control of such spaces could be dispersed, there should be central agencies concerned with maintaining the "openness" of the region as a whole, constantly monitoring the quality, quantity, and use of the open lands.

The open space system is a clear subject for action. But in the city we wish to make possible, we can go further. We can think of the entire environment as a means to education, a place where learning and working are indistinguishable and absorbing activities. Such an environment would be highly diverse, offering rich sources of information and experience in the midst of everyday life: working processes and styles of life exposed, human and natural history explained, unusual trips and experimental actions facilitated. It would invite exploration but allow periodic withdrawal. The awareness of things and people, direct perception and communication, would be encouraged. Small groups should be able to build and care for their own surroundings. This would be a manipulable world, inviting action and responding thereto; a domain where people could see the results of what they do; a social world with open niches; an array of teaching machines, through which people might gain and structure skill and information at their own pace and for their own purposes.

Surely this redefinition of working and learning will not be brought about by changes in city form, but form can reflect and support it. These policies may sound innocuous but are in fact dangerous. Change and growth are disturbing; they upset vested interests and are painful (as well as exhilarating) to undergo. If we engage in them, we must be prepared for trouble.

Experimental Communities

Just as we look for an environment conducive to growth and learning by its inhabitants, so we also want one that will itself "learn," that will respond to the varying needs of its users and provide a stream of new possibilities for trial and evaluation. Think of a room which responds to the man who enters it: his preference for temperature, his need for light according to the task, his mood for color. We already have some of these devices: the light switch, the thermostat. At the city scale, the task is technically far more difficult, and complicated by the variety of simultaneous users.

We can conceive of large environments which respond to outside changes to maintain some average preference, as the facets of a geodesic dome become opaque or translucent as the sun moves across them, or as street lamps turn on when darkness falls. It would also be possible to build public spaces that would respond to the cumulative effects of users: opening up, or decreasing the acoustical reflectance, or lowering the temperature, as crowds change in size. Alternatively, we might amplify an effect, as by re-projecting views of a crowd to itself, or re-broadcasting its noise, or by allowing its actions to program changes in light and sound. Where the outdoor environment can be controlled on a fine scale, and users are relatively sparse, there are other openings: outdoor radiant heat or light which can be turned on or off at will (or even "track" a traveller), retractable shelters which open out at need. Over a longer time interval, buildings might grow, contract, or otherwise adapt to the activities they contain. People should be able to take on environmental control as they wish, up to the level of intrusion on their neighbor. Ingenious design and technology could open some new possibilities for us.

The symbolic environment might be similarly organized; signs could expose only the most general information to the casual viewer, and respond with details when queried (a directory, a map with locations that light up on call, a programmed teaching device, are examples). The creative use of ambient factors: artificial light, sound, modified climate, even smell, is a large and unexploited realm in city design. For example, much of the city experience is a night-time experience, but no city has yet attempted to design the nightscape. City people are vocal about their climate, but no efforts are made to provide a varied outdoor climate, not even an indoor one which is more than a single monotonous standard. A rich and varied responsiveness is what we mean when we plead for a more "human" environment.

If environment should respond to the user, it should also suggest to him new modes of action and perception. New shared experiences may bring men together over the gulf of traditional divisions. We should be trying out settings which offer the possibility of different styles of life:

residential areas based on new ideas of family organization; new systems of space organization; new ways of sensing the surroundings; schools completely dispersed throughout other activities of the community; mobile temporary and shifting environments; very high density areas using new techniques for communication and privacy; moderate density zones in which families have the independent control and access now associated with the single family house; or "isolated" rural settings in the midst of the urban region. Once built, they must be evaluated for their effects, indeed the means of evaluation must be built into their design. They will improve our skill in constructing environment, while expanding the choices that people have. They could be the "museums of the future."

To take one example, new technology will soon allow us to occupy marginal areas on which increasing wealth and population will as soon place mounting pressure. We should prepare for the rational exploitation of these hitherto "waste" areas. This means exploratory design and pilot experiments for settlements in the desert, on (even under) the water, in extensive swamps, high mountains, arctic regions, underground. Use of these areas may be forced upon us, here or elsewhere in the world, but they may also turn out to be highly desirable habitats, once the adverse conditions are removed. We shrink at the thought of such places—they would be strange, artificial. But the problem is not one of a natural versus a synthetic world; all human environments are natural, and most of them are synthetic. The problem is how to make these new worlds humane, by taking account of our psychological limits and abilities; and how to give them a rich and stable ecology. Occupation of sea or mountain may increase the diversity and delight of our landscape. Certainly we should like to prevent their casual spoliation. Important new technical systems should never be employed before they have been tested for their human and environmental side effects.

Thus there are cogent reasons why we should begin now to make environmental experiments on a substantial scale. They will be expensive. They will be seen as disturbing to the existing order (indeed they are), even immoral. They may have to be geographically isolated, or located in areas where tolerance is high, or restricted to spatial experiments without obvious social connotations. They will attract peculiar people, making generalizations to the rest of the populace more difficult. Experimentation will have to be undertaken with care. The risk is high, and the period of fruition uncertain. Yet this is a most effective way of keeping our future options open. The combination of risk, requirements, and importance means that this work must be institutionalized by government, foundations, or universities. Experimental communities might become the laboratories of our society, a new sort of university, where people are not experimented upon, but join in conducting experiments in which they learn about themselves and their own possibilities.

New Cities

It may be apparent from this that, while I see metropolitan growth as a magnificent future opportunity for the improvement of our environment, I do not advocate a special form nor a single strategy. On the contrary, I propose a plurality of actions, and many levels of control. I do not emphasize restriction of size, nor starting with what seems to be a "clean slate." The critical problem is to manage the metropolis as a vast ongoing system, monitoring the growth and quality of the environment as a whole, and concentrating public efforts at the key points of development. There are a number of strategic opportunities, of which the most attractive seem to be planned development and resettlement at the fringe; creating new open space and transportation systems; organizing a new set of intensive centers; building a sophisticated disposal and maintenance technology; developing the techniques and institutions which will facilitate environmental change and also justly allocate its costs; and conducting environmental experiments. These opportunities are easily lost, but the act of changing the environment can be a potent weapon for mobilizing hope and social action.

The deliberately planted, independent new city has been much discussed as a remedy for urban ills. In the United States, however, "new towns" are simply planned chunks of the existing metropolitan regions, and are functionally integrated with those regions. They illustrate how new growth can be better organized physically, but they do not deal with our more refractory social problems. It seems unlikely that new cities, in their original sense, will be an important device for development in this country, unless we are prepared to program them to grow at the rate of, say, one million people in a decade—unless, that is, we are ready to build new metropolitan regions. Such a task would require a national effort, based on a policy to change the national distribution of the population. We would then be seeking to exploit some potential, human or physical, that could only be unlocked by this means. At present we are unable to say whether such a massive effort is indicated, whether we can concentrate the resources for development at that scale, and whether we know how to do it well. The need for considered national policy of that kind is evident.

New cities are likely to be more important elsewhere in the world, where urbanization is just gaining momentum, and where there are glaring regional inequalities. Planting a new city can be a critical weapon in revolutionizing a backward economy. Were there to be a serious world-wide attack on poverty (and how can we face the possibility that there might not be?), then international consortia for new cities would be a potent device. One or more of the developed nations might join with a host country, furnishing technical aid and part of the capital but leaving political control in local hands.

New cities could be built for political reasons, as they have been in the past. Cities cut by national boundaries are thought of as disturbing anomalies. And yet, if we had more of them, joint action on urban problems might tend to keep international communications open. Urban regions could deliberately be planted across boundaries, either where current relations were reasonably amicable, or even as internationalized buffer zones between nations in conflict. New cities have been suggested as an alternative to American destruction in Vietnam, to turn war expenditures to productive ends, to offer a haven for refugees, and to give us a less embarrassing means of exit. New urban regions might be a constructive way of settling Arab refugees in the Middle East.

This paper has focused on the problems of the city in this country. I do not imply that we can ignore the convulsive changes occurring elsewhere in the world. Morally, we cannot turn our back on the poverty of the colonial world, nor refuse to support the awakening of its people. Realistically, if we do, we will spend our attention and our resources on destruction and "defense." Urban policy is tied to foreign policy. Our predicted affluence and decline in the need for human labor is either chimerical or fragile, in the face of the desperation inside and outside our borders. Whether due to commitments for international aid, or cost for war, we can expect that our resources for internal urban development will continue to fall short of need. Our aim must be to use those limited resources to encourage human growth, and not to find ways to "use up" goods or leisure time. Urbanization in the developing countries poses problems at a different material level, and yet the basic purposes and dangers seem surprisingly similar. Indeed, in the midst of social revolution, those purposes may there be easier to attain.

In the United States, however, the core problem is the quality of the metropolis, as a device for supporting the activities of a complex population, and for promoting the growth and autonomy of the individual and the small group. This requires an open, adaptable, diverse, autonomous, responsive environment. The necessary actions range from national policies, through the guidance of metropolitan development and the development of certain kinds of large environmental systems, to experimentation and the creation of new prototypes at the site planning scale.

Opportunities and Actions

I have outlined some opportunities for future city form. Do we have the leverage for them? The strategic impression is imposed at the point of development. We need to build the agencies which can carry out development at the scale now required, while avoiding the centralized control over detail that such large scale action seems to imply. To concentrate the necessary skill and capital, these agencies will probably have to be mixed public and private authorities, with special powers of acquisition and development, but operating under local and national regulation. They need not be tied to one locality, but should be free to apply themselves throughout the nation, and perhaps elsewhere in the world.

I have indicated the crucial points of intervention: the growing edge, the open space system, the circulation system, the intense centers, the insertion of new activities at under-used places in the existing fabric, the building of experimental communities and of new cities in the underdeveloped world. Development agencies would probably specialize in particular kinds of problems, and there should be a sufficient number of such agencies to encourage competition.

They would be called in by localities—cities, small neighborhoods within cities, or metropolitan regions—or perhaps by other nations, to carry out specific development tasks. Some authorities might be quite large and comprehensive in their abilities, others small and specialized. All of them, by virtue of their public component, and in return for such powers as condemnation, would have mixed criteria of performance, including the well-being and development of the user as well as the return on capital. They would, moreover, be constrained to work within the policy guidelines of the locality engaging them. In any event, they must be motivated or constrained to build with adaptability, diversity, and openness.

Regulatory and planning agencies, tied to units of government, will still be essential, recommending broad policies, monitoring the environmental system and disseminating information about it, proposing controls and using economic devices such as user charges and user subsidies, or the allocation of block grants to local units. Thus a city, following its general policy, might call in a development agency to acquire and build a new center, or a part of the open space system, which would afterward be turned over to the control, partly of public agencies, partly of special institutions, partly of private owners. The center, or the open space, would then operate within the general controls and incentives of the governmental unit.

Planning agencies, attached to a public base of power at that scale, are particularly needed at the metropolitan level, the functional unit where a new environment is actually being built, and where the opportunities therefore lie. Their functions will probably include recommendations for the application of user charges and the allocation of federal grants to minimize inequalities and bring out-of-pocket costs closer to social costs; as well as recommendations for key development actions in the region. Similar agencies will be wanted at the other end of the scale—the local intra-city neighborhood. These local areas, working within the constraints imposed by the larger units, should also be able to call for, and control, development and change within their own territory. Finally, since policies for urbanization at the national scale and for international development assistance are prerequisites for action on new cities and for the intelligent use of federal grants as a lever for environmental improvement, the environmental planning functions are also required at the national level.

We need a means for accomplishing environmental experimentation. Work must be done on new techniques for adaptability, as well as on the innovative design of centers, of open spaces, of circulation systems, and of local site planning. Exploratory design should be underway on possible new habitats, and experimental communities must be designed, built, and tested. Laboratories should be engaged in fundamental research on the interaction of user and environment, developing new criteria, and acting as "look outs" to discern new opportunities and possible futures.

Some of these activities may be carried out by the development authorities in their own area of specialization, since they would now be large and flexible enough to make in-house research reasonable. But much of the exploratory and basic work is too risky to fit into their calculations. Environmental design laboratories and exploratory planning units must therefore be established by universities, foundations, and governments, with sufficient funds and abilities to test their explorations in actual use.

Environmental research and development will not come cheap. The yearly bill for the new urban development and redevelopment that we should be doing will rise to the order of $250 billion per year in the next generation. If 1 percent of this were to be devoted to research and development, then $2.5 billion per year would be devoted to basic and developmental research on the city environment.

There are severe administrative problems to be met, particularly in regard to metropolitan planning and government, but also in developing national urbanization policy, and in making possible semi-autonomous development at the neighborhood level. We will suffer from shortages of skilled manpower when we seek to staff these agencies. However difficult, this is a secondary problem, which will be met once a decision is made to embark.

When massive new powers or funds are applied to a problem, there is always a danger that they will be diverted to ends far removed from their original ones. Urban renewal is a well known example. Many of the above proposals could be deflected in ways not now foreseen. Their exploration must therefore include a study of how they could be turned to other purposes. The proposed development agencies, for example, might become centers of irresponsible power, unless they were carefully regulated at the national and local levels, and numerous enough to be affected by competition.

A fundamental difficulty will be the resistance to change that will be encountered: the privileged interests, the fears of racial integration or of other social change, the just apprehensions of the displaced. Since our possible city is based on change, there must be provisions for identifying the social and economic costs of change and for fairly allocating them by charges, subsidies, or replacements. Since we will also encounter less rational fears, we will be constrained to begin at points where there is already some consensus: circulation, open space, new suburban development, insertion of new activity into unused interstices in the existing fabric, attacks on pollution, climate, and noise, experiments with new possibilities for the physical fabric of the city.

I have not tried to program the necessary actions, at various scales, for periodic times throughout the next fifty years. I believe that a long-range program of that kind is both impossible to construct (given our present state of knowledge about environment), and useless if constructed (given our inability to control the programmed actions at the scale and over the time suggested). I think it more useful to scan the future for likely dangers and constraints, and particularly for appealing possibilities, and then to suggest present actions calculated to meet those problems and to keep open those opportunities. The opportunities I have outlined above. The critical present actions are to establish the developmental and experimental agencies which will begin to unfold those opportunities; to imbue them with positive attitudes toward growth and diversity; to give them the backing of finance, power and skilled men that they need for the task; and to begin to prepare environmental policy at the metropolitan, the national, and the neighborhood levels.

If I seem to prophesy a bright new technological future, I am misread. My purpose is to encourage human beings to grow into their diverse potentialities, and to find a possible city to do it in. Technology and environment might be exploited to that end. They will subvert it, if left to develop in their present course.

Comments on
Lynch

VICTOR GRUEN
Victor Gruen Associates

Let me establish first of all a frame of reference for my critical remarks. I regard this paper as one which is supposed to make a positive contribution to the deliberations of a conference of planners, in the widest sense of the word, a conference which deals with the problems of our urban areas and their future solution. If the theme of the conference were purely esoteric, the paper's tendency to be original for originality's sake, capricious in order to keep the reader or listener awake, frivolous in order to create psychological shock effects, would be forgivable—maybe even laudable. But the theme, "The Future of Our Urban Areas," is one which calls for an earnest, sincere, and constructive attitude based on deepest concern about matters of distressing urgency.

The urban crisis, which expresses itself in ever more serious manifestations —from race riots to ghettoism, from pollution of air, water, and land to the deterioration of the public environment—which includes the inability to provide a decent individual environment for the economically or racially underprivileged—must be the point from which all thoughts on the future have to begin. Therefore, the measuring sticks which are used in forming my opinion about this paper are: Does it assist, either through well founded criticism or through positive and imaginative proposals, the efforts of shaping a better future environment to a degree commensurate with the eminence of the author? Or does it not?

In reading and rereading the paper, I have found that as a whole it is unassailable. It is not possible to "tear it apart" because the author has taken care of this task himself. In all those cases where suggestions for actions are made, the fabric of thought is immediately interrupted by loopholes of sufficient size to make the escape from any stand speedily possible.

There is, of course, always the possibility that the author had something important to say but that the average reader (and this critic flatters himself as belonging to this category) just cannot get the message. If this were the case it would be extremely regrettable—but also inexcusable. If someone has something significant to contribute in matters of great importance, then he is saddled with the responsibility of communicating his ideas in a manner understandable to others.

In the framework of a short critique, it is not possible to discuss every one of the issues which could be raised. Instead of this, I will lift out at random some statements which appear to me either: capricious, inconsistent or contradictory, loopholes for statements advanced, or critical of efforts of others without providing a basis for such criticism.

Under the category of capricious could be included the statement, "It may be unrealistic (even undesirable) to hope for a fine-grained mix of social groups." I believe we *must* hope for a fine-grained mix, especially as it would be inconsistent not to hope for it but still to try, as the author says we must, to "destroy the one-color school district and the single-class town."

Later Lynch says, "If the car kills, if it pollutes the air and occupies big space, it also confers a new personal freedom." This certainly is a statement of existing conditions but inasmuch as nothing is recommended to prevent the car from killing, polluting the air and occupying big space, it doesn't add anything to our arsenal of possible countermeasures.

The author proposes a number of measures which could be used instead of an "efficient mass transit system." Some of them, for example, the proposal to build "challenging routes to test your skill," seem to be unnecessary. Anybody who has driven one of our urban freeways has ample opportunities to test his skills today. The paper proposes roads which would be "scenic corridors" and, in addition, suggests "Highways might move through giant sculptures." There seems to be a concept of converting the roadscape into a kind of continuous Disneyland for the amusement of drivers. I wonder why we don't worry about scenic corridors for subway users.

"We could use rights-of-way for many other purposes than circulation; for example, for housing, for recreation, or commerce." After years of hard work we are just beginning to separate the utilitarian activity of travel from human activities. Does the author really propose to turn the wheels back? Does he really think the highway would be an ideal playground for children?

In the section, "An Open Environment," the author recommends the use of "ambiguous places of ill-defined ownership and function" for recreational purposes, such as "marshes, canals, dirt piles, junk yards, aerial runways, undersea gardens, ruined buildings." Well, a look into the existing urban landscape will show that we are saddled with millions of such ambiguous places providing a serious threat to the safety and health of the underprivileged. The paper argues for the use of such places by saying, "The guerillas of the future will need a base of operation." One paragraph later he says they will "learn to care about things and people." If they really care about people, they will make pretty poor guerillas.

In his description of locations for experimental communities, the author says about his own ideas, "We shrink at the thought of such places—they would be strange, artificial." But then he says, "There are cogent reasons why we should begin now to make environmental experiments on a substantial scale." He proposes this in spite of the statements which follow the previously quoted sentence. In his words, "They will be expensive. They will be seen as disturbing to the existing order (indeed they are), even immoral. . . . They will attract peculiar people. . . . The risk is high, and the period of fruition uncertain." As localities for the experimental communities the paper recommends "settlements in the desert, on (even under) the water, in extensive swamps, high mountains, arctic regions, underground." Yet the author acknowledges in another part of the paper that only about 7.5 percent of the total land of the United States is urbanized and there would be plenty of perfectly habitable, agreeable, and not "immoral" areas available for settlement. (The 7.5 percent figure, incidentally, appears very high. According to data based on the 1960 census, the total area covered by cities and their fringe areas, but excluding towns of less than 50,000 inhabitants outside such fringe areas, covered less than 1 percent of the total land area of the United States.)

This leads us to the second category on which I base my critique: *inconsistency and contradiction.* After proposing that we should prepare ourselves for the exploitation of the "hitherto 'waste' areas," the paper deals with the idea of planning new towns or new cities. Lynch says, "It seems unlikely that new cities, in their original sense, will be an important device for development in this country, unless we are prepared to program them to grow at the rate of, say, one million people in a decade—unless, that is, we are ready to build new metropolitan regions. Such a task would require a national effort." This critic agrees completely that a national effort would be required, but he also believes that a national effort is necessary and essential to solve any of our urban problems. The author questions seriously whether we in the United States can concentrate the resources for development at that scale. One paragraph later, however, he recommends such development for other areas, especially in countries with a backward economy. The question arises in the critic's mind whether it is not inconsistent to claim that what the richest country in the world may not be able to achieve should be recommended to the poorest countries.

The paper says, "Our cities might take on a porous texture, embracing open and rural uses, so that the boundary of city and country is erased." This erasing of the boundaries between citified or man-made areas, between landscaped or man-influenced areas and nature (areas free of human interference) exists today, and we have learned by bitter experience that by erasing the boundaries we have created vast stretches of unattractive development which is neither city nor suburb, nor landscape nor nature.

Lynch states, "We should have a free transit system, operating over extensive regions." Immediately thereafter, however, he goes on, "Rather than dream about a return to 'efficient' mass transit, we should build a diversified system of small-unit, flexible transport." Earlier he has noted, "We are spending large sums on highway systems and are encountering increasing resistance from those who are dissatisfied with highway performance." I am troubled by the sentence which immediately follows the one which criticizes the highway: "Despite troubles of parking and congestion—he can go from door to door at will . . .—the car owner is far more mobile than he ever has been." Well, anybody who has tried to go from the door of his house in the suburbs to the door of the department store in which he wants to shop has found out a long time ago that he cannot do so. (In downtown Boston, for example, the average walk from a parking place to the place of final destination is around 1,000 feet.)

"One reasonable response," Lynch says, "is to make sure that any new environment is highly adaptable, able to accommodate new functions at low economic or social cost." This sentence is followed by a loophole sentence: "We know very little about how to do this. We can only make vague guesses." This statement is followed by the suggestions: "Building at low density, providing growth room or surplus capacity; . . . using temporary or movable structures," followed by the loophole comment, "(only if we are later able to control their disposal, however)." Now it is obviously inconsistent to ask for "low economic or social cost" and at the same time to demand "Building at low density, providing growth room or surplus capacity; providing a high capability for circulation and communication." You can't have your cake and eat it too.

Lynch criticizes *efforts undertaken by others*, as when he says, "Strenuous efforts are being made to 'save downtown,'" and "The danger lies in the attempt to cling to the present—to save the downtown, for example, or to congeal our problems by rebuilding at higher densities." Interspersed between these two statements is the loophole argument, "Indeed there is something lost, if we should no longer have places of diverse services and opportune encounters. The outward dispersion of high intensity activities to widely scattered sites deprives us of social and visual meeting points, as well as of the opportunity to live close to the action or to enjoy a rich array of support-ing facilities." In spite of this statement the paper proposes, "Rather than straining to entice the middle class to return to the central city they have left behind, we should make it possible for others to move out to the suburbs that they would like to reach."

If we don't entice the middle classes to return and if we encourage all the others to move out, who is going to remain in the city? And who is then going to use the "underused space" about which the paper talks, such as "rooftops, empty stores, abandoned buildings, waste lots, odd bits of land . . . parking lots, expressways, railroad yards, and airports"?

I agree, that "Building or rebuilding the important focal points is another crucial development task which might be undertaken by public authority." But then why, of all things, except the existing central city, which is, after all, the most important focal point?

The author writes, "but to maintain a single center as the dominant focus of employment and services is to swim against the flood." First, I believe that no thoughtful planner proposes that in a vast metropolitan area there should be maintained a single center, though it may very well be argued that one of the centers might be dominant from many points of view. But what I really take issue with is the statement that we should not swim against the flood. Reversing or modifying trends which are operative is in many ways the quintessence of planning. If we want to swim with the flood, we might just as well forget about any planning activity and watch the spectacle of urban anarchy as amused observers.

The "possible city" as described in Kevin Lynch's paper looks, after one eliminates some of the frills, amazingly similar to the existing city. And of the existing U.S. city we know enough to realize that it is an "impossible city."

Finally, I want to cite a statement with which I fully agree, namely, the last sentence of the paper, "If I seem to prophesy a bright new technological future, I am misread. . . . Technology and environment might be exploited to that end. They will subvert it, if left to develop in their present course."

JACOB BAKEMA
Van den Broek en Bakema, Architects

After reading Kevin Lynch's paper and rereading my own, which follows after these comments, I got the feeling that we are alike; we are making wonderful menus for a good restaurant, leaving the user in a situation of not knowing how to choose. Knowing that one cannot eat all he likes on the menu, I have made the following choices.

The first thing we have to do is to change the conditions of the actual slum areas. These areas can be the test-grounds of research for art-of-living conditions on an urbanistic-architectural scale. Planning should be concentrated at test-ground operations and their connections. Until now, the element of variation in urbanization has been the house, the block, the building. I think we are leaving this period of putting together houses and buildings and approaching the period in which test-ground groups can be the element of variations and scale of operation.

We have to offer space-qualities instead of types of houses. Space-qualities have to be produced, advertised, and distributed, as is done for all other productions in our society, like food, clothes, television, refrigerators, cars. Space-qualities might be advertised by such words as: open, closed, under, over something, gray, dug-in, yellow, cantilevered, round, square, rough, glittering, clustered around subway stations, kind, brutal, lonely, together, black, white, stone, steel, plastic, red brick, concrete, diagonal, along streets, in the air, with air-wall curtains, up, down, in and over the ground, at the horizon, lasting fifty years, disposable.

Man likes to choose space-qualities fitting to his own wondering about what space is. Houses so far are protectors against nature, but this function becomes extended and overlapped by the additional function of being and space detector. The political administrative production of houses around Washington, The Hague, and Moscow more and more is resulting in a worldwide monotony fitting for nonexistent monotype man.

Man has the right to have an individual way to believe and wonder about existence and space. We assist in the planning of Asian and African countries and we fill them up with houses. Doing so, we become housing missionaries, denying the right of changing man to trust his own wondering and the manifestation of it by choice of a particular space-quality fitting to a particular person in a particular situation.

Each test-ground action could be done by a particular association of users and designers and producers and should result in realization of a particular space-quality inside and outside which can be tested by using them. Each test-ground action for change of slums could be financed by giving 1 percent of the annual national building budget for research into space-quality by a group of users, designers, and producers. In chemistry, food, clothes, cars, television, spacecraft production, more would be done by research. But research in space-qualities has to be done on the art of living by people who are qualified, despite our not knowing what are the qualifications for carrying on such research.

All societies on earth are making road networks, radio and television stations, knowing that we are in the period of the architecture of connections. But it is also the period in which the greatest client of all times who is using these roads—the anonymous man—has the right to express his individual wondering about life and space by personal choice of space-quality.

Urbanization by test-ground action for space-quality research on slum sites could make weak countries really believe in strong countries, because weak people living in slums would be being helped. If we do not give help, it will be sought by force. We should step out of the museums, magazines, art galleries, and go with our latest architectural movements to the field, where help is needed. The magazine *Kenchiku Bunka* devoted its January, 1967, issue to several groups that were experimenting with space-urbanization systems. Each of them could realize space-quality research on its own test-ground site. How many principles and systems never are published and remain unused, and how many could come to exist if urbanization became an inviting condition for man to show, by his choice of built space-quality, his individual wondering about universal space?

Evolution of the structure of towns is based on the evolution of the structure of society. Evolution of the structure of society is the growing awareness of man about what existence truly is. Part of existence is universal space. During the past sixty years the anonymous man achieved basic rights in society. In the Netherlands the first housing act, giving conditions for mainly state-subsidized housing, was made in 1902.

In the coming fifty years the anonymous man will have to develop enterprise responsibility. He should be responsible for the planning and building of his own environment. He will only get the kind of environment he wants if he knows what space-quality has to do with his life-quality, and how this can be produced.

In the U.S. the crucial part of the planning and housing problem is how to replace slums by a good environment. In slums live people who are poor, and being poor in the U.S. often means that you are black. The weakest part of the population still is a big part which has the least opportunity for improving its own environment. It is a universal law that the weakest part of existence, if ignored in evolution, can grow to revolutionary force. This happened in Russia and is now happening in China. The slogan of those days became "Proletarians of the world, unite" (and the proletarians were the weakest part of society, those populating the slums!). At the moment the colored part of the population is economically and politically the weakest part, and I think that the towns of America can only be improved if we concentrate on methods of change for these parts. Only this approach can avoid revolution.

The evolution of planning and architecture in Europe since 1910 has been part of the evolution of living conditions in workmen's quarters (the anonymous client). Examples include the Garden City movement of England, Zeilenbaublock of Germany, community centers (Peckham Health Centre in London of Dr. Williamson, opened in 1935 and closed for lack of funds in 1951), neighborhood planning, and new towns. Housing for the great number was what Berlage, Tony Garnier, Corbusier, Gropius, Oud, Rietveld, and Wright tried to do. In the end they had to give up and make houses for rich clients who were spiritually ahead of the institutional housing officials.

At the moment it seems to me that the evolution of U.S. architecture has become too much a free-lance action, not engaged in the real problems, instead making "great-statement" buildings at university campuses or along Park Avenue-like streets while ignoring the critical part of the problem, which is housing for those who really need help. How is it that almost no school of architecture is a center of study to help those who need it? The education of many students in planning or achitecture becomes increasingly abstracted from the real problem: that we have to produce in the next fifty years more cubic meters of built volume than were produced by the whole civilization in the past 1,950 years! We know we cannot do this by using usual methods.

And we have to do it for a type of man who can be characterized as the changing man, changing from living in African and Asian jungles and deserts into inhabitants of towns, from agricultural to industrial man, from man working a whole day in workshops and plants into man working in a push-button process some hours a day and for the rest having free time. It is the changing man (the biggest client and consumer of all times) who is trying to find self-identity, what I call "ownness," by using food, clothes, transport, communication, space, sound, light. If we go on trying to produce for him types of houses multiplied a million times, we will never produce enough and will end up with just the opposite of what we pretend to be. We will produce a monotype man.

More and more, built environment becomes a main function of man's evolution toward awareness of what life and space are. Finally, built-form for changing man becomes a religious value. We shape our dwellings, and afterwards our dwellings shape us (Churchill). Man's need for identification in space by a built environment corresponding to his own self-identity has more to do with the kind of space he uses than with the amount of space he owns. And I think this is true for all scales, as wide-ranging as from house to region. The relationship of space-quality and life-quality is an underdeveloped part of science and art activity.

In 1945, Adelbert Ames of the Hannover Institute reported, "The insights gained in the study of visual sensation can serve as indispensable leads to better understanding and more effective handling of the complexities of social relationship." So, if building for the weakest part of society is the crucial part of our planning problem, and if knowing that for the big program ahead our methods of type-repetition do not fit, and if use of built-space becomes one of the essential conditions for "ownness," what can be done? (1) We have to restrict our planning to not more than we can realize architecturally in the next fifty years. (2) We must not design by architecture what can be done by man himself. This can result in the design of minimal condition-making elements which can then be extended if necessary by the users into more, thus fitting realistic, individual changing circumstances.

The condition-making elements could include all of what is equally needed by everybody: energy and water and sewer systems, private and public means of transport and other communication systems, perhaps a vertical and horizontal traffic system in high density areas. A minimum project of house or office or workshop can be built by coordinated combinations of big enterprise working during pushbutton, short-time, daily working hours. The user can extend this program by creating a smaller enterprise in which he participates for free-time activity. The condition-making structures with minimum fill-in programs have to be started with public money. The extension into an individual environment should be financed by the economic capacity of the users (who also give free-time activity support).

This process has to start in the slum areas and high density regions; and experiments—as in other industry—must be carried out before big production is started. In the preparation of these experiments, graduate students and faculties of architectural schools should participate. From 1900 to 1960, in the whole world there were only three well-known experimental projects realized on the urban scale: The Weisenhofsiedlung at Stuttgart in 1927, the Wiener Werkbundsiedlung at Vienna in 1932, and the Hansa-Viertel project at Berlin in 1957. Before 1940, there were no predictions for a world population such as we are now familiar with, and there was no human right formulated by a United Nations Institute saying that everyone has the right to his own belief (religion), roof, and food. We teach our children at primary school how to clean their teeth and how to cross a street; why don't we teach them that use of space-quality is a value conditioning the quality of mental health?

Are we building a stereotype, or can we accept Robert Frost's statement:

> All men are born free and equal
> equal at least in their right to be different
> Some people like to homogenize all in society
> I am against these homogenizers in art and politics
> In every walk of life
> I like that the cream can rise. . . .

Planning is providing conditions for an architecture that is a three-dimensional expression of human behavior. It is the anonymous man, the youth group, the Negro, who tries to identify himself by built-form in space. Planners and architects have to provide condition-making structures in which the user can build with his own initiative his identifying forms using disposable elements of short-term investment.

Transportation: An Equal Opportunity for Access

This paper was commissioned to examine how transportation fits into our lives as well as into our communities. This is a matter of both applying technology and restraining it. What sort of access to what do we want? Perhaps nowhere is the clash between engineering and human environment more evident. We can make a supersonic jet, but should we? We can run expressways through cities, but is the human way of accomplishing this able to combat the economic way? Is there more human transport? For various distances, what transporter?

How are the great advances being made in the electronic modeling of traffic demands to be utilized to the fullest, consistent with aesthetic or physiological choices? With greatest access to opportunity for all?

In cities and between cities, what comfort, convenience, and safety in transport is consistent with human needs and with human environment, both inside the transporter and on the adjacent land? There are many side effects of transport that are difficult to measure but are nevertheless important to acknowledge. We need to consider these before we earnestly apply the new electronic technology in ways that simply project the past into the future but call themselves scientific. The question comes up eternally, not only "What can we do?"—What do we *want* to do?"—thinking in terms of the next fifty years.

What is the most desirable mode of commuting to work, to study, or to recreation? What form of transport is to be provided for the aged, or the teenager, or the rest of us? Is personalized mass transit possible? What is the role of mass and personal intercity transport by air and over the ground?

When is a scenic road not a scenic road? What amount of pleasure and what amount of direct control of driving can appropriately be given the driver under different circumstances? Does taking electronic control of his car remove most drivers from their one prime remaining area of decision-making?

Author: Max L. Feldman, General Electric Company, TEMPO Center for Advanced Studies

Chairman: Alan M. Voorhees, AIP, Alan M. Voorhees and Associates

Committee: Alan Temko, School of Environmental Design, University of California, Berkeley; Athelstan Spilhaus, Franklin Institute; George Hoffman, Institute for Traffic and Transportation Engineering, University of California, Los Angeles; Roger L. Creighton, President, AIP, Creighton Hamburg, Inc.; Rev. H. Conrad Hoyer, Associate Executive Director, Department for Council of Churches, National Council of Churches; A. Scheffer Lang, Deputy Undersecretary for Transportation Research and Undersecretary of Commerce for Transportation

VII

Max L. Feldman

General Electric Company
TEMPO Center for Advanced Studies

Transportation:
An Equal Opportunity for Access

Introduction

From the time man invented the wheel until the middle of the nineteenth century, the animal-drawn, wheeled vehicle was the best man could do for continuous, high-speed travel. In the short century since the invention of the steam engine, the average rate of speed that man could maintain continuously has increased at an exponential rate to about 25,000 mph. Now speeds approaching the physical limiting speed of 670 million mph appear to be within reach. Fortunately this ability to move at ever more rapid rates of speed has been confined largely to movement in the air and outer space. Even with vehicles restricted to 65 mph, few pedestrians succeed in crossing a Los Angeles freeway.

Soon after the invention of the steam engine and the construction of railroads, trains were moving at speeds up to 60 mph. Although the speed record for steam engine locomotives is about 120 mph, this speed could not be maintained for long because of limited boiler capacity. For the last two-thirds of a century, 90 mph which is the speed that electric interurbans used to attain, has remained as a sort of "sound" barrier for trains. Much effort is now being directed toward the elimination of this barrier. Japan has succeeded on one rail line where trains run at 135 mph, and the U.S. has been successful with an experimental 150 mph train. Wheeled vehicles can travel at significantly greater rates of speed than those normally associated with them. Automobiles have been driven up to 500 mph. However, vehicle stability becomes a primary concern and power consumption increases exponentially when wheeled vehicles are operated at speeds in excess of 150 mph.

Obviously we have made striking progress in transportation, but there are glaring gaps between what we could accomplish on the basis of available technology and what we actually are accomplishing on the basis of applied technology. Our long distance transportation systems have been improving at a spectacular rate, while our short distance (urban transportation) systems have been deteriorating. We appear to be developing a law of transportation to the effect that the further one has to travel the easier the transportation problem and the faster he can go.

The weakness in U.S. transportation resides primarily in our inability to look at U.S. transportation as a complex and interrelated system network comprised of a variety of transportation modes serving a wide range of transportation needs. Because we have never undertaken a comprehensive systems analysis of U.S. transportation network, we have been unable to define an optimized system or to prepare a plan of action that would permit us to launch a program that would result in the establishment of such a system.

Since transportation is concerned with the movement of people and their things and since people tend to fall into political categorizations, it is convenient to break transportation down into levels of transportation networks, with different levels identified with generalized political categories. Five levels of transportation networks have been identified: (1) international, (2) national, (3) multistate regional, (4) state, and (5) multicounty regional (urban-suburban).

Two appendices have been attached to cover portions of the subject that are of general interest, but which do not logically fall within any particular section of the paper. Appendix A discusses urban transportation alternatives and Appendix B briefly covers the aspects of modern technology related to transportation.

1. International Transportation

Technologically international travel is not faced with any serious or insurmountable obstacles. The world has been shrinking in time-size ever since Nellie Bly's 72-day trip, and recent technical developments such as jet aircraft and communications satellites have served to hasten the process. Supersonic aircraft will make near neighbors of all the world's people.

National politics and customs and duties have more effect on the free movement of people and things than does transportation technology. World tensions show every indication of continuing. They will remain as a key restraining influence on the free international movement of things and people.

Since, in the past and for the foreseeable future, most United States transportation development money was and will be spent for the development of equipment for faster long-distance transportation, the equipment that evolves will be almost universally applicable to world transportation needs. For example, supersonic jets will have international transportation significance, and high speed ground transportation systems will have great significance for international travel in Europe and Scandinavia.

There should not be any significant changes in world or international transportation by 1975. Supersonic jets will reduce the longest international trips to short travel times which will serve to bring opposite portions of the world much closer together. High speed ground transportation and subsonic jet aircraft will continue to dominate the transportation market for relatively short international travel and shipment distances, because the lower fares of subsonic jets will be more attractive than the shorter travel times of supersonic jets. The convenience of high speed ground transportation will make it competitive for the relatively short distance city-center to city-center trip market. The sonic boom, which is associated with supersonic flights, is receiving a great deal of research and development attention. Any success in reducing the intensity of sonic booms can result in the rapid acceptance of supersonic commercial jets, assuming, of course, favorable passenger-mile economics.

During the 15-year period from 1975 to 1990, we should witness significant changes in world transportation patterns. The development of a low-fare sky-bus should result in a great increase in the volume of international travel. The jet-set will be outnumbered and overshadowed by a great horde of middle class people from all nations exploring their world. This travel will be stimulated by international television programs broadcast via communication satellites and by spreading affluence. These trends will stimulate international trade, which will further stimulate international travel. This will have a significant effect on world affairs. More of the mystique about foreigners will disappear. More people will learn to understand people of other lands, and, hopefully, genuinely appreciate mankind's interdependence.

Obviously this international travel will have only a limited effect on newly developing nations. Comparatively few people will choose to visit those countries and very few people in these countries will be able to travel. However, improved international travel conditions will contribute to a greater interchange of people between developing countries and developed nations, with the hope that there will be a growing realization within developing countries that the solution to their problems must come primarily from within their own borders. Transportation problems within developing nations will remain severe and will represent one of their most pressing problem areas. They will need to develop efficient and widespread internal transportation networks to permit them to move people and goods inside their own borders. This will make more of their locally produced products available to more of their own people and will facilitate moving these products to world markets.

Centuries of progress cannot be crammed into capital-less, developing societies in a decade. Great progress will not be made in aiding developing nations until more programs are established to overcome superstitions, until more facilities are installed to educate the people of these nations, and until the developed nations make available more technical aid and other knowledge required to permit these developing nations to attack their problems in a systematic fashion with a well conceived, well planned, orderly, and realistically time-phased approach. This is a challenge for the leaders of these nations, as well as for the United Nations.

The United Nations can serve a vital role as an international transportation information center. Knowledge, technology, and lore developed around the world can be assembled, categorized, and catalogued in this center. To make the most effective utilization of this knowledge, the United Nations should establish a permanent commission charged with the responsibility for providing expert technical and management transportation assistance to developing nations.

The turn of the century should see trends in the direction of a more united world. The concept of regional common markets will have spread widely. Some interregional markets may have been established. Fast economical air transportation and inexpensive bulk shipment modes should tend to encourage development within the world of the same degree of specialization that has occurred within nations. For example, as the Ohio-Pennsylvania area became the center for heavy manufacturing industry within the United States, in the same fashion a world heavy manufacturing center might develop, perhaps in the Ruhr Valley. In addition to other specialized activities centered in these two countries, the United States and Canada may become—even more than now—the world's breadbasket.

At this time it is too early to set policies and to propose the establishment of specific development programs for the world's transportation needs, but the need for faster, more economical systems will continue to grow.

2. National Transportation

The past century has seen the development of a large gap between the transportation capabilities of developed nations and those of developing ones. The United States was fortunate during this period because it was populated with an industrious, aggressive, ambitious, profit-seeking people led by educated, dedicated individuals with a zealous interest in their country and its citizens. The roads, canals, and railroads that this country's citizens built and which government encouraged to be built and contributed to, formed the solid foundation that permitted the rapid growth and development of the United States. This rapidly expanding transportation network, even though the history of its development is colored with every known form of financial and political chicanery, permitted the United States to pull away from other emerging and developing nations and to close the gap between itself and more mature nations. The U.S. was fortunate also because its early growth coincided with the invention, development, and exploitation of railroads and steamships. They remained as efficient and modern transportation modes throughout the critical growth period of the nation and are valuable national transportation assets today.

As the United States has grown into a heavily industrialized and urbanized nation, we have not continuously and critically evaluated our transportation needs and existing facilities and proposed new facilities as required to assure an integrated national transportation system. Consequently we have not treated national transportation as a systems problem. Instead, we have emphasized seeking solutions to specific but poorly defined and inadequately documented transportation problems without giving adequate consideration to where these problems fit into the context of a national transportation network. We have concentrated our money and consequently our talents in the high speed, long distance transportation field, probably because technologic developments favored improvements in this area. However in so doing we neglected a critical portion of the national network and as a result are slowly destroying our urban areas with vehicle congestion and poisoning urban residents with polluted air.

We must structure a set of national transportation objectives based on transportation needs. Although it would be nice to be able to design an optimized national network from scratch, for obvious reasons this cannot be done. Therefore these objectives should be realistic. They must recognize the existing framework of vested interests and high investment facilities within which a national transportation system must operate. We are now going to have to learn how to encourage and achieve cooperation between the private and the public sectors and among vested interests representing a variety of transportation modes, if we are to make any progress at all with respect to a truly effective national transportation network. We must learn how to encourage free competition in transportation, but at the same time we must learn how to give to transportation modes and systems credit for their national defense value. We must learn how to provide a mixture of transportation services based on need, on ability to pay and on desire to pay for additional speed, comfort, pleasure, or status.

By 1970 the Department of Transportation should be staffed, organized, and operating out of suitable quarters. It should have established a set of goals and long range objectives and should have structured research, development, and analytical programs designed to assure that the Department of Transportation achieve its objectives. It should also, by 1970, have identified promising transportation systems and technological developments that could be put to use to aid it in being responsive to the transport needs and wants of people.

By the year 1980, the Department of Transportation (DOT) should be a well established government agency with responsibility for coordinating all federal activities in the transportation area. U.S. transportation cannot be properly treated as the complex system problem it is, unless there is complete cooperation among all federal agencies involved with transportation. By 1980, the Department of Transportation (DOT) should have established, built, and operating a Research and Development (R&D) Center where new technology and newly developed components could continuously be tested for their applicability to U.S. transportation systems needs. Experimental operating models or prototypes of feasible and practical new systems should be under test. These tests must include the collection of data on the reaction of people to these new systems.

By 1980, air freight should be exerting an influence on the U.S. economy. Readily available and dependable air freight service can have a marked effect on warehousing and inventory levels and practices. Air freight deliveries tied in with efficient urban freight movement and package delivery systems should permit the delivery of products from distant factories as rapidly as purchases are now delivered from the local store to the consumer's home.

By the beginning of the twenty-first century, at least one new high-speed, long-distance transportation mode should have been developed and added to the nation's stockpile of new transportation modes. High speed systems should be speeding air travelers from all large U.S. airports to interfaces with local distribution systems. At least one east-west and two north-south automatic highways should be guiding and controlling individual passenger vehicles speeding from coast to coast and border to border.

Freight should be moving through at least one completed, continuous, freight system which completely separates freight from people. The original development work for all these systems should have been projects conducted either in-house at the Department of Transportation's R&D center or as a result of contracted R&D conducted by some industrial organization. These systems, the electronic highways and the freight system, would probably be owned and operated by a transportation network company, similar in structure to Comsat, with private industry and the U.S. public owning the company in much the same manner that Comsat is owned.

The year 2020 should see us well on the way to a complete national transportation network capable of transporting both people and things, apart from each other, from any point in the United States to any other point. (The development of the subdividable uniform container concept for the movement of things from automated warehouses to a transportation mode such as a train, to another such as a barge and back to another automated warehouse will make a great contribution to the development of this capability.) Progress must and will be made in multiple access computers, in the technology of moving things, in new approaches to conveyorized systems and in control equipment before such transportation systems can be built. These individual developments will frequently be forthcoming as a result of industrial research and development, other than transportation research. Their application to transportation systems and the development of prototype systems will probably be the result of government supported projects.

Professor Galbraith[1] astutely remarked that costs and risks associated with technical developments can be reduced significantly if the government will foot the development bill. This is the emerging pattern in transportation. Therefore it is expected that the aerospace and defense industry, which is oriented toward complex systems problems with government research and development support will strive to fill the vacuum that currently exists relative to the development of new transportation modes and systems.

3. Multistate Regional Transportation Networks

Obviously transportation systems will grow from short demonstration systems installed in or near the research and development centers where they are developed to complete systems serving some pressing, but initially limited scale, need where actual operating experience with the system can be gained. Once a system grows to the multistate scale, it will be a significant part of the national transportation network. The only significant new multistate system expected by 1970 is the Northeast corridor high-speed ground transportation system. Hopefully, this will be the last of the piecemeal approaches to solving U.S. transportation problems. In order to develop a system that truly resolves the transportation needs in a multistate area, we must consider a great deal more than a point to point high speed ground transportation. For example, for a family that wants to go from a small town such as Catskill, New York, to Washington, D.C., to do some sightseeing, the high speed system, as currently conceived, does little because it only covers a small part of their travel needs. This system makes no provision to assure them individualized, immediately-available, comfortable, inexpensive transportation in Washington to all the places they might wish to visit during their trip. Certainly, they can ride taxis or buses or even rent cars, but the overall transportation cost to them must be competitive with the cost and convenience of going in their own automobile. A high speed corridor system does little to alleviate street and highway congestion because 80 percent of all auto trips are for 20 miles or less. We must learn to use more comprehensive analyses in planning transportation systems before we commit additional billions of a very limited resource, the taxpayers' dollars, to transportation projects out of the context of an overall national transportation system need.

When 1980 rolls around, some of the new systems concepts developed by the Department of Transportation should be undergoing tests on a multistate scale. A complete multistate transportation network should have been designed, built, and tested by the end of the twentieth century. Multistate tests of systems will be necessary, because a test of this size will permit exposing the system to a wider variety of climatic extremes and use requirements than one could find within a smaller area.

Pipelines fall within this regional category and will remain as a rather specific transportation mode for a particular and narrow range of products. A few new products, such as slurries and suspensions, can be added to the list of products moved in pipelines, but in spite of talk about gravity cars in tubes and pneumatic-tube vehicles, pipelines will not become a dominant mode for the movement of things.

4. State

State transportation networks are becoming less and less significant as independent transportation networks. As more and more economic activity becomes interstate in nature, the state transportation systems attain greater significance as links in multistate and national networks— particularly highway networks. Exclusive of highways and road building materials, states have consistently played a minor role in the development of transportation modes and in encouraging the development and testing of new modes.

There will be few if any noticeable changes at the state level with respect to transportation between now and 1970. The states will exert their maximum influence in the political arena. The period 1970 to 1980 should see the beginning of massive efforts devoted to the removal of "local jurisdiction" roadblocks blocking the formation of the metropolitan or regional governmental structures required to assure the establishment of requisite urban transportation systems. Individual states can maintain life and death control over these transportation systems by the attitude of state legislatures toward the passage of the necessary legislation.

Some transportation experts suggest that the individual states must accept responsibility for the establishment of metropolitan transportation systems because states rather than cities have access to sources of tax dollars that grow with increasing affluence. Cities by virtue of their reliance on property taxes are tied to a relatively constant tax source. The redistricting of state legislatures will aid in bringing this type of state aid about, but the suburban resident, who will control state legislatures, must be educated to want this type of state aid for metropolitan transportation. All states will not accept responsibility for transportation within the state with equal degrees of enthusiasm, initiative, and financial commitment. Some states like New York and Pennsylvania have already recognized the need. However, events that occur at the state level relative to transportation will not develop the new transportation modes that are necessary to supplement existing modes nor will they result in the development of systematically planned and developed, integrated, complete transportation networks.

It should be mentioned that vehicles powered by internal combustion engines will be with us through the end of the twentieth century. An expanded network of rural and state highways will be required to permit this continued use of automobiles and trucks. Automatic electronic highways for long distance travel by automobile will be federal systems rather than state. The heavy electronic content and the complex maintenance and reliability requirements of electronic highways will probably require a federal control organization similar to the FAA's aircraft control system.

Rental cars may have an unexpected effect on long distance traveling. Since the same models are available all over the U.S., the renter of a particular model in Ohio would probably be willing to turn his Ohio car in to the leasing company if the company were to make a similar car available to him in Texas, or Florida, or wherever he was going. Therefore, as people turn to car rentals in larger and larger numbers, this should reinforce the market for high speed transportation systems that can move people from their rented car in one location to an identical one in another location.

Airport congestion is becoming the rule, rather than the exception. Since regional airports may be required as one way of alleviating this congestion and since these airports must be linked to local airports and to urban and suburban centers by high speed transportation links, this could well be an area in which states and state transportation agencies can play a significant role.

5. Metropolitan Transportation

In spite of a strong national awareness of the need for good transportation, a history of cooperation between government and industry in this field, and a history of demonstrated progress in the provision of transportation facilities and modes and generations of experience of governmental control over transportation, today we find ourselves in the midst of a paradox. We have the most advanced transportation complex in the world. We have highly engineered transportation equipment and systems, yet for a two- to four-hour period in most urban areas and the better part of the day in some, our systems are incapable of moving us at speeds any greater than those attainable at the turn of the century. Sometimes the systems collapse completely as did the automobile-street system in Boston for five hours several years ago.

In the past century, man has been changing his status from rural animal to urban animal. William Robson identified 21 great cities.[2] In 1850, only 15 of these cities were in existence. These 15 cities had a population of 4 million people in 1850; by 1950 the 21 great cities had 52 million residents. This figure does not include the additional millions of people residing in the suburbs. This tremendous growth must be attributed to the industrial revolution, which created jobs in cities. However, the agricultural revolution, the results of which are most evident in the U.S., freed millions of people from agricultural types of work and made it possible for them to move to cities to fill the labor needs of the new industries.

Today, the word city is synonymous with congestion. Actually, cities have always been congested because one function of a city is to bring people into close contact to facilitate the interactions that occur between people. In the past, the heavily congested portions of cities were relatively small because cities themselves were small in area. As mechanized transportation vehicles and systems evolved, cities grew appreciably in physical size and congested central areas became more extensive because of the large numbers of people the transportation systems were able to deliver to and around the core of the city.

Starting in 1950, most of Robson's 21 great cities either stopped growing or their rate of growth slowed appreciably. Within the context of unchanging urban transportation service, city growth appears to be a self-limiting process. There are statistics on numbers of automobiles entering the central cores of large U.S. cities which indicate that once traffic in a city becomes congested, additional automobiles entering the central core of a city cause the volume of business in proportion to the number of additional cars to decrease. For example, as the average number of cars entering New York City rose from 382,000 in 1948 to 590,000 in 1960, the average number of people entering fell from 3.7 million to a little over 3.3 million. We have not yet learned how to quantify or express this as a mathematical relation. However, this could be a significant statistic in determining the optimum size or density for existing cities.

Urban transportation is the crucial transportation problem of the United States. This is due to the great concentration of people in these areas and to the fact that all the interfaces between transportation modes occur in urban areas. These interfaces occur at places such as airports, rail terminals, sea and river ports, bus stations, and large markets. The manner in which these transportation interfaces function determines the effectiveness of the U.S. transportation system. The major difficulties associated with urban transportation can all be traced to these interfaces.

The interface has been the neglected area of U.S. transportation. It is not unusual for the trip from airport to hotel to take longer than the airplane ride. The trip from commuter train to office can be difficult, particularly on a cold or rainy day. Moving about in a strange city after detraining or leaving a bus can be a frustrating experience. In spite of federal emphasis on many aspects of transportation such as the development and improvement of aircraft and flight control equipment, on subsidizing the construction of merchant vessels and on building limited access highways, we have missed the real problem areas. We have given inadequate attention to problems such as getting the traveler to the airport, loading and unloading a modern, automated freighter, and handling the cars that pour off a limited access highway into the downtown area of a city.

Assuming a continuation of current trends:

1. In the next fifty years, the U.S. population will increase to about 390 million people. More than 300 million of these people are expected to reside in urban areas. This represents an increase of almost 200 million urban residents.

2. Projections indicate that by the year 2020, there will be about 158 million additional autos in urban America. This is almost as many more cars as people, but it is doubtful that these trends can be allowed to continue.

Serving the transportation needs and wants of this number of people and providing for this number of automobiles will require more than skillful juggling. This growing horde of people combined with each one's desire for the full flexibility of individual transportation is frightening. Current modes of transportation will not be able to handle the movement of large numbers of additional people. The comedian who suggested that we are heading for a massive traffic tie-up where we will all starve to death while sitting in our cars blowing our horns may not be far from wrong.

There is no combination of insufficient and inadequate transportation that provides adequate urban transportation. More variety in transportation systems is required before we can begin to look for optimum combinations of systems to serve the needs of specific urban areas. For example, most people do not ride the New York subway because they want and like to but rather because it is necessary. For some of the 20-cent fare is a burden; others would be happy to pay more for a more dignified mode, and still others would be willing to pay a high premium for dignity, comfort, convenience, and speed. Some people do this to an extent today in choosing between their own car, a taxi, or a chauffeur-driven limousine. Future demands for transportation may come from contrasting groups of social and economic classes who may not be willing to accept the same service or even travel together.

In discussing urban transportation, it is convenient to consider at least six related subjects: these are congestion, air pollution, new transportation modes, changing aesthetic, moral, and economic values, people's needs and wants, and land use.

1. *Congestion.* Urban congestion will eventually affect currently accepted values on the freedom of movement of people within urban areas. For example, extreme freedom, the ability to go where you want to, when you want to, in your own vehicle by the route of your own choosing, as we now do with our own automobiles, will eventually have to be limited in order to prevent the complete collapse of urban circulating systems and to save the cities themselves. This congestion may accelerate the acceptance of more costly but more satisfying communications media, such as visual phones.

Not only has the automobile created vehicular congestion in cities, but its incessant need for additional rights-of-way has placed unreasonable demands on cities that cities cannot continue to meet. Urban expressways can cost over 50 million dollars per mile. In addition to this first cost, there is a continuing expense due to taxable property removed from the tax rolls to make way for expressways. Urban road building displaces more people and businesses than urban renewal, and urban expressways destroy the aesthetics of cities as well as property values near them. San Francisco stopped all freeway construction when the State Highway Department defaced the Embarcadero with an elevated structure. Santa Barbara has been fighting off the State Highway Department's efforts to build an elevated freeway for five years. New York has had to restrain Mr. Moses in his efforts to scar Manhattan with an elevated cross-town expressway. This type of protest will become the rule rather than the exception.

2. *Air Pollution.* When the American public becomes sincerely concerned about the effects that the exhausts from internal combustion engines have on its health, it will support the imposition of restrictions on the use of these vehicles within and near congested areas. When the average urban resident has been convinced that the exhaust from someone else's car has a deleterious effect on his health, great social pressures will arise to force the imposition of restrictions on the use of automobiles and other motor vehicles in congested areas. Years ago we forced railroads to change to electric engines before entering some of our cities. It would be perfectly feasible as an interim measure to have large freight terminals outside cities where tractor trailers could be unloaded and their loads transhipped in smaller, less offensive vehicles or via specially designed freight moving systems. For example, cities with rapid transit could utilize rail cars with removable seats, similar to those on some of the newer jets, for the movement of freight during off-peak and night hours.

3. *New Transportation Modes.* A few creative and concerned people have proposed novel ideas and novel approaches for new transportation modes and systems for urban areas, but for the most part these ideas were ignored. Some experts shrugged off the problem because urban transportation was expected to be bad, because people were flocking to cities, and, according to Meyerson and Wilfred Owen, because cities are synonomous with crowds and congestion.

Senator Williams attempted to break through this barrier with his transportation bill. None of this money was spent either to develop or to encourage the development of the new transportation systems so desperately needed to attack problems associated with interfaces between transportation systems. In addition to seeking and developing new transportation equipment and systems to fill needs inadequately served by existing transportation facilities and sources, our society must develop a data base that will permit conducting accurate and meaningful, economic and technologic analyses of new transportation systems and that will permit making accurate and meaningful comparisons of new systems with each other and with existing systems.

4. *Changing Aesthetic, Moral, and Economic Values.* The transportation planning process must consider and weigh changes that have occurred in America's aesthetic, moral, and economic values. These changing values coupled with developing technology and emerging national goals and objectives could have a profound effect on the direction taken by transportation research and development effort. For example, recognizing the role that mobility plays both with respect to poverty and to the concentration of minority groups in deteriorating urban areas adds a degree of urgency to the necessity for making striking improvements in urban transportation. Urban transportation has made the transition from a readily available service that contributed greatly to the growth and viability of cities to a deteriorating, marginal service contributing to the demise of cities. The automobile has had a far greater impact on the lives of people than most people realize. It shaped some cities—Los Angeles is the classic example—but many U.S. and foreign cities are now beginning to assume the shape of Los Angeles.

In affecting the shape of our cities, the automobile has also contributed to the deterioration of public transit. Obviously an inanimate object could not cause these events by itself, but the auto priesthood, those who pave the way for automobiles and who remove obstacles interfering with unrestricted rights-of-way for automobiles in all parts of our cities, has set the forces in motion that have caused these events to occur.

Specialization of land use in our cities has resulted in the conversion of the core of many cities to office and financial centers. This combined with traffic congestion has encouraged manufacturing industry to move at least to the fringe of cities and in most cases even farther. Since most urban transportation systems are designed to serve the automobile or to bring commuters into a city, it has become either too expensive or even impossible for the unskilled poor to reach manufacturing employment opportunities out of the city. Gardening, yardwork, and other job opportunities have developed in the suburbs as the affluent have moved to suburban homes. However, inadequate transportation has also made it extremely difficult or impossible for the unskilled poor, who traditionally filled these jobs, to reach the places where these jobs exist. The decay of public transit in many areas has also immobilized the young and the old. This hurts the senior citizens most, because often they don't have someone who can transport them. It is imperative that we recognize these problems in planning for future urban transportation needs.

It might be possible through the judicious use of modest amounts of subsidy funds to create a few jobs that would make it possible for thousands of unskilled minority group people to find rewarding employment. For example, this service could provide work for many bus or jitney drivers. A bus service primarily for the unskilled minority group probably could not be economically justified on the basis of the low fare that should be charged. However, if it were equated to welfare cost reductions, it could indicate a good dollar return. Subsidizing this service would create jobs because it would assure that workers could reach places with employment opportunities. The availability of help would open up many domestic, gardening, and other job opportunities for the unskilled. The use of this transportation service by teenagers and senior citizens would reduce the size of the subsidy that would be needed to keep the system in operation.

5. *People's Needs and Wants.* Planning efforts will be wasted and otherwise seemingly attractive transportation systems will fail unless the planning process gives greater consideration to factors such as convenience specifications, frequency of service expected, amenities desired, fare that can be paid, the role of the automobile, and controls that can be instituted. Improved inputs are required to permit predicting with accuracy what people will pay for levels of transportation service and how much automobile owners will pay for the privilege of operating their cars on city streets. We must also learn how to calculate actual costs associated with different transportation services and how to communicate to people real out-of-pocket costs, indirect costs, and levels of inconvenience associated with different systems or modes. We must be able to quantitatively establish the levels of congestion and traffic delays that will force various percentages of people out of their automobiles. We must determine the parking charge rates that will either keep cars out of the city or will reimburse the city for the true cost of the space utilized by vehicles. The Bay Area Rapid Transit system may provide answers to some of these questions.

6. *Land Use.* The design of a city that represents the optimum utilization of land and provides for matching transportation to land use is every planner's dream. The ability to enter the picture in city design where this degree of planning could be effected would permit maximizing the flexibility of transportation systems and minimizing incon-

veniences to residents. However, this type of optimized design can be implemented only if it is done during the very beginning stages of a new city or as a very long range, carefully planned, and carefully controlled rebuilding effort carried out over a period of several generations. This latter approach can be successful only through the application of more local governmental control over the pattern and rate of growth than we are currently accustomed to or willing to permit.

The existing cities in our democratic society have developed in the directions dictated by economic pressures and will continue to respond to these pressures in the future. Government will have to exercise the greater control required in the future through the more astute use of taxes and through the imposition and enforcement of controls such as regional zoning. Our approach to long range planning must evolve the ability to plan in such a way that transportation systems and land use patterns established now will remain optimal into the future.

Land is the most valuable commodity a city has. Consequently, cities must take steps to assure the optimum future utilization of the space available to it. One evolving trend toward improved land utilization consists of making full use of air space through the design of structures that provide for multiple use of the land. Transportation can then be vertical, which an elevator can handle easily. This type of land use makes it possible both to achieve higher land use densities and to provide open space closer in. It also makes it possible to think in terms of new ways of laying out cities because the conventional street and city block structure becomes obsolete. The typical block-street layout would be replaced by high density centers connected by low density areas. High density centers would be served by horizontal transit. San Francisco is beginning to zone this way.

Mixing many types of activities in small areas permits people to engage in activities of interest to them without their having to travel long distances. This makes people's time more productive and provides for fuller utilization of a city's facilities. It also reduces the load on a city's transportation network. Jane Jacobs was right when she said that cities must learn to design for 24-hour use of their facilities. In the future cities must also learn to control their growth. There is no law of nature or economics that states that cities must grow continuously to provide an attractive environment for living or to be economically healthy.

A city is a highly complex structure assembled from many interrelated parts. The transportation network of a city cannot be modified without this change having an effect on the entire city, i.e., its communication network, circulatory system, business community, administrative structure, and revenues. Congestion, air pollution, the cost of providing roads and parking space, and the true cost of vehicular congestion will force the older central cities such as New York, Philadelphia, and Boston to gradually impose restrictions on the use of automobiles and trucks within cities. Early restrictions will consist of severely limited street parking, high license fees for unrestricted entry to cities, high parking fees and trucks restricted to night operation. Changes in transportation policy and systems will have to be carefully factored into the overall city system and must be made to conform to the basic plan for the city itself. However, we cannot lose sight of the fact that breakdown of a city's transportation network could lead to the demise of the entire city.

The very beginnings of progress can now be seen in the urban transportation area. The Housing and Urban Development Department (HUD) has let four study contracts to explore ways and means of improving urban transportation both in the near term and through the foreseeable future. These study contracts, although small, should delineate the boundary or interface problems and should help to identify programs that could lead to the development of systems uniquely constituted to assure a smooth uninterrupted transition for the traveler and for things from the terminus of one mode to a connecting system. Hopefully, these studies will result in the identification of the need for downtown distribution systems, for downtown to airport systems, for diffusion capabilities that permit travelers to reach their ultimate destinations, and in specifications for systems to serve these needs.

The recommendations resulting from these studies, if implemented, may lead to the development of both high density, low cost per ride urban distribution systems and low density, high cost per ride systems. As far as the future of the large U.S. central cities is concerned, a great deal hinges on the outcome of these studies and the action initiated as a result of them. The results should also be exportable to many of the world's large cities.

The rate of growth of the United States' population and the movement of people to urban areas will complicate efforts to bring about significant changes in urban transportation. The period from 1970–80 will be the development and evaluation period. It can be hoped that changes and improvements will be evident by 1980. New systems growing out of HUD studies now underway may have been installed to move people from airport to downtown in some of the larger cities such as

Washington, Los Angeles, New York, and Philadelphia. Cleveland, of course, is already running a rapid transit line to its airport. In a few isolated cases, some activity may be underway to install systems to feed people to transit system stations.

By the year 2000 there should be some significant changes in urban transportation. The larger U.S. cities may have converted completely to electric transportation and several completely new cities should have been built incorporating the most recently developed transportation systems and offering maximum convenience. It is highly conceivable that in those cities, both old and new, where the individually owned vehicle passes from the scene, all transportation will be free.

It is easy to fail to recognize that transportation can have a significant and unanticipated effect on the way in which the United States' population will divide itself between urban and non-urban America. The availability of fast, efficient transportation service from rural areas to urban areas could encourage a significantly larger than anticipated percentage of the population to remain in rural areas, because those people who enjoy spending their leisure time in bucolic surroundings will find they can utilize this time more effectively if they reside in open areas. Improved communications systems, which will make it easy for people from non-urban areas to enjoy cultural experiences and to communicate remotely with others, could also reverse the trend toward the concentration of people in urban areas.

Efficient transportation will encourage the further dispersal of industry. Since a system that moves rural dwellers quickly and comfortably to urban areas can be designed to operate as effectively in reverse, people will be able to make the decision with respect to where they live independent of transportation.

Viewed in the context of good transportation systems, current projections of the numbers of people within urban areas may be significantly too large. As Lewis Mumford said in his testimony to Senator Ribicoff's Senate Subcommittee, just because Jean Gottmann said everyone was going to live in cities doesn't necessarily make it so. This agrees with several recently conducted sociological studies, including a University of Michigan study for the Bureau of Public Roads and a Herbert Gans study, which indicate that people are interested in moving further away from the central city in order to have more social interaction with other people.

In general, then, the next fifty years will see great changes in the urban-suburban regional transportation field. The way will be led by the federal government, presumably by the Department of Transportation. Private industry will build and develop components for systems and will vie for contracts to build systems. However, the systems development costs will be borne by the federal government. This is almost a certainty, because developing new transportation modes and systems can be extremely costly and there is no assurance that a system developed out of the overall national transportation context will be accepted. The fact that all new transportation systems will have to be designed to fit into a national transportation network, and many of the national sub-networks will be urban and regional metropolitan systems, will complicate modal and system design and will add greatly to development cost.

Conclusions and Recommendations

Conclusions

Transportation is very closely related to people. Since people's needs and wants change with time, transportation planning must be treated as a continuing process.

Transportation planning cannot be performed in a vacuum. Transportation can and does have both anticipated and unanticipated effects on growth patterns and rates and direction of growth of cities and urban areas.

We are not yet able to plan transportation networks or systems with adequate sophistication to preclude the occurrence of unanticipated results in land use patterns, nor have we been able to plan and implement land use patterns that assure the continuing adequacy of installed or proposed transportation facilities.

We do not yet have sufficient analytical capability to anticipate the long range implications of subsidies for transportation modes.

We have not developed either the data base or the set of quantitative value criteria that permit us to make valid economic comparisons between existing or proposed transportation modes.

Future changes in transportation will be evolutionary. The rapid acceptance of the road vehicle powered by an internal combustion engine and its movement into the role of dominant U.S. transportation mode was largely an extension of the industrial revolution to transportation.

Future changes in transportation modes and systems will be forced by crises resulting from urban air pollution and vehicular congestion rather than technological developments.

The federal government must play a leading role in the development of technology related to transportation needs because the large expense and great risk involved will either preclude or seriously restrict privately financed efforts in this field.

Higher levels of government must enter into transportation planning to assure coordination of all transportation modes and networks into integrated systems.

Rapid, comfortable, convenient, and frequent transportation must be made available for all people to permit everyone to capitalize on widespread employment and education opportunities, and to make full use of medical, recreational, cultural, and other facilities.

Greater cooperation between industry and government is required. Transportation represents about 20 percent of the gross national product. Any development that drastically affects transportation could have a deleterious effect on the national economy. Changes in transportation must be gradual and planned in the context of a healthy national economy.

Recommendations

To assure the efficient and timely development of new transportation equipment and systems based both on evolving technology and on identified needs, a national Transportation Research and Development Center should be established. This center should have an "in-house" research and development program of its own and should also serve as the contracting agency for all federally sponsored ground transportation study and development programs.

All federal activities related to transportation should be coordinated within the government to assure minimal duplication of effort and the treatment of all forms of transportation as interrelated portions of a complex system network.

Transportation planning must be completely coordinated to assure participation by all levels of government, evaluation of all transportation alternatives, and consideration of long range land use planning and regional zoning objectives.

Land use plans and regional zoning controls should be designed to permit people to minimize distances traveled and the number of trips required in the course of a normal day's activities. This will require putting land to multiple uses as well as overcoming certain superstitions, traditions, and habits with respect to where and how certain functions such as education and recreation are provided for.

Plans should be prepared to cover long time periods to assure long term suitability of implemented plans.

Future transportation systems should be designed with system flexibility in mind so that systems can be readily modified to match changing environmental conditions.

Congress should appropriate adequate funds both to assure the development of novel and promising transportation ideas and to permit conducting evaluation tests on equipment and systems already developed.

New concepts for and attitudes toward freight movement and distribution systems in urban areas should be developed. These new approaches to the movement of goods in urban areas should be concerned initially with improving the aesthetics of cities, reducing noise and pollution levels, and alleviating congestion by removing large trucks from city streets.

Complete new cities should be built to demonstrate, among other things, new concepts in urban transportation as well as the long range benefits of integrated land use planning for transportation.

Transportation planning should involve more participation by social scientists both at the planning and the evaluation stages.

The true costs of providing automobile rights-of-way in urban areas should be determined and automobile users should be charged the full cost both for use of rights-of-way and for space occupied for parking.

New transportation systems and modes must be sold to people just as any other new manufactured product is sold to people. The "marketing or advertising" program must be carefully factored into the overall plan for any new transportation system or any significant change in a transportation network.

A series of programs should be instituted to test available downtown distribution systems by blocking off downtown areas to automotive traffic and installing and evaluating these systems in actual need environments.

Appendix A

Urban Transportation Alternatives

Individual Automobile

The automobile as we know it now will remain with us for a long time. We have not yet learned how to design a replacement transportation mode that has the comfort, convenience, flexibility, reliability, or appeal of the automobile-road system. As indicated elsewhere, pressures are building for the imposition of restrictions on the use of automobiles in urban areas. However, great social changes must occur before the automobile can be dislodged from its present position in the U.S. transportation system.

The contribution of the internal combustion engine to air pollution will receive increasing attention during the next ten years. Blow-by control devices, currently required in California, and catalytic after-burners, are not a suitable solution to controlling air pollution resulting from the widespread use of internal combustion engine powered vehicles. Impurities in gasoline can rapidly poison and render catalysts ineffective. Catalysts cannot prevent the escape of hydrocarbons from vented fuel tanks or when vehicles are refueled. Considerable progress should be made, within the next ten years, in reducing the volume of emissions per automobile, probably to the extent of eliminating 70 to 80 percent of total emissions. Since these efforts will fall short of "solving" the problem, it is expected that alternative automotive propulsion systems will also play a role in reducing smog emissions. These should include the gas-turbine engine and battery propulsion systems.

Automotive transportation will continue to be the dominant city-to-city, city-to-resort, and rural-area-to-city form of transportation for at least the next twenty-five years. The pressures, air pollution and congestion, which exist to restrict or control the auto's penetration of cities, do not exist over 95 percent of the United States' land area. Significant progress toward electronic highways will occur over the next quarter century. A demonstration stretch of electronic highway may be built during the next ten years. This could be based on the electronic highway system components demonstrated by RCA and General Motors. The high cost of the RCA system will limit the extent of its application over the next twenty-five years. The new Department of Transportation may elect to devote some of its research and development efforts to overcoming the high costs associated with the RCA-GM electronic highway system. As a result a large percentage of new highway construction by 1990 or 2000 will be for electronically controlled highways.

Electric Vehicles

The internal combustion automobile, as currently designed, is not intended to function optimally in a congested urban environment at low speeds with frequent stops. Yet it is used primarily for this purpose. For example, Bureau of Public Roads statistics indicate that 50 percent of all automotive trips are for 10 miles or less and that more than 80 percent of all vehicle-miles travelled are for trips less than 20 miles in length.

These data suggest that the automobile may be vulnerable to competition in the short-distance, slow-speed transportation field from a vehicle designed specifically for this service. It is for this supplementary function—as distinct from the long-distance, high speed transportation need, which today's automobile serves so well—that the electric vehicle has a strong potential.

A forerunner of the type of electric vehicle which can satisfy the short-distance, slow speed requirement is the electric golf cart. This vehicle has been used for many tasks other than transporting golfers and the list of applications is steadily growing. Another existing vehicle is the electric shopper that is popular in Long Beach, California.

Recent technological advances now make it possible to design small electric vehicles with improved characteristics. It is now feasible to design a two-passenger vehicle capable of speeds up to 20 to 30 mph with a range of 30 to 50 miles per battery charge. The technological features of such a vehicle would include solid-state speed controllers which permit stepless speed control and can also serve as the battery charger circuit; lead-acid batteries guaranteed for five years of deep discharge service; high impact, long-lived plastic bodies; inexpensive, comfortable-riding, independent wheel suspension systems; and electric differentials. These vehicles can carry two adults with additional space for packages or small children. They could be serviced by conveniently located battery stations where batteries could be charged in a matter of seconds for a nominal fee. In effect, these battery stations would provide an energy service by leasing batteries to vehicle owners and fleet operators.

This concept was not feasible a generation ago because most families owned only one automobile. Today, however, the multi-car family is commonplace and the primary function of the second and third cars is to provide short-distance, slow speed transport. Under these circumstances a sensible second car option could be a specially designed electric, slow speed, short-range vehicle.

The type of electric vehicle discussed above will be developed and marketed in volume within the next ten years. Westinghouse has already announced the limited availability of such a vehicle. However, electric vehicles cannot compete on the basis of first cost economics and performance, but must gain acceptance because of concern over air pollution and congestion and the hope that they can capitalize on relatively low operating costs of about 1.5 cents per mile and the inherent low-maintenance and long-life characteristics of electrical components. (Operating costs include .5 cent for electricity and 1 cent per mile for battery replacement.)

It is unrealistic to expect or to predict the sudden emergence of a trend that will sweep all internal combustion engine powered vehicles out of urban areas and replace them with electric vehicles. This could be accomplished or aided by legislation, but any politician who stuck his neck out on this at present would soon be out of office. It is more sensible to think in terms of the gradual appearance of electric vehicles in cities accompanied by gradual substitution of electrically powered urban distribution systems for automobiles and buses.

Two types of power sources are currently available for furnishing electrical energy to an electric vehicle—batteries and fuel cells. Batteries have been used for over sixty years for the propulsion of electric vehicles. Fuel cells have just begun to be used experimentally for this purpose.

The most commonly applied battery for electric vehicle propulsion is the lead-acid battery. This is the same battery used the last time electric vehicles were in vogue. However it has been greatly improved. It is not expected that more than a 10 to 15 percent improvement in energy storage per unit of weight (which is the weak feature of lead-acid batteries) can be made in lead-acid batteries in the next ten years.

Lead-acid batteries already perform some vehicle propulsion functions adequately. All milk deliveries in London are made by electric vehicles. The average route is only about 8 to 10 miles, but the longest route is 52 miles. There are 40,000 electric road vehicles licensed in England.

The nickel-cadmium battery is another mass produced, secondary battery that is periodically considered for motive power applications. This battery offers several advantages over lead-acid batteries. It is completely sealed, can be recharged within one hour, and will permit a 30 to 40 percent improvement in energy storage density. Unfortunately, this battery costs about ten times more than a comparable lead-acid battery.

Recently there has been a great deal of research and development effort applied to the secondary battery field in an effort to develop batteries based on unconventional battery couples that offer the potential of storing ten or more times as much energy per unit of weight as the lead-acid battery. These batteries under development include the metal-air batteries, such as magnesium-air and zinc-air, the sodium-sulphur battery, and a lithium battery. Periodically there are optimistic reports on some one of these projects but then other difficulties arise and the researchers return to their benches. However, continuing development work on battery systems will result in greatly improved, lower cost batteries in the next twenty five years. This will improve the economics of electric vehicles and will extend their range and speed capabilities enough to make them competitive for all urban-suburban travel needs.

Economically feasible fuel cells for widespread motive power applications are not expected in the near or intermediate term future.

Individualized Mass Transit

During the period from 1975 to 1990, some progress will be made in individualizing transit. There are about fifty proposals around for systems to accomplish this. Some are ideas on the backs of envelopes but some have been well thought out and conceptually analyzed. The development of individualized transit which combines the freedom of the automobile for short movement and the speed of mass transit for longer distances will require a great deal of money, time and good work. Control, propulsion, and guidance systems must be developed on the basis of frontier technologies.

The introduction of small electric vehicles will stimulate the next evolutionary step toward the development of individualized urban transportation systems. These are systems involving electric vehicles operating on roadways where power is fed to the vehicles and their speed, entry and exit is controlled by the system. This approach was first proposed by GE in about 1960. It was followed by the Alden StaRRcar proposal. Within the next twenty-five years this type of system should be widely used for intra-airport transportation, downtown distribution, transit in moderate sized communities and around large shopping centers.

No one urban transportation mode will satisfy all people. It is doubtful that one mode can be developed that will be capable of satisfactorily serving all urban transportation needs. For example, to meet commuting needs, systems are required that can move tens of thousands of people from one part of an urban area to another part in a half-hour or less. For downtown distribution there is need for a system that can move thousands of people around central business districts at slower speeds. Although the technology is available for the lower density systems, and preliminary prototypes have been demonstrated, no full-scale systems have been installed.

The Stephens-Adamson-Goodyear Carveyor system could serve as a downtown distribution system. It is a combined passenger-vehicle, conveyor-belt system that carries passengers seated in vehicles carried by the belt. Passengers enter the system from a dynamic station. The Carveyor system is limited to operation in a closed loop and has a 15 mph top speed.

Another interesting new system is the Disney WEDway which has been installed in the new Tomorrowland, at Disneyland. The four-passenger vehicles can climb steep grades, negotiate sharp curves, and ascend a helix. They are propelled by powered wheels mounted in the system's roadway. It also is loaded from a moving station.

Bus Transit Systems

General Motors appears to have chosen the bus as its vehicle for serving the mass transit needs of urban areas. The bus represents "instant transit" because the "rights-of-way" are already in place. The bus has a diffusion capability at one end of the trip. It can circulate through a neighborhood, pick up a load of people for downtown and deposit them at a central terminal. At that point the system faces the same problem as rail rapid transit or the monorail. Bus systems are very flexible in capacity and can serve communities with populations ranging from tens of thousands to millions.

Bus transit is a highly labor-intensive system with a high maintenance requirement. As buses age they become noisy and emit copious quantities of unpleasant fumes. In general, they are not as comfortable as other transit systems. If special roadways are required in urban areas for the exclusive use of buses, the cost of providing and maintaining these rights-of-way can easily spoil the economics of a bus transit system.

Rail Transit

In large cities urban transportation systems have been dominated by rail rapid transit. It is generally accepted that rail rapid transit can only serve urban areas with populations in excess of one million residents.

No major technical innovations are expected in rail rapid transit systems within the next twenty years. The most modern rail rapid transit system in the U.S., the Bay Area Rapid Transit system (BART), is an electric railroad system. BART will use steel wheels on steel tracks, will travel at 80 mph, and will be equipped with air-conditioned cars and seating arrangements not unlike current subway trains. It will proceed over rights-of-way that are elevated, at ground-level, in subways, and in tubes.

Two major technologic advances are incorporated in the BART system. Automatic electronic control circuitry will permit shorter time intervals between trains (90 seconds) than are common on other systems and an automatic fare collection system will be installed. The automatic fare collection system will permit basing fares either on zones or on distance traveled. This approach to fare collection requires a high initial investment in equipment but it permits a greater revenue income and lower system operating costs.

If rail rapid transit systems could be used during night and off-peak daytime hours to move goods around cities, traffic congestion could be alleviated. Transit cars could be designed like jet aircraft with seats on removable roller platforms. The installation of freight elevators during the construction of stations should not add significantly to station or system costs. This double use of transit systems could make them economically attractive.

Appendix B

GARTH LEETH

General Electric Company, TEMPO Center for Advanced Studies

Technology

A graphic way of comparing various modes of transportation that was first used by Von Karman is shown in Figure 1. Von Karman curves are obtained by plotting the thrust to weight ratio of a vehicle versus speed. This can be done for any vehicle, since it is equivalent to the ratio of the force resisting vehicle motion divided by the vehicle weight. If this technique is followed for many vehicles, a family of curves is obtained which permits comparing the inherent efficiencies of modes of transport.

In general, the curves are time or "state-of-the-art" dependent. Normally, the curve for any particular vehicle should move down and to the right with time. This statement implies that improvements in technology result in better performing vehicles. This figure provides only general information about vehicle types. Since any vehicle type can be designed with different characteristics to meet a specific application, there could be a family of curves for each vehicle type. However, all of these curves would be of the same shape and would all fall close to the line in Figure 1 for that type of vehicle.

Certain generalizations can be drawn from Figure 1:

1. At speeds below 30 to 40 mph, a ship or submarine is the most efficient vehicle.

2. At speeds above 150 to 200 mph, some type of aircraft is the most efficient vehicle.

3. At speeds between 50 and 150 mph, a typical railroad train is most efficient.

4. At speeds in the range of 150 to 500 mph for aircraft, the most efficient vehicle is the subsonic jet using a fixed wing.

There are many factors, other than efficiency, that enter into the process of selecting a transportation vehicle or mode. For example, it is difficult to run a ship or submarine on dry land, therefore, low speed land transportation needs are not served by ship or submarine. However, one need only look at the burgeoning profits of the barge companies to realize the correctness of the Von Karman curve with respect to the advantages of a ship for slow speed transportation needs.

Subsonic Jet

For the time period between now and 1980, the majority of passengers and air freight will move by jet-powered fixed-wing aircraft at subsonic speeds. This vehicle type has reached a high state of development, is reliable and efficient, and most of the supporting ground facilities are in existence.

The only significant change to be anticipated during the next ten years in this vehicle type is a size increase.

VTOL

VTOL is an acronym for vertical take-off and landing aircraft. A helicopter satisfies this definition, but the label is usually reserved for an aircraft using thrust devices for take-off and landing lift and a fixed wing for cruise lift. Undoubtedly some form of military VTOL will be operational within ten years. It is unlikely that commercial versions will be of significance in the same time period. Since there is a very great incentive for the military to develop VTOL, it is practically certain that this will be done. VTOL's may capture almost all of the intercity air passenger traffic under 700-mile distances by 1985–90.

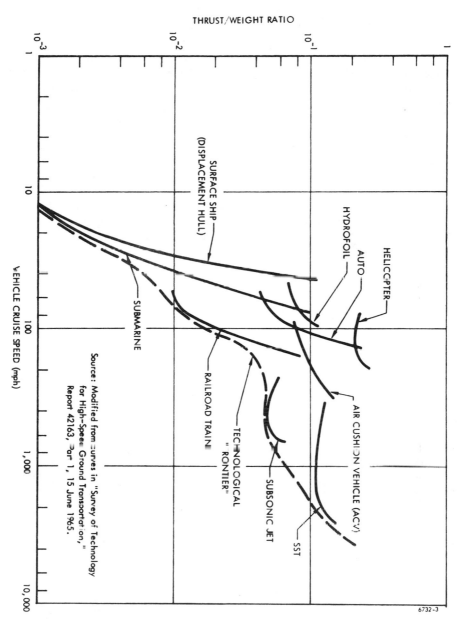

Figure 1.

Von Karman Curve (1965)

Supersonic Transport

There is no doubt as to the technical feasibility of SST aircraft. The B-70 has demonstrated that supersonic flight in large aircraft is practical. One of the major uncertainties related to supersonic flight is the allowable overpressure or "sonic boom." The actual flight capabilities of the SST depend upon how this matter is finally resolved. SST's are expected to have only a very slight effect from now to 1975.

Hypersonic Aircraft

This is a loosely defined term implying aircraft with cruise speeds above Mach 3, probably in the Mach 5 to 10 range. If a hypersonic transport (HST) can be developed, it would be more attractive than the SST (Mach 2 to 3) because the high cruise speeds could actually be utilized without on-the-ground "boom" problems because of the very high cruise altitude, 100,000 feet. At this time the HST is in a very early research and development phase.

Private Aircraft

By 1980, many new private aircraft will be jet craft. However, the VTOL may have a large influence on private flying. When this type plane becomes readily available, congestion in the air could become a severe problem requiring the institution of stringent controls over all flying.

Downtown Distribution Systems

Our current technological capabilities will permit the design of attractive, functional downtown distribution systems. Several such systems have already been demonstrated. These include the Conveyor and Disney's WEDway.

Rail Vehicles

It is difficult to do better than the coefficient of rolling friction of a steel wheel on a steel rail. At speeds below 150 mph, the flange on the steel wheel provides excellent guidance. However, at speeds above 125 to 150 mph, other forms of suspension and guidance will be required.

Air Cushion Vehicles

Air cushion vehicles (ACV) are supported on a film of air. Essentially they can be considered as flying very close to the ground. The cushion of air can vary from several thousandths of an inch to several feet. In general, high speed ACV's used for ground transportation will travel on several millimeters of air over special roadways. This type of ground transportation has many problems associated with it. No long operating systems are expected in the near future (1980). Currently available data indicate that tracked ACV's cannot be economically successful except in unusual applications requiring very high speeds and very high passenger densities.

Displacement Hull Vessels

No significant change in vehicle type is expected for water transport. The displacement-hull surface ship operating at speeds less than 25 knots will dominate ocean shipping. Ship size will increase, especially for bulk transport, but also to some extent for all types of cargo.

Hydrofoil

The only anticipated future uses for hydrofoils are specialized military missions such as antisubmarine warfare and unique short-distance commercial passenger movement such as from Santa Barbara to the Channel Islands or across Lake Michigan.

Amphibian Air Cushion Vehicles

These vehicles will have specialized applications, but are not expected to become general service vehicles. Their major advantage is their ability to operate over tidelands, swamps, marshes, and other inaccessible areas.

Submarine

The nuclear powered submarine is not currently competitive with the displacement-hull surface ship for freight or passenger service. This is due to the cost of the pressure hull required for underwater service. When nuclear propulsion becomes competitive with fossil power, probably not before 1990, the cargo submarine will be able to compete with surface ships for a few specialized cargo applications.

Propulsion Systems

Air. Basically propulsion systems for aircraft will consist of hydrocarbon burning, gas turbine engines. Various types of gas turbine engines will be used for different speed regimes. The turbofan will dominate for subsonic uses and the pure turbojet probably will be used only for supersonic flight. However, the HST will be powered by some form of ramjet, probably hydrogen or methane fueled. A nuclear powered fanjet may be developed and applied by 2000 for use in a very large subsonic aircraft.

Land. The piston engine will continue to dominate the automotive field through 1980. When gas turbines appear in land vehicles, it will be in large ones such as trucks and buses. The major disadvantage of the gas turbine is its low efficiency at low speeds. This could be overcome by combining a gas turbine with batteries as a power source for vehicles. Proper selection of the gas turbine size would permit the gas turbine to be constantly run at its optimum operating speed.

Propulsion systems for locomotives will gradually become electric. In the East the railroads will be electrified. In the West, the locomotives will be gas turbine electrics.

Sea. A major substitution of conversion devices is foreseen for marine propulsion systems. Current surface ships now use either steam turbines or diesel engines. Diesels are rapidly replacing the steam turbines because of lower fuel consumption and easier installation. Regenerative gas turbines, with equivalent power ratings but weighing one-twentieth as much as a diesel, can be built. Therefore by 1980 gas turbines will be used to power marine vessels.

Other Technologies

Developing technologies that may be of significance with respect to propulsion are linear motors, fuel cells, microwave power distribution, silicon controlled rectifiers for DC to AC inversion, and arc type, noncontact power pick-ups. It also is obvious that eventually, perhaps by 2020, transportation will be all electric.

Linear motors are an exciting concept; however, they are expensive because a great deal of motor material must be spread out along the road bed. There are other critical problems related to considerations such as tolerances and the need to keep air gaps small.

Microwave power distribution can be accomplished readily within wave guides, but over long distances wave guides become expensive. Our ability to transfer power without direct contact has not progressed rapidly. Therefore, any indirect method of transferring power is extremely inefficient.

Solid-state silicon controlled rectifiers (SCR's) have advanced a long way in a short period of time. These devices are used to control diesel-electric locomotives as well as electric fork lift trucks. This is a useful technology that makes the control of DC motors relatively simple and will have widespread utility in future transportation systems.

Miscellaneous

There is a variety of technologies that may be applied to transportation in general. These include lasers, magnetic tape coding of information, pattern recognition, electro-hydraulic rock fracturing, information display, remote sensing, automatic control, and time-sharing computers.

These new technologies may be applied with value to transportation in a wide variety of ways. For example, electro-hydraulic rock fracturing and lasers may be of value for tunneling. Magnetic tape coding of information is essential for automatic fare collection. It could also be of great value for use in preparing credit cards for transportation system users. Pattern recognition can be used for system control, for vehicle spacing, and for identification of credit card users. Remote sensors can be of great value for guidance systems and for control systems. Information display can be of inestimable value for control of transportation systems as well as for informing users of the system about the status of the system. Automatic control techniques are required for automatic individualized transit and time sharing computers will make it possible to further reduce mass transit vehicle headways without sacrificing overall control of the entire transit system.

Notes

1. John Kenneth Galbraith, *The New Industrial State* (Boston: Houghton Mifflin, 1967).
2. William A. Robson, ed., *Great Cities of the World* (New York: Macmillan, 1957).

Comments on

Feldman

COLIN BUCHANAN
Professor of Transportation
Imperial College of Science and Technology, London

Max Feldman, in his extremely interesting paper, first points to the paradoxical situation in which, in recent years, spectacular improvements have been achieved in long-distance transport while short-distance transport (especially in cities) has steadily deteriorated. In reviewing the situation and likely development in fields ranging down from international travel to city movement he casts doubts on the wisdom of spending money on the development of supersonic aircraft as well as on the suggested high-speed ground transport system in the northeast corridor. But he returns inevitably to the problems of city transport as being the most obdurate of all. By year 2020, based on present trends, the population of the U.S. will be 390 million, of whom 300 million will live in urban areas. This will represent 200 million extra urban residents, and they will be likely to desire the use of 158 million additional autos—nearly as many more autos as people. How can this situation be handled?

There is nothing in the paper with which I would disagree. Feldman is absolutely right in pointing out that long-distance transport technology has advanced spectacularly whereas short distance movement (which is the essence of urban travel) staggers into increasing difficulties. Perhaps it would be helpful if I were to try to explain *why* this has been the case. The answer in a nutshell is that advance in the long-distance field has presented comparatively easy right-of-way problems, whereas the short-distance movements typical of urban areas have presented very difficult right-of-way problems. The oceans, the skies, and the open terrain between cities have presented few distractions to the development of long distance transport systems; but the shorter movements in urban areas take place, by definition, in areas beset with solid buildings where right-of-way improvements are fiendishly difficult. Moreover, as cities have grown and taken to the automobile, the movements have been multiplied, intensified, and complicated, yet by the same token the improvement of rights-of-way has become even more difficult because buildings have become bigger and more solid.

This leads me to the main comment I wish to make on Max Feldman's paper. He stresses several times that transportation is concerned with people, with activities, with the use of land, and that it cannot be pursued in isolation from these—a very sound point. But for full understanding of the urban transport problem the argument needs to be taken a vital step further. Where do virtually all urban activities take place? The answer is in *buildings,* provided the definition of that term is enlarged to include places such as yards, depots, sports grounds, zoos, and so on. So the proposition now becomes "Transportation is concerned with buildings." Unless this is understood and accepted I do not think there can be any progress made with the urban movement problem.

Let me try to explain this further and to mention some of the implications. In the first place the broad spread of buildings coupled with the kinds and intensities of activities inside them, is what produces the movements that have to be discharged by some combination of movement systems. This is a more realistic way of expressing the matter than to say "land use begets transportation" or some such phrase. It rams home that what estate developers, industrialists and their architects *build* on their land is what matters. It is what they have already built, mindful of many matters but ignorant of the insidious accumulation of movement needs as building followed building, which is largely responsible for present difficulties.

But there is more to it than this. If you consider the journeys which building development produces you find one widespread characteristic. Many of the journeys consist of three distinct parts. First there is a "wriggle out" from a building or group of buildings; then there is a "main run"; then there is a "wriggle in" to a building or group of buildings. One can think of a truck extricating itself from a warehouse area, proceeding along a main road, then inserting itself into a group of retail stores. Now the so-called land use-transportation studies have restricted themselves entirely to the study of "main runs"—anyone familiar with the zone-to-zone techniques of these studies will appreciate this. And what has been constructed in the way of new transport facilities has been largely to assist "main run" journeys. The "wriggle journeys" have been utterly neglected. Now the importance of the wriggle journeys is that they are intimately associated with buildings—this is the sector where trucks cast around for discharge points and loading bays, where autos mill about after leaving freeways searching for parking places and waiting bays, where buses nose up to buildings to discharge their loads, and where multitudes of pedestrians move between buildings and bus stops, parking areas, and stations. These movements are not the less "transportation" just because they are short journeys, and it is around them that some of the worst problems arise. This is where the dirt, the ugliness, the noise (why does Feldman not mention noise, that most baneful byproduct of city traffic?), the stink, and the confusion lie; this is where pedestrians run for it and sometimes die for it. This is where, as I often think, urban civilization ends—in the streets.

Yet dealing with these problems is not solely a question of transportation. It is *urban design*—it is designing buildings, controlling their size and what goes on inside, and contriving the circulations and the access, all as part of one combined operation. So this is the main rider I would add to Feldman's paper: to the extent that your new Department of Transportation is involved with *urban* transport, see that it understands what cities are made of, and how they function and why. See that it grasps that cities are incredibly complex conglomerations of buildings in which people undertake a multitude of activities which in turn involve movement patterns of great complexity and intricacy around and between the buildings. Unless this is understood I fear that the obsession will continue as before with the technology of longer movements to the complete neglect of the approach-to-buildings-movements which have such powerful implications for city design. I can speak here from experience in Britain—for sixty years we have had a Ministry of Transport roughly corresponding to your new Department of Transportation, but it is only just beginning to understand that urban transportation is as integral a part of city design as the communication system of a hospital is an integral part of the hospital design.

A few further implications of this approach. In view of the amount of attention which has been paid to identifying the longer zone-to-zone movements, I think it is no bad thing to go to the other end and to consider the more intricate random movements associated with buildings. I would start myself with the pedestrian. This brings to light a curious void in Mr. Feldman's paper—he nowhere mentions walking as a form of urban transport. Yet surely walking, in a sense, is the most important form of all: walking accounts for a vast amount of movement—all the final distribution from bus stops, parking places, and stations, and a multitude of casual comings and goings, some of which (window-shopping, for example) are almost the essence of urban life. Nor is walking to be neglected as a medium for carrying goods— small in individual loads, but vast in aggregate. A city can struggle on when its mechanical transport breaks down or is strike bound, simply because people can walk. Imagine the effect if walking were to break down. Walking is important all through cities, in residential as well as downtown areas. Owing to the way we lay out residential areas we are having to resort to school buses, thereby depriving children of one of the most important journeys of life—the walk to nursery school, the child's first unaccompanied venture into the world and an invaluable step in its education. I would say to city designers and transportation experts: start by considering the needs of walkers and all the subtleties that derive therefrom, work outward from this and you will find that many other matters will fall into place, and you will not have missed the essential humanities of urban design.

Another implication, which I will mention only briefly, concerns the need for inter-professional understanding and cooperation. Unless transportation study teams contain planners and architects and sociologists who understand cities, I think there is a serious risk of faulty conclusions an abortive work. Let me pinpoint a specific risk arising out of Mr. Feldman's suggestion that the aerospace and aviation industries will increasingly turn to the urban transportation field. That is fine, their expertise is needed, but personally I would not let a single aerospace engineer loose on the problems of cities until he had been given a six-months' course about cities so that he had some idea of what he was dealing with. The risk, otherwise, is that money and effort will be expended on producing movement systems which, when put to the test, satisfy no known human desires for movement, or are inassimilable into the physical structure of cities. Recently in Britain, in an official report, there has been a serious proposition for introducing elevated gantries along many of the principal streets of London for the conveyance of special mini "city cars." I do not think this would have happened if there had been town planners and architects in the team, or someone who knew about cities.

To summarize my own comments, I congratulate Max Feldman on a far-ranging paper, a wonderful summary of many aspects. It is no fault of his that the questions of international, national, and even state transport leave me personally a little cold. The great problem for the world is cities, these extraordinary agglomerations into which, for better or for worse, the greater part of mankind seems destined to concentrate. The form and organization of cities is now coming into view as the major social problem for humanity with an infinite number of relevances to human happiness and welfare. Transportation is important to both form and organization—crucially important. But unless transportation is treated as an integral facet of the whole and unless this philosophy is reflected throughout the process—in design teams, in federal, state and city departments, in political bodies—then there is more than a risk of city design going tragically astray.

HARMER E. DAVIS
Director, Institute of Transportation and Traffic Engineering
University of California

Max Feldman has presented a comprehensive overview of transportation in relation to the business and pleasure of living; he provides a synopsis of the existing situation and a preview of the potentialities of the future. He capsulizes the major problems and issues currently confronting society, stemming from the present state-of-the-art of providing transportation, and insists that the application of evolving transport technology be increasingly directed to support an improved overall future environment for living.

After examining the interactions of transport and society on the basis of several "levels" or geographic scales of movement, ranging from global to local, he very appropriately directs major attention to urban transportation. He indicates that the most crucial problems of movement in the upcoming years are those in the urban regions.

Appropriately, also, he recognizes that mere vehicles and devices do not make or guarantee the provision of a viable transport service. How transport activities are organized and conducted, and what policies and incentives are conducive to more effective organization of transport activities may be as important as, or more important than, improvements in technology. We may deduce that many of the difficulties now apparent in the performance of our urban transportation systems could be overcome through better organization of transport activities without recourse to new exotic hardware. This is not to say, however, that new transport technology will not be useful in improving some features of our total transportation complex.

Feldman attributes the "weakness" in U.S. transportation to "our inability to look at national transportation as a system network" in order to tie all modes into "an integrated national transportation system" and states that inability or unwillingness to conduct a systems analysis has prevented moving toward the establishment of an optimum system. This diagnosis raises a number of questions, two of which I should like to explore. One has to do with systems analysis as being the key requirement for the resolution of the "transportation problem." The other has to do with an optimized, integrated national transportation system as being the appropriate objective in future transport development. These questions are interrelated.

There is a growing and increasingly widespread recognition of the importance of regarding our total complex of transportation networks, facilities, and services as a single system for purposes such as estimating the allocation of economic resources, certain general aspects of transportation planning, and some stages in designing facilities and programming services. The now frequently used term, "systems approach," serves as a useful reminder, to the policy maker, to the planner, and to the designer, of the pitfalls of too narrow a view of his problem. It emphasizes the necessity of avoiding the conflicts, inconsistencies, loss and malfunction that can result from the design and optimization of components (subsystems) without regard for their influence on the performance of the overall system of which they are a part. It is a reminder that every system is in some respects a subsystem of some larger, more comprehensive system. But what we choose as the system with which to deal depends on what we wish to do with it, or about it.

In recent years there have been systems analyses attempted, using models devised to approximate transportation systems of very large extent. To make such analyses manageable, at least within the capabilities of present-day computers, a high degree of simplification has been required, however, relative to the extremely large number of variables that are characteristic of real-life transportation systems. We do need to improve our capabilities for making such systems analyses, as an aid in better estimating the consequences of adopting one or another course of action among important transportation alternatives. But that the ability to make a sufficiently sophisticated systems analysis of the total transportaion complex is a necessary and sufficient condition to achieve an optimal integrated overall system is open to question.

Some of the difficulties in attempting to analyze and plan "transportation" as a system derive from the "facts of life" about transportation. In the first place, transportation takes place because of needs for movement; it is not an end in itself; something else comes first and is not controllable by the transportation system planner. Second, in an ongoing society, new transportation is provided as an addition to an existing complex of investments and services; some existing services may be gradually superseded but we do not start over and displace an entire transport complex with a completely new and different one.

Third, the multitude of segments of the transportation complex are related in many different ways with different segments of the socioeconomic environment they serve. There is no single, isolatable set of policies that uniquely governs the functioning of the transport complex. The policies which condition how transport develops and functions are deeply rooted in the social, political, and economic mores which guide the general course of our national life. Be that as it may, however, a consistent body of national policy which would encourage coordination of transportation planning and services could go far toward reducing the gaps and losses for our now largely nonarticulated transport activities, even without having attained a capability for large-scale systems analysis. Feldman recognizes and comments on this.

A first step in the planning of a system is the identification and selection of the system objectives. Then, after the usual intermediate steps of a formal systems analysis, an optimum plan is selected. The choice of what is optimum would be made with respect to criteria such as cost, safety, comfort, amenity, flexibility, etc. Now suppose we did proceed to plan the total national transport complex as a system, and we were able to delineate and bring into being an optimum system. It is quite likely that we would not be happy with the optimized system—for a very old and fundamental reason: an optimum transportation system would not necessarily optimize the national economy nor maximize the national welfare.

The implications of a goal of a completely integrated, total transportation system need also to be examined. One implication is that a strongly regulated society would probably be a prerequisite. Another is that the economy served by such a system would presumably be fairly static; but in a dynamic society, patterns and levels of activity, use of resources, and even values are ever changing; such basic changes are inevitably reflected in the demands upon and thus the response of the means of transport. And finally, if the controls were such as to continuously maintain such a system, the response to innovation and new transport potentials would probably be sluggish.

Now these comments are intended in no way to depreciate the value of systems analysis in dealing with transportation problems. Indeed, a scientific basis for study of transportation problems is developing through the techniques associated with systems analysis. Further, if the processes of transportation planning and design are to be improved, the capabilities for analysis of transportation systems must be greatly broadened and extended. And additionally, the concepts derived from viewing transportation in terms of systems have great value. Rather the point is that to deal with the problems associated with transportation something more is needed than an analytical methodology or a technique of planning.

It has become popular in recent years in conferences and symposia concerned with transportation and urban problems to dwell on the terrible state of urban form and growth, the massive paralytic congestion of the urban arterials, and the pernicious role of the individually owned automobile in causing both. A sort of standard set of cliches has developed for describing this now customized model of the urban "mess," and a standard solution is usually proposed in the form of superimposing a high capacity transport scheme on the congested corridors.

As is probably proper for a paper which should reflect a cross section of thinking about conditions and trends, Feldman's paper includes a sample of this standard recital of symptoms. Unlike many papers on the urban transportation problem, which just leave us with the (same) problem, his paper provides a number of helpful insights into the underlying nature of the problem and offers a number of thoughtful leads concerning directions of development that could alleviate what is seriously recognized as a major deficiency in urban life. I should like to pursue a line of thought suggested by his observations.

Let us consider some of the aspects of urban functioning as related to accessibility and needs for movement. We might observe first that the magnitudes and patterns of movement that take place, at a given point in time, in an urban region are a reflection of the social and economic activities of people as they are distributed throughout the region at that particular time. In systems terminology, the output of the transportation subsystem is conditioned by the requirements of the functioning urban complex as a physical and socioeconomic system.

On the other hand, the location of the socioeconomic activities in the urban region is a result of a composite of decisions by people, made in the past, as the result of weighing various sets of values, or costs. Among the sets of costs affecting location, sometimes in considerable degree, were the costs of movement among the various locales of activity. We can thus note that the patterns of activity are some function (involving other variables, however) of past relative accessibility.

It has long been recognized that lack of mobility, or cost of transport (in the sense of real or economic cost), places a limit on socioeconomic activity. Removal of this limit, however, does not necessarily result in new or expanded socioeconomic activity: other prime socioeconomic potentials and forces must be present. Jungle growth on the unused pavements of some highways built in undeveloped regions, or weeds growing between the ties of some overextended suburban electric railway lines of a former day, have given mute evidence that providing the means of transportation is not a unique causal factor in inducing economic growth.

Over the course of previous history the cost of movement appears to have been a strong determining factor both in the size of cities and in the arrangement of activities within them. It seems fair to conclude that until recent decades cities were severely transportation-limited as regards potential size and arrangement. Some parts of a region simply could not be used because they were not accessible, which is to say that the costs of transportation that would have been required to use them were more than the economy of the urban region could meet.

But we seem now to have entered a state of economic and technologic development in which limitations imposed by transport availability and cost have been greatly relaxed. The size of our present-day great urban complexes and the locations of socioeconomic activity within them bear witness to this as a fact.

This situation has implications of the utmost significance both for the planning of transportation systems and for decisions concerning the arrangement of the urban plant.[1] To illustrate this, consider a hypothetical end point at which transportation would be costless and instantaneous. In such a situation, there would be no premium (insofar as influenced by costs of movement) on any particular location. This would mean that decisions concerning the location of activities needed or desired for the functioning of an urban complex could be based entirely on considerations other than transportation.

We certainly have not reached this non-transport-limited condition, and probably will never do so. But compared with the conditions in all of previous history we have, one might say, edged up on it.

While the availability of transportation currently seems, to some extent, to be taken for granted, it does not mean that all locational decisions are not affected by transportation considerations. In the first place, there are in fact differences in accessibility which do still affect the locations of some kinds of activity (or inhibit the functioning of others). Second, necessary additions to the transportation system do change, for some period at least, the relative accessibility of some parts of the region. And third, with the process of continued growth of the urban regions, together with the processes of decay, rehabilitation or conversion of use in older parts of the regions, the patterns of socioeconomic activity change, both locationally and in intensity; with changes in transport demand, which increase the load on some segments of the transportation system, congestion develops as the capacity of those segments is approached. This in effect increases the cost of transportation in those segments and thus also changes relative accessibility of some key parts of the region.

Although the location of regional activity is in a number of respects much less restricted by transportation costs than formerly, the very fact of possible wider latitude in locational decisions, together with continued changes in nature and intensity of land use in parts of the region, owing to the pressures of growth, will make the demands which the transportation systems must serve more varied, more complex, and more dynamic than ever before. For the planners of transportation systems, it is placing crucial importance on the need to relate the function over time of a growing urban region to the performance of the development.

For those who have the responsibility of trying to shape and improve the urban environment during this next half-century, the implications of the mobility explosion are enormous. Transport as a longer range constraint to the arrangement of socioeconomic activities has been greatly relaxed. We can begin to think in terms of the location and spatial organization of urban functions subject to only relatively small inhibition by transport; we can begin to think in terms of design of the urban complex which permits greater emphasis on other considerations than ever before in all of history. But along with this is the consequence that the addition of new transport capacity will no longer be the crucial stimulus of urban change. Freedom from constraint does impose new responsibilities.

Note

1. I use the term urban plant to describe the collection of sites, buildings, and other structures and physical facilities and devices which house the activities of an urban region and the physical processes by means of which the urban complex functions.

Housing in the Year 2000

This paper was commissioned to define what a good home consists of, how many people really have one, and what can be done to help assure good homes for all. In this we are talking of the technology and cost of housing, what a home should be for various stages of life, and how the optimum home—under all the different circumstances—might be achieved for all within the next fifty years.

At the rate people move from house to house and at the rate technology for housing could be changed—how permanent should a house be? Freedom within a house, lack of conflict between individuals, is a major aspect of house design, not often adequately considered. How important is this, for example, to the development of a creative child? How important was it at Watts?

Further, how are the optimum mixtures of housing types to be determined? What is the optimum use of the freestanding house, the town house, garden apartment, and elevator apartment? How is that optimum achieved in each case (privacy, space, view, ceiling heights, neighbors, etc.)? What is the optimum compact house, family house, or personal house? What densities for neighborhoods should exist and at what scale? What mixture should there be of land uses?

Author: Charles Abrams, AIP, School of Architecture, Columbia University
Chairman: Bernard J. Frieden, AIP Associate Professor, Massachusetts Institute of Technology
Committee: David Barry, New York City Mission Society; Robert Gladstone, AIP, Economic Consultant; Bernard Spring, Department of Architecture, Princeton University; Roger Montgomery, Department of Architecture, Washington University; Edward P. Eichler, Kaplan Gans Associates

VIII

Charles Abrams

School of Architecture
Columbia University

Housing in the Year 2000

Prophecies usually make sad reading when the time for judging them arrives, and prophecies on what housing will be like in the year 2000 should prove no exception. The predictions of population decline that colored the economic tomes of the 1930's were nullified by the postwar baby boom and forecasts of housing needs have too often suffered similar disappointments. The human animal being what he is, there is no sure way of predicting the outcome of the battle between pills and passions or the vagaries of man's capabilities for building or destroying.

Despite its shortcomings, however, forecasting has become a respectable trade. Its practitioners include the pessimists who gamble on a downward trend and the optimists who venture on an upward one. The forecasting game is being played in housing as it has been played in the stock market and roulette.

If the forecaster takes the grim view of housing's future, he can muster ample support for the claim that man's shelter will be little different in the year 2000 from what it is today. Of all the commodities that have been touched by the industrial revolutions, the house has remained the most impervious to change. It has resisted the assembly line and the organization of a building industry capable of producing homes most of the world's people can afford. American technicians can show the less developed nations how to put up a steel mill or a dam, but even in their own country they have failed to mass-produce a cheap shelter. In the United States, a quarter of the population still lives in slums while people in the less developed nations build with their own hands as they did 5000 years ago.[1] With urban populations in Asia, Africa, and Latin America expected to rise five or six times their present numbers by the year 2000 and with building industries unprepared to meet even a small fraction of the need, it is a safe bet that slums, bustees, street-sleeping, and squatments will be the retreats of most of the world's human beings three decades hence.

Under this grim view of the future, the disparity between house cost and income will show no sign of abating even in the United States.[2] Improvements in construction will continue to be held back by land speculation, and the stubborn handicraft of the building industry. A generation ago, the United States, the most technologically advanced of nations, was "experimenting" and "demonstrating" how to lick the slum; today it still experiments and demonstrates. It has, in fact, re-signed itself to reclaiming its older housing stock which only a few years back had been consigned to the wrecking crews. If present trends are any guide to the future, the United States should have put houses on the moon long before it has given all its families decent houses in decent communities on its own soil.

The housing optimists can make an equally good case for a technological revolution in housing. They point to the new uses of plywood, steel curtain walls, plastic panels and foams as well as concrete and dry-wall construction. Though little progress was made in plumbing from ancient Rome to the nineteenth century, the Western world has now acquired the flushing apparatus to dispose of its wastes and builders have adopted the radiant heating used by the Romans in their baths. Though four walls and a roof are still much the same as they were in the Stone Age, we have discovered the elevator and learned how to pile units atop one another to conserve ground space. After continuing failures, the optimists also see the beginnings of apartment house prefabrication in Europe as well as mass on-site building and mobile housing in American suburbs, all of which they contend are sure-fire harbingers of the long overdue assembly-line homestead.

Both optimism and pessimism have their gradations, and among the optimists may be found the more exuberant optimists who anticipate discoveries far more significant than those that ushered in the revolutions in iron, steam, and electricity. As automation and nuclear power forge ahead, these and other innovations are seen as spilling off gains on the sluggish housing economy. In their estimates, the fall-out from these technological advances will bring thousands of self-contained new towns to our countrysides; modular, fully equipped rooms will be bought in department stores; sonic cleaning devices and air-filtering systems will be banishing dirt; computerized microwave ovens will automatically mix ingredients from preselected recipes that will make Julia Child the relic of a forgotten age. Everything will be "instant," as it is today in building rehabilitation and oatmeal. Kitchen equipment will produce disposable dishes of powdered plastics and electronic devices will make the housewife work-free so that after her husband leaves his three-dimensional television set for his three-hour work day, he will be whisked to his destination on an unmanned tube in a split second. A glance at the sky will reveal helicopters transporting geodesic domes to distant places where they will be tacked to the ground complete with utilities while compact sewage systems will be turning dishwater into drinkwater as pure as from a mountain spring.

From Plato's republic to our own day, the dream has been a propelling force in the march of progress and there should indeed be considerable advances in public utility and transportation techniques as well as in the production of those housing appliances which can be produced in quantity and mass-marketed through television. The latter include new variations of electric irons, toasters, percolators, and kitchen grills; more and more of the nation's rooms will probably be heated by dust-free electricity which may even power-drive a kitchen computer that will ring an alarm when the bank account is overdrawn.

The main trouble with the dream house and the dream world as with the age of gadgetry has been that, despite miracle discoveries in almost every field, technological advance in housing has never been able to bridge the gap between income and shelter cost. A low income family will own a vacuum cleaner but must live in a slum; an Alaskan Eskimo family will have a kerosene washing machine but its ten members must huddle around a tiny stove in a 7- by 10-foot hut to keep from freezing. The more an underdeveloped nation industrializes, the more intense its housing problem becomes; the greater the descent of people upon the world's cities, the tougher are the housing challenges they must face. Even in the United States, which has experienced the greatest industrial expansion of all, good new housing is still a luxury product, and despite the blessing of the assembly line, the gap between shelter cost and income persists. What hope then, in countries where annual per capita income is under $100?

Whether one be bull or bear about the future of man's shelter, one thing seems certain—there is a widening pressure upon governments to improve man's environment and provide housing where private effort defaults. Whether the country be capitalist, communist, or socialist, there is a growing commitment to meet housing need by direct operations through subsidies to entrepreneurs or by underwriting risks. In Europe and North America as well as in Japan, Singapore, and Hong Kong, the firm commitment to government-assisted housing has already been made, while in less developed countries, massive squatter invasions of urban land as well as political collapse are seen as inevitable unless these nations provide the shelter their people are demanding. In short, it is probable that the world's future housing revolution will be political rather than technological. If it is partly technological as well, the gains will be incorporated into long range government-assisted programs.

This view of political inevitability sees two divergent trends manifesting themselves in the more and the less developed countries. In the former, the commitment to better housing is taking form both in the provision of publicly assisted housing for lower income families and in the renewal of its slums. On the other hand, in most of Asia, Africa, and Latin America, where urban population is rising 400 percent higher than population as a whole, no amount of housing assistance can stay the onrush of squatterdom and slum life. With hundreds of thousands of families already sleeping in the streets or hallways, with millions seizing land in the desperate effort to get roofs over their heads, and with half the people in these continents living in housing described by the United Nations as an "affront to human dignity," it is doubtful that people in these places can ever be sheltered decently, at least by the year 2000. These countries should therefore be providing land for controlled slum formations and stop demolishing what exists. They should be currently planning not for short term urban renewal but for long term urban renewability. This means a greater concern for layouts and provision of utilities than for the standards of the houses themselves. A gradual improvement of the initially substandard houses can be expected if tenure is assured to the settlers and financing is made available for improving their houses.

Irrespective of whether they are more developed or less developed, all countries are feverishly looking to each other for the magic formula that will transform castles in the air into houses on the ground. One reason for this growing interdependency is that there appears to be a similarity of symptoms among all countries—population increase, mass migration into cities, housing shortage, a disparity between shelter cost and income, racial and class frictions, a growing competition for land, growing social problems due to housing distortion, and the universal backwardness of building techniques. This similarity in symptoms is putting a particular highlight on the policies and programs of the more industrially advanced nations who are thought to have the answers. Though many of their policies are still unproven experiments, they are nevertheless being embraced as though they were sure-fire solvents.[3]

It is the United States in particular that is being looked to for the example and many of its devices have been adopted with little or no change. Unfortunately its housing aids are little more than a mixed bag of tricks, experiments and often inconsistent devices contrived over three decades of Congressional improvisation and compromise. If the United States is to be the example of what a great democracy can achieve, it must produce something better than the promise of "a decent home and a decent environment for every American family," and the way to begin is with a statement of objectives, backed by a program to implement them. The first objective should be *a realistic land deployment program.*

Both in the more and the less developed nations, the factor that will condition man's future homes and environment will be the control and disposition of the world's urban land resources. Fortunately urban land represents only a tiny fraction of the world's surface and whatever may be the need for more foodlands, the fact is that there is but never should be a quantitative urban land shortage. (Such places as Malta, Gibraltar, and Hong Kong may be exceptions.) There will be, however, a steadily intensifying competition for the land radiating from the world's urban cores.

As more and more people move into the metropolitan regions, the competition for land will stiffen, the traffic flow slow to a halt and the general problem of getting around, finding a bit of open space, breathing good air and getting enough drinking water will move up as public concerns. The land currently harnessed into use and the services and utilities being presently placed on the land will, moreover, condition the environment a century ahead just as man's first cities continue to affect his environment today. As urbanization continues to confine people to small and compact agglomerations of land and as houses are built closer together and to greater and greater heights, they will also be more costly to demolish and it will be more difficult to displace the growing number of occupants.

What is built in 1970 will thus have an impact on what can be built in 1980 and what is built in 1980 will affect what can be built in the years 2000 and 2020. In short, urban development is a continuum, its product the archive of misjudgments and masterworks competing for influence on the shape of things to come.

Assuming continuity of present trends, the United States will have some 350 million people a generation hence. To meet their needs, we shall have to build as many structures of all kinds as we have built since our earliest immigrants first moved from their hillside dug-outs. These structures will be consuming at least a million additional metropolitan acres each year and it is this land that must somehow be brought under constructive control if decent homes and environments are to be more than promises. The land to be converted to urban use accounts for only a small fraction of the total cost of the houses and public improvements that will be placed on it—5 to 15 percent at most. The land currently in urban use represents only about 1 percent of the nation's total space and by the year 2000 should be no more than two or three times that.[4] But how the land is deployed will influence the height, cost, and types of houses and shops; how and whether man will use his feet for negotiating distance; the length of his work journey; the expenditures for roads and throughways; the proximity to friends and recreation; the future appearance of our cities and how people will be functioning in them.

Land regulation with nothing more has proven of limited value. If we are really concerned about the future of the American environment, direct acquisition of the land needed for homes, factories, and services is an imperative. The land could then be planned, the schools, water, drainage, and open spaces provided, and the improved lots for private investment subject to suitable conditions governing its future development. This procedure would be no more than an extension of the urban renewal program to vacant land—it encompasses slum prevention instead of clearance. Unlike the current version of urban renewal, it enforces no mass displacements; it would entail no lesser role for the private builder than he has under existing land development operations; only the sequence of the public and private efforts are reversed. By making the improved land available for private home building, contiguous land would be assembled and planned, waste and shrapnel development avoided, more convenient journeys to work would be assured, and substantial economies in road building would be achieved. Local autonomy would be subordinated at first but be restored thereafter, since upon completion of each development, the public land would be turned over to the existing city or county, to a newly incorporated local government, or to a federally chartered regional agency. Land would be sold for the homes of the rich and the middle class while federal low-interest programs and family subsidies would provide for the lower-paid workers as well. Proper enforcement of the expanded federal nondiscrimination order would bar exclusion because of race or color. What would be built would fulfill the concept of a regional city—a place in which people of all walks of life could work and live with comfort and dignity.

To accomplish this objective, a federal Urban Space Agency (URSA) —comparable in organization to NASA—should be chartered by Congress and funded for the purpose. It would operate through the states where possible, but have superior jurisdiction where regions cross state lines. It would be empowered to buy land to round out the development of existing neighborhoods, to acquire and release land for new neighborhoods, to acquire or finance the acquisition of land in central cities for redevelopment and to facilitate the proper planning of land for housing, commerce, industry, and recreation.[5] Its annual requirements would probably not be greater than its astronomical counterpart.

A second objective should be *to make our existing suburbs better places in which to live.* Since the suburb will be the next generation's main encampment, its proper development should be a prime national concern. Only a generation old, however, the suburban structure is already exhibiting serious fissures. One problem is that by 1980, a quarter of a billion people may be weaving in and out of our urban and suburban areas in some 90 million automobiles, making it virtually impossible to negotiate the work journey. As the years go on, we shall either have to earmark enormous sums and great swathes of precious space to road building, or replan our future neighborhoods into tall, compact centers, negotiated by foot, elevator, and mass transportation.

It is also probable that many of our people relegated to suburban formations that are simply more of the same, will have found life increasingly dull—at least some of our younger folk will. Suburban development programs however, have demonstrated little capacity for dealing with the human aspects of community life, and programs like FHA have found little room in their manuals for such commonplace things as meeting and mating, or walking and browsing, or giving people a sense of belonging, or adding something of ourselves to the prepackaged community, or expanding the opportunities for adult education, or providing escape hatches from the sameness of living. In the creation of our environments, we are becoming a nation of real-estate men warped toward mortar instead of mortals and concerned about house values more than about those human values that make life tolerable. By the year 2000, we shall therefore be paying the price of our omissions in a massive program of suburban renewal with no guarantee that the new will be any better than the old.

Many of our suburbs are already feeling increasing pressure to provide apartment sites for industries, their menial workers, and the aging. With the shift of industry to the suburbs, the movement of Negroes suburbanward in quest of jobs will bring challenges to suburbia no less serious than the central cities have had to face. Simultaneously, the existing stock of suburban houses is beginning to look so worn and seedy that it is taking on the appearance of some of our older cities but with less of their resiliency and staying power. These developments may not all be preventable, but some are.

Instead of permitting sprawl, skip-over subdivisions, and the wanton destruction of green spaces and orchards to make way for small speculative subdivisions, we can preserve what open lands or green spaces should be preserved for our future settlements while simultaneously acquiring and planning land for new downtowns with room for apartment dwellers, workers, industries, commerce and all the other services that any working urban settlement requires.

We can also merge or bring under planning controls the thousands of disparate little governments that surround the central cities and keep their regions from growing sensibly. These little governmental units have common problems in water, transport, sanitation, education, parks, air pollution and hospitals. Yet they compete with each other for industries, revenues and people as though they were no part of the main. A single hamlet in the constellation can veto an improvment affecting the whole region. Workable units must be created out of these conflicting jurisdictions so that they can function more efficiently in their own, the regional, and the national interest. The nineteenth century shibboleth of local home rule which has been sheltering these little autonomies should no longer be permitted to forestall the emergence of decent, functioning urban environments for the generations to come.

A third objective is to *make our central cities sound*. There are those who look upon the old central city as passé and who would let it die. But the urban civilization for which the United States is irrevocably destined requires these central cities to play a vital part in it. Most of the 160 million people who will be added to the nation's population by the year 2000 will be carving out niches for themselves in the burgeoning suburbs, but a sound national environment is more than simply a stockpile of houses on well-cropped lawns. Our central cities are the buttresses of our new urban civilization, the cores around which the suburban communities will be polarized. These cities will educate and shape the future recruits for the suburbs. They will provide the essential contrast to suburban life; they will be the frontiers of the young in search of new horizons, the escapes to anonymity, the refuges of the immigrant, the poor, and oppressed. They will be the main forums of civil rights and the crucibles in which our democratic faith will be getting its critical tests. If these cities will no longer be the exclusive centers of commerce, they will continue to hold an important share of it. If they will not suit the tastes of all, they may satisfy the desires of many. If the central city will no longer be the only type of environment by the year 2000, it must still be preserved as one of the options in a society of diverse environments in which to live and love, work and play.

Many of these cities however, will undergo major racial and social changes. Disorder and insecurity as well as economic considerations will not only speed white emigration to the fringes but industrial emigration as well, making more of these cities the beleaguered cores of swelling metropolitan formations. Already in 1967, the loss of the city's more affluent taxpayers has made the cost of servicing impossible to bear. A generation ago, municipalities were collecting more taxes than the national and state governments combined, but their revenues, which were 52 percent of the total as recently as 1932, had dropped to 7.3 percent by 1962. Unable to finance their requirements from taxation, the cities have resorted to borrowing, and between 1946 and 1964, when federal debt per capita actually declined, local debt per capita more than trebled. The federal government has failed to share the growing costs of education and safety, and when it has proffered new forms of aid in housing, urban renewal, or welfare, it has always required its cities to contribute a share, thereby increasing the burden of already sagging local treasuries. When the cities have tried to meet the costs of these new services (or of existing services) by raising taxes, they have simply accelerated the flight to the suburbs. We have not yet learned that the housing problem is more than houses—it is also a safe and solvent community, the existence of good schools, the proximity to the better jobs, social services, and transportation. If the Congressional goal of decent houses in decent environments for everyone is to be realized, the federal government will have to assume the consequences of the shift to an urban society with all the economic and social distortions it has brought with it.

A fourth objective is a *housing inventory in both city and suburb providing a variety of electives to every family*. Neither family composition nor housing needs are constants. They vary with the life cycle, with the health, age and changing fortunes of families and with the births and deaths of people. They change with the decisions of industry and with job locations, building costs, and incomes. They depend on mortal whims and human restlessness, on the desires for change by a people, 35 million of whom shift annually within, from, and into cities, farms, villages, suburbs, mobile parks, warm and cold climates, mountain and sea-level terrains—these people require every variety of house and environment in which to make their choices.

There are those who believe in a stabilization of human movements and they proffer scores of "self-contained" new towns of 35,000 to 50,000 people as the new design for life. The towns would be independent of the city and would have their own built-in shops and industries for their own built-in residents. The proposals would bring us stability—and sterility as well. "Perfect order" can be the prelude to tyranny. New towns should be part of the new environment, but the idea of a nation of 10,000 grooves into which our future generations will all be neatly fitted is consonant neither with a Great Society nor even with a middling one. A nation composed entirely of New Lanarks and New Harmonies would be as dull as a nation that is just one big Texas. A sprinkling of the unordered and unorganized would help keep us from becoming just that.

Between now and the year 2000, the number of people will increase in every age grouping,[6] and there will be a growing demand for housing of every variety. Most of our older and more of our younger folk would like apartments, if they were something more than the vertical caves they are today.

The economics of apartment house investment, however, dictates provision of an absolute minimum in space, height, and amenity. Yet with projects set to grow larger in the years to come, it is at least physically possible to supply the same amenities in apartment projects that resort hotels provide for their guests, i.e., swimming pools, exterior and interior playgrounds, club-rooms, etc. Since this aspect of the operation cannot always be profitably provided by the entrepreneur, it should be supplied at public expense. The concept that parks and playgrounds must always be on separate publicly owned lots or that they must always be open to the sky is obsolete. Leasing interior space to the public for these purposes or dedicating the yard space to public use are some of the possible arrangements that could make apartment living more tolerable.

A fifth objective should be to *provide variety and security in the forms of home tenure*. The generation to come will still have many among them who will not want to sink lasting roots into a given community. At least twice as many families as do today will prefer owning a mobile or demountable home, set either on its own lot or in a vertical structure. Still others will choose a furnished unit in an apartment motel from which they can check out on an hour's notice. Freedom of opportunity implies mobility to seek that opportunity and this in turn calls for an inventory of houses that can be rented, owned, leased, or held under any one of a number of other arrangements.

The 90 to 100 percent mortgage effected a major revolution in the system of mortgage finance. By reducing the stake in ownership, it simultaneously cut down the buyer's risk. It also gave the American homeowner a unilateral opportunity either to surrender possession or cash in on a price rise.

One of the main troubles with our 90 to 100 percent mortgage system, however, has been that its opportunities have been withheld from America's poorer folk. They have not only been looked upon as bad risks but the fiction has been officially created that they deserve tenancy only in a public housing project. Yet if the exodus to suburbia continues and the poorer folk are the principal candidates for central city homes, prices of houses in many central cities will drop to a level that will afford a signal opportunity for ownership by these families. A recent Philadelphia study made by the writer showed that thousands of row houses in move-in condition could be purchased at $1,500 to $5,000 per house and carried at as little as $40 to $60 a month. All that was needed was a mortgage fund to facilitate a flood of purchases.[7] Similar conditions are indicated in St. Louis and other cities in which low income families are now the only potential bidders for such houses.

The risks of such ownership could be minimized by requiring only a nominal down payment. Such a program would be far less costly than public housing. While home ownership can be no cure for poverty, it would diminish vandalism, give a stake to many families, a roof they could call their own, and perhaps even give them an opportunity to become members of the next generation's middle class.[8] Public housing should be simultaneously built for those who prefer rental, but it should never be the only type of housing available to the less privileged. The units should also be sold to the occupant when earnings permit.

Nor should home ownership any longer continue to be precarious— either for the poor or for any other group. Many a family has built up a seasoned equity only to face loss of it because the breadwinner's unemployment, illness, or death prevented the family from making a single mortgage payment. An insurance scheme to protect against such hazards is long overdue.[9]

A sixth objective should be *a national building industry capable of producing efficiently at low cost.* Home building (including home repair) is one of the nation's key industries, not only because of its dollar volume, but also because it spurs construction of schools, streets, roads, utilities, and shops. It was not a concern for the poor that first prompted federal support of housing programs but concern for the economy. And it is the same concern that is responsible for the huge commitments now being made to the federal mortgage agencies and to savings and loan associations.

The home-building industry however, is important to the nation for other reasons as well. It shapes the nation's physical environment; a fifth or more of a family's income is required to maintain every home that is sold; the taxes levied on houses are the main support of local governments; the failure to provide houses for minorities is one of the main causes of social conflict in the nation; finally, how much the home builder charges for his product determines whether the house remains a luxury product or whether it becomes available to every American family.

Despite its importance, however, the industry is small, fragmented, undercapitalized, and victimized by all sorts of obstructions. A California study in 1963 showed 85 percent of the builders with less than 9 persons on their staff.[10] A survey by the National Association of Home Builders a few years ago showed three-fifths of their members building only 25 or fewer houses a year; no more than 1.5 percent built 500 or more houses. They undertake little research, carry no land inventories for continuous operations, and make little effort to reach a mass market.

The industry will be more vital to the economy in the years to come. Assuming current trends in the rate of household formation, about 1.2 million houses will be required annually between today and the year 2000, not allowing for vacancies and the needs of the two-house family.[11] If the average durability of houses is calculated at 30 years and if we allow for the ravages of age, obsolescence, and disaster, some 10 million additional units will have to be replaced in the next decade, rising to 16.5 million units by the 1990's.[12] Based on these assumptions, we will be needing 2.4 million new housing starts by 1970, rising to 4.2 million by the century's end. By 1980, expenditure for residential construction should be $55 billion, or $32 billion more than in 1960, rising about 2⅓ times more between the years 1980 and 2000.[13]

Despite the massiveness of the nation's social and financial stake in the industry, there is little prospect of an early mutation in the nature of building entrepreneuring. Big industry continues to supply the materials that go into the house—steel, cement, wood, plumbing, glass, gypsum, etc.—but shuns the actual home-building. The trend in industry is to look for smaller profits per unit in large volume, not large profits per unit in small volume; but in supplying materials to the homebuilder, the materials industry often wants big profits as well as big volume.

A few symptoms of big-line entrepreneurial interest in house building have recently appeared. Alcoa has been unwittingly lured into some urban renewal investments; General Electric, Westinghouse and a few oil and insurance companies have given backing to some new towns entrepreneurs. U.S. Gypsum has made a well publicized start at remodelling a few tenements in Manhattan's slums. These examples are claimed to be the forerunners of a take-over by the Leviathans of capital. But a similar spurt in interest was manifested by them before (Metropolitan's Stuyvesant Town and Parkchester in New York City, the Rockefellers' Carver Houses in Harlem, New York Life's investment in Chicago). After reams of publicity that promised billions in investment, their interest petered out.

The evidence today is that Alcoa's interest is surfeited; Westinghouse, which bought out a Fort Lauderdale builder, including his 11,000 acres on which it hopes to build a new town, has still to cut its eye teeth on the building business (its executives say the investment was prompted partly by a desire to get closer to the consumer); Columbia, the new town between Baltimore and Washington, will smartly sell off land to small builders instead of mass producing and retailing its own units; Reston, Virginia, has still to demonstrate that building a new town provides bonanza profits to its oil company backer—or any profit at all.

Among the reasons for the hesitancy of big business are that land and land improvements (representing 15 to 25 percent of cost) cannot be standardized; local zoning and archaic building codes and the vested interests of their protectors frustrate the venturesome; vested labor interests will oppose introduction of new materials. We can probably expect some additional standardization, a few more Levitts, and a few joint ventures with these Levitts by those with more capital but less know-how; more mass on-site production and more mobile housing manufacture participated in or taken over by the big-timers. But more than this in the next decade or two would be a welcome surprise.

A bigger interest by the capital pools could come with a national land policy and the organization of an URSA. The release of land in large parcels could provide enough good sites to make more wholesale operations profitable, manageable, and cheaper. Zoning and other local impediments would be removed and better deals might be negotiated with unions looking for year-round employment.

A seventh objective should be to guarantee *freedom of movement by eliminating all restrictive barriers preventing people from living in areas of their choice.* An apartheid threatens the United States, and unless it acts now, it may be irreparable by the century's turn. The difference between the South African variety and our own will be that our Negroes will be confined to the cities instead of the outskirts; the threat to democratic principles will probably be no less.

If current trends continue, Negroes by the year 2000 will outnumber whites in 8 of the nation's 10 largest cities.[14] Such predictions can be nullified by labor shortages in other areas, by unanticipated breakthroughs into suburban enclaves, or by a cessation of the northward migration as the Negro, having obtained the vote, decides to stay put in the South. But Negroes are already a majority in Washington, D.C., and Newark, while their numbers range from 25 to 35 percent of the population in Philadelphia, Cleveland, Detroit, and Baltimore.

Although a nationwide division into black and white communities will firm segregation for a time in schools and public facilities, it need not be the disaster some people fear, provided the cities are given top-flight schools and services and provided the channels of opportunity and escape from the ghetto are kept free and open.

The indications, however, are that the cities will not get such schools and services and that the channels of opportunity will not be kept free and open. In the nation's most liberal era, i.e., from 1935 to 1950, exclusion of minorities from neighborhoods was not only sanctioned by federal manuals and judicial decisions, but was exhorted by officialdom; withdrawal of government mortgage assistance was threatened unless exclusion was practiced[15] and some of our most respectable national leaders wrote restrictive covenants into their title deeds.[16] The covenant was finally struck down by the courts but the public attitudes that gave them support survive.

As more and more all-white suburbs are developed, the proportion of voters with a stake in exclusion will grow and it will need only the right kind of demagogy to spur a mass descent into prejudice, bringing with it a collapse of all the gains laboriously won in the last two decades.

There are already ominous political signs that this is happening. In Berkeley, the center of California's intellectual liberalism, an anti-bias law for housing was voted down decisively in April of 1963, and soon thereafter, "Proposition 14," a constitutional amendment to bar adoption of any law that would outlaw housing discrimination was passed by the state itself (November 3, 1964). It rolled up a surprising 4.5 million votes in its favor to less than 2.4 million opposed, and the votes for the proposition exceeded those polled by President Johnson by more than 350,000.

Nor is this the aberrant exception—the signs are increasing that California only expressed what is now a going national trend in attitudes. This was indicated in 1966 when Congress decisively turned down a law to bar private housing discrimination, and though inroads have been made by Negroes into a few suburbs, the evidence is overwhelming that suburban opposition to Negro entry is firming. The Negro riots of 1967 did little to relax white fears. If in fact the right to exclude were to be made a national issue in 1972, it is by no means improbable that the housing backlash that made its initial swing in California could complete its course in metropolitan New York and the whole eastern seaboard.

To halt the spread of prejudice that is sweeping steadily through the nation's burgeoning suburbs, a mighty effort must be made to sustain the gains and maintain the moral climate that made them possible. This calls for continued leadership by the President; for an expansion of the President's Executive Order to ban exclusionary practices in housing by all mortgage lending agencies benefiting from government assistance; for continued pressure on state legislatures to enact state anti-bias laws.

Above all, it requires the sensible support not only of the Negro community, but also of churches, civic associations, and other groups to whom equal access to shelter is the indispensable link to the democratic faith.

Anti-discrimination laws, however, will not bring the millennium to America's minorities, for even if all suburban homes were opened to them, most could not afford them. The most subtle and most effective form of discrimination, in fact, has been government's failure to provide realistic subsidy programs and ample mortgage facilities to enable minorities to buy or rent homes within their means.

If private builders or the state refuse to build or the local governments persist in maintaining their exclusionary practices, the federal government must be prepared to go in and build the housing itself; only then can one of the most stubborn links to poverty and discrimination be disengaged and access to shelter be maintained as a civil right.

An eighth objective should be the *assumption of leadership by the United States in the improvement of urban settlements in the world's less developed areas.* The world in the year 2000 will be a predominantly urban world. The urban population of Africa will probably grow from 58 million in 1960, to 294 million by the year 2000; that of Asia from 559 million to 3.4 billion; and that of Latin America from 144 million to 650 million. In that world, all areas will be no more than two or three hours' distance from each other, so that no nation can remain insensitive to the problems of its ever-encroaching neighbors.

The American indifference to the world's emerging urban problems changed abruptly with the rise of Fidel Castro, after which appropriations for mortgage aid and home building swelled. But it was confined to Latin America and little money for urban development has found its way into the rest of the world from the United States, the other more advanced nations or the international aid agencies.

As masses of people keep pouring into the cities, they are seizing public and private land, threatening the rule of law. Industrialization, urbanization, and political change have all arrived precipitously in nations lacking the experience, traditions and capital with which to cope with their surging problems. Their industrial, urban, social, and political revolutions have all come at once, and are taking place in an arena in which three great ideologies are competing for preeminence—the American based on the theory of private enterprise, individual land ownership, and individual choice, the other two based on summary revolution, state hegemony, and subordination of the personal freedoms.

In this contest of ideologies, the underdeveloped countries are trying to carve out their own values while resolving the sensitive relationships between government and property, between the public and private spheres of interest and between central and local controls, all of which will determine the kind of political systems under which their people will live. It is in the urban sector, particularly in the housing sector and in the laws governing the ownership of houses and real property, that the nature of the emerging political systems will manifest itself. But by 1967 there was no evidence that the older democracies had even sensed either the dangers or the potentials for rescuing democratic norms out of the gathering chaos.

The emerging urban world is the frontier for new ideas—in the building of new communities, in the creation of a democratic land policy, in the development of savings mechanisms for home ownership, in the production of international financing schemes for urban development, in the standardization of building parts, in the provisions of land and utility projects and core housing techniques, and in the conversion of tribal relationships into cooperative tenures. What is lacking, however, is the essential international concern with urban development[17] as well as the existence of the international and local skills with which to bring sensible urban development into being. The field requires people who have a grasp of multiple disciplines—economics, housing and land policy, public administration, sociology, city planning, finance, law and legislation, transportation, architecture, building and building materials, and public relations—plus a large gift of common sense. Finding the proper candidates and training them will not be easy. The challenge is to the world's universities and to the whole field of education which has become too specialized to qualify. It cries for a new discipline, for the integration of disciplines and for the initiation of new varieties of research, for the training of the right kind of personnel and for the development of a new type of leadership and responsibility that can not only see the emerging urban world from its new, broad, and challenging perspective but which can generate progress with limited tools and resources toward making the world a safer and a better place in which to live.

A personal postscript for the year 2000. By January, 1, 2000, I shall be 98 years old, an age in which my hindsight will be better than my eyesight. I shall be watching the celebration of the second millennium of the birth of Christ, delivered in a stable during a housing shortage.

I suspect that there will still be a housing shortage in most parts of the world and that more nations, not yet ready to heed the Sermon on the Mount, will have the capacity to clear areas far more effectively than any urban renewal program.

Fortunately, the tendency of world urbanization to confine people to concentrated settlements will make all nations vulnerable to destruction and therefore more reluctant to employ their awesome prerogatives. At least this is my hope.

World urbanization will bring another blessing. One of the main forces making for war in the past has been the necessity for expansion on the part of increasing populations—war was simply one of the special manifestations of the biological struggle for existence. This manifestation spurred conquests since early times, underlay Malthusian doctrine and Hitler's more recent drive for *lebensraum*.

Yet logically, while world urbanization is no insurance against either cupidity or stupidity, it should bring with it a subsidence of some of man's compulsions to conquer and kill, for in an urban world, his drives for space will be inward and intensive rather than outward and extensive. It is not the land of a neighboring nation that is needed for urban expansion but the land within a nation's own borders. The competition for this land will be intense but it will be mostly internal, not external.

This, of course, will not dispense with the competition for the foodlands or the need for birth controls. It will, above all, not dispense with the necessity for the most intelligent planning of the urban cores and the land around them. In this respect, the present and future concentrations of people and industry should be highlighting the overriding need for rationalizing the world's urban land resources.

If the rule of law is to survive, if rebellion is to be avoided and a measure of human happiness secured for the urban society to come, it is this resource and its proper planning that should be engaging universal concern. In this sense, resolving the mysteries of the space problem on earth is, I believe, at least as important as resolving the mysteries of space in the outer regions of the universe.

Notes

1. Bernard Spring comments that our slums would be considered rather good housing by the poor urban population of Asia, Africa, and Latin America and that the two types of slums should not be lumped together. "The slum of the underdeveloped areas is much more serious than ours, . . . qualitatively quite different," he says. All slums are of course different even in our own country. But contrary to current thinking, I believe a slum should be viewed as a condition rather than simply as a deficient building. If it prevents the functioning of a decent family life, it is a slum even if physically sound. In that sense, a room in a New York City sixth floor tenement occupied by a whole family may

have worse impact on family life than a one story house in a squatter community set in a clement climate. Slums are as "qualitatively different" in Asia as they are in America but they may be more serious in their overall implications in some of the Negro areas of the United States than they might be in the squatter areas of Turkey, Venezuela, or Peru. At the same time, no comparison can be made between the average American slum and some of the slums, say in Calcutta. It is the impact on the people in the slums that should be the measure of a slum's banefulness in all cases, and qualitative comparisons give only a fragmentary picture.

2. As I point out later, there are already a number of cities in which perfectly good houses in Negro areas are purchaseable at prices well within the means of low income Negro families. A sharp drop in prices has occurred in slum areas due to the continuing exodus of white families, the low purchasing power of Negroes, the undesirability of these properties as investments, particularly since the recent rioting, and the absence of mortgage money and fire insurance in these areas. But the average Negro family could not afford a house in a good suburb where he might find a better school for his children. In short, where the bulk of good neighborhoods are located, the disparity between house cost and income persists.

3. FHA mortgage insurance has been adopted in the Philippines, parts of Latin America, Barbados, Trinidad and other places. Our mutual savings and loan prototype has spread throughout Latin America. New towns have been called one of Britain's "main exports." Zoning and building regulations as well as planning laws are being copied and enacted in one country after another without change of a comma.

4. It is also probable, as family formations grow, that the free-standing house will give way to the semi-detached, the semi-detached to the row house, and the row house to more and more multiple dwellings. This will vary between small and large cities.

5. It has been estimated that by 1985, the New York region alone will have 5 to 6 million additional people and that the region's capital requirements for transportation, communications and utilities, recreation, education, and other public and social services will be $75 billion for housing, $12 billion for private utilities, $40 billion for commercial and industrial structures. The total required capital investment will be $175 billion. Harvey S. Perloff and Henry Cohen, "Urban Research and Education in the New York Metropolitan Region," Regional Plan Association, July 31, 1963.

6. Projections by the Hudson Institute show comparative U.S. population by age as follows:

	1965	*2000*
20–24	13,023,000	26,430,000
25–34	22,374,000	44,480,000
35–44	24,462,000	41,390,000
45–54	22,067,000	35,141,000
55–64	16,973,000	22,260,000
65+	18,102,000	28,200,000

7. Charles Abrams, *Equal Opportunity in Housing* (Philadelphia Redevelopment Authority, December, 1966).

8. Indeed millions of white families are now members of the middle class because the houses they had bought in the 1940's for $5000 with a few hundred dollars' down payment are now worth $20,000 or more.

9. For an amplification of the proposal, see *The City Is the Frontier* (New York: Harper & Row, 1965), p. 262.

10. Housing in California, Appendix to Governor's Advisory Commission on Housing Problems, p. 521.

11. Plato's Utopia called for everyone having one house in the city and another in the country, and though few have been able to attain the ancient prosperity of Cicero who had six houses scattered about Rome, there is a growing number of American families to whom Plato's dream is now a reality.

12. These estimates are based on the study by the Resources for the Future, Hans H. Landsberg, *Natural Resources for U.S. Growth* (Baltimore: Johns Hopkins Press, 1964), p. 44.

13. Ibid., p. 46.

14. *U.S. News and World Report,* February 21, 1966.

15. Charles Abrams, *Forbidden Neighbors* (New York: Harper & Row, 1946), p. 227.

16. Charles Abrams, *The City Is the Frontier* (New York: Harper & Row, 1965), p. 62.

17. The report of the Delos Symposium of 1967 urged that the rich Atlantic powers should contribute annually at least 1 percent of their GNP to the urgent tasks of world development. As one of the signers, I considered this a minimum, as did others signing the report.

Comments on

Abrams

JOHN P. EBERHARD
Director, Institute for Applied Technology
National Bureau of Standards

To equate technology with gadgetry, as Charles Abrams does, is to mistake both its nature and its potential. To mistake its nature is to attempt to seek solutions to problems in spite of technology. To mistake its potential is to seek solace in what the world might have been if only man had been wiser or better. It tends to be what Marshall McLuhan has called "the rear-view mirror" approach to the future. The pity is that Professor Abrams' eloquence, which is so well demonstrated in his personal postscript, is not linked to more advanced concepts of technological potential than "computerized microwave ovens."

Technology is the sum of the *ways* in which a society provides itself with the material objects of its civilization. One of those material objects is a house, but another and much more complex object is a city. Neither the house nor the city is technology, but the *processes* which are used to bring them into existence are. Therefore, the nature of technology is inherent in the concept "process," not the concept "product." The potential for advancing the processes of housing or urban technology is very large and a cause for optimism. How well our technological potential will have been utilized, to advance the quantity of our built environment and the quality of the lives which can be lived within that environment, depends on the aspirations of our collective will. We are probably not in a position to afford guns, butter, and the moon at this point in our history.

I agree with Professor Abrams that if we are "to be the example of what a great democracy can achieve," we must first be clear on our objectives. I concur in the list of objectives he has outlined as far as they go. They seem to me, however, limited in two ways. Either they are "timeless" objectives like: "1. Having realistic land development programs . . . , 4. Providing a variety of electives . . . , 5. Providing variety and security in the forms of home tenure . . . , 7. Removing all restrictive barriers to locational choice," in which case the list needs to be extended in important ways; or they are limited in value to present concepts of cities. In these cases, they are "rear-view mirror" objectives of what we should have done, e.g., "2. Making our existing suburbs better places in which to live . . . , 3. Making our central cities sound . . . , 6. Having a building industry capable of producing low-cost housing."

There is no reason to suppose that by the year 2000 the forms of the urban environment will be capable of being described by terms like "suburb" and "central city" or that we will need "low-cost" housing.

One of our mistakes has been to assume that there is presently a technological solution to low-cost housing which we should be vigorously pursuing. We should have been conscious of this mistake when we realized that our "bag of tricks, experiments, and often inconsistent devices" were almost exclusively designed around financial innovations and land use policies. Overriding any narrower objective like low-cost housing, we have decided that our form of capitalism would maximize the opportunities for "free enterprise" and "private property." This has been one of our strengths. If it has as one of its consequences the lack of institutional and political mechanisms for inducing technological solutions which will provide low-cost housing, we should recognize it as a limitation. We might consider the alternatives available to us to provide housing to low-income families such as: (a) providing supplemental income to such families in order that they can afford to buy housing; (b) providing rent supplements to such families so that they can rent housing; and (c) publicly acquiring the land to remove this high cost item from housing programs for such families.

Many of these policies would not be popular with those who oppose the separation of benefits from the ability to earn such benefits. In any event they are, and would only need to be, short-term solutions to a *present* inability to match the output of our home-building technologies to the income levels of all of our citizens.

By the year 2000 it is likely that we will have taken two different approaches to removing this problem in this country. One is to continue to raise the income potential of all of our citizens so that none is considered to be within the boundaries of "poverty," even on a relative scale. (The problem on a worldwide basis is much different and much less likely to be solved by this means.) Another is to raise the potential of our building technologies. We know now how to shift processes from ones that are labor-intensive to ones that are capital-intensive. We have a history of two hundred years to mark the evolution of such developments. Beginning in 1760 in England the industrial revolution began replacing hand tools with power-driven machines, like the power loom and the steam engine, and by the concentration of industry in large establishments changing the size of business firms. In the early part of this century, the development by Henry Ford of mass production introduced processes based on the standardization of components manufactured by assembly line techniques and the concept of paying workers sufficient wages to make them consumers of the goods which they produced. This latter concept provided the large-scale markets necessary to warrant large-scale production. In World War II, in the Manhattan Project, we essentially invented the process of "invention." We found ways to invest large amounts of capital in "brain power" harnessed to specific objectives in ways which practically guaranteed solutions given time and funds. With the Polaris project we demonstrated an ability to link performance requirements to large programs that required manpower and capital at a scale not previously attempted. The systems approach, developed from this program, has now permeated all large-scale programs in space and defense.

The systems approach, based on computer-aided design, engineering and management techniques, and linked with well organized research and development efforts, gives us the potential for large-scale, capital-intensive programs which in the next thirty-five years will likely reshape the role of those who address themselves to designing our physical environment. The nature of this effort is embodied in the natural evolution of advancing our *processes,* but the impact on the *products* which make up our built environment from houses to cities should be enormous. By the year 2000, we will be prepared to pass on to the generation who will inherit from us the twenty-first century an adaptive, physical environment capable of responding to the highest aspirations of a great democracy—individual initiative and choice for the full life in a context of excellence.

GLENN H. BEYER

Director, Center for Housing and Environmental Studies
Cornell University

Charles Abrams has presented a sound, comprehensive, and well defined set of objectives for housing to achieve by the year 2000: (1) create a realistic land deployment program, (2) improve our existing suburbs, (3) make our central cities sound, (4) add to our housing supply in both city and suburbs so that families may have a choice of electives, (5) provide variety and security in the forms of home tenure, (6) develop a more efficient national home building industry, and (7) eliminate restrictive barriers to free choice of place of residence.

Most of these are not new goals. It is to Abrams' credit that he has restated them so succinctly. In some instances, he has suggested some intriguing new ideas for their implementation: I refer especially to his suggestion of a Federal Urban Space Agency (URSA).

This reviewer detects more pessimism than optimism in Abrams' remarks. In fact, his reasons for a lack of optimism are in many instances quite adequately documented. Among others, he cites Alcoa's surfeited interests, Westinghouse's lack of progress, and he makes some less-than-optimistic remarks concerning Columbia City and Reston. He gives the impression that cities and housing of the future are still the concern of small and perhaps non-influential groups. In the long history of housing in the United States, there is much more evidence than Abrams cites which supports and gives credence to a pessimistic point of view.

Nevertheless, within the last 7 to 10 years, a number of happenings have impressed this reviewer as auguring well for optimism concerning the Future of our Cities and our Housing. These happenings, taken together, constitute a revolution. Individuals, public agencies, and private industry, by combining their efforts, are responsible for it. Their new approach to old problems is being made in the strong belief that the means to resolve housing and urban difficulties now exist and that it is their concern to discover them and put them into effect. The most conspicuous aspect of the combined effort is its orientation to the future. This revolution has come about so rapidly—and possibly so quietly—that many planners, architects, sociologists, economists, and housing professionals have not heard of it, or if they have, they have not had time to adapt themselves to it.

The fact of the matter is that the Future of the House and the City is now the concern of many colleges and universities, influential government groups, and top executive staffs of leading American corporations. Today almost all the principal centers of higher education (Harvard, Massachusetts Institute of Technology, the University of California at Berkeley, the University of Michigan, among numerous others) are engaged in top priority, future-oriented urban research.

Today, we also have the new "look-out" organizations, whose principal business is the future. Systems Development Corporation and Rand Corporation in Santa Monica, G.E. TEMPO in Santa Barbara, Litton Industries in Culver City, McDonnell Aircraft in St. Louis, and the Hudson Institute in New York are examples.

The 1966 Woods Hole Conference, sponsored jointly by the Department of Housing and Urban Development and the White House brought together leading authorities from throughout the United States for a summer of study on science and urban development. In October, 1966, an international meeting on "Inventing the Future Environment," sponsored by the American Institute of Architects and other groups, was held at the Massachusetts Institute of Technology. In 1966, many individuals on top executive staffs of leading

American corporations attended a conference organized by the California Institute of Technology in Pasadena to discuss the next 90 years. Concern for the future, likewise, was the focus of a conference held that same year at the University of Pittsburgh, sponsored by IBM and the Carnegie Corporation of New York, for the purpose of discussing "The Impact of Technological Change upon American Values."

Because this revolution has been so recent, we cannot accurately predict its consequences for the year 2000. They could, however, be drastic. The gap between income and cost of shelter, as Abrams rightly points out, keeps us from owning not only our "dream house" but also, frequently, any house suited to our needs at any point in our lives. The reaction of the futurists to this situation would most likely be to stress that the extrinsic values of a society can change over time. The Society of the Future may well forgo the strong emotional appeal and sometimes economic advantages of home ownership in favor of the convenience and other advantages of rental housing. Higher income groups, especially, appear to be leaning toward "rental facilities like the telephone," as Buckminster Fuller predicted more than thirty years ago.[1]

But the householder of the future who wants to own his own home may find it easier than it is today to indulge and support his preference. The low-cost house is not being forgotten. Thomas Paine (G.E. Tempo) has developed some very specific proposals for "hardware" system methodologies (including items from pre-plumbed and prewired low-cost kitchen units and security systems for slum dwellings) and "software" system methodologies (including, for example, alternatives to slum-lord ownership such as cooperatives and condominiums) for the $5,000 house.

John H. Rubel of Litton Industries has proposed a new way of creating our new cities. He suggests setting up *ad hoc* projects to carry out their creation, development and administration, in much the same way that we build our bombers and our missiles and put men and machines in space. He suggests "creating a marketplace, a wholly new marketplace, one that does not now exist and never has, where private industry can come and sell the development, creation, and administration of new cities."[2] His ideas have some things in common with the idea, suggested at the Woods Hole Conference in 1966, that a Comsat Corporation be established for housing. The Housing Comsat Corporation would be a joint stock corporation in which individual dwelling ownership would be transferred to a more valuable share of neighborhood ownership.

Abrams quite properly points out the importance of land development programs, as against housing of middle-class standards, for developing countries. However, the developing countries look to the developed countries for leadership. When modern science and technology are brought to bear on urban problems in developed countries, an overflow of technique to the developing countries can be expected.

As the Department of Housing and Urban Development gains greater maturity, one of its primary roles most certainly should be to develop significant avenues for problem solving through research, experimentation, demonstration, and administrative action. It will need to develop greater long-range reliance on the scientific approach to advance housing technology in its broadest sense. This it has set out to do.

The theme of these remarks, in summary, is that something different in housing has been happening during the last 7 to 10 years—something very important and resolute. While we cannot predict the exact nature of the impact for the year 2000, we can predict that the activities of the individuals and groups mentioned, as well as others, bodes well for bringing about a betterment in our housing and our cities. There has never been a time in our history when so many individuals and groups concerned with housing and related areas were so future-oriented; much less has there been a time when so many were in such a good position to do something positive about the quality of the future.

Notes

1. This idea has been brought up to date in a paper commissioned by the Task Force on Economic Growth and Opportunity, Chamber of Commerce of the United States, prepared by the Stanford Research Institute (William K. Wittausch), to be published as a part of a Task Force report.

2. John H. Rubel, "Defining the Role of the Private Sector in Overcoming Barriers to Urban Betterment," paper delivered at symposium on "The Troubled Environment" sponsored by Action Council for Better Cities, Washington, D.C., December 10, 1966.

P. I. PRENTICE

Retired Vice President and former Publisher
TIME, Inc.

I have a question to ask, and I'm afraid it's the $64 billion question or perhaps $640 billion question. I've wanted to ask this question after each of these stimulating, hope-raising papers about what better urban planning could do to better the American way of life in tomorrow's almost completely urbanized America. I've wanted to ask this question not just of the authors who have painted this cheering word picture of life in a better-planned America; I've wanted to put this question to every planner, to every architect, to every builder, to every developer, to every government official, to every urban economist, to every educator I have met.

My question, my $64 billion question, is this: Now that city planning has made such wonderful progress in the past fifty years, now that everyone is coming to recognize that better city planning is absolutely imperative, now that you city planners have learned so many ways to make city life so much pleasanter and so much more rewarding, why, year after year, despite all the planning, all the efforts and all the dreams, why do *most of our big American cities seem to be getting so much worse instead of better?*

Why is two-thirds of the most valuable downtown land in almost every city preempted by obsolete buildings that every planner knows should have been torn down and replaced long ago?

Why in this age of vastly accelerated obsolescence, does the replacement rate on housing still average less than once in a hundred years?

Why is the heart of every big city ringed around with miles of slums left standing in what every planner would recognize should be among the choicest residential locations?

Why is the middle class fleeing en masse from the cities your planning could make so much better? Why, except for small enclaves of the rich, why are so many central cities being abandoned to the nonwhite poor?

Why is nearly half the land in our cities wasted? Why are so many millions of close-in acres needed now for planned and orderly urban expansion being held off the market, forcing developers to leapfrog further and further out and blight the countryside with premature subdivision? Why are so many cities just disintegrating in suburban sprawl instead of growing and expanding in a planned and orderly and economical way?

And this brings me to the second part of my $64 billion question:

Why is city planning in every city still so completely dependent on government action, government regulation, and/or government subsidies? Why, if better planning could make our cities so much better, is private enterprise doing so little to translate better planning into actual construction? Why on the contrary, is private enterprise obstructing and fighting and making a mess of so many plans?

If I were a city planner, if I had spent years learning how to plan cities that would be far pleasanter for people, far more economical for government, and far more efficient for business, I would be so frustrated by the mess private enterprise is making of my plans and dreams that I'd be tempted to just go jump in the river—if the river weren't so polluted.

Unless and until that $64 billion question is answered, I am afraid trying to find answers to all the other questions in planning for the future will be a waste of time. Until that question is answered and the answer applied, I am afraid too many other efforts will continue to be almost fruitless and too many cities will continue to get worse and worse.

For so big a question and so complex a problem I would be last to suggest that there can possibly be any one, any simple, any easy answer. In detail there must be almost as many different answers as there are different cities and different neighborhoods. But it has often been said that if you can restate a complicated problem simply but still correctly you will find it much easier to solve, and I think we may find it much easier to see that all these local planning problems and disappointments have at least *one* common cause if I describe how the problem has been restated by two urban experts overseas.

One of them is an Englishman, the veteran editor of the *Estates Gazette*, who restated the problem in its shortest possible form. Said he, "Planning is by its very nature a restrictive process." In other words, you can restrict property owners from doing what they ought not to do, but (unless you can pay them off with a big government subsidy) there is no way you can make them do what they ought to do if they think it will be more profitable not to spend their money to carry out your plan.

The problem was restated a little differently but to very much the same effect by Dr. Van Ettinger, director of the famous International Housing Center in Rotterdam, who has spent many years watching and studying the successes and failures of city planning on every continent. Says he, "It is impossible to make good planning effective in the face of land speculation if the landowner finds it will be more profitable for him to misuse or underuse his land instead of following your plan."

That, I believe, is one of the most basic problems, and I believe the best and perhaps the only answer to that basic problem was suggested elsewhere by Charles Abrams, when he said, "We have never coupled the taxing power with the planning power." What Abrams said in eleven words was also stated by former Senator Douglas in his report of the Joint Economic Committee of Congress: "State and local governments have failed to make use of the enormous potential inherent in the property tax for the cure of blight conditions." It was spelled out more belligerently in the report of the New York mayor's special adviser on urban renewal: "No amount of code enforcement and tenement rehabilitation can keep pace with slum formation until the profit is taken out of slums by taxation." It was echoed and expanded by Dr. Netzer's long and learned research report to the Brookings Institution: "Today's property tax discourages construction and rehabilitation. A change to location value taxation would encourage rehabilitation, increase the holding cost of underused land, and so encourage more intensive utilization." And it was put into perhaps the most succinct form by Robert Hutchins: "Today's property tax promotes almost every unsound public policy you can imagine. It encourages urban blight, urban sprawl, and land speculation. It thwarts urban rehabilitation, building investment, home improvement, and orderly development.

"The remedy is absurdly simple. Take the tax off improvements and put it on the land. The owner would then be taxed on what the community had done for him by multiplying the value of his land. He would not be punished for what he had done for the community by putting his land to good use."

This tax impact is so important that now I would like to share with you the recent advice of a number of urban experts.[1] After laying it on the line that it is absolutely essential to enlist the participation of private enterprise in the almost unbelievably costly task of rebuilding our cities not just twice as big but also twice as good—a task whose cost was estimated at *more* than $3 trillion, 500 billion, after laying it on the line that "it is just plain nonsense" to hope that any such sums for urban betterment can or will be supplied by any government, Federal, State or local, the experts suggested that, "Cities will find it a lot easier to interest private capital in urban betterment if they modify their system of property taxation to encourage new construction and better land use instead of (as now) penalizing improvements with overtaxation and subsidizing blight, slums, and sprawl by undertaxation."

So it was the almost unanimous consensus of these urban experts that today's property taxes are "almost unbelievably foolish." Specifically, they said, "If you want private enterprise to make its maximum contribution to rebuilding our cities bigger and better, it is foolish to penalize and discourage that contribution by overtaxing improvements. As all bankers can figure, but too few planners seem to realize, a 3 percent-of-true-value tax on improvements actually costs improvers almost as much as a 50 percent sales tax would cost them if they were able to finance it and pay it off on the installment plan over sixty years at 5 percent interest. And it should be obvious to everybody that, in an economy where every business decision must first be checked against its tax consequences, the equivalent of a 50 percent sales tax can be a mighty powerful and effective deterrent. No other industry's product—except hard liquor and cigarettes—is taxed as heavily as the building industry's product."

These experts also said, "If you want to get rid of slums, it is foolish to subsidize slums by assessing and taxing slum properties only half or a third as heavily as good housing with the same market value. If you want to lessen the cost of slum clearance, it is almost unbelievably foolish to inflate the price of land needed for urban renewal by undertaxation.

"If you want to speed up the replacement of obsolete buildings such as now preempt so much of the downtown land in every city, it is foolish to keep them standing and profitable by taxing not only the aging buildings, but also the land under them, less and less as the buildings get older and more and more rundown. Tract-by-tract research conducted for the Urban Land Institute, with the cooperation of the Milwaukee tax commissioner, showed that it would be profitable for private enterprise, *without any subsidy*, to tear down and replace practically all the obsolete buildings downtown if the property tax were put all on the valuable land they cover, so the tax burden on the replacement would not be many times heavier than the tax burden on the relic. Says Professor Gaffney, who conducted the research: 'Today's property-tax practice is slowing down the replacement of obsolete structures by 20 to 30 years.' "

These experts further suggested, "If you want to minimize suburban sprawl and stop blighting the countryside with premature subdivision, it is foolish to assess and tax fringe land so lightly that its owners will be under no tax pressure to release their land at a reasonable price when it is needed for orderly urban growth. Today, with the Federal Government absorbing half the local land tax as an income-tax deduction and assessors assessing idle land at not more than 20 percent instead of the theoretical 100 percent, the effective yearly tax cost of holding a $100,000 tract off the market is not the $3000 it is theoretically supposed to be, but a quite negligible $300.

"If you want to make low-density living possible closer to downtown, it is foolish to subsidize the waste of central-city land by undertaxation. The Urban Land Institute research referred to before showed that full utilization of the land close to the center would satisfy most of the demand that is now proliferating sprawl, thereby making land available for low density less than half as far out as now."

In brief, the urban experts would tell you, "There is hardly an urban development and urban planning problem today that is not aggravated by toady's practice of undertaxing land and overtaxing improvements."

And that is only half of what today's practice of undertaxing underused land does to make it harder to translate better planning into better cities. It is only half of it, because today's practice of undertaxing underused land not only gives its owners an almost free ride on the enormous community investment needed to pay for the urban infrastructure of roads, schools, water supplies, sewage systems, fire protection, etc., needed to make their land accessible and livable—an infrastructure whose cost around New York the Regional Plan Association estimates at $16,850 per added family; worse than that, today's practice of undertaxing underused land lets landowners capitalize into the price of their land everything the community has spent to make the neighborhood more livable and more desirable, so the community has to pay twice over for every improvement. First the community pays for the improvement; then it has to pay the nearby landowners for the same improvement a second time, in higher rents or higher sales prices.

Of this twice-over cost for better planning you can find a fine example in that widely publicized center of better planning, Philadelphia, where the regional urban renewal director says, "The situation is desperate." Last year the Philadelphia Redevelopment Authority had to raise its capital budget $100 million, or roughly 80 percent, because, as it euphemistically (and I'm afraid optimistically) explained, "Redevelopment has been so successful in Philadelphia that we are having to pay much higher prices for land." Less cheerfully and less euphemistically the renewal director said: "Our program is being limited by rising land prices"; and at Ed Bacon's planning agency they were still less euphemistic and called the prices they were having to pay for the land to carry out their plans, "a scandal."

No one, certainly not I and certainly not any of the urban experts would be foolish enough to suggest that today's crazy misapplication of the property tax is the only reason why the performance of better planning is lagging so far behind its promise. There are many other reasons, not least of which is the preposterous amount of official red tape in which redevelopment is all tied up. For example, I know to my sorrow as Vice President of the National Association of Homebuilders Research Foundation, it took the Washington Redevelopment Agency 67 days to write a 65-page contract for a quarter-acre redevelopment in the Northeast Washington Redevelopment area, on which the National Association of Homebuilders and the Portland Cement Association are prepared to lose $80,000 to demonstrate a better site plan and a better building method, and now I'm told it's a miracle we were able to get this quarter-acre contract cleared in six months instead of the usual two years.

Likewise neither I nor any of the experts would be foolish enough to suggest that untaxing improvements and shifting the entire burden of the property tax to the community-created and community-paid-for location value of the land is a magic formula that would overnight achieve the miracle of making better planning as effective in the future as it has been ineffective in the past.

But I will say that private enterprise is not going to put up all the billions of dollars that will be needed to carry out plans if our cities continue to penalize and discourage private investment in improvements with the equivalent of a 50 percent sales tax, and our cities are not going to get rid of slums, blight, obsolescence, and sprawl as long as they continue to subsidize slums, blight, obsolescence, and sprawl by undertaxing underused and misused land and continuing to let landowners translate into soaring prices for their land the enormous investment of both public and private money that will be needed to carry out your plans for a better urban tomorrow.

The very first and most urgent recommendation I would make to planners, therefore, would be that they line up solidly behind the tax reform needed to harness the profit motive forward instead of backward to better planning. Without such a tax reform you cannot expect or even hope that private enterprise will put up all the thousands of billions of dollars that will be needed to build and rebuild America's cities, not just twice as big, but twice as good and twice as well planned.

That reform is a lot more important to the achievement of better planned cities than pushing for a few more billions of Federal subsidy, for those subsidies will never be more than a drop in the bucket of the more than $3500 billion that rebuilding our cities will need in this generation.

Note

1. From a round table discussion held at the Washington Conference, October 5, 1967.

Manpower Needs for Planning for the Next Fifty Years

This paper was commissioned to attempt the definition of the critical skilled manpower needs for the planning and development of our future environment over the next fifty years. The term environment (an exact definition is impossible—the publications to be provided will supply the best concepts available so far) is being used in all of its physical, social, and economic meaning. Planning and development mean implementation as well as theorizing and blueprinting.

How is this subject to be approached then? It is hoped that the quantity, type, and working interrelationships of the various skills needed will be explored. These estimates need to be related as best they can (without any explicit specification of the future environment) to the public and private sectors and to the various geographic scales at which skilled persons would work.

This paper is intended to take into account the production of skilled environment planning manpower needed from: graduate schools—for professional personnel; special college courses—for those in allied professions; four-year colleges—for semiprofessional technicians; two-year colleges—for technical aides; continuing education—for professional personnel, semiprofessional technicians, and technical aides; and adult education—for lay decision makers. It cannot totally avoid handling definitions of the sort of education and training courses that are needed at the various levels and how they are to be provided. While saying this, it is well recognized that there is no general agreement on what sort of education and training is "the best." Professional judgment of a high order and a well-developed ability to analyze is called upon here. This is not work for empirical researchers. If no comprehensive statement seems feasible, that too is useful information.

If it is possible to prejudice the authors, we would urge consideration of *planning and development* as an indivisible term. Community and regional development, conservation and renewal and new town construction are ways of alluding to the great scale and new ways we will plan and develop, utilizing skilled manpower to realize the great growth ahead. Man must attempt to envision a totally new national and worldwide environment planned and built in a lifetime. At the great scales and rates of environment building predicted, yet carried out in a way sensitive to the needs of the individual, planning must be tempered by susceptibility to development and vice versa. That probably means participation by laymen of a totally new order.

Author: Jack Meltzer, AIP, Director, Center for Urban Studies, University of Chicago

Chairman: Richard May, Jr., AIP, Raymond and May Associates

Committee: John A. Parker, AIP, Chairman, Department of City and Regional Planning, University of North Carolina; Henry Cohen, Deputy Director, Human Resources Administration of New York City; Lawrence M. Orton, AIP, Commissioner, New York City Planning Commission; Alan Pritchard, National League of Cities; Seymour L. Wolfbein, Dean, School of Business Administration, Temple University; Eli Ginzberg, Conservation of Human Resources, Columbia University; Walter K. Johnson, Director, Department of Resource Development, Wisconsin; Jean Fourastie, Professor, Conservatoire National des Arts et Metiers, Paris

IX

Jack Meltzer

Director, Center for Urban Studies
University of Chicago

Manpower Needs
for Planning for the Next Fifty Years

Introduction

The process of projecting manpower needs for planning over the next fifty years necessitates a philosophical and theoretical examination of the nature of the changing role of planning in terms of the evolving character and pattern of society and government, the probable future governmental and administrative forms, the transformations within higher education, and the impact of emerging technology. While current comparative statistics on manpower supply and demand provide a useful indication of foreseeable needs, they have limited value for purposes of ascertaining threads of anticipated or certain change, and they have even less applicability for shooting a crystal-gazing snapshot of the pattern of manpower need at some moment in time fifty years hence. As a matter of fact, from this vantage point, statistics on supply and demand simply constitute another unweighted factor in the array of available material which will undoubtedly influence the nature of planning practice and, therefore, its manpower needs.

If city and regional planning maintains its present course with only modest extensions of its current jurisdictional service and disregarding profound functional alterations, it seems likely that there will be no more than 20,000 to 30,000 full-time planning positions fifty years from now (see Appendix). Although this is more than three times as many planners as now exist (assuming 7,000 practicing planners currently), the profession is small and the net increase, therefore, is modest. Moreover, even if the total demand for planners is increased to one planner for every 10,000 persons—a figure which is above current and anticipated ratios—the total demand for professional planners would be only 32,000 people. This represents an increase of only 25,000 people, plus a modest number of replacements, over a fifty year period, or an average addition of about 500 persons per year. To make a relative comparison, at least 2,300 graduate school students have earned master's degrees in foreign languages or psychology each year for several years running, and more than 40,000 educators earn master's degrees each year.[1] Thus, even when ample allowances are made for the replacement of existing planners and for mortality resulting from retirement, death, and occupational mobility, the magnitudes of the potential academic output suggest that the satisfaction of the planning demand will be a product of the profession's own capacity to retain and strengthen its relative position in terms of the ability to attract talented people to the field.

Simple Demand Projections—Summary

Although the future role and function of planning will largely determine the magnitude and character of the manpower requirements over the next fifty years and beyond, there is justification for examining the dimensions and straight line projections of current planning manpower patterns, as a prelude to a more thoughtful and hopefully more profound deliberation. Two purposes are thereby served. The first is to determine —even in gross terms—whether the manpower requirements, in fact, present a substantive and qualitative issue or a crisis in quantitative supply. Since functional changes tend to occur slowly and sometimes imperceptibly over time, the second purpose is to determine the manpower accommodations which are likely to constitute erratic adaptations of existing projected patterns.

The formidable task of dimensioning planning's manpower needs in the light of uncertain future social, economic, governmental, and technological patterns is compounded by the imperfections and inadequacies of existing data for nearly all aspects of planning and its practice.

Complete information concerning the number and the character of planning agencies or their staffs is not available. Moreover, the information that is available is more or less limited to an examination of the membership of the two major planning organizations—the American Society of Planning Officials and the American Institute of Planners. Consequently, the existing materials on the technical personnel engaged in planning activities is only a partial characterization of the total universe. More importantly, the lack of definition as to what constitutes planning tends to further limit the value of existing material and statistics. This is highlighted by the large percentage of people classified as professional planners, by both planning organizations, despite the fact that they do not have academic degrees in planning. A planning degree, therefore, constitutes an uncertain absolute, delineating criterion.

On the whole, two tendencies appear to define the planning professional's universe. One tendency is self-determinative. An agency or individual is generally assumed to be and accepted as engaged in planning if the claim is independently asserted, particularly if this assertion is accompanied by the appropriate agency or job title classification. The assertion is made binding if the agency and its principal staff join one or both of the two planning organizations.

The second tendency is to limit the planning identification by the stated or unstated assumption that planning has a pivotal concern with environment, particularly with spatial relationships, including the provision and location of land uses and facilities, and the movement among them. Health planners, welfare planners, school planners, and the like, who are on the staffs of health, welfare, school, and other agencies, are assumed to be outside the more defined planning universe, although individuals so engaged could presumably elect to be identified as planners for professional organizational purposes. These individuals, often performing tasks identical to those which they would normally perform if on the staff of their "native" professional agency, would most probably be considered planners if on the staff of a planning agency.

The need for classification to prescribe the planning universe for purposes of manpower estimation is further complicated by the existence of a number of agencies which are similarly characterized, in whole or in part, by their environmental focus and who draw on the identical group of planners to meet staff needs in varying, although substantial, degree. These activities include, but are not limited to, housing and renewal, transportation, college, university, and hospital campus development, economic development, human resources, and related activities, all of which have distinct organizational structures and an expanding urge for professional separability.

Granting the discomfort of advancing a series of premises in the face of the lack of widely accepted limits as to the universe encompassed by planning and granting the inadequacies of the statistical measurement of current, more traditionally defined planning practice, certain assumptions can be made and are essential even for a simple projection of manpower requirements.

The material which is summarized below is based on the classifications and designations used by the American Society of Planning Officials and the American Institute of Planners, as reflected and incorporated in their published and unpublished surveys and reports. Their material is augmented by a limited number of other publications and sources, such as the Municipal Manpower Commission, the U.S. Census of Municipalities, the Municipal Year Book, selected theses and dissertations, and papers and volumes by planning scholars and practitioners which are generally of a reflective rather than an exhaustive nature. Detailed elaborations underlying the simple demand and supply projections that follow are included in an appendix to this paper.

Although the surveys undertaken by both professional planning organizations are heavily weighted toward the local public planning agency and individuals classified and identified as professional planners, this factor is, in part, compensated for by the adjustments made in using their data.

Selecting the most conservative national population projections to the year 2015, among a series of alternatives provided by the U.S. Bureau of the Census, and applying a continuously upwardly adjusted percentage as constituting the increasing number of the "urban" population permit a series of alternative simple projections based on the current ratio of planners to the urban population. Since the current urban population will slightly more than double within fifty years, using the conservative census estimates, the application of the existing ratio of .56 full-time professional planners per 10,000 urban population will result in a need for over twice as many full-time professional planners by the year 2015 as now exist (an increase from approximately 7,000 to over 14,000). If the planner-urban population ratio were to increase by

.04 per decade to a ratio of .76 by 2015, the need would rise to about 20,000 full-time professional planners per 10,000 urban population; and if the ratio were increased to one planner per 10,000 people, the number would increase to 32,000 by the year 2015.

Were we, in the alternative, to project planner demand by relating probable urban population increase to agency staff expansions, and to staff needs resulting from projected new agency formations, the demand for new professional planners would be nearly identical to the above recited numbers which flow from extending population ratios alone.

Sources and Estimates of Probable Supply—Summary

When we examine current planning school enrollments and make certain assumptions with respect to future planning school enrollments, it seems likely that 35,000 planners will be produced over the next fifty years. This projection is based on the extension of current ratios of planning students to future total enrollments at four-year colleges and graduate schools, and on the assumption that only slight increases over 1965–66 ratios will occur in the percentage of persons enrolled in planning schools in the future who will graduate. Thus, even if 1966–67 planning schools expand their enrollments only enough to maintain their relative position in the academic structure, they can produce the increased numbers cited.

It might be added that the annual enrollment in planning schools awarding undergraduate degrees would have to increase by only about 100 students per year between now and the year 2015, master's degree enrollments would have to increase by only about 650 students; and Ph.D. enrollments by only about 50 students to achieve a level of 30,000 to 35,000. Assuming a ratio of one teacher to 10 students or one teacher to 20 students, between 40 and 80 new college teachers could very likely train the additional students. It would appear that over the next fifty years, planning can fill the teaching requirements from the pool of practitioners who wish to teach full- or part-time and from advanced-degree graduates. Although these teacher-student ratios are higher than currently exist,[2] new teaching techniques and the demand for student output will inevitably lower existing ratios in planning schools to ratios prevalent in other graduate schools and departments.

The number of existing graduate schools with planning programs comprises approximately 5.3 percent of the accredited universities with graduate programs in the United States.[3] The number is likely to increase over the next five decades. The opportunity clearly exists, as does its likelihood, for the increased number of students to be accommodated not only by additions to existing planning school loads but by the initiation of planning programs in schools which do not provide such training now. Even at existing average ratios of students per school, only about twenty universities would need to add planning programs to realize the estimates without any increase in the existing average current student pattern.[4] Undergraduate experience is even more dramatic.

Of equal pertinence is the outlook for providing other planning personnel. Currently, about 20 percent of all professional planning staff work is done by persons without a college degree.[5] On the assumption that technical school, junior college, and community college training would be sufficient to start work on these tasks in planning agencies, such programs would further reduce the pressure on the planning schools to meet the total manpower need. If approximately 20 percent of the demand could continue to be met by people without advanced degrees, this need could be filled by less than .5 percent of the projected junior and community college graduates with a terminal education commitment.

In addition, if the ratio between full-time professional planners and specialized professionals continues to fall, which is likely, to an assumed ratio of 1 to 5 (the current city planning staff ratio is 1 to 10), the need would still represent an extremely small percentage of specialized professionals graduating in fields related to planning (.4 percent of those graduating with a B.A. degree, 2 percent of those graduating with a master's degree).

A Possible Challenge

Despite these recitations, existing demand, reflected in numbers of unfilled positions reported annually (see Appendix), constitutes a possible and troubling contradiction in the material heretofore discussed.

There appears to be a series of explanations for this seeming contradiction (inadequate data precludes more definitive assessments). The vacancy rates may constitute new positions not yet filled, turnover resulting from income or political dissatisfactions, and velocity of job change among a mobile and restless profession. No material is available on job vacancies in other professions to ascertain its relative significance, which would help establish whether the vacancy ratio is peculiar to planning or a universal phenomenon.

Another possible explanation is that the vacancies represent a sudden burst of demand (reflecting the heightened status of planning) to which the planning schools are only belatedly adjusting. If this is the case, demand is likely to level off into a more normal relationship between demand and academic supply. This is suggested by the table on vacancies (found in the Appendix) in which total positions increased at about twice the rate in the years shown as did vacancy rates.

It is also possible that planning graduates and related professionals are being attracted to non-planning agencies at a rate which could cause concern for planning. The plausibility of this explanation is reinforced by the pattern of federal expenditures in a variety of fields requiring planning talent, many of which were earlier recited (housing, urban renewal, natural resources, highways and transportation, economic development, and the like) and by the probability that young people are most likely to be attracted to "where the action is."

Finally, the vacancies may not reflect an inadequate supply quantitatively, but rather qualitatively, in which new and rapidly developing skills are being demanded that are not possessed by conventional planning school graduates. The assumption is that the training establishments are and will fashion their curricula to the needs of the planning marketplace. The current universal absorption of planning schools in a process of self-evaluation suggests that appropriate adaptations are now in fact being generated.

Perhaps more pertinent to the question of manpower needs in planning over the next half century are (1) the type of training necessary for planning in the twenty-first century in light of the changing role of planning, possible rationalization of government, the emerging technology, and new decision-making instruments; and (2) the changes in planning education implied by challenges to current planning practice.

Some Demand and Supply Observations

The demand and supply data heretofore discussed is an essential element in any manpower exploration. In spite of the lack of adequate and conclusive statistics with respect to the planning professional, the public and private employment channels, and the educational institutions which prepare professionals, some sense of the demand and supply scale can be derived. More importantly, the data will hopefully shatter a series of myths which obscure the need for more critical attention to the character of the planning agenda.

These myths have tended to create an attitude in which professional planners derive smug satisfaction—perhaps even a comfort—from reciting statistics on the unfilled demand for planners, the growth of the planning organizations, or the scarcity of trained planners being produced by the existing planning schools. These recitals apparently reinforce the planner's sense of status and being needed.

Narrative elaborations on the urbanization of the nation and the problems associated with it have provided the planner with assurance of his continued well-being by creating a sense of euphoria as to societal dependence on his services. The steady stream of research output and reflective essays on governmental structure and administrative reorganization, although frequently contemplating and occasionally requiring professional accommodation, is rationalized as a byproduct of the profession's increasing importance.

More unsettling to the planner have been social confrontations challenging long-held professional beliefs about the significance of environment, and gnawing uncertainties which introspectively emerge about the planning profession's capability to deal with universal social issues and complex technical questions with profound political and economic implications.

The relative balance among the supply and demand data presented is consistent with the research conclusions of manpower specialists who are persuaded that the "expanded number of college graduates anticipated in the next decade will be sufficient to maintain the rise in the educational level of each occupation, to replace workers leaving the labor force, and, among women, to provide a modest surplus for further accelerating the rising educational levels of the white collar occupations."[6] Furthermore, the President's Report on Manpower (1966) and similar studies indicate that, for the period from 1965 to 1970, the number of people who will graduate from college will be "about in balance with the estimated requirements for additions and replacements of graduates during the five year period" and that, for the period from 1970 to 1975, the number of male graduates will exceed projected requirements.[7]

The manpower challenge clearly, therefore, is not a problem in "numbers matching" or statistical quantification, but is directly related to the character and role of planning, societal need, and the academic capacity to prepare the professional planner. The issue, in sum, is one of professional preparation, competence, and function. The issue is not the shortage of planners.

The Impact of Future Change on Manpower Needs

The above material assumes both an even national distribution of the urban population and the retention generally of existing governmental forms. Although the precise number of urban agglomerations are variously estimated, it appears likely that America's urban population will be concentrated in a limited number of areas over the next fifty years, even though we may see the development, on an experimental basis, of a selected number of new cities in currently underdeveloped parts of the country for the purpose of redistributing a portion of the urban population. One study[8] advances the proposition that four major urban region zones (each encompassing subregions) in the United States—the Atlantic Seaboard, the Lower Great Lakes, California, and Florida—will contain 60 percent of the nation's population by the year 2000; and that, in addition, thirteen outlying urban regions and six free-standing metropolitan areas with populations of one million or more each will exist in the year 2000, approximating 17 percent of the nation's population. Consequently, 77 percent of the country's total population will probably reside in these urban goliaths which will comprise only about 11 percent of the nation's land area.[9] Such a pattern will have obvious effects on the pattern of transportation, communication, resource management, and recreation.

When these events are linked with the probable accompanying changes in existing governmental forms and the new forms which will inevitably emerge, certain manpower implications are identifiable.[10] Despite new governmental forms, consolidations, and probable reductions in the number of local governmental jurisdictions, however, the urge to intensify and extend voluntary and semi-official instrumentalities which attract more citizen participation, involvement, and influence on the decision-making process will expand rather than diminish the demand for planning professionals. The urban concentrations, the associated technical, economic and social problems, and the governmental forms thereby demanded will result in a refashioned and newly created tier of public responses that will provide the setting for the planning professional. Although the dominant or actual patterns of governmental levels in the year 2015 are uncertain, the following administrative and governmental jurisdictions will probably exist: (1) neighborhood or small town jurisdictions (with a voluntary or semi-official status); (2) major or central cities; (3) consolidated counties or metropolitan areas; (4) subregions, regions, or interstate arrangements (with the accompanying intensification of the role of the individual state); and (5) the nation.

The increases in population, the probable distribution of that population, the attendent problems and their increasingly complicated interrelationships, and the interdependency of their possible and available solution will profoundly affect the planning function and its organizational location and role in government. It is likely that the most significant changes in planning will occur in this connection, with simultaneous change in the academic structure and content, rather than in overwhelming challenges to spiraling manpower demands.

The principal intent of this paper is to point out that planning is synonymous with the process of change. Therefore, planning's reliance on rigid institutional forms or instruments (such as zoning, subdivisions, and the like) and concentration on specific subject areas (such as land use, spatial relationships, or transportation) comprise self-perpetuating seeds of the profession's own destruction, or, at the least, the relegation of the profession to highly specialized functional performance. On the other hand, the capacity of planning to constitute the profession which facilitates societal adaptation and accommodation in the face of probable major changes in life style born of new technology assumes that the planner is (or will be) equipped with the skills critical to comprehending the process of change and possessing the capacity to digest, integrate, and incorporate those elements which influence growth into manageable and achievable plans and programs.

From this vantage point, the future is not simply a modestly adjusted extension or straightforward projection of the past. Although the future's dimension may belie precise quantification and preclude time scaling by decennial periods, certain probable events will clearly intervene which will profoundly affect the character, role, and function of planning by the year 2015 in discernible ways. These events will sharply and perceptibly vary the present planning patterns.

A series of changes in the nature of the planning function is already evident, and the tendency toward change will accelerate sharply. The four most significant future functional adaptations are referred to briefly below:

1. The transformation of planning from an activity dominated by and absorbed with space utilization and with the channels of communication among space users to an activity carried on by professional environmentalists, who, over time, will combine indivisible social and economic realities and goals with the occasion to use space and allocate resources as reciprocal and unified acts in a solitary process. This phenomenon is dramatized by the evolving history of urban development, which began as an instrument of physical change in which the provision of community facilities and social institutions comprised detached opportunities and constituted little more than making available resources whose incorpora-

tion depended on the acquiescence of the sponsoring private or public agency. This pattern was sharply altered in the large neighborhood and conservation urban development projects in which the facilities and institutions, while still viewed as separable and distinct quantities, were acknowledged as being interdependent. Indeed, interdependence was required and frequently demanded as an essential element in a project's ultimate success.

The new Model Cities program, while applying to the disadvantaged areas, will have more universal effects. This program—or a successor, if the process of political accommodation results in the need for a sequence of digestible mouthfuls—will reinforce the current of change by weaving a fabric in which the threads of social and economic dynamics and purpose are interwoven with the physical instruments of change in a total planning process, in which physical planning, social planning, and economic planning will no longer have isolated identities. Illustrations can be drawn from the relationship among air and water pollution, recreation, housing and economic development, etc.

2. The increasing reliance of planning on methodological skills, techniques, and processes in lieu of its conventional reliance on universally applied environmental and public health spatial models. These interdependencies will accelerate planning's transformation into society's professional instrument for comprehending and programing the urban complex holistically, without sacrificing the identity of the constituent subsystems. Viewing the urban complex systematically and as a methodological challenge is discussed in detail and persuasively by John Eberhard (among others) in "Technology for the City" (*Science and Technology*, September, 1966). While not claimed by Eberhard, the methodological and systematic role is likely to shape the planning function and differentiate the future role of planning.

Accompanying and accelerating this transformation is likely to be the problem reorientation of the planning practice. Increasingly, planning will be charged with responsibility for resolving complicated confrontations and will seek to systematically recommend diverse public and private activities (in housing, employment, education, and all other fields) in various combinations as constituting available tools of intervention. These changes will thereby tend to diminish the current dominant and competing role of each of the separable, cited activities. The existing pattern, which emphasizes a community's historical construction and fashions public and private programs in terms of the physical, social, and economic shortcomings that characterize an area and its population will be replaced by an approach oriented toward those external obstructions, interferences, and institutional practices which limit choice and aspiration. Thus the prevalent approach, which assumes that the correction of either environmental or personal deficiencies (or the imposition of predetermined standards of performance and excellence) constitute the profession's principal thrust, will be replaced by a process which deals systematically with the channels of resource allocation and with the trade-offs among the compensatory benefits and liabilities associated with separately identified problems and solutions, and combinations among them.

3. There is growing recognition of the integrative and highly specialized character of planning's role in government. Evidence is already observable in the assignment to the planning agency of programmatic responsibility for relating the multiple and diverse actions affecting the environmental construction flowing from public urban development activity. The limited coordinating responsibility will perforce expand laterally (in the face of the expanding public commitment) and will be paralleled by a growing responsibility for, and charge to, integrate the range of programmatic resources through a systematic process of planning, as a prelude to the activation of constituent action elements. Aside from the needed methodological skills and the new interdisciplinary content which the planner will need in his academic preparation, the coordinating and integrating capacity may require attracting a different order of student to the planning profession.

Coordination and program integration suggest a need for distinctive human qualities, along with the acquisition of transferable skills. The failure of planners generally to either inherently possess, or to have acquired such capacity may explain why an increasing number of executives in command of planning or related agencies come from other professional ranks—most notably law. The future planning agency will absorb highly skilled and specialized professionals trained in a number of applicable fields, e.g., systems analysis, natural resources, communications, transport, and other fields, who are distinguished (a) by extensive training and experience and (b) by a capacity to comprehend, relate, and integrate the impact of their particular sphere to the total system and its subsystems.

4. There is an emerging view of planning as a critical ingredient in the enhancement of the executive capacity. This suggests a horizontal (comprehensive) role for planning, related to the executive role and

encompassing the entire spectrum of activities which shape and influence the change and growth directions of any given political jurisdiction.

This anticipated pattern would replace the traditional role of city and urban planning, which has been largely vertical in organizational placement, generally tied to space utilization, and coordinate with other vertical activities (like education, social welfare, health). Each of these vertical activities influences growth directions at least as significantly as the designated planning agency itself. Consequently, the planning function is fractured by the existence of multiple, diverse, unrelated, and frequently uncoordinated planning agencies. Once again, evidence of anticipated future changes is beginning to be observed, in organization, through the creation of departments of development and planning and in programs, through such new activities as the Model Cities program, which in conception is dependent on the highest order of coordination and program integration.

The entire array of factors which have been suggested as shaping the future character and function of planning (and therefore the emerging manpower need) will elicit sharp academic adaptations. It is likely that no one academic form will predominate, nor, probably, will any single form meet the radically altered need. Variations in academic form and content are likely to be the only desirable recourse for accommodating the diverse requirements and testing possible academic constructions. Thus, highly specialized undergraduate programs with a subsequent overlay of more general graduate training will provide an alternative course to specialized graduate training following general undergraduate preparation. Future planners are likely to be produced not only by traditional planning schools but also by urban and regional centers and institutes, which are variously associated with ecology, environmental health, regional science, urban studies, and the like. Furthermore, the current ratios in planning agencies, which weigh heavily toward those trained in planning schools as against those professionals without planning degrees, are likely to undergo sharp equalizing adjustment by the significant addition of people drawn from the fields of social science, social welfare, health, education, and natural resources, and by people with regional science and systems analysis backgrounds. Many of the activities traditionally associated with city planning, particularly those nut-and-bolt functions generally related to such matters as zoning administration, subdivision review, or traffic and circulation, will probably be performed by professionals and semi-professionals generally trained in technical institutes, junior and community colleges, mass-oriented universities, and the growing number of continuing education and extension programs.

The impact of the ongoing "technological revolution," which will massively alter our patterns of existence and profoundly affect the character of manpower needs in planning, is the most difficult area to assess. There are two levels of inevitable impact, technological influences on the mechanical aspects of planning and technological influences on society's life style.

The former influences include the use of the computer in data processing, graphics, traffic generation, economic forecasting, capital improvement budgeting and similar advances which will result in a shift in the job categorization of the manpower needed and in the academic preparation and type of personnel required in the performance of traditional planning functions.

Of more sweeping significance are the other, more profound technological changes. It is well within reasonable expectation that technology will alter societal patterns and life styles and reorder the structure and pattern of problems in a way that cannot be anticipated except by reasonable fantasy. A series of illustrations may dramatize the character of the future technological revolution. The impending capacity to utilize the manifold opportunities in communication might well alter the nature of the educational system and diminish or even eliminate the need for school structures. The pattern of commercial, office, and banking communication may be sharply reduced by substituting intricate communication systems to transmit visually catalogues of goods between points. This in turn could seriously affect the pattern of transport, which in its own right lends itself to significant technological change. The use of atomic power for energy and heating and the laser beam for sewage disposal may eliminate the need for conventional power plants, chimneys and power stacks, and sanitary sewers.

Together, these changes would remove many of the existing constraints in land use development, such as structural location, lot size, building layout, and right-of-way alignments, and it could well revolutionize economic locational theory and other pivotal conceptions in social science. Similarly, it may be possible to create vertical cities (assuming social and political sanction), which would markedly alter communication and transport patterns and create accompanying opportunities for new methods of material and product distribution. These changes would result in radical shifts in marketing and plant locational practices. Furthermore, climatological and pollution control, and a variety of other consequences, would flow from the experimental, and ultimately selective use of geodesic domes. The possible emergence of megastructures which would incorporate all major daily functions within a single building or complex would radically refashion social patterns and land usage and, in the process, require a massive reordering of traditional professional performance, e.g., the emergence of a socio-architect, or other new, and as yet unknown, professionals.

In contrast to the latter pattern of increasing densification, an alternative redistribution of population would have similar profound implications for conventional professional practice forms and associated academic training requirements.

It is contended here that executive capacity will be reinforced by the transformation of planning into an instrument which is (1) oriented toward methodology and systems, (2) geared to problem confrontation and resolution, (3) located horizontally in the governmental structure, and (4) responsible for preparing plans and programs that affect and shape the significant elements of change and growth. This transformation will comprise the most effective means available to society to absorb, digest, and adapt to technological change over time and to the resulting associated problem combinations. The number of people involved are at a scale well within the society's and the planning profession's statistical capacity to provide. The more significant challenge is to planning's capacity to adapt its functional performance, supported by a refashioned academic form and content, as part of a process of continuous accommodation to the needs of government and its citizens, along with the dictates of technological change, at critical stages in time.

The anticipated scale of governmental activity and technological change clearly constitutes a challenge to the planning function and its performance. However, much more is at stake than professional identity or integrity.

The increasing growth of government (one in four of the new jobs created since World War II has been in government); the urbanization of the nation (a study at the Center for Urban Studies at the University of Chicago, conducted by Professor Brian J. L. Berry for the Social Science Research Council, indicates that 95.85 percent of the nation's population lives within commuting distance of central cities); the administrative and governmental jurisdictional formations existing or likely to emerge; and the mechanization and professionalization of nearly all activities will, among other things, tend to increase the alienation felt by the governed toward the governing and will compound or paralyze executive capacity.

The challenge, therefore, is not only to planning, but to democracy itself: to find the means to absorb and cope with the massive and inevitable impacts, as part of a pattern which is more, rather than less, responsive and sensitive to the needs of an increasingly affluent and aspiring population.

The new and emerging directions contemplated here are viewed not as mechanistic devices matching corresponding technological and scientific innovations, but as focusing on the accelerating need to reinforce and enhance executive capacity in their wake. It grows increasingly clear that there is a need to create executive capability at appropriate geographic scales, because it is the only effective means of achieving social purposes. Even today, the dilemma is not a lack of professional and technological capacity, but a lack of capacity (1) to isolate and define goals which reflect interaction between citizens and government and (2) to develop integrated plans and programs which allocate resources and activate program instruments in a fashion which will assure achievement of these goals. Current frustrations are largely a product of governmental fragmentation, in which programs are viewed as separable and in which social, economic, and environmental activities are at best superficially coordinated. The result is that the executive—ergo the citizenry—is unable to assess alternative combinations of programs and activities and attendant resource allocations against consistently applied goals; or to evaluate the effectiveness of diverse combinations of programs and resources.

Charles Merriam has said that free enterprise (and I would substitute democracy) has more to fear from lack of planning than from its effective and appropriate use. Planning can provide the means by which the public, and ultimately the executive, can assure its supremacy in the decision-making process in the face of massive technological change, increasing professionalization and mechanization, the expanding distance between the individual and enlarged governmental jurisdictions, the overwhelming increases in the size of the population, and heightened personal and family expectation and aspiration.

Through these societal transformations planning can bring about its greatest achievements, if it will discard traditional constraints and fulfill its promise as professional facilitator of change and growth. Failing this, other professional adaptations will emerge. The need to find and fashion a "professional" instrument to harness programmatic opportunities and resources will sharpen the demand for improved management and programmatic capacity.

This is the only foreseeable means available to the public to contain and control the vast network of activities, enterprises, professional establishments, and administrations which otherwise threatens to determine and dominate governmental purpose and widen the rift between social goals on the one hand and the bureaucratic tendency toward aimless self-perpetuation on the other hand. Currently, legislatures are relegated to the status of dignified advisory boards, and executives to the status of conveners, coordinators, or chairmen of the board, as a result of their dependence on and domination by bureaucratic and professional establishments. In this context, planning would constitute the means by which political determinism could be restored.

New dilemmas and new issues, many of which cannot now be foreseen, will emerge from and be caused by the future patterns herein discussed. These byproducts will demand fresh societal, governmental, and professional adaptations. But planning, if it is to fulfill its destiny as the profession born of society's need to influence and manage change, must come to view adaptation and accommodation as the fuel which generates its continued existence.

Appendix
Supply and Demand Projections

Simple Demand Projects

In 1966 the American Society of Planning Officials mailed 821 questionnaires to city, county, and combined city-county, metropolitan, or regional agencies, all of which had populations of 10,000 or more. Included were a limited number of agencies in Canada. Since the list is acknowledged to be incomplete with respect to local planning agencies and other appropriate local planning entities which employ planners as defined by AIP and ASPO, a base figure of 1,000 (rather than 821) is used as the appropriate starting point from which projections of planning agencies are calculated. Similarly, since each of the planning groups reports between 3,500 and 4,500 professional positions—both groups report many of the same positions—an arbitrary figure of 7,000 professional planners, or about twice as many as the reported number of planning positions, are assumed to be currently engaged in planning practice or in related tasks involving professional and technical planning capacities. This figure is doubtlessly a close approximation to the existing number of practitioners as defined by the respective organizations.[11]

Thus, while the tabular and statistical material which follows reflects the actual number of people and agencies surveyed by the two organizations, the distributions and relationships thereby obtained have been assumed to extend to the expanded universe above recited. A degree of safety is provided by the statistical extension, in that a number of related planning agencies—including those at the federal level and a number of planning professionals engaged by special functional units—will be absorbed in the estimates. Unavoidable distortions, however, may be reflected in the assumed equivalent distributions among the extended universe.

An estimate of manpower requirements for planning, even on a tentative basis, requires at least a minimal recitation of certain national phenomena against which to juxtapose the present experience patterns. As noted earlier, more profound societal directions may intervene and substantially alter the future course of planning and the accompanying character of the manpower need. The most recent U.S. Bureau of the Census projections predict that between 482 and 324 million people will live in the United States in the year 2015, barring a disastrous world war, a widespread epidemic, a major economic depression, or other catastrophe. Demographers currently tend to advance the lower projection because of recent and anticipated declines in fertility rates.[12] If we accept the more conservative estimates, the following population projection will result:

Table 1

Decennial Estimates of Urban Population, 1960–2015

U.S. Census Projections (in millions rounded) (low fertility rates)		*Estimated Urban Population (%)*	*Estimated Urban Population (in millions rounded)*
1960	180	70	125
1970	200	75	150
1980	230	75	170
1990	250	75	190
2000	280	80	225
2015	320	80	255

Source: Population projections taken from U.S. Department of Commerce, Bureau of the Census, *Current Population Reports: Population Estimates*, Series P-25, No. 359, February 20, 1967.

The materials that follow are based on these projected data. Although there is considerable evidence which contends that the country's urban population will rise to 80 percent by 1980, a more conservative base point has been taken using the 1960 census definition of urban.

Table 2 summarizes planning staffs by jurisdiction and population group and provides a frame of reference against which urban population forecasts can be evaluated and tested.

Table 2

Summary of Planning Staff by Jurisdictions and Population Group, 1966

Jurisdiction and Population Group	Number of Agencies Reporting	Full-Time Professional Planners		Mean Number of Employees (based on agencies reporting employees in 1966)					
		Range	Median	Professional Planners	Specialized Planners	Drafting	Clerical	Other	Total Staff
Cities	389								
1,000,000 and over	6	14–89	39	46.8	17.0	15.8	26.7	3.5	109.8
500,000–999,999	20	9–38	16	19.4	3.5	7.8	9.5	2.7	42.9
250,000–499,999	21	6–24	12	12.3	.7	4.2	6.1	2.5	25.9
100,000–249,999	57	2–19	6	6.7	.3	2.2	2.7	.7	12.6
50,000– 99,999	133	1–10	3	3.2	.2	.9	1.5	.4	6.2
25,000– 49,999	98	1–6	2	2.1	.1	.5	1.1	.2	4.0
10,000– 24,999	54	1–3	1	1.5	a	.3	.9	.2	2.9
Counties	123								
1,000,000 and over	7	4–89	14	25.1	1.1	5.4	9.7	2.4	43.9
500,000–999,999	16	4–25	12	12.8	1.2	4.6	5.1	2.4	26.0
250,000–499,999	23	3–24	7	8.7	.4	3.0	4.2	1.3	17.6
100,000–249,999	42	1–15	4	4.8	.3	1.6	2.2	1.1	10.1
50,000– 99,999	25	1–6	2	2.3	.1	.7	1.3	.6	5.0
25,000– 49,999	10	1–6	2	2.7	a	1.1	1.5	.1	5.4
Combined (city-county, metropolitan, and region)	96								
1,000,000 and over	9	10–62	19	22.1	3.8	7.3	13.1	8.2	54.6
500,000–999,999	13	2–36	9	12.0	2.8	5.9	6.0	6.5	33.2
250,000–499,999	20	2–17	8.5	8.7	1.6	4.7	4.1	2.1	21.1
100,000–249,999	24	1–8	3	3.9	.7	1.8	1.9	.4	8.8
50,000– 99,999	15	1–11	3	2.9	.2	.7	1.5	.1	5.4
25,000– 49,999	11	1–4	2	1.9	.1	.5	.8	.2	3.5
10,000– 24,999	4	1	1	1.0	a	.3	.8	a	2.0

a. Less than 0.1.
Source: Leopold A. Goldschmidt, "Expenditures, Staff, and Salaries of Local Public Agencies," *ASPO Planning Advisory Service*, Report No. 208, March, 1966, p. 28, Table 4.

Reconstructing the basic data included in the 1966 ASPO report which underlies the Table 2 summary, results in a distribution of full-time professional planners and specialized professionals among local planning agencies, in jurisdictions over 10,000 in population, as follows:

Table 3

Full-time Professional Planners and Specialized Professionals, 1966

	1 million or more population group	250,000 to 899,999 population group	50,000 to 249,000 population group	10,000 to 49,999 population group	Total
Cities					
Full-time professional planners	291	570	734	220	1815
Specialized professionals	99	44	28	15	186
Counties					
Full-time professional planners	209	428	274	10	921
Specialized professionals	4	23	14	3	44
Combined (city-county, metropolitan, and region)					
Full-time professional planners	139	331	152	14	636
Specialized professionals	64	51	15	4	134
Total: full-time					
Professional	639	1329	1160	244	3372
Specialized professional	167	118	57	22	364

Source: Leopold A. Goldschmidt, "Expenditures, Staff, and Salaries of Local Public Agencies," *ASPO Planning Advisory Service*, Report No. 208, March, 1966; adapted from various tables.

There is a series of simple methods for calculating the increased demand for full-time professional planners, without reference to more profound changes in professional practice which would reflect major alterations in governmental forms, technology, or other basic factors which influence planning.

If we assume that the number of full-time professional planners is 7,000 and apply this figure against the current urban population, we obtain a ratio of .56 full-time professional planners per 10,000 urban population.[13] Although the method is crude for a number of reasons—including the fact that many planners included in the calculation are employed by non-urban local planning agencies and that there is great disparity in staff size among local agencies within and between various population groupings, it provides a useful rule of thumb. If this ratio is mechanically applied to the urban populations at each decade over the next fifty years, approximately 7,280 full-time professional planners would be required in addition to the current estimated supply of 7,000 by the year 2015.

Table 4

Estimated Number of Full-time Planners Required to Serve the Urban Population 1960–2015, based on .56 ratio, per 10,000 Urban Population

	Urban Population (in millions rounded)	1960+ Ratio of .56 Full-time Planners per 10,000 Urban Population	Full-time Planners (estimated)	Cumulative Number of Full-time Planners (estimated)
1960+	125	.56	7,000	7000 (base point—existing supply)
1970	150	.56	8,400	+1400 over base point
1980	170	.56	9,520	+1120 over 1970
1990	190	.56	10,640	+1120 over 1980
2000	225	.56	12,600	+1960 over 1990
2015	255	.56	14,280	+1980 over 2000

These data would suggest that a doubling of urban population within the next fifty years will also result in slightly more than doubling the number of full-time professional planners required during the same time span.

An increase in the ratio of full-time planners on the basis of a changing and increasing ratio over time, per 10,000 urban population, would result in a need for 19,380 full-time planners by the year 2015 (see Table 5).

Table 5

Estimated Number of Full-time Planners Required to Serve the Urban Population 1960–2015

	Urban Population (in millions rounded)	Ratio of Full-time Planners per 10,000 Urban Population	Cumulative Number of Full-time Planners (estimated)	Full-time Planners (estimated)
1960+	125	.56	7,000	7000 (base point—existing supply)
1970	150	.60	9,000	+2000 over base point
1980	170	.64	10,880	+1880 over 1970
1990	190	.68	12,920	+2040 over 1980
2000	225	.72	16,200	+3280 over 1990
2015	255	.76	19,380	+3180 over 2000

Another factor that can be calculated in determining planner demand involves a more careful examination of the urban places. While nearly all places of 100,000 population and over have full-time planning staffs, the range of staff sizes is widely disparate. In 1966, ASPO reported staff size ranges in cities over 100,000 population from two to eighty-nine full-time professional planners. If the average number of full-time professional planners for each of the city population groups increased by one-half, this would generally raise the average to a level no higher than two-thirds of the current staff range among planning staffs in cities classified by population size. The result would be an increase in the demand for full-time professional planners of 654 over current levels, even assuming no increase in the number of cities in each of the population groups.

Table 6

Increased Demand for Full-time Professionals Based on an Increase in the Average Number of Such Employees in 1966 for Cities over 100,000 in Population as of 1966

Cities	Total in Survey	Adjusted Average— Full-time Professional Planners (50% above 1966 average) (rounded)	Net Addition over 1966 (rounded)
1,000,000 and over	6	70	140
500,000–999,999	20	30	200
250,000–499,999	21	18	126
100,000–249,999	57	10	188
Total			654

Source: Leopold A. Goldschmidt, "Expenditures, Staff, and Salaries of Local Public Agencies," *ASPO Planning Advisory Service*, Report No. 208, March, 1966; adapted from various tables.

Assuming an even distribution of population increase by decade among each of the cities within each population group and a rising ratio of planners to population (see Table 5), the demand for full-time professional planners would rise by the year 2015 to about 20,700, or 1,320 above the straight line projections (see Table 7).

Table 7

Increased Demand for Full-time Professional Planners in Cities over 100,000 as a Factor of Urban Population Increase by Decade, Assuming Even Distribution of Population Addition

	Percent Increase in Urban Population over 1960+ by adjusted average	Absolute Increase in Planners Needed (to meet growth needs of new and enlarged planning staffs)	Cumulative Demand Beyond Normal Increase Shown in Table 5
1960+	—	—	654 (base addition)
1970	+20	131	785
1980	+13	101	886
1990	+12	106	992
2000	+18	179	1171
2015	+13	152	1323

In addition to the estimated increase in the number of full-time professional planners required by cities over 100,000 population, additional assumptions may be warranted in establishing planner manpower demand for the next fifty years.

The number of full-time professional planners on the staffs of local agencies in cities with populations under 100,000 falls sharply at each step-down in population class. While planning for these cities may be performed by planning consultants and/or increasingly incorporated in the planning agenda of counties and metropolitan and regional planning agencies, the fact is that the number of equivalent full-time professional planners is likely to grow, as a product of population growth and the problems associated with age and change. If we assume that the approximately fifty cities in the 50,000-99,999 population class without full-time planning staffs will seek to create such staffs in a quantity equal to the average for this class city in 1966, the demand would equal 160. If, in addition, 150 of the approximately 250 cities in the 25,000-49,999 population class without full-time professional planning staffs seeks to provide such staffs equal in amount to the average for this class city in 1966, the demand will be about 315 planners. Finally, if only 250 cities in the approximately 1,000 in the 10,000-24,999 class seek to establish planning staffs in an amount equal to the average for the cities in this class with planning staffs, the demand will be 375 planners. The total for these three classes of demand would be 850 planners. If this figure is similarly subjected to the urban population percentage increases on the premise that the additions to the urban population will be evenly distributed, an additional 1,720 estimated planners will be required by the year 2015 to meet this demand. It should be noted that many of the urban places in the categories just described are suburban in character and are likely to grow in concert with their metropolitan parent areas.

Table 8

Increased Demand for Full-time Professional Planners in Cities Under 100,000 as a Factor of Urban Population Increase by Decade, Assuming Even Distribution of Population Addition

	Percent Increase in Urban Population over 1960+ Population	*Absolute Increase Per Decade*	*Additional Cumulative Demand for Planners*
1960+	—	—	850 (base addition, by adjusted average)
1970	+20	170	1020
1980	+13	133	1153
1990	+12	138	1291
2000	+18	232	1523
2015	+13	198	1721

The most significant increases in demand for full-ime professional planners is likely to occur in the county, "combined" (city-county, metropolitan, and regional agencies), and state planning agency categories.

There are about 3,000 counties in the United States and 212 Standard Metropolitan Statistical Areas, yet the ASPO survey reports only 123 counties with local planning agencies and 96 combined agencies (either city-county, metropolitan, or regional). Of the agencies reporting, the average number of full-time professional planners is below the average number reported for each equivalent class of city by population class. While some readjustment may occur in the distribution of full-time professional planners in cities over 250,000 and in larger geographic units, the number of, and demand for, professional planners is likely to persist in large cities because of the dimension of city problems. Moreover, there will probably be a substantial increase in the demand for professional planners within existing county and metropolitan agencies, while the creation of new, large-jurisdiction planning agencies will also increase the demand for planners. The prospects will undoubtedly be enhanced by increased public sophistication and will be reinforced by the federal government's growing requirement that much of its aid is dependent on metropolitan and regional planning.

An increase in the number of full-time professional planners on the staffs of the "combined" agencies (city-county, metropolitan, and regional), up to the median number existing within city planning agencies for jurisdictions with comparable population, and the creation of an equal number of new combined agencies, with staffs containing the median number of full-time planners for cities of comparable population size would result in a need for 2,740 planners (see Table 9).

The total increased demand over the next fifty years resulting from the addition of the series of projections based on local jurisdictional examinations is over 5,700 new, full-time professional planners, which would undoubtedly increase to about 7,000 (for a total of about 14,000 including the estimated current number of planners) when the state, interstate, federal, and special agencies are included. The 1966 ASPO survey, for example, reported 556 planners on the staffs of 37 states which are not included in the recited data. Interestingly, this estimated added demand of about 7,000 based on urban population extensions applied against governmental jurisdictions compares remarkably well with the approximately 7,000 additional (or 14,000 total) demand earlier recited, derived from straight-line urban population extensions (on the basis of a ratio of .56 planners to 10,000 population) applied against adjusted current numbers of professional planners reported in national surveys.

The United States Department of Labor, "Report on Manpower Requirements, Resources, Utilization and Training," March, 1966, sought to translate the series of goals incorporated in the 1960 report of the President's Commission on National Goals into projections for fifteen areas of national activity

Table 9

**Increased Demand for Full-time Planners in Selected County and "Combined"
Agencies in Jurisdictions over 100,000 as a Factor of Urban Population
Increase, by Decade, Assuming Even Distribution
of Population Addition[14]**

	Staff Increases in Existing "Combined" Agencies up to City Median Equivalents	*Staff Increases Resulting from New "Combined" Agency Forma- tions up to City Median Equivalents*	*Percent Increase in Urban Population*	*Absolute Increase*	*Additional Cumulative Demand for Planners*
1960+	+413	+943	—	+1356	+ 1356 (base addition, by ad- justed median)
1970	+ 83	+189	+20	+ 272	+1628
1980	+ 64	+147	+13	+ 211	+1839
1990	+ 67	+153	+12	+ 220	+2059
2000	+113	+258	+18	+ 371	+2430
2015	+ 96	+220	+13	+ 316	+2740

(later increased to sixteen by the addition of space exploration). One of these areas, Urban Development, was intended to include adequate metropolitan transportation systems, housing, cultural and recreational facilities, schools and hospitals, industrial and commercial buildings, public buildings and utilities, and control of air and water pollution. The report sought to establish the dimensions in manpower of the goal at "levels of achievement regarded as reasonable and within reach on the basis of present knowledge and in a free enterprise system." Based on a manpower projection to 1975, the report estimated "an increase in public and private expenditures—largely private— from $64 billion in 1962 to $130 billion (in 1962 dollars) in 1975, and in- cluded in the manpower estimate both the direct and indirect employment resulting throughout the economy. . . ." The report projected a demand of 10 million jobs by 1975 to achieve the urban development goal, of which just over 920,000 were estimated as professional and technical workers. This latter figure covers a wide-ranging number of professionals, including special- ist professionals in education, recreation, resource fields, architecture, engi- neering, and the like, and provides no specific separate information for planning. However, based on the application of the sparse evidence earlier discussed, if we assume that .5 percent of this projected professional category consists of planners, the absolute demand which is derived would be well within manageable statistical proportions.

Because the data on the need for planners is so incomplete, comparative magnitudes of increase were examined between planners and social welfare supervisory and administrative personnel. Social welfare workers are an integral part of all levels of government. They have an extensive dual public and private structure that extends from the neighborhoods to the federal government. Planning, although an accepted part of city and federal government, is just beginning to expand its activities at the level of state and regional jurisdictions and community organizations. Therefore, it is not possible to compare absolute increases, but the relative magnitude of the increase may be of interest. It should also be noted that the value of the comparison is enhanced by the fact that the social welfare field is included separately in Department of Health, Education, and Welfare statistical reports and by the existence of a Bureau of Labor Statistics manpower study on social welfare undertaken in 1960 which provides a relatively accurate comparative base.

The 1965 Department of Health, Education, and Welfare study which reported on the social welfare profession estimated that non-caseworker social welfare personnel will increase by about 50 percent between 1964 and 1975 in public assistance and public child welfare areas.[15] According to the planning projections previously discussed, the total—among the probable net increase in 1970 for cities and "combined" agencies plus a yearly average for five years of the estimated additional planners not accounted for, is about 1,200, or a 41 percent increase over 1966. Allowing for the relatively limited size of the planning field, the inadequacy of the data, and the conservativeness of the estimates, it appears that projections outlined here are reasonable.

Sources and Estimates of Probable Supply

In order to determine whether the demand for trained planners over the next fifty years can be met, current planning school enrollments and graduates have been projected to the year 2015. Let us assume that (1) there will be a slight increase over 1965–66 ratios in the percentage of persons enrolled in planning schools who graduate[16] and (2) the current percentage of the total increased magnitude of four-year college enrollees will elect to secure planning degrees, the same percentage of the total master's degree candidates will elect to obtain master's degrees in planning, and the same percentage of Ph.D. candidates will elect to obtain a Ph.D. in planning. The estimates that follow were obtained by using the least squares equation, adjusted by Marie G. Fullam in *Projections of Educational Statistics to 1974–75*, and the U.S. Bureau of the Census Series D population estimates issued in February, 1967, in order to project four-year college and graduate school enrollments. In addition, the ASPO "Survey of Planning Schools" was utilized to provide current and past planning school enrollments and graduation statistics. However, while their data show percentage increases in planning students, the information available on planning students in relation to total students that would be necessary to establish a trend is erratic and imprecise. Consequently, projections were based on a fixed percentage relationship of planning students to other students.

The projections suggest that, even if existing planning schools increase their enrollments only enough to maintain their relative position in the aca-

Table 10

Projections of Undergraduate Enrollment and Bachelor's Degree Awards in Planning During Decennial Years, 1970–2010, Assuming the Relationship Between Planning School Enrollments and Total Four-Year College Enrollments Remains Constant

Year	Bachelor's Degree Planning School Enrollment Per Year	Projected Bachelor's Degrees in Planning Per Year
1962–63	151	76
1963–64	150	61
1964–65	302	69
1965–66	302	73
1966–67	352	80
1970–71	368	111
1980–81	382	115
1990–91	390	117
2000–1[a]		127
2010–11[a]		139

a. Gaps in years are due to difficulties in data assembly.

Sources: The 1966 ASPO "Survey of Planning Schools" was used for 1963–66 enrollments; the 1965 ASPO "Survey of Planning Schools" was used for 1962 enrollments. Earlier surveys could not be used because of lack of correspondence to more accurate, recent surveys. John F. Folger, "The Balance between Supply and Demand for College Graduates," *Journal of Human Resources*, Vol. 2, No. 2, p. 146.

Table 11

Projections of Master's Degree Enrollment and Degree Awards in Planning During Decennial Years, 1970–2010, Assuming the Relationship Between Planning School Enrollments and Total Graduate School Enrollment Remains Constant

Year	Master's Degree Planning Enrollment Per Year	Projected Master's Degrees in Planning Per Year
1962–63	559	200
1963–64	649	274
1964–65	819	306
1965–66	956	347
1970–71	1,387	554
1980–81	1,435	574
1990–91	1,465	586
2000–1[a]		644
2010–11[a]		706

a. Gaps in years are due to difficulties in data assembly.

Source: 1965 ASPO "Survey of Planning Schools"; 1966 ASPO "Survey of Planning Schools" was used for planning school enrollments. Master's degrees in planning are calculated at 40 percent of enrollment in planning schools. This figure compares favorably with experience between 1960 and 1965. Planning school enrollment figures as 3 percent of the graduate school enrollment in fields related to planning. (A 2.9 percent ratio existed in 1965.) Fields related to planning were selected among fields of study listed in U.S. Department of Health, Education, and Welfare, Office of Education, *A Fact Book on Higher Education* (1965), p. 92.

demic structure, they can produce more than 35,000 planners over the next fifty years. If we adjust our figures to account for possible double counting caused by bachelor's degree winners also earning master's degrees and master's degree graduates being counted in Ph.D. statistics, it will still be possible to produce 30,000 planners—most of whom would have at least a master's degree—without any appreciable acceleration in other fields of specialization or professional training.

Table 12

Projections of Ph.D. Enrollment and Awards in Planning During Decennial Years, 1970–2010, Assuming a Constant Relationship Between Ph.D. Enrollments in Planning and Ph.D. Enrollments in Graduate Schools

Year	Ph.D. Planning Enrollment	Projected Ph.D. Degrees in Planning Per Year
1962–63	52	5
1963–64	68	10
1964–65	82	15
1965–66	92	10
1970–71	124	16
1980–81	129	21
1990–91	131	28
2000–1	132	28
2010–11	135	31

Source: 1965 ASPO "Survey of Planning Schools"; 1966 ASPO "Survey of Planning Schools" for planning school enrollments.

Table 13

Projected Enrollments and Graduates from Public Community and Junior Colleges, 1970–2010

Year	Total Opening Fall Enrollment Each Year[a]	Graduates[d]	Yearly Graduates Available for Employment upon Graduation[e]
1970[b]	1,086,000	434,400	238,920
1980[c]	1,138,667	455,466	250,506
1990[c]	1,197,746	479,098	263,503
2000	1,319,938	527,975	290,386
2010	1,515,354	606,141	333,377

a. Used least squares equation, adjusted by Marie G. Fullam, *Projections of Educational Statistics to 1974–75.* Assumes rates for men and women aged 18 to 21 in junior colleges will follow the 1954–64 trends.

b. Given in *Projections of Educational Statistics to 1974–75* and based on U.S. Census Series B population estimates.

c. Based on U.S. Census Series D population estimates, because they appear to be made accurate after 1970.

d. Based on 75 percent of the difference between the total enrollment and the first time enrollment. This 75 percent difference is arrived at by taking the full time students, which make up 50 percent of enrollments, and adding one-half of the returning part-time students. Figure given only allows 1.5 percent of difference for dropouts.

e. Assumes 45 percent go on to four-year institutions or military service.

As planning considerations become increasingly more complex, planners become more reliant on what ASPO calls specialized professions or subject matter specialists. This is illustrated by the 1967 ratios of specialized professions to planners. In "combined" agencies, the number of specialized professionals in relation to planners has been steadily dropping. Using a relationship of one specialized professional to every five planners, which is slightly above the current "combined" planning agency ratio, the number of specialized professionals necessary to assist planners in urbanized areas will increase from 1,800 in 1970 to 3,876 in 2015. On a ratio of one specialized professional to every ten planners, which is the current city planning staff ratio, the demand for specialized professionals on planning staffs will increase from 900 specialized professionals in 1967 to 1,938 specialized professionals in 2015. Assuming a ratio as high as one specialized professional to every five planners, only .4 percent of those graduating in bachelor's degree fields related to planning or 2 percent of those graduating with master's degrees in fields related to planning would be required to fill the demand for specialized pro-

Table 14

Projected Enrollments and Graduates from Four-Year Colleges and Universities with Estimates of Graduates in Fields Related to Planning

Year	Yearly Total Enrollment[a]	Yearly Bachelor's Degrees Granted[b]	Yearly Number of Bachelor's Degree Graduates in Subjects Related to Planning[c]	Yearly Number of Bachelor's Degree Graduates in Related Subjects (after allowance for graduate attendance)[d]	Graduate School Enrollment
1965		557,280			
1970	6,139,000	736,680	132,594	79,556	53,038
1980	6,365,012	763,801	137,484	82,490	54,994
1990	6,498,977	770,077	140,378	84,227	56,151
2000	7,066,050	847,926	146,408	87,845	58,563
2010	7,741,525	928,983	160,404	96,242	64,162

a. The least squares equation, adjusted by Marie G. Fullam, *Projections of Educational Statistics to 1974–75*, was used to project enrollment. Our projections are based on U.S. Department of Commerce, Bureau of the Census, *Current Population Reports: Population Estimates*, Series P-25, No. 359, February 20, 1967. Our projections assume that the trends from 1954 to 1964 will continue.

b. The average number of degrees conferred between 1960 and 1965 was 11 percent of enrollment. It has been estimated, however, that the percent will increase to 12 percent by 1970. We have estimated that 15 percent will graduate after 1990. See John K. Folger, "The Balance Between Supply and Demand for College Graduates," *Journal of Human Resources*, Vol. 2, No. 2, Spring, 1967, p. 146.

c. Approximately 18 percent of all four-year college graduates have subject matter training which will enable them to work in planning and related programs. See U.S. Department of Health, Education, and Welfare, Office of Education, *Earned Degrees Conferred, 1963–64* (Washington, D.C.: U.S. Government Printing Office, 1966), p. 7. See also American Council on Education, *A Fact Book on Higher Education* (1965), p. 85.

d. About 40 percent of college graduates go directly to graduate school (within a year). Folger, p. 148.

fessionals on planning staffs over the next fifty years. Obviously, even a 100 percent increase over the one-to-five ratio could be easily absorbed.

Draftsmen currently have a ratio to planners of about one to three, and the number of draftsmen would triple over the next fifty years if we disregard the major changes already underway as a result of the introduction of new techniques in cartography and in the use of computers.

Table 15

Projection of Graduate School Graduates in Fields Related to Planning[17]

Year	Master's Degrees	Ph.D. Degrees
1970	26,622	3,978
1980	36,801	5,499
1990	46,966	7,018
2000	51,836	7,744
2010	56,791	8,484

Table 16

Projection of the Demand for Persons to Fill Vacancies in Selected Planning and Related Positions

	Number of Planners Employed Without Bachelor's Degree[a]		*Number of Specialized Professionals Based on a 1:10 Relation to Planners*[b] *(based on planners to urban population)*	*Based on a 1:5 Relation to Planners*[c]	*Number of Draftsmen*[d] *Based on a 1:3 Relation to Planners*
	20%	*15%*			
Year	*(Cum.)*	*(Cum.)*	*(Cum.)*	*(Cum.)*	*(Cum.)*
1960 to 1970	1400	1050			
1970 to 1980	1800	1350	900	1,800	2,970
1980 to 1990	2176	1632	1,088	2,176	3,590
1990 to 2000	2584	1938	1,292	2,584	4,263
2000 to 2010	3240	2430	1,620	3,240	5,346
2010 to 2015	3876	2907	1,938	3,876	6,395

a. Two separate projections were made to show a range of demand for persons in the planning process who do not have a four-year college education.

b. In 1967 the ratio of planners to specialized professions in combined city-county agencies was 1:9.65 and going up; ASPO Files.

c. In 1967 the ratio of planners to specialized professionals in city planning departments was 1:4.7 and going down; ASPO Files.

d. In 1967 the ratio of draftsmen to planners is 1:3 for all agencies; ASPO Files.

Technology, however, will doubtlessly affect these estimates, perhaps drastically. Drafting machines, data banks, and related developments already in use can be expected to alter the numerical requirements and the functions assigned to specialized professionals, draftsmen, and other personnel and thus radically alter their relationship to the planning process.

Table 17

**The Cumulative Production of Graduates Available for Planning
and Planning Related Job Opportunities**[18]

		Graduates					
	Junior College Graduates Available for Employment	*Bachelor's Degree in Fields Related to Planning*	*Bachelor's Degree in Planning*	*Master's Degree in Related Fields (terminal)*	*Master's Degree in Planning*	*Ph.D. in Related Fields*	*Ph.D. in Planning*
1965 (base)	167,887	100,310	73	19,980	306	2,754	15
1970	839,435		365	99,900	1,530	13,770	75
1980	3,228,635		1,475	366,120	7,070	53,550	235
1990	5,733,695	3,202,330	2,625	734,130	12,810	108,540	445
2000	8,368,725		3,795	1,203,790	18,670	178,720	725
2010	11,272,405	6,070,190	5,065	1,724,626	25,110	256,160	1,005
2015	12,939,290	6,872,210	5,760	2,008,581	28,640	298,580	1,160

The strong, existing demand based on simple mathematical applications of the current experience as represented by the evidence of unfilled positions reported in the 1966 ASPO report constitutes a possible and troubling contradiction. These implications have been discussed above.

Table 18

**Number and Rate of Unfilled Positions by Jurisdiction,
1964–1966**

	Positions			Vacancies			Vacancy Rate (in percent)		
Jurisdiction	*1964*	*1965*	*1966*	*1964*	*1965*	*1966*	*1964*	*1965*	*1966*
City	1,474	1,556	2,019	187	200	295	12.7	12.9	14.6
County	617	694	868	89	72	106	14.4	10.4	12.2
Combined	396	560	690	47	123	159	11.9	22.0	23.0
Total	2,487	2,810	3,577	323	395	560	13.0	14.0	15.7

Source: Leopold A. Goldschmidt, "Expenditure, Staff, and Salaries of Local Public Agencies," *ASPO Planning Advisory Service,* Report No. 208, March, 1966, Table 4.

Despite this possible challenge, however, the absolute capacity of the universities to produce (and exceed) the number of planners needed seems clear and is further facilitated by the increasing numbers of people that can be produced by junior and community colleges and by the growing number of specialized professionals that can be drawn from related fields.

These facts indicate that supplying enough planners to meet the demand is not the major problem facing the planning profession. A conservative demand of between 14,000 to 20,000 planners, cumulatively to the year 2015, could be increased to as much as 30,000 to 40,000 planners, cumulatively, and still represent a manageable achievement.

Planning is a small field and projections that increase planning job opportunities by 100 percent involve few total jobs. Furthermore, current scales of efforts are likely to be sufficient to meet projected demands for planning, provided existing planning schools simply maintain their current relative position with respect to total college and graduate school enrollments or provided new planning schools, about equal in number and in size[19] to those that now exist, are created.

Notes

1. U.S. Department of Health, Education, and Welfare, Office of Education, *Projection of Educational Statistics to 1974–75* (1965), p. 23.
2. The current average ratio in planning schools is about one teacher to six or seven students.
3. Office of Education, U.S. Department of Health, Education, and Welfare, *Earned Degrees, 1964–66* (1965), and 1965 ASPO "Survey of Planning Schools," American Society of Planning Officials, 1965.
4. In 1965 the average enrollment capacity of bachelor's degree-granting planning schools was 56 students each; for master's degree-granting institutions it was 37 students each; and in Ph.D. programs it was 17 students each (adaptation of "1965 ASPO Survey of Planning Schools" data).
5. John Moeller, "Expenditures, Staff, and Salaries of Local Planning Agencies," *ASPO Planning Advisory Service,* Report No. 196, March, 1965, p. 27.
6. Folger, et al., "The Balance Between Supply and Demand for College Graduates, A Symposium on Manpower Theory," *Journal of Human Resources,* Vol. 2, No. 2, Spring, 1967.
7. Ibid.
8. Jerome P. Pickard, "Future Growth of Major U.S. Urban Regions," *Urban Land Institute,* February, 1967, Vol. 26, No. 2.
9. Ibid.
10. For a detailed discussion of the implications of urban growth on governmental forms, see, for example, *Modernizing Local Government* (Committee for Economic Development, July, 1966), which proposed that the approximately 80,000 local governments in the United States be reduced by about 80 percent; and that of the approximately 3,000 counties in the nation, the 350 in standard metropolitan areas be retained, and the residual outside metropolitan areas be consolidated into no more than 500 new county jurisdictions.
11. A figure of about 7,000 professional planners is suggested by interviews and the best inferences that can be drawn from available literature and observations.
12. See, for example, Donald J. Bogue, "The Demographic Moment of Truth," *Chicago Study,* Vol. 4, No. 1, Winter, 1967, pp. 37-41.
13. This is a method suggested by Richard May, which May then tested against the staff patterns among selected city planning agencies.
14. These figures have been adjusted upward for future urban population increases on the premise that the urban population will increase evenly among jurisdictions.
15. U.S. Department of Health, Education, and Welfare, *Closing the Gap,* Report of the Departmental Task Force on Social Work Education and Manpower (November, 1965), pp. 23, 24, 39.
16. Planning degree graduates are assumed to be a constant percentage of total degree graduates as projected by Folger in *Journal of Human Resources,* Vol. 2, p. 146. This assumption is necessary because the enrollments in planning schools have been

increasing so rapidly that new classes have generally been much larger than previous classes and hence serious distortions result if corrections are not introduced.

17. Ph.D.'s are 13 percent of total advanced degrees, *Earned Degrees, 1963–64* (Washington, D.C.: U.S. Government Printing Office, 1964). According to these projections, the number of Ph.D.'s is 3 percent of bachelor's degrees in 1970, 4 percent in 1980, 5 percent in 1990 and thereafter. A figure of 3 percent for 1970 is given by Folger (p. 146) and he assumed advances of 1 percent per decade. We extended the ratio to 1990.

18. These data do not take into account retirements, deaths, and losses to the profession. Consequently, the cumulative data do not necessarily represent the cumulative number of planners available at any given time, but these data do assume the replacement of planners trained prior to 1965. Compensatory margins are reflected, however, in the fact that existing planners are not included, and graduates from related fields and from junior colleges are separately shown in the cumulative statistics.

19. The average enrollment among planning schools is currently about 100 enrollees per year.

Comments on
Meltzer

COLEMAN WOODBURY
Department of Urban and Regional Planning
University of Wisconsin

Number of Planners

In roughly the first half of his paper (and in the Appendix) Mr. Meltzer seems to me to have done a commendable job on an almost impossible assignment—almost impossible because the information he has to work with is so fragmentary, unreliable, and often contradictory. Moreover, nearly all of it lacks an adequate time dimension that might have enabled him, for example, to judge more confidently what ratios of professional planners to urban population or of planners to specialized professionals in planning agencies are most likely to obtain in the future.

I see only one possible development in planning practice that might raise doubts about his less than doubling of the ratio of planners per 10,000 urban population, with the resultant estimate of 32,000. At recent meetings of the National Commission on Urban Problems in some dozen major metropolitan areas I have been impressed by how much local officials (including some planners) and others concerned with current issues are talking about and experimenting with ways to increase public participation in local public affairs. Fifteen or twenty years ago, I know from experience, anyone even tentatively suggesting this was met almost everywhere with incredulity or suspicion. To be sure, even today some urban planners are still skeptical, but others are trying to find out more about the potentialities as well as the limitations and the dangers of this part of the planning process in a democratic society. Although the methods and techniques to this end are still in embryonic, experimental stages, one thing seems certain: if urban and regional planning agencies move measurably in this direction, the number of intelligent, trained, and skillful planners needed will rise sharply.

It seems to me that Mr. Meltzer's estimate of between forty and eighty additional instructors in university departments of planning is much too low. The assumed student-teacher ratios of 10:1 or 20:1 are too high for a subject so complex and for the quality of product that I know Mr. Meltzer favors as strongly as I do. Besides, the future of planning education almost surely holds a much larger component of "continuing education." We have hardly begun to move on this front. One of the weakest parts of the programs of existing departments, research, must be encouraged in many ways, including lighter teaching loads. Finally, it seems reasonable to look forward to a greatly increased volume of university instruction for students preparing for careers in local government other than as professional planners—e.g., city managers, finance officers, assessors, police commissioners, welfare and recreation directors. Although in traditional terms these are not essentially planning jobs, certainly university preparation for them should include a more than casual introduction to the principal ideas, the outlook, and methods of central or professional planners. Thus I see a possible heavy addition to the student body in many planning classes and, therefore, a need for additional teachers.

In short, relying necessarily and openly on intuition, I would guess that Mr. Meltzer's estimate of the number of professional planners needed in 2017 might be doubled, and his higher figure, eighty, for additional university teachers of planning might be quadrupled. Even so, I would concur strongly with his conclusion: "The manpower challenge clearly, therefore, is not a problem of 'numbers matching' or statistical quantification, but is directly related to the character and role of planning, societal need, and the academic capacity to prepare the professional planner."

Character and Role of Planning

If in the first half of his paper Mr. Meltzer faced an *almost* impossible assignment, in the latter half he presents this commentator, who has limited space, with a *completely* impossible task. This I feel very keenly because I find nearly all of this second part of his paper stimulating and provocative; some of it I could second heartily, but much I have to disagree with, at least in emphasis. How can one deal with such a situation in a few hundred words? At the serious risk of exaggerating my differences with Mr. Meltzer and of doing less than justice to the ideas I prefer, I can mention briefly only three points of difference that seem to me significant—significant in the perspective of a generation or two in the evolving profession of planning.

1. *Technology and change.* Mr. Meltzer presents, in fairly extreme form, the common view of technology or technics as a powerful but rather disembodied force producing social changes that often disrupt established patterns and institutions, a force so strong that adaptation and adjustment to it are the only practicable possibility. In my view, this is simply incorrect and misleading as well. Technical developments—whether they be television, the diesel powered bulldozer, the jet airplane, the communications satellite, the electronic computer, or the septic tank—are, in and of themselves, socially inert and almost powerless. It is the human organizations and institutions that command and own and use them that produce the social effects. This, I suggest, is more than a nicety of expression. Although I cannot spell out here the differing implications of these two views for the future strategy of American planning, I think that they may be fairly obvious to anyone who thinks a little about the question.

2. *The essential roles of planning.* In his plea for flexibility and new horizons for planning in the future, Mr. Meltzer speaks of "the capacity of planning to constitute the profession which facilitates societal adaptation and accommodation in the face of probable major changes in life style born of new technology." I suggest that as a characterization of central or professional planning this statement is both too broad and too limiting.

Several other social institutions—e.g., the day-to-day political process, the educational system from kindergarten or Headstart to the university, many civic organizations—also play very significant parts to this end. Planning is distinctive not in its concern with these matters but in the process by which it deals with them, including its attempt to be reasonably explicit as to goals, its exploration of the principal (not necessarily all) possible courses of action, and the care with which it considers probable side effects or byproducts of these actions—in other words, in its ecological or systems orientation.

On the other hand, planning should be engaged not only with adaptation and accommodation to change; it should be at least equally concerned with physical, economic, political, and other social environments that serve and sustain some of the deep-seated needs of man as a social animal, e.g., the needs for security, the respect of one's fellows and oneself, a range of real choice, at least occasional relief from the imposed routines of mechanized production processes, a feeling of "knowing the score" and having some voice in determining one's destiny, etc. In this role the planner will often be helping to initiate change or to lay the groundwork of fact, understanding, and concern from which change may arise, rather than adapting to or "managing" change already underway or impending.

3. *New skills.* In his fervent plea for a revised and broader definition of planning and his questioning of the adequacy of present planning curricula, which certainly deserve to be read and pondered by all planners and teachers of planning, Mr. Meltzer refers several times to new "methodological skills."

Clearly he includes in this term more than simulation models, computer programing, and systems analysis, but he does not mention one skill that seems to me crucially significant. In my opinion its rareness among planners is the profession's most crippling weakness; its mastery would do more to strengthen central planning as a servant of the public good than any other one thing.

For its most effective explanation to date we must turn not to a planner but to a sociologist, Professor Herbert Blumer of the University of California at Berkeley.[1] He thinks that human group activity and structure are determined primarily by "a vast interpretative process in which people, singly and collectively, guide themselves by defining the objects, events and situations which they encounter . . . , a vast digestive process through which the confrontations of experience are transformed into activity." He goes on to argue for "a markedly different scheme of sociological analysis . . . [that] relies on a distinctive form of procedure. This procedure is to approach the study of group activity through the eyes and experience of the people who have developed the activity. Hence, it necessarily requires an intimate familiarity with this experience and with the scenes of its operation. It uses broad and interlacing observations and not narrow and disjunctive observations. . . ."

Although these brief quotations do scant justice to Mr. Blumer's argument, I hope they may induce some planners as well as many teachers and students of planning to read his article. He, of course, urges this conception of group life and this research procedure on professional scholars, who wish to understand and perhaps to predict. It seems to me equally pertinent to the needs of planners who, in addition, wish to be and, in fact, often are charged with the responsibility of trying to influence, more or less directly, the course of events. And planners, properly and professionally concerned with human environments, may need to remind themselves from time to time that much of the product of this "vast digestive process" in the minds of individuals and groups *is* their environment, regardless of what the census enumerator, the land use mapper, or the model builder may think or say.

Note

1. From his 1956 presidential address to the American Sociological Society, "Sociological Analysis and the 'Variable,' " *American Sociological Review*, December, 1966, pp. 683-90. The quotations are from pp. 686 and 689.

HERBERT E. STRINER
Director of Program Development
W. E. Upjohn Institute for Employment Research

In his paper Professor Meltzer has undertaken a monumental job. Although he had to work with the most tenuous of data and the assumptions had to be based on variables which are hazy at best, the result is a very useful document.

In dealing with the likely manpower situation for planners in the year 2017 and attempting to assess the factors which impinge upon supply as well as demand, it is easy to see why Professor Meltzer has listed many caveats. Peering ahead fifty years is a terribly hazardous business and quite frequently is met, not as a professional challenge, but as an opportunity to display one's resourcefulness as an expert in the artful use of jargon. Indeed, I am reminded of one of Piet Hein's short poems, called "Experts,"[1] in which he says:

> Experts have
> their expert fun
> ex cathedra
> telling one
> just how nothing
> can be done.

Hein also points out, perhaps as a source of encouragement in dealing with just such complicated topics as the paper I am discussing, in his poem "T.T.T.":[2]

> Put up in a place
> where it's easy to see
> the cryptic admonishment
> T.T.T.
>
> When you feel how depressingly
> slowly you climb,
> it's well to remember that
> Things Take Time

Professor Meltzer's paper has to be read in two ways in order to appreciate its usefulness in our efforts to discern where we are going in terms of the quantitative need for city planners as well as the types of individuals who should be trained to fill this function. If we accept the 7,000 figure which is used in the paper as the contemporary number of planners, Professor Meltzer's point that even if the total demand for planners is increased to one planner for every 10,000 persons, a figure which is above current and anticipated ratios, the total demand in the year 2017 for 32,000 professional planners would still represent only a modest increase over a fifty-year period. In all fairness, Professor Meltzer is quite careful in indicating that the assumptions on which these extrapolations must be made include a number of serious cautions as to the possibility of major social changes which can take place, and therefore change radically the order of magnitude of this figure. This point is well taken.

I believe that I can serve a more useful function if I am less concerned with smug criticism of a paper which I believe most of us would be hard put to improve upon, if I focus on an extension of some of the theoretical and philosophical considerations to which Professor Meltzer refers as factors which can have heavy impact on the nature of our demand for and the magnitude of the supply of city planners by the year 2017. As the author put it (see page 248):

> The manpower challenge clearly, therefore, is not a problem in "numbers matching" or statistical quantification, but is directly related to the character and role of planning, societal need, and the academic capacity to prepare the professional planner. The issue, in sum, is one of professional preparation, competence, and function. The issue is not the shortage of planners.

I take exception, however, to the last sentence in this quote. The issue may indeed be a shortage of planners, but the factors which affect the shortage may be those which have only too briefly been touched upon in the Meltzer paper.

The paper seems to assume that competitive forces in the economy which bid against each other for skilled manpower will remain in relatively the same position in 2017 as in 1967. To differ from this assumption, one either must talk in terms of quantitative differences or merely raise as a form of speculation the conceptual possibilities underlying changes in our structure which will change the competitive forces affecting the demand for resources which could go either into the planning profession or other types of activity.

During as brief a period as the last decade, there has been a major shift in the level of concern in this nation with social problems. Many solutions for these problems call upon increasing use of social scientists and technicians from such fields as economics, sociology, psychology, political science, and geography. These fields call for the same types of skill and interest which we find among planners. What we have been seeing in recent years is an increase in the demand for the very types of individual and skill which must over the next fifty years be in increasing competition with those individuals who would normally go into the planning profession. Hence, I would contend that in any effort to project what the nature of the demand is for planners by the year 2017, we must also take into account the nature of demand for the various types of professional skill which will probably prove to be attractive to the very individuals who would ordinarily also be attracted to the professional planning field. As a result then, I believe that in the next several decades, competition for these human resources will increase and the degree to which we will be able to supply even the limited number of planners envisioned in Meltzer's paper will depend on the degree to which the planning profession is able not only to provide competitive incomes but also the manner in which they are able to match the challenge and the professional satisfaction to be found in these other fields.

There is another caution about the ease with which we will be able to supply the number of planners necessary to deal with the increasingly complex problems of our large population centers. The 7,000 planners now making up the professional population represent a number in a professional field which has only relatively recently begun to grow in popularity as a profession. While concern with city planning is old, the profession as a major professional increment in our policy and decision-making population is a rather young one. Recent demand for city planners has increased radically and in two different ways.

First, as a result of the demographic shift away from rural areas into larger concentrations of populations, there has been a tremendous increase in the numbers of individuals needed in this profession. This is represented not only by the number of professional planners directly involved as planners, but also by the increasing numbers of individuals in supportive roles, in addition to which we have, of course, increasing vacancies for positions. There is, however, an interesting additional factor on the demand side which complicates this whole problem of training and influences what types of individuals can be enticed into the field. This grows out of a qualitative change in the nature of planning and the training necessary for a city planner.

Professor Meltzer has alluded to the fact that there has been a transformation of planning from an activity dominated by and absorbed with space utilization into an activity best described as increasingly concerned with the indivisible social and economic realities and goals of the society and an attempt to meld these interests with the use of space and the allocation of scarce physical resources. This is a most complicated field of endeavor and increasingly has had to resort to highly scientific and quantitative techniques growing out of systems and operations research. To prepare planners adequately for this new type of methodology and technique calls, I believe, for a longer period of either graduate or on-the-job training in situations which permit the individuals to acquire skills far beyond those viewed as sufficient only a few short years ago in the planning profession.

What does this do to our supply-demand situation? I believe the demand must increase possibly beyond that envisioned by Professor Meltzer, as a result not only of the Great Society programs, but also of the increasing demands by the middle and upper income segments of our metropolitan populations for model cities, transportation, land use, and educational programs which they quite properly feel should more adequately represent our increasingly sophisticated society. This trend will probably increase during the balance of this century well into the next century. But, in addition, with the increasing restiveness of disadvantaged sectors of our population, there will be increasing demands made on our local and federal policymakers to do something which is far more effective and long lasting in dealing with the ills of our communities. Thus, the demand must grow, but the increasing demand called for can only be met adequately by planners who because of the greater needs for more sophisticated education will be much longer in preparing themselves in training programs than their professional forebears. The result must be a bottleneck in supply. Professor Meltzer properly warns that:

Future planners are likely to be produced not only by traditional planning schools, but also by urban and regional centers and institutes, which are variously associated with ecology, environmental health, regional science, urban studies, and the like. [See p. 253.]

This lengthier period of preparation occurs at the very same time that the demands of our society will be for a more rapid preparation and a larger supply of planners to meet with the increasing demands of our shorter and shorter tempered society.

I must conclude, then, that I am far less optimistic than Meltzer about the ability to produce the numbers and types of planners which I think will be needed by the year 2017. I am convinced that, as is true in many fields, we must begin to evolve a completely new approach in order to provide the skills needed for a function we now call "city planning." I am certain that increasingly the city planner will not use other city planners as his support staff, but rather, the city planner, more broadly trained and more intelligent about inputs which must come from other disciplines, will as a matter of fact look to the other disciplines as his source of professional help. The city planner will increasingly be less viewed as a source of productive ideas and more and more viewed as a source of productive coordination and management of teams of individuals who possess highly technical skills which must be fed into the management process. Putting it most bluntly, the beginnings of the educational process of the planner-coordinator of these teams will have to start with a recognition of the true meaning of omniscience. Again I refer to Piet Hein, and the Grook called "Omniscience":

> Knowing what
> thou knowest not
> is in a sense
> omniscience.[3]

Notes

1. Piet Hein and Jens Arup, *Grooks* (Cambridge: M.I.T. Press, 1967), p. 23.
2. Ibid., p. 5.
3. Ibid., p. 6.

PART III

A National Policy for Development

National Development and National Policy

This paper was commissioned to question: Just how far should this nation go with optimistic serendipity as a policy for development of 300 million people by the year 2000? What national policies will be needed through the next fifty years? What distribution of jobs and people? What population? What scale of communities?

How are the energies of an open society to be harnessed to build toward optimum environment, including the maximum free choice consistent with responsibility?

Is indicative planning for a national perspective necessarily bureaucratic? To take responsive federalism into the twenty-first century is a whole new order of regionalizing the United States necessary? What price tax can be put on America's goals? What new criteria might be needed to resolve conflicts in the competition for GNP dollars to achieve goals as set?

Author: Lyle C. Fitch, President, Institute of Public Administration
Chairman: Henry Fagin, AIP, Professor of Planning, University of Wisconsin
Committee: Scott Greer, AIP, Director, Center for Metropolitan Studies, Northwestern University; Wilbur Thompson, Department of Economics, Wayne State University; Calvin S. Hamilton, AIP, Director, Los Angeles City Planning Commission; James Alcott, Economist, Midwest Research Institute; Rev. William Spurrier, Professor of Religion and Chaplain, Wesleyan University; John Rubel, Vice President, Litton Industries

X

Lyle C. Fitch

President, Institute of Public Administration
New York

National Development
and National Policy

The people of the United States have always been of two minds about planning, including planning for national development. There is the long history of antipathy to planning which involves interference by government with the decisions of private individuals and organizations. Within the private sector (it has been supposed) the need for planning is minimized by the beneficent operation of the market system, whose signals provide information for decisions respecting such matters as levels of production and fair wages for labor, and which distributes society's product in at least rough proportion to the contributions of its members.

While it is probably fair to say that the free enterprise, market-oriented ideology has been the predominant ideology of social organization, Americans, being highly pragmatic, have not hesitated to depart from the ideology whenever it suited their convenience and to follow a quite different ideology of collective action for national development.

Indeed, a comparison of American nineteenth century experience with the travails of today's less-developed countries makes plain that Americans have possessed a genius for social cooperation, in matters large and small, of a degree equalled by few other societies. Throughout its history the United States collectively has been vitally concerned with national development. National development goals have always played a large part in shaping policy and public action, and have provided much of the cement which has held the society together.

This paper explores some of the responsibilities of national development policy in the next few decades as they appear in the perspective of 1967. It discusses some dimensions of national development planning and proposes some goals for development policy. It then examines implications for goal implementation of various growth rates of population and of national economic output. It looks briefly at arguments for and against a major program of building new cities, for bringing about a different geographic distribution of urban population than would otherwise obtain, and/or for other reasons. Finally, the paper considers possible ways of expediting some of the institutional changes which may be required to realize the nation's full potential.

Implicit in the discussion is the idea that change can and will be substantially guided and assisted by purposive national policy. "Policy" here implies more or less consistent pursuit of more or less specific goals (allowing for the fact that nearly all policy processes, particularly in the political sphere, are subject to short-term setbacks and perturbations). "Planning" implies a more structured pattern—"a formal, ordered process in which men seek by forethought to effect action so as to bring about more desired states than would otherwise obtain."[1] It connotes more than the systematic pursuit of goals and objectives through the routines usually associated with planning—gathering information, using such information in program formulation, and searching out and evaluating alternative means of attaining objectives. To be meaningful, planning must be associated with action and with the political process. Its responsibility does not stop with decisions or with setting programs in motion; it must continuously observe the administrative process and evaluate program results, and feed back the information, along with information on trends and changing needs, into successive rounds of decision-making. One more stipulation: planning is conceptually innovational. Once a policy or program becomes routine administration, planning goes out the window.[2]

The first essential in the policy-planning process is to establish goals and objectives which can command working consensuses. Such consensuses underlay the expansionist policies that opened the West and promoted the settlement of the frontier—provision of land, protection of settlers, construction of roads, canals, and railroads; provision of communications, establishment of law and order, provision of education and other public services. Of particular interest is the chain of developments which began with the passage in 1862 of the Morrill Act establishing the land-grant colleges. This was the first of a series of acts to foster the development of agriculture through research, education, and dissemination of information by means of a widespread apparatus reaching from the federal government down through state agriculture departments and state universities to counties and county agents and finally to individual farmers. This apparatus was supplemented later by market and pricing arrangements designed to protect farmers from the vicissitudes of the free market, and unplanned production and price fluctuations. That the benefits of this "intervention" have not been completely salutary does not alter the fact that the agricultural development policy in large part has been a smashing success—American agriculture is the productive miracle of the world. And to judge by results, most other development policies have been similarly successful (with some conspicuous exceptions, such as the merchant marine).

Great events ordinarily are associated with storm and turbulence, and the nation's development policies have been no exception—most have been evolved in controversy rather than sweetness and light. One reason for this is that most policies have been designed to benefit directly particular groups or geographic and economic sectors—the West, agriculture, manufacturing—and only indirectly the general welfare of the country as a whole. Most policies have been hotly opposed by individuals and interests not directly benefited; indeed, the pre-Civil War coalition of the West and the East to further development policies considered by the South to be inimical to its own development was one of the causes of the Civil War. Even such broad social welfare policies as the social security measures of the 1930's were for the benefit of a special group—the indigent or potentially indigent—and were opposed by those who fancied that their own interests would be damaged thereby.

The Full Employment Act of 1946 was one of the few instances of a momentous national development policy which promoted the immediate interests of nearly all groups and directly damaged few or none. The hot opposition to this "watershed" planning measure rested almost entirely on the free market ideology, not on adversely affected group interests. Indicative of the characteristic American ambivalence toward national development policy, in the same period that the Full Employment Act was being conceived, gestated, and born, the free market ideology was renewing itself by loud outcries and bitter denunciations of planning. The National Resources Planning Board was abolished by Congress in 1943 with firm pronumciamentos that no such subversive organ should ever again sully the federal scene.

But backstage, planning was taking an increasing hold in American society and American management. Several factors contributed to this subversion of ideology. One was the vast planning effort required by the Second World War and the planning skills developed thereby. Another was the very size of the giant corporations which were increasing their proportionate control of large sectors of the American economy and the necessity for extensive planning in the operation of any large and complex organization. Third was the nature of the technological process which, for complex projects, may require long and intricate preparation involving millions of operations, many of them sequential. For instance, the proposed supersonic transport will require a decade of decision-making and production before the first plane flies, with participation by several giant and many small corporations and many government agencies. The process of the market, flexible and extensive as it is, cannot possibly provide the components for a supersonic aircraft, most of which—new power systems, metallurgy, intricate electronic controls, and the rest—must be invented for the purpose. By contrast, the Wright brothers built their first airplane from materials bought mainly from stores in Dayton, Ohio.[3]

The federal government, and to a lesser degree state and local governments, are widely, heavily, and inextricably involved in modern economic management and hence necessarily with the planning-action nexus. There is the continuing concern with high employment and stability, hence with checking inflationary and deflationary trends, and hence involvement with wage bargaining, price setting, and other matters popularly supposed to be the province of the private sector. Only the federal government can assert the public interest where great oligopolies and labor unions find they can agree on wages and working conditions and pass the bill on to the consumer, with no thought given to the consequences for the rest of the economy. It is expected and demanded that the federal government will take responsibility for promoting development and for lending assistance to socially desirable projects involving great risks. And there is the ever-widening involvement with all dimensions of urban development. The need for planning, including self-conscious monitoring, evaluation, and innovation, leads to increased dependence on the "technology" of modern planning and management, such as program planning and budgeting systems.

A strictly political interpretation of the great national development policies would see them not as expressions of the national will in any meaningful sense, but rather as the vector of forces representing the various groups contending for advantage. In its most extreme form, this interpretation holds that social goals, aiming to promote the general welfare, play no significant part in mobilizing national action; that at best they are formulated by planners and others seeking to advance their own limited perception of the national interest, and that at worst they are perverted by special interests to serve their own purposes. My own view is that this is too cynical and narrow an interpretation of social idealism in general and, in particular, of the great national goals which mobilized generations of effort in such fields as education and public health. To put the matter another way, the forces generated by broadly accepted national goals and concepts of the general welfare generate forces which influence the direction of the national policy vector. Moreover, it would appear that the formulation and pursuit of explicit national goals is increasingly important in the sociopolitical process. The sponsor of the Eisenhower Commission on National Goals was, after all, the least interventionist-minded President of modern times. Daniel Bell points out that the reaching for a rationalistic view that transcends group interests is associated also with the increasing importance in government policy of matters that transcend group interests, such as foreign policy and economic growth.[4]

The recent enlarging of state and local government perspectives on planning, for example in the recognition of "economic" and "social" planning, also has historical antecedents. It is true that state and local government planning has been identified mainly with regulation of land uses, and that it was originally developed largely to protect the environmental comfort of the middle and upper classes (planning controls have been based mainly on police power). The larger interests of designing cities for efficiency, variety of choice and aesthetic quality have taken a back seat. There have been, to be sure, great city planners —the Olmsteads, Daniel Burnham, Thomas Adams, Clarence Stein,

Henry Wright, to name a few—and there have been such triumphs of city design as the Chicago lakefront, Radburn, New York's Central Park and Grand Central Station, and more recently such planned projects as Radio City, Penn Center, Constitution Plaza, Gateway Center, Century City, and the United Nations complex; also such suburban developments as Reston and Columbia. But these and other notable instances that might be mentioned are still no more than oases in a desert of urban mediocrity.

Economic development, which is beginning to be recognized as a legitimate interest of state and city planning, is a revival of a traditional concern of state and local governments, many of which bankrupted themselves in the canal and railroad building booms of the nineteenth century. And social planning, which addresses itself to raising the economic and cultural status of people, is an extension of the traditional responsibility for education. The reason we think of economic and social planning as innovational lies in the redefinition of goals and objectives and the gaining of new insights and perceptions, with formulation of new approaches that depart from established ways of doing things.

By and large, however, state and local governments have done little planning and introduced little innovation—their bureaucracies and political officials have been resistant to change. Most of the recent spurt of planning activity in these fields has been fostered and financially assisted by the federal government, for instance, through the workable programs and other planning requirements posed as a condition for federal grants-in-aid. These conditions are imposed both as measures of self-protection for federal administrative agencies and, more profoundly, as an attempt to increase the effectiveness with which resources are used. Despite the anguished howls (in many cases justified) of state and local officials over the arbitrariness of federal requirements, we can be reasonably sure that federal pressure for more and better state and local planning will continue and increase. There are signs, however, that the middle- and upper-class groups which have tended to dominate the control of state and local government are taking an increased interest in social action for urban improvement. One index of interest is the number of citizens' goal-study commissions that have been created in cities as diverse as Los Angeles, Dallas, Phoenix, and Minneapolis-St. Paul, and by such potent business organizations as the Committee for Economic Development. State, regional, and local planning agencies have at least contributed to public education in the matter of urban needs and goals, although with a few exceptions their efforts have produced little tangible payoff. Demands for greater efficiency, particularly in transportation systems, have been creating a new awareness of the need for broadening the scope of city design. Aesthetic quality is beginning to command attention, particularly when it can be shown to increase market values.

Although it is too early to be able to say for sure, we may be breaking out of many political and social institutions, taboos, and shibboleths which hitherto have impeded new concepts and approaches to urban planning and development.

The Uncertainty of Conventional Wisdom

Not the least of our uncertainties are those having to do with a lack of patterns of thought and behavior behind the accumulation of knowledge and technological potential. Future rates of progress will depend in part upon the ability to identify and discard what is irrelevant and mistaken in our conventional wisdom and social morality respecting such matters as causes of poverty, work and the distribution of income, population control, and role of the family and perhaps, in the longer run, genetic measures for improvement of the human species. To illustrate the point: when the economy was at the bottom of the great Depression a third of a century ago, very few people had any notion of what to do to get out of it short of overthrowing the existing political and economic system. J. M. Keynes, one of those very few, observed:

> If our poverty were due to famine or earthquake or war—if we lacked material things and the resources to produce them—we could not expect to find the Means of Prosperity except in hard work, abstinence and invention. In fact, our predicament is notoriously of another kind. It comes from some failure in the immaterial devices of the mind . . . , nothing is required and nothing will avail, except a little, a very little, clear thinking.

As it turned out, the conceptual solution to the problem of smoothing out business cycles was of the simplest: business recessions result from a lack of spending—the remedy is to increase spending. This simple proposition has had more far-reaching consequences for both domestic and international society in the post-World War II period than any other "breakthrough," except possibly the atomic bomb. World War II was the first of the great wars of modern times not to be followed by horrendous depression. Instead, all of the more developed and many of the less developed countries have maintained high growth rates.

It may be that we are on the verge of breakthroughs that will be as important for the final third of the twentieth century as was the discovery of how to eliminate calamitous depressions for the second third. Thus, the solution to the poverty problem may turn out to be as simple in essence as that of the business cycle: since poverty is inadequate purchasing power, the indicated remedy is to provide the poor with more income either directly or through the opportunity for higher earnings. Just as conventional wisdom thirty years ago shuddered at the notion that spending is the remedy for depression (economy rather than spending was thought to be the way out of depressions), today's conventional wisdom shudders at the notion of providing anyone with "unearned" income. It is thought that this would sap the morale and fatally impair the incentives of society. Conventional wisdom may be correct, but we are not sure it is correct. There is little solid research evidence to support its position, which tends to lean on such irrelevant historical analogies as those which attribute the decline of the Roman and British Empires to free bread and the dole. We need much more research and experimentation on this question.

The survival capacity of myths and questionable assumptions, however, depends upon their serving a widely accepted purpose. Thus conventional wisdom holds that income is about the only motivation for work. Many students of the question, sociologists and others, point out that the nature of work and motivation for work are far more complex. First, an increasing proportion of society's work holds out interest and challenge and other rewards transcending mere income; much of today's work is neither the curse of Adam or even a "disutility." Second, in contemporary American society holding a job is a central part of the male role (and the generalization applies increasingly to unattached females). The simple income-work notion, however, furnishes a rationalization for tolerating the existence of dire poverty, but once a myth or assumption starts to endanger the welfare or peace of mind of a large number of people, it must fall or the society itself will be endangered. Notions about work and income distribution may be changed if the poor can make enough of the non-poor sufficiently uncomfortable. But overt social conflict is the hard way to reduce a cultural lag and increases the danger that the notion will be used to overturn valid as well as invalid concepts and practices. A better, if little-used, way is through research and experimentation, and exploitation of the latent sense of humanity that, we trust, resides in most people.

A few of the other existing myths and dated institutions that might be mentioned include the beliefs that poor people are that way because they are lazy, shiftless, incompetent, or otherwise undeserving; that race is a simple biological phenomenon and that there are great differences in mental and other capacities among the "races"; that desegregation can be the main vehicle for improving education of children from low-culture backgrounds; that all land not immediately needed for public purposes should be in private hands (with private owners entitled to speculative gains therefrom); that "progress" or "public welfare" justifies taking private property for public purposes without full compensation for losses (including costs of relocation); that private individual decisions are always "better" than government decisions in matters concerning spending and the allocation of resources; that "traditional" government functions are always performed best by governmental agencies; and (peculiar to America among Western nations) the belief that private is private and public is public and never the twain shall meet.

Planning Under Conditions of Uncertainty

I have observed that planning is concerned with innovation and with the uncertain and the unknown. This definition is at odds with the view that we cannot plan where things are uncertain. But the exercise of preparing for foreseeable needs in habitual ways, like packing one's razor and toothbrush when preparing for a trip, is not planning as the term is used here; it is better called "preparation-making" or some similar term. If the essence of planning is dealing with innovation and conditions of uncertainty, the pace of change and the uncertain shape of the future challenge as never before the creativity of those who would call themselves planners. Most of us are not sure of what we as individuals want, either for ourselves or for society. How much less sure can we be of what the American people will want twenty-five or fifty years from now?

There are several strategies for dealing with uncertainty and reducing the cost of uncertainty, including:

1. Making projections which set reasonable limits on uncertain magnitudes (thus one might place the growth rate of a gross national product over the next three decades between 3 and 4 percent, discarding as unlikely a growth rate as low as 1 percent or as high as 10 percent).

2. Making careful choice of what is to be decided.

3. Choosing lines of action that will preserve later flexibility. Hedging. Converting uncertainty to risk by grouping future planned events in such a way as to take advantage of probabilities (as opposed to staking everything on the outcome of single events).

4. Formulating and articulating social goals that can serve as broad policy guidelines, recognizing that goals themselves will evolve over time.[5]

Urban Goals and the Social Climate

Let us accept the proposition that the greatest national developmental task of the next few decades is getting accustomed to and raising the standards of urban life.[6] The prevalent tendency of contemporary society is to depend upon the market and steadily rising purchasing power for things which we do want, while being forced to turn to collective action to eliminate things we do not want such as congestion, pollution, crime and delinquency, restrictions on choice, and the ugliness of the urbanscape. It is for this reason that many of our social goals have to do with eliminating abominations. The reason we have not gone further is that not enough people deplore them sufficiently.

We are told that the reason for this apathy is that, in the experience of the ordinary American, things are getting a bit better all the time.[7] The middle class escapes the most severe urban troubles by moving to the suburbs. The upper-income people can wall themselves off from the city's unpleasantness or can flee to suburbia or exurbia along with the middle class. In both central cities and suburbs, dominant political control has tended to be held by the middle class.

The people who require most from government—those at the lower end of the income-cultural scale who are heavily dependent on welfare and related bureaucracies—exercise relatively little control over it. However, there are signs that new political winds are beginning to blow; protests over deprivation are being listened to; at least in some cases the lower-income groups are assuming a more active political role. And, as previously noted, there are signs that middle- and upper-class groups are showing a new interest in public issues of urban improvement.

I personally subscribe to the article of faith which says that initiative for urban social and physical improvement should come primarily from the urban areas themselves. Centrally planned change almost inevitably entails uniformity—in rules and regulations, standards of design, financing mechanisms, and so on. With urban development, variety is preferable to uniformity, first because needs and conditions vary widely and second because in most fields we need to experiment with a great variety of approaches. However sound the principle that innovation should come from the grass roots, local governments have been pitiably weak in practice; most innovation has come from the federal government. The grass roots have lacked imagination, technical skills, and finances. Such weaknesses might be made up in some degree by calling upon the well advertised innovational genius of business and industry, but local government bureaucracies have been timorous (they tend to dislike innovation anyway) and money has been lacking.

Clearly, the great need of the times is for applying American genius for innovation to fields where innovation has been tardy or lacking—in the social field, to the problem of raising the productivity and cultural status of people now caught in the poverty trap; in the physical field, by applying technologies to problems of transportation, housing, and new concepts of urban design; in the field of government, by creating new governmental and political arrangements needed to serve effectively the emerging urban society. But if innovation is going to take hold at the grass roots, it must be generated therefrom. Experience thus far, however, indicates that this will happen only if there is vigorous stimulation of and financial support for innovation, and this, so far as we can see, must come from the federal government.

An important aspect of the national development task, therefore, is creation of an atmosphere which will support exploration and innovation. Plainly, innovation in the public sector must be based upon public demand. One basis of demand is public dissatisfaction with existing conditions, but, given the fact that the majority is not as yet crisis-minded, it is highly likely that national development policy in the foreseeable future will be a series of incremental steps and adjustments, rather than quantum leaps.

I believe, however, that development can be guided and accelerated by a conscious effort to build consensus around development goals. I here suggest an agenda focusing on two very broad goals and several supporting sub-goals, as a basis for further discussion. The list is exploratory, not definitive. In any rapidly changing society, goals must be as protean and evolutionary as the society itself.

Two Broad Goals for National Development Policy

Eradication of Poverty

This is a goal which commands general support in principle but which runs into difficulties over specific measures for implementation. The goal necessitates equipping individuals with the essentials of productivity—good health, aspiration and incentive, lifelong opportunities for education and training, jobs for everyone who wishes to work. Underlying these should be a policy for a national minimum income, designed to replace as much as is feasible of the present congery of income-maintenance programs and to reinforce incentives for self-improvement and productive work and family stability.

The Great Society and the War on Poverty have never mounted a general attack on the poverty problem. The antipoverty programs have concentrated mainly on upgrading skills and increasing opportunities of the potentially employable, giving less emphasis to the majority of the poor, including the old, the young, the handicapped, and women with fatherless families. These groups can be adequately provided for without impairing work incentives, since most of them are not in the labor force. The working poor, whose poverty results from intermittent work, low wages or large families, also need assistance which can be provided in various ways without raising the great bugaboo of spoiling the incentive to work.

But what if machines take over a large proportion of society's routine work, and perhaps braintrusting as well? How then would we distribute income? Is this likely to happen on any considerable scale over the course of the next fifty years? About all that can be said now is that machines have not as yet created a general shortage of jobs; blue-collar job shortages thus far have stemmed more from deficient aggregate demand than from the impact of machines. An increasing proportion of jobs requires skilled professional training, these are increasingly in the service industries as opposed to manufacturing, and there is no indication that they are being taken over by machines, in the large. Over the next quarter century, at least, these trends are likely to continue.

Along with poverty, discrimination and caste based on racial differences have to go. In the present institutional system, discriminaton contributes to poverty and makes the escape from poverty more difficult. But poverty also contributes to discrimination—if we can help the minority groups to raise their economic and cultural status we can expect less difficulty with discrimination *per se*.

Environmental Improvement

This second broad goal includes all the things that need to be done to make urban (and rural) areas most efficient, convenient, and aesthetically pleasing. It comprehends such subgoals as:

1. A variety of ways of life and opportunities to choose among them, such as a greater degree of choice for all income groups as between living in central cities or suburbs without sacrificing essential amenities

(such as educational opportunities, physical safety, fresh air, or mobility).

2. The elimination of aggression, such as criminal aggression against person and property, and environmental aggressions such as noise, pollution, congestion, and obtrusive ugliness.

3. The maintenance of central cities as vital, healthy centers of knowledge and culture, of management and commerce, and of residence for city-lovers.

4. Planned metropolitan development outside central cities with population and activities grouped in urban subcenters designed for efficiency and aesthetic appeal.

I make no suggestions as to priorities, and in any case all the goals mentioned require immediate attention. We are not yet so affluent a society as to be able to afford all at once everything we want or even need, but pursuit of some of the above goals requires no more resources than would be used by proceeding in a helter-skelter, unplanned fashion. And some of the goals, such as effective educational opportunities, are essential for maintaining and increasing economic productivity over the long run.

Two factors over which society has at least some degree of control will vitally affect the capacity of the American economy for goal achievement over the coming decades. These are the increase-rates of population and of the gross national product. The following section considers the quantitative implications of these factors for national development between now and the year 2000.[8]

I project the quantitative demands on GNP which would be created by specific "levels of attainment" of the above broad goals. In connection with eradicating poverty, we "increase" consumption, housing, and various government services. For environmental improvement, there is (again) improved housing, urban infrastructure, and allowance for gross private business investment to reduce various kinds of social costs. These projections, it should be emphasized, are an exercise in analyzing what we might expect to achieve in various aspects of the suggested goals, given varying rates of economic growth.

Population and Resources

Population Growth

We had barely become accustomed to the post-World War II population upsurge after the low of the 1930's, and the notion that the urban population would double between 1960 and the end of the century, than evidence of falling birth rates began accumulating. The Census Bureau's four-level projections of year-2000 population now range between 283 and 358 million, whereas high projections a few years ago were running over 400 million. If the decline in birthrates continues, as seems quite likely, the lowest projection is the most probable and even it may be too high. But for the moment let us specify a range of population between 280 million and 360 million, an increase over 1967 figures of from 40 to 80 percent. All of the increase will be in urban areas.

The year-2000 population will be remarkable in several respects. First the proportion of people in the working-age bracket—20 to 64 years—will be higher than it is today.[9] Second, the size of the working-age group of the year 2000 would vary relatively little between the two population projections. It will not be affected greatly by what happens to the birthrate from here on because two-thirds or more of it already has been born.

Assuming that birthrates increase again to give us a higher population, where and when would this occur? The increase might not take place among the present generation of families, which is reducing its birthrate, but among their children. If it is true that the generation born in the period 1947–60, when birthrates were high, has been impressed by crowding and high cost of maintenance and education sufficiently to plan for smaller families of their own, birthrates would rise again only if their children opted for larger families. The impact would not be felt until the middle 1980's; none of the larger crop would be of working age by 2000.

The differential population (over the low projection) thus would require high expenditures on education in addition to high costs of housing, infrastructure, and ordinary maintenance. The marginal contribution of the differential working force at best would fall considerably short of supporting the differential population; this means that the smaller population would enjoy a larger product-per-person than the larger.

In fact, there are reasons for supposing that the total GNP for a population as large as 360 million would be little larger than that for a population of 280 million. First, because the incremental population would not be self-supporting, the pool of funds for savings in capital formation would be larger for the smaller than for the larger population. Second, because the labor force differential would be relatively much smaller than the population differential, a relatively high proportion of the differential labor force probably would come from the low-income, low-culture groups; their productivity in 2000 may still be under average, no matter what we can do in the meantime.[10] Third, continued technological progress may deplete the number of jobs for low- and semiskilled workers, and make part of the differential labor force redundant.

These considerations all point to the conclusion that the suggested goals can be achieved more fully for a smaller than for a larger population. In itself, this might seem an inadequate or even a selfish reason for national policies to promote, or at least not to inhibit, family planning. But in the long run, much more is at stake. With the prospect that the Earth's scarce resources will be used up in a flash of geologic time, population limititation is essential to the welfare of future generations, of which, we hope, there are a great many yet to come.

GNP and General Well-being

In recent years, the GNP (roughly defined as the market value of all goods and services produced) has been used as the leading indicator of economic performance and progress over time. Several factors are making the GNP as now measured less adequate as a measure of changes in general well-being. It leaves out of account such uncompensated services as those of housewives and of do-it-yourself activities. It takes no account of leisure time, and ignores the value to the user of recreation except insofar as recreation involves services which are specifically charged for. Withal, present measures are valuable, if not all-inclusive, indicators of capacity. Many of the goods and services with which the above goals are concerned, such as health and medical services, urban development and renewal, and environmental improvement do show up in the GNP. If the GNP as now defined should stop rising, many goals would have to be abandoned.

What GNP increase rate can be attained? The annual growth rate between 1929 and 1966 was about 3 percent, but growth was interrupted for nearly a decade by the Depression. The rate in the postwar period—1946–66—has been nearly 4 percent, but again there was an interruption in 1952–60 when the rate was relatively low (about 2.6 percent). The rate between 1960 and 1966 has been approximately 4.9 percent.

Many analysts think that an average rate of 4 percent can be sustained, and some think that a high-driving policy of expansion could achieve 4.5 or 5 percent. Some, impressed by their reading of long-term trends, would put the probable rate closer to 3 percent.

These apparently small differences will make an enormous difference in the amount of resources available for goal achievement. A 3 percent growth rate for the rest of the century will give us an aggregate GNP of about $42.5 trillion over the 33 years. A 4 percent rate will give us $51.5 trillion in 1966 prices. The difference, $9 trillion, is equivalent to about *13 years'* GNP at present levels (about $750 billion per year). A 4.5 percent rate would yield an aggregate of $57.0 trillion.

These magnitudes make clear that the most important requirement for achieving national goals is to keep up the rate of economic growth. This will require high rates of investment in productivity-increasing factors—plant equipment, research and development, education. Raising the productivity of the present low-productivity groups is an important element —the Council of Economic Advisers' 1965 report estimated that if the nonwhite population were at the level of the white in education and earnings, the GNP in 1965 would have been $27 billion higher. Over the rest of the century, this difference would accumulate to some $1.5 trillion.

Denison's study for the Committee for Economic Development, *The Sources of Economic Growth in the United States and the Alternatives Before Us* (December, 1961), attributes 23 percent of GNP increase between 1929 and 1957 to advances in education, 20 percent to advances in knowledge, but only 15 percent to increase in the stock of capital *per se*.[11] Even if his estimates are only roughly correct, the fact that knowledge and technological potential continue to accumulate at increasing rates may indicate that the end of productivity potential is nowhere in sight. The experience of the last few years teaches us that continuous high demand is necessary to call forth high increase rates in the GNP.[12]

I next posit, more or less arbitrarily, some quantitative objectives for the purpose of examining whether they can be covered by projected levels of GNP and what their possible implications might be for national policy respecting GNP allocation. I have not here undertaken, however, to explore the much more difficult question of strategy to attain these or other quantitative objectives, but if the productive potential is there, the main obstacles in the way of goal achievement will stem from the impediments of the mind compounded by the inflexibility of sociopolitical institutions.

Consumption

Consumption in the GNP is measured largely by personal expenditures on consumer goods and services, but these include expenditures on health and medical services, education, and housing, each of which contributes to skill and energy and thereby to economic productivity. Although they are labeled consumption, such expenditures might well come under the rubric of investment as a means of increasing public understanding and acceptance of their implications. (The same is true of government expenditures on the same items now classified under the uninformative title, "government purchases of goods and services.")

The principal immediate goal with respect to consumption is to raise consumption levels of the poor and near-poor who constitute more than 25 percent of the present population. We cannot stop with increasing consumption at the bottom levels, however; political expediency dictates that consumption be increased all along the line. As a rough exercise, let us consider the implications for increasing consumption by various percentages, which are taken as targets to be reached by the year 2000.

Table 1

Quintile	Assumed Consumption Increase by 2000 (in percentages)	
	Low	*High*
First (lowest)	150	250
Second	125	200
Third	100	150
Fourth	75	100
Fifth (highest)	50	50

In the top quintile, the per-household consumption figure would go from an average of approximately $15,200 per annum to approximately $22,800. Increasing consumption for the lower quintile by as little as 150 percent over 33 years is a slow train for the very poor. The average consumption per household now is in the magnitude of $2,800; it would rise to $7,000 by 2000, and the average annual increase per household would be approximately $130. Under the higher formula (giving the lowest quintile an increase of 250 percent), the annual increase would average about $215 per annum, with an annual per-household consumption figure of approximately $10,000 by year 2000.

The total cumulative amount required, of course, would depend upon the level of population. The figures are presented in Table 3, p. 303; the higher increase, even for the smaller population, would consume 73 percent of a GNP growing at 3 percent per year. (Actual percentages, consumption of GNP, ranged between 66 and 63 percent in the postwar period.) The higher consumption goal is not, for technical reasons, consistent with a 3 percent GNP growth rate; however, it is consistent with a 4 percent growth rate. The higher consumption goal for the higher population would preempt 63 percent of a 4 percent growth GNP, approximately the 1967 figure.

Achievement of consumption patterns anywhere near those projected here (high or low) would require a very substantial leveling of consumer incomes. The solution, if there is a solution, lies in part in measures to accelerate the productivity of those labor force members, or potential labor force members, now at the bottom of the income and productivity scale. But it would require also proportionately greater income transfers (i.e., redistribution) through increased welfare and social security grants, and perhaps new forms of income maintenance (the much-debated negative income tax is one alternative).

The political and economic difficulties of such a shift in consumption and income distribution are indicated by the fact that since the end of the war there has been no trend toward greater equality of incomes; on the contrary, the trend seems to have been toward greater *inequality*.[13]

Housing

In projecting housing costs for the remainder of the century, I have used the following standards: (1) a dwelling unit for each added household; (2) replacements sufficient in number to bring down the average age of the housing stock to 25 years. This subgoal could eliminate housing now classified as substandard. It would account for approximately half the total demand;[14] and (3) second dwelling units equal in number to 25 percent of year 2000 families.

I assume also that the real cost of dwelling units would gradually increase from the 1967 average of $14,000 to a year-2000 figure of approximately $22,500 with the proviso that the cost of second units will average $10,000 apiece less than other dwelling units. The goal would necessitate an annual average production of nearly 3 million units per year, nearly twice the average output over the last decade.

Education

I assume virtually universal enrollment of the 5 to 17 age group, slightly over half of the 18 to 20 age group, 30 percent of the 22 to 24 age group, and 15 percent of the 25 to 34 age group, with the targets to be reached by 1975. This gives us the following demand for education, in terms of pupil years, to the year 2000.

Table 2

School Level	Aggregate Pupil Years 1967–2000 with Population Projections (in billions of pupil years)	
	360 Million	280 Million
Elementary	1.67	1.30
Secondary	.63	.53
College and university	.54	.47

Real costs of education will undoubtedly rise owing to the necessity of pouring enormously more funds into the education of low-income, low-culture groups, the advent of new and costly teaching technologies, and the continuing need for the overall improvement of education. A goal which contemplates doubling average expenditure for elementary and secondary school education by 1975, and holding it constant thereafter, is not unreasonable. (Average present costs per pupil year from $450, elementary, to $900, secondary.) Higher education costs also are assumed to double in the same period.

Public Infrastructure

Infrastructure includes public transportation facilities, water and sewer lines, recreational and cultural facilities, public health centers and hospitals, etc.

I have used a cost figure for new infrastructure of $30,000 per new household, and for modernization and renewal $10,000 per household as of 2000. These figures allow a fair margin for such things as improved pollution control, development and introduction of new transportation devices (separation of vehicular and pedestrian traffic, moving sidewalks, new transportation technologies) and generally higher standards of design for the entire urban environment. The total comes to a figure of between $1.5 trillion and $2 trillion; the magnitude might be increased by another 5 percent without greatly changing the aggregate demand on GNP.[15]

Domestic Private Business Investment

This category is an amalgam of increasing capital stock and technological improvement.[16] It is the most difficult figure to project because of the high uncertainty respecting the functional relationship between private gross business investment and GNP. Throughout the postwar period the figure has stayed close to 10 percent of the GNP; the average in the ten-year period 1956–66 is almost exactly 10 percent. A part of this outlay, however, represented investments in the space and defense industries.

Meanwhile it appears that many American industries are obsolescing technologically and that in a number of fields American industry is falling behind foreign competitors.[17] Obsolescence is speeded up by the pace of accelerating technology and the probability of demand for new types of consumer goods, for public as well as for personal consumption. The very large investment required to produce a supersonic transport is a straw in the wind. Increased emphasis on labor-saving devices, to reduce labor costs and accommodate demands for more leisure, is another investment-cost-increasing factor. Still another is the rapidly growing demand for reduction of social costs imposed by industry, which involve among other things pollution control and higher aesthetic standards. The day is passing when smelly, ugly factories will be tolerated simply because they provide jobs.

Finally, there is the problem of maintaining a high rate of growth over an extended period of time—this may require substantially larger capital inputs than we have been accustomed to in the past. Resorting again to the technique of reducing uncertainty by specifying ranges, I show two figures for investment in plant and equipment—one an aggregate figure of 10 percent of GNP, which is close to the historic average; the other, a figure of 15 percent.

Federal Government Purchases

Here the problem centers on what will happen to military expenditures, which are by far the largest federal government demand on the GNP. (Federal expenditures for nonmilitary goods and services in 1966 were only $17 billion compared with $60 billion for military.)[18]

The federal government's purchases of goods and services have not been rising rapidly, in contrast to the zooming rise of federal transfer expenditures.[19] There is nothing on the horizon, save possibly a vast increase in the space exploration program, which seems likely to change this picture. I have therefore projected federal non-defense purchases at the prevailing 1967 proportion (2.3 percent) of the GNP.

Defense expenditures can be viewed pessimistically or optimistically. Two projections are used here: first, that defense expenditures will average $130 billion a year for the rest of the century; second, that they will average $65 billion a year. This makes a difference of approximately $2.1 trillion in federal expenditures over the period (equal, incidentally, to almost three years of GNP at the present rate).

State and Local Government Purchases

State and local government purchases in recent years have been the most rapidly increasing segment of GNP. Two major components, however, have already been projected under the headings of public infrastructure and education. The remainder is largely personal services such as services of law-enforcement officers, firemen, inspectors, sanitation workers, health and medical services, along with the administration of the various welfare (consumption-increasing) functions. In the 1960's, the period of most rapid recent growth, such service expenditures per person have been increasing at the rate of about 4.0 percent per year. I have projected this rate for the rest of the century.

Foreign Expenditures

Foreign expenditures represent (1) overseas assistance for development and (2) overseas investment. Assistance for development at present is running at a very low figure—less than 0.3 percent of GNP—whereas several years ago it was in the magnitude of 1 percent of GNP. A goal of 1 percent of GNP has repeatedly been urged and is projected here—it would use approximately $500 billion. Foreign investment may reasonably be assumed to take another 1 percent of GNP.[20]

Table 3

Projected Aggregate Demands on Gross National Product: 1967–2000

Demand

	Year 2000 Population of 280 Million Projections[a]		Year 2000 Population of 360 Million Projections[a]	
	High	Low	High	Low
	(trillions)		*(trillions)*	
Consumption	$31.0	$26.3	$32.5	$29.2
Housing	1.6	1.6	1.9	1.9
Education, total	4.1	4.1	5.3	5.3
Urban public facilities (infrastructure)	2.0	2.0	2.5	2.5
Business investment (plant and equipment)	7.7	4.3	7.7	4.3
Federal government				
Defense	4.3	2.2	4.3	2.2
Other	1.2	1.0	1.2	1.0
State and local government (excluding education and public facilities)	2.5	3.1	2.5	3.1
Foreign expenditures	1.0	.8	1.0	.8
Totals	$55.7	$45.7	$58.9	$50.3

Supply

Assuming Various Growth Rates

Aggregate GNP with Annual Growth of
$$\begin{cases} 3 \quad \text{percent} = \$42.5 \text{ trillion} \\ 4 \quad \text{percent} = \$51.5 \text{ trillion} \\ 4.5 \text{ percent} = \$57.0 \text{ trillion} \end{cases}$$

[a] Principal differences between the low and high projections are as follows:
1. The amount of per capita consumption increases in all but the top quintile of consumers (see above, pp. 299 and 300.)
2. Business investment in plant and equipment, assumed to be 15 percent of aggregate GNP in the high projection, 10 percent in the low.
3. Federal defense expenditures, assumed to average $130 billion a year in the high projection, $65 billion a year in the low.

Conclusions from Table 3

A 3 percent growth rate would not be adequate to meet the low goals for the low population projection. A 4 percent growth rate would fall short of meeting the high goals for the low population projection, and to meet them for the high population projection would require a growth rate slightly in excess of 4.5 percent.[21]

The largest items are consumption, defense, education, and private investment in plant and equipment. Of these, only consumption and defense can be held below projected figures without some risk of reducing the GNP growth rate. However, we do not know how much the growth rate would be affected by expanding or contracting expenditure in either the education or private investment categories by, say, a trillion dollars.

The items most important for improvement of the urban environment are housing, infrastructure, other state and local government expenditures, and private domestic investment. The first three items are relatively small—any of them could be increased by a substantial percentage without much effect on aggregate demands on GNP.

We have noted that several of the suggested goals presumptively will pay for themselves in increased productivity, such as the raising of educational levels of those who otherwise would be caught in the low-culture, low-income trap. Increasing the economic efficiency of the urban environment pays off almost by definition, and in many cases so does aesthetic quality—people will pay more for homes, travel facilities, and workshops with pleasant surroundings than with unpleasant.[22]

Some of the bolder notions in urban development now going around, such as developing new towns in towns and building new cities outside established urban centers, would involve no great expenditures over what will be spent in any case to accommodate the increased urban population and to improve environment. The essential point lies in how the growth is planned, organized, and directed rather than in the additional resources necessary to achieve growth.

Urban Concentrations and New City Building

Should the distribution of the urban population be a concern of national development policy? In particular, should we undertake to build new cities away from the present and projected concentration as, for example, in northern California, New Mexico, Appalachia, or other sections?

Experience of governments elsewhere does not hold out great promise that government policy can have a marked effect on the flow of people and investments except under favorable economic circumstances (as those involving the exploitation of natural resources). Potential measures that might be used include provision of water for areas where it is in short supply; manipulation of government contracts, particularly those involving new plants; incentives such as low-interest loans for location in stipulated areas; and provision of transportation and other infrastructure. Any of these measures, however, can be expected to raise intense political opposition from areas less favored or areas whose resources might be tapped for the benefit of other sections. Thus the northwest can be expected to fight to the death any attempt to divert its water supply to, say, the southwestern desert regions.

I shall use as a point of reference the results of Jerome Pickard's studies for the Urban Land Institute of population distribution in the United States projected to the year 2000.[23] The studies take the Census B population projection of 312 million for 2000 (lower projections would change the absolute amounts but would not much affect the main conclusions).

The projections show the urban population concentrating in three major regions (the California region, Florida region, and the metropolitan belt which clusters around the Great Lakes and along the Atlantic seaboard) thirteen "outlying urban regions,"[24] and six "free-standing" metropolitan areas with a population of one million or more each.[25]

In all, the total population of the three giant regions, the thirteen outlying regions, and the six free-standing metropolitan areas is projected at 239 million—77 percent of the total population of the forty-eight mainland states, occupying 11 percent of the land area. Average density of population on the mainland outside of these urban areas is projected to drop from 29 persons per square mile in 1960 to 27 persons per square mile in 2000. The density of the urban regions and metropolitan areas comes to 708 persons per square mile. Densities would be higher in some regions, as the Atlantic seaboard region (1,050 persons per square mile) and within the New York zone (1,863 persons per square mile). In limited areas, densities would go much higher. Thus New York City already averages 25,000 people per square mile. Overall densities in urban regions, however, are less than those now prevailing in England and Wales (810 per square mile) and the Netherlands (768 per square mile).

The economic forces which determined the location and growth of urban areas in their formative stages, such as the location of cities around harbors, on rivers, at the crossings of transportation routes, and the location of industries with respect to natural resources, markets, or labor supply, are being superseded by other forces. A large proportion of industrial expansion occurs near already existing plants. For this reason and because of other factors having to do with economies of scale and "externalities," already established regions tend to keep growing. The second factor which will be increasingly important in the future is climate, particularly warm climate. For example, the growing industry of research finds an advantage in being able to offer climate as an attraction in recruiting scientists. Climate is also associated with recreation and retirement, both increasingly important as locational factors.[26]

The main constraint on urban development, it would appear, is water, but this constraint can be surmounted in most areas with the possible exception of the southwest which must depend upon importation of water to reach projected dimensions. The greatest potential source, the Pacific northwest, is unlikely to give up its water, and thereby damage its own prospects for development, without a struggle. The population configuration of the western belt, therefore, may depend somewhat upon the outcome of the struggle over water, but this prospect could be altered by development of low-cost techniques for desalinization.

The projection techniques used by Pickard depend heavily upon extrapolation of past and current trends, both in population growth and land use densities. Both presumptively reflect strong locational forces and preferences which express themselves mainly through the market. Altering this pattern in any substantial way requires countering already operative forces with stronger forces and locational attractions to people and industries. Any policy for decentralization can be supported, therefore, only if there is reason to think it would produce great advantages.

Proponents of decentralization and new-city building advance several arguments. First, urban settlements of high or low density which extend indefinitely are undesirable in that they separate people too far from the countryside, green space, and outdoor recreation. The very prospect of endless megalopolis is depressing. Concentrations may become so high as to produce adverse psychological and physiological effects.

On the other hand, urban densities within the projected megalopolitan areas will be lower than in present urban areas and, as noted above, densities for the entire complex of the year 2000 would be lower than those which already prevail, without apparent adverse effects, in England, Wales, and the Netherlands. The nearly nine-tenths of the U.S.

land area outside the urban concentrations would offer opportunities to escape from the stresses of urban living, and escape will be facilitated by increases in both leisure time and ease of transportation.

Another argument points to the high cost of building in urban areas, and of maintaining the projected urban densities, including land costs, the problems of water supply, pollution control, recreation facilities, and so on. Aside from the one item of land cost, however, these can be largely discounted. Control of pollution, from whatever source, will be necessary and there is little reason to suppose that it will cost much less for any feasible alternative distribution of population than for the ones projected. Such relatively isolated urban areas as Kansas City and Phoenix already have serious air pollution problems, and so might new cities. Inducing people and industries to locate in new areas and overcoming possible adverse climatic and other environmental conditions might add substantially to the cost of new-city development.

As for possible economies in land costs, it should be noted that such costs ordinarily represent a transfer of income, which in many cases contributes to the concentration of wealth, rather than withdrawal of GNP. Avoidance of concentrations of wealth is a desirable objective, particularly in a society where so many fortunes accrue from real estate holdings, but this objective can be achieved by means less drastic than spreading out urban settlements. A more important consideration is that very high land prices make it difficult to assemble development tracts of the size needed for modern integrated urban developments, particularly new towns of the scale of Reston or Columbia or larger.

We should note in this connection the school of thought that holds that trends toward lower densities of land use are increasing the costs of urban development and consuming land at a profligate rate. This school would increase densities by putting working, recreational, and residential facilities in close juxtaposition in high-density areas.[27] Although this approach would not necessarily preclude building new towns, it would call for a national policy of quite different emphasis.

New-city enthusiasts argue that radical improvement of existing cities and new development in their suburban ambits is out of the question because of already existing commitments to physical layout, institutional patterns, political structure and traditions, and other rigidities of long-standing organizations, not to mention the impossibility of assembling land holdings large enough for efficient planning and building of new towns and cities. Thus, John Rubel says:

Nearly every projection about our cities points to a worsening of the environment for people. The traffic will get worse. Air pollution will be more frequent and worse. . . . Useful and accessible open spaces will be gobbled up until a good part of both sea coasts will be paved with contiguous urban conglomerations for hundreds of miles. Anyone who is sanguine about the prospects for curing smog in Los Angeles or over-crowding in Harlem or the imminent erosion of the San Francisco Bay does not understand the problem.[28]

The plain fact is that, no matter what we do to divert population away from settlements in areas already dictated by powerful locational forces, much of tomorrow's urban population will be living in and around existing concentrations. The largest part of the development task, there-fore, is environmental improvement where the mass of the people will be.

If land for agricultural or other valuable non-urban uses becomes scarce, there might be a genuine economy in diverting newer urban developments from such land to land less valuable for non-urban pur-poses. Except in a few areas, however, there is no indication of any such encroachment and there is no indication of any impending shortage of agricultural land overall.[29]

It appears that the most useful purpose to be served by building complete new cities somewhat apart from other urban concentrations is that of technological development and demonstration. Thus John Rubel has called for a "new city technology, created by methods analo-gous to a very big missile and space project." These projects "represent important innovations in at least two fundamental ways: they call for a novel articulation of public purposes with private means—it was this that led to the creation of the aerospace industry in the first place—and they evoke the accelerated development and swift refinement of 'systems engineering,' 'systems analysis,' the 'integrated systems management approach,' 'operations research.'"[30]

Rubel continues, "If you could set up a project for the creation of a new industry from scratch, and offer the job to private industry, and set up project goals in terms of the performance of a dynamic system, you would see new industries spring up within the framework of existing firms to meet new needs. Soon the multidisciplinary teams would be assembled. The relevant analytical techniques would be applied. The new methods, the new technologies, the new insights would begin to emerge."[31]

Other crucial elements of the Rubel approach involve the assembly of land sufficient for an entire new city and its environs (the technique also used by English new town development corporations) and public-private cooperation to provide the large amounts of funds which will be necessary to develop a new city of substantial size. Counting gross private domestic investment, the development of a new city of, say, half a million people would require a total outlay in the magnitude of $100,000 per household or an aggregate of approximately $16 billion, about $8 billion of which would be required for housing and public facilities. Given the fact that housing, infrastructure, and jobs must be provided for some 26 million new urban households by the end of the century, it would seem only prudent to explore the potential of such an approach by undertaking to build several new cities of various sizes as rapidly as possible.

As previously noted, it seems highly unlikely that new cities could be built on a scale that would significantly alter the projected pattern of urban settlement. But the issue is not closed—this is one of the uncertainties that can be reduced only by gaining knowledge through research and experimentation.[32]

Incentives for Technological Innovation

We have noted that urban governments generally have been slow to initiate or stimulate innovation, including technological innovation, and that there are several reasons, including financial, for their inertia. But urban governments have responded where there have been incentives and resources.

For example, the urban development and renewal programs have been utilized by many cities with some failures but with some notable successes. In the process, there has been a considerable conceptual development (more significant than the physical development that has occurred thus far) and a great improvement in planning and development standards and in the number and quality of planners employed at the urban, state, and regional levels. The model cities program, less than six months old, already has evoked many applications (though few, if any, thus far manifest much original thinking or innovation). Federal participation in airport financing helped municipalities enter the air age. The War on Poverty has mobilized a substantial national effort, with the participation of both public and private sectors.

The competition for the proposed giant accelerator for high-energy physics research, involving a construction cost of several hundred million dollars and an annual payroll of some $60 million, drew in all of the major regions and many individual states and localities, which spent millions of dollars preparing and presenting their cases.

All the above cases have in common (a) clearly defined objectives and (b) awards of federal funds for innovational programs sufficient in scale to evoke major efforts on the part of the urban communities.[33]

These precedents suggest that a series of national competitions and awards for best "plans-and-programs" dealing with various urban needs could supply the motivation for significant breakthroughs in these fields by human improvement, not only in hardware but also in organizational improvement and political acceptance thereof. For example, awards might be made for the best plan and program to be submitted by a government, or consortium of governments, representing a metropolitan area, and in a number of functional fields. Award programs could be established for a number of objectives; some examples follow:

1. A comprehensive innovative intra-urban transportation system; such a system exists nowhere at present.

2. An integrated, area-wide health and hospitals program.

3. A 20-year housing development plan that takes into account not only the immediate need for low-cost housing but also such factors as (a) the efficient location of housing with respect to employment centers, (b) probable increases in incomes and housing standards over the planning period, (c) feasible approaches to integration.

4. A comprehensive social development plan for an urban area, including such elements as income and educational objectives for various segments of the population, particularly people who would be prone to stay in the poverty trap.

5. A recreation development plan to make recreation facilities available to all inhabitants of the urban area on approximately equal terms.

6. A plan for the development of a business area to separate (a) pedestrian, (b) private motor vehicle, and (c) mass transportation movement.

The losers in any such competition would benefit from the stimulation of interest in their urban problems and the mobilization of their resources to attack problems. It is likely that meritorious plans which did not win awards would be eligible for federal assistance, either under already existing programs or newly enacted programs. The competitions themselves, if successful, would stimulate and guide the federal government in expanding its participation.

Such competitions would present many technical problems, but probably none greater than those presented by the decision of where to locate the giant accelerator or the space center—there is already a body of precedent and experience in handling such problems. The greatest problem, which may make the whole idea impractical, is the political problem. Competitions of the kind proposed would be very costly, since the awards would have to be very large to induce urban areas to plan and carry out significant projects. (Financing a transportation program for a major urban area, for example, might run to a billion dollars or more.) Congress is unlikely to vote the sums required without some assurance that the funds would be widely distributed, and this would defeat the basic purpose of the program. Nonetheless, the concept may be worth pursuing further—it has already been employed to a limited degree in the model cities program and in HUD's annual "Urban Development Intergovernmental Report."

Modernizing State and Urban Government

The proposition that local areas are the principal arbiters of their own destinies falls athwart the generally low level of competence displayed by local governments as now constituted to cope adequately with the issues of today's and tomorrow's urban development. The criteria underlying this statement are primarily those having to do with state and local governments as service-rendering machines as opposed to political machines, or as job-providing machines, or as protectors of middle-class or other interests. The capacities for service and for adaptation are the primary criteria used by the Committee for Economic Development (CED) in its recent policy statements, *Modernizing Local Government* and *Modernizing State Government*. These reports concluded, in brief, that state and local governments as now constituted are not capable of meeting the problems created by the expanding urban society or of moving constructively to formulate and build consensus for urban goals, or to foster innovation. With respect to local government, there are too many local jurisdictions; their functions overlap in crazy-quilt patterns; they lack planning and administrative expertise; they are unable to expand either with the needs or the geographic territory of growing urban concentrations.

There is a tendency in some quarters to rationalize the multiplicity of jurisdictions found in most metropolitan areas on the ground that small governments have a greater capacity to meet consumer preferences because they are closer to the people and because, with many jurisdictions to choose from, people can more easily locate in jurisdictions

offering service levels best suited to their particular desires. It is supposed also that collective decisions reached by small aggregations of
individuals are likely to be more nearly "optimal" than decisions by
larger aggregations. This rationalization, however, runs into the fact that
smaller governments tend to be less efficient and to command less
constituent interest than larger governments. The smaller government
jurisdictions are not necessarily responsive to need; it appears that the
smaller the government, the stronger is likely to be the veto power of the
negative elements.

The CED prescriptions in *Modernizing Local Government* offer an
agenda of local government reform:

Reduction in the number of local governments by at least 80 percent,
and severe curtailment of overlapping layers of local government, with
townships and most types of special districts being obvious targets for
elimination.

Limitation of popular election to members of legislative bodies and
the chief executive in the "strong mayor" type of municipal government.

A single strong executive—elected mayor or city manager.

Much stronger staffing and use of trained professionals.

Use of county, or combinations of county, jurisdictions to attack
metropolitan problems.

Use of federal—and state—grants-in-aid to encourage local government administrative reforms, particularly reforms having to do with
consolidation and organization to meet metropolitan problems.

A parallel set of prescriptions is presented in *Modernizing State
Government*.

The last recommendation suggests tying a system of federal grants
(possibly per capita block grants to states as proposed by Heller and
Pechman) to local and state government reform. This is not as simple as
saying to the states and localities: "Reorganize; eliminate corruption;
introduce program planning and budgeting systems; hire good personnel, as a condition for getting per capita grants." In fact, administrative
problems are most difficult. One formula for administering such a
concept was set forth in a bill introduced in the House of Representatives
by Congressman Henry S. Reuss of Wisconsin, in January, 1967. Under
the Reuss bill, block grants would be made conditional upon the sub-
mission by states of acceptable programs of government modernization;

the review and evaluation bodies would be regional coordinating committees and the federal Advisory Commission on Intergovernmental Relations, which would certify as eligible programs reflecting "sufficient stated creative initiative so as to qualify that state for federal block grants." Among the items suggested for consideration in drawing up such programs are:

1. Arrangements for dealing with interstate regional, including metropolitan, problems.
2. Strengthening and modernizing state governments.
3. Strengthening and modernizing local, rural, urban, and metropolitan governments.
4. Proposed uses of federal block grants, including provisions for passing on at least 50 percent to local governments.

The federal government took an important step to stimulate metropolitan organization with the Metropolitan Development Act of 1966, which provides that local governments seeking federal grants for certain development projects must have their grants reviewed by metropolitan planning agencies composed of or designated "to the greatest practicable extent" by elected local officials. This provision will for the first time give substantive powers to metropolitan planning agencies as well as encourage the organization of metropolitan government decision-making agencies—already more than three dozen regional councils have come into being as a result of the requirements of the Act. The Association of San Francisco Bay Area Governments recently requested from the California State Legislature formal metropolitan governmental status with authority to administer four functions: metropolitan planning, regional airports, solid waste disposal, and regional parks and recreation. The Twin Cities area has been moving to establish a metropolitan council (which might alternatively be elected or appointed by the governor of the state) to assume control over planning, transportation, sewerage, and various other functions.[34]

County governments in a number of states are gradually taking over metropolitan functions, Dade County, Florida, and Davidson County, Tennessee, being the most advanced.

The difficulty in these proposals is the continued role accorded the state governments. They are, to be sure, most difficult to get around, being among our most deeply imbedded institutions. But with respect to the needs and problems created by rampant urbanism and rising expectations, they have tended to be, with a few exceptions, willfully blind. Professor Roscoe Martin observes that "only a few states have ever assumed significant program responsibilities [in the urban area]. The states have been slow to take meaningful hold of urban problems in the past, and there is little sign of any real intention to do so now."[35] *The Eighth Annual Report of the Advisory Commission on Intergovernmental Relations* (1967) comments that only a handful of states has moved to meet the problems of their urban areas and that state governments are on the verge of losing control over the mounting problems of central city deterioration and the rapid growth of metropolitan areas.[36] And there is a serious question as to whether, even with the best of intentions, many of the states have the geographic jurisdiction, resources, and general sense of unity to deal adequately with the problems of their cities and growing metropolitan areas.

The picture of urban concentrations in the year 2000 drawn by Picard poses still further questions about the incapacity of the states. Two of the great megalopolitan areas, to be sure, will be contained within the boundaries of single states (California and Florida). But the "metropolitan belt" will encompass a dozen or more states. Aspects of many of the problems now plaguing metropolitan areas will be transferred to the larger areas of the future—problems such as water supply, air and water pollution control, and transportation. Despite their incapacities, the states offer the only organizational building blocks below the federal level for coping with megalopolitan problems. In some cases, they may be able to organize into regional blocks (as through the device of interstate compacts) for dealing with interstate megalopolitan problems. An interesting if small-scale precedent is offered by the Delaware Valley Authority compact encompassing the states of New York, New Jersey, Delaware, and Pennsylvania with the federal government as an equal partner. This may be the megalopolitan counterpart of the emerging federations of municipal governments at the metropolitan level.

We should note finally that the federal government itself is not a model of organization, least of all with respect to urban programs. The scores of urban-oriented programs and grants administered by the Departments of Housing and Urban Development, Labor, Commerce, Transportation, Interior, Health, Education, and Welfare and other departments and agencies, including the Office of Economic Opportunity, Army Engineers, and General Services Administration still suffer from a lack of centralized planning and direction. Down below, state and local governments are handicapped by the number of and administrative requirements for the federal programs ostensibly established to spur, not hog-tie, local initiative. The several coordinating devices established in the last few years have made little impact and the situation overall is still much as described by Robert Connery and Richard Leach almost a decade ago.[37]

A number of more muscular measures have been advocated, including establishment of a special urban programs unit in the Executive Office of the President. Another is to put specific responsibility for coordination with the Bureau of the Budget which might use, as one important planning and administrative tool, the developing program planning and budgeting systems (PPBS) approach. Also needed, however, are radical changes in the administrative philosophy of the programs. A few promising beginnings have been made, notably the simplification of health programs administered by HEW.

Most policy, as Lindblom and Braybrook and others have pointed out, is incremental. Progress is made in short steps. It does not follow, as some seem to think, that planning and goal-making are fruitless, if pious, exercises. I have argued, on the contrary, that most of our great national achievements have rested on well articulated, nationally accepted goals and that, increasingly, these goals are supported by formal planning and implementation machinery (this is the meaning of much of the federal government reorganization of recent years). And national policies such as the full employment policy do represent quantum leaps forward, even though they involve relatively minor and incremental measures for implementation.

Incremental decisions, after all, are not governed by a deus ex machina but by national goals and objectives. And finally, as we learn from the infinitesimal calculus and Xeno's paradox about Achilles and the Tortoise, a large number of even small incremental decisions can add up to very large finite sums. The point is not that progress accrues incrementally, but rather the rate at which the increments occur; and with the expanding population, the accelerating rate of knowledge-accumulation, and our growing expectations, we can expect that the rate of incremental decisions and adjustments also will accelerate. In the long run this is likely to be our best hope, for the experience of the last 200 years teaches us that very few quantum changes in social organization, traditions, and goals have produced either happiness or prosperity for the people concerned.

Notes

1. John R. Seeley, "Central Planning: Prologue to a Critique," in *Centrally Planned Change: Prospects and Concepts*, Robert Morris, ed. (National Association of Social Workers, 1964), p. 43.

2. By this test much of the work of many so-called planning agencies, including such functions as capital budget preparation, are not planning at all but routine administration.

3. See John Kenneth Galbraith, "The New Industrial State" and "The Manipulated Society," *The Atlantic Monthly*, April and May, 1967.

4. Daniel Bell, "Notes on the Post-Industrial Society" (II), *The Public Interest*, Spring, 1967. See also Walter Heller, *New Dimensions of Political Economy* (Cambridge: Harvard University Press, 1966).

William A. Spurrier, reviewing this paper, commented: "It has almost always been a small, noisy, and sometimes pesky minority which has initiated significant reform. The problem for both our culture and our political structure is to make sure that such individuals are not only tolerated but encouraged."

5. For this list I have drawn on an unpublished manuscript by Ruth P. Mack of the Institute of Public Administration, *Uncertainty in Municipal Decision-Making*. Dr. Mack lists numerous other techniques for coping with uncertainty.

6. In reviewing this article, James Alcott remarked: "Relatively few people think in national development terms at all. . . . There is not much awareness of national development in the sense that there was when we were still opening the West. Therefore, the concept of national development may be more of an intellectual difficulty than is planning."

7. Thus real income per capita has increased 50 percent in the last two decades, city life has improved in many respects, educational and cultural standards are rapidly rising.

8. The time period examined, a third of a century, is shorter than the half-century span which is the theme of the conference, but quantitative projections being hazardous at best, I would feel uncomfortable about going beyond the year 2000. And in any case, the conclusions would not be changed, since I could only project more of the same.

9. The year-2000 projection ranges from 52 to 56 percent for the high and low populations respectively, compared to the present ratio of 46 percent.

10. Over 21 percent of the difference between A and D projections for 1990 is nonwhite. By contrast, nonwhites in 1966 were approximately 12 percent of the total U.S. population. (See U.S. Department of Commerce, Bureau of the Census, *Current Population Reports: Population Estimates*, Series P-25, No. 359, February 20, 1967.)

11. Denison's own projections, incidentally, indicate a 3.33 percent increase in GNP over the period 1960–80.

12. This is not to ignore the dangers of inflation, nor the structural factors that hold down productivity (low skills, poorly functioning labor market, geographic separation of jobs and potential workers, etc.). Maintenance of high growth rates depends upon both increasing demand and eradicating structural obstacles.

13. See Jesse Burkhead, "Vietnam and the Great Income Reshuffle," *Challenge*, May-June, 1967. Burkhead's thesis is: (1) income redistribution has not changed in any basic way since the close of World War II, but (2) in the 1960's, and particularly since the advent of the Vietnam war, a disproportionate amount of incremental income has gone to non-wage shares and to the non-poor.

14. With respect to the figures for housing replacement and various other data for

these projections, I have drawn upon a number of sources, including particularly Hans H. Landsberg, Leonard L. Fischman, and Joseph L. Fisher, *Resources in America's Future* (Baltimore: Johns Hopkins Press, 1963).

15. Estimated costs of furnishing infrastructure vary substantially. The Regional Plan Association's estimates of cost in the New York region for new growth were in the magnitude of $18,000 each for all households existing in the region as of the target year, 1985 (*The Spread City*, New York, 1962). More recent estimates, compiled for the Joint Committee on Economics Report for the period 1966–75, indicate a new-growth magnitude of about $20,000 per new household and a figure for modernization of $1,400 per household, as of 1975.

16. To the extent that research and development expenditures are capitalized, they are included in this figure; otherwise they are included with consumption.

17. See Seymour Melman, *Our Depleted Society* (New York: Holt, Rinehart & Winston, 1965).

18. The bulk of the federal government's nonmilitary expenditures consists of transfer expenditures rather than purchases of goods and services. Transfer expenditures include grants-in-aid to state and local governments and social security, welfare, and other income maintenance payments.

19. Between 1964 and 1966, federal purchases of nonmilitary goods and services (deflated for price changes) rose by 3.5 percent while transfers to persons and state and local governments (also deflated) rose by about 18 percent.

20. The principal other component is accumulated inventory, which for any given year might be positive or negative. For technical reasons, inventory can be ignored in aggregate figures such as are presented here.

21. Leonard Lecht at the National Planning Association has made a somewhat more elaborate projection of the cost of meeting the main goals called for by the Eisenhower Goals Commission, in terms of the demands on GNP in 1970 and 1975. See *Goals, Priorities and Dollars* (New York: The Free Press, 1966). The amounts required to meet Lecht's projections total about 10 percent more than the amount of 1975 GNP, assuming a GNP growth rate of 4 percent. Lecht's cost projections for goals differ from the ones presented here in that they are aggregated only for selected single years. The conclusions, however, are roughly comparable.

22. In his remarks on this article, Wilbur Thompson commented, "Would not a higher population cause some shift from the private to the public sector? I would expect some shift toward user charges, and away from general taxation, in financing some types of public services." The first of these shifts, if it occurred, would raise public expenditures relative to consumption. The second shift would have the opposite effect. The extent of either can only be a matter of conjecture at this time.

23. Urban Land Institute, *Urban Land*, February, 1967.

24. Carolina-Piedmont, North Carolina-Georgia, North Central Alabama, Central Gulf Coast, Texas-Louisiana-Gulf Coast, North Central Texas, South Central Texas, Missouri-Mississippi Valley, Salt Lake Valley, Colorado-Piedmont, Puget Sound, Willamette Valley, metropolitan Arizona.

25. St. Louis, Louisville, Memphis, Oklahoma City, Twin Cities, Albuquerque. In addition, Honolulu is projected to have more than one million inhabitants.

26. For a discussion of locational forces and trends, see Harvey S. Perloff, Edgar S. Dunn, Jr., Eric Lampard, and Richard F. Muth, *Regions, Resources, and Economic Growth* (Baltimore: Johns Hopkins Press, 1960).

27. Chicago's Marina City puts forty stories of apartments on top of twenty stories of parking on top of two levels for shopping over a marina for 200 pleasure boats, all integrated with sixteen floors of offices, theaters, bowling alleys, tennis courts, and swimming pools.

28. John H. Rubel, "Defining the Role of the Private Sector in Overcoming Barriers

to Urban Betterment," a paper presented at the ACTION-Urban America Symposium on "The Troubled Environment," Washington, D.C., December, 1965. Daniel W. Cook in *The New Urban Frontier: New Metropolises for America* (1964, mimeo.) takes much the same view.

29. See Landsberg et al., *Resources in America's Future*, chapter 18.

30. Rubel, "Defining the Role of the Private Sector."

31. Ibid.

32. A beginning has been made with the exploratory study of the feasibility and problems of building a new Minnesota city north of Minneapolis under the aegis of the University of Minnesota and Minneapolis business interests.

33. For example, an award might take the form of federal financing of the entire cost of a winning program, over what would be supplied by already ongoing grant programs.

34. A bill passed by the Minnesota State Legislature in the spring of 1967 unfortunately sidetracked the effort to establish a council with significant powers.

35. Roscoe E. Martin, *The Cities and the Federal System* (New York: Atherton Press, 1965).

36. See also the CED policy statement, *Modernizing State Government* (1967).

37. Robert H. Connery and Richard H. Leach, *The Federal Government and Metropolitan Areas* (Cambridge: Harvard University Press, 1960).

Comments on
Fitch

JEAN LABASSE
Professor, University of Paris

Three hundred million Americans by the beginning of the twenty-first century: at first, this possibility appears neither surprising nor alarming. A population density of 32 people per square kilometer seems low when compared to that of the coastal areas of Asia and Europe, and, due to the advanced stage of technology in the U.S., better housing and working conditions seem to be guaranteed.

However, the geographical distribution of this larger population raises a problem. The cumulative processes inherent in a market economy lead to congestion. This surburbanization of industry and housing will probably affect the manufacturing belt and the Pacific coast more than the Middle West and the highlands of the West. Furthermore, as industry, housing, and recreation increase their needs for space, the consumption of space per individual will rise accordingly. By the year 2000, while probably not reaching Europe's state of overcrowding, Americans will still run the risk of experiencing some restriction in the free use of their territory. The art of managing space will probably play an important role within fifteen years, although it contradicts the deeply rooted myth of "free open space."

The consumption needs in an affluent society will eventually clash with the biological rhythm of renewal of natural resources, both vegetable and mineral. To deal briefly with the question of water supply of urban areas: If progress in the desalinization of water will solve many local difficulties, the development of urban zones far from the seashore may be restricted. While today the concept of protecting nature has only a limited scope (parks and lake shores, for example), it is bound to be expanded considerably in spite of the increasing artificiality of the production of raw materials and energy. Those in charge will be forced to ensure the control of air and water pollution, the reconstitution of agricultural and forest soils, and that more care be taken in the extraction and processing of rare metals. Because "the era of the finished world starts" (Paul Valéry), that of the economy of waste is coming to an end. We will have to learn to use sparingly and to renew that which in nature recuperates slowly or with difficulty. And this is bound to influence the extending and functioning of man's installations.

In this context, the city is of primary concern. Certainly the possibilities of improvement brought about by science, in terms of comfort, communication, and culture, are both difficult to measure and unforeseeable to a large degree. The possibility of improvement that will be brought about in the physical environment through mastering urban micro-climates is, however, an example that our grandchildren may witness. Still, worry about the future often haunts the conscience of city dwellers. Why? Because the accumulation of technical means of exchange such as transportation, and social means, such as mass media, threatens our nerves and our bodies. It incites this depersonalization of which anomy, as denounced by David Riesman, is a precursory symptom. The Promethean pride of the metropolis has already reached its limit within each one of us.

The cities' explosion into residential suburbs and recreational areas is but a temporary and questionable palliative to congestion and to the unhealthy atmosphere of urban centers. Is not the hope placed by Gutkind in the "twilight of cities" tainted with medieval reminiscences? The renovation of these centers which remain the depositaries of the essential qualities of the city will call for ingenuity and immense financial sacrifice. It seems obvious that, for such efforts and sacrifices to be meaningful, drastic action must be taken against the automotive frenzy, and there must be planned use made of the surfaces, volumes, and movements. These salutary trends will take some time to develop as they contradict individual initiative. It is probable that the illusion of an electronic solution to the problems of moving men and things will continue to be nurtured during the coming years. But won't the excessive evils of the megalopolis cause the birth of a new way of urban life during the next ten or fifteen years? A new style? Maybe even a new morphology. A clearly differentiated morphology in which reinforced autonomy of districts and suburbs—the latter becoming the basic political and social units of collective life—will balance the reinstated prestige and authority of centers. The Old Continent, which owes so much to the New Continent, might be in a position to make the latter benefit from the fruits of some planification experiences forced upon them by congestion.

Will American society's extraordinary ability to change affect geographical repartition of economic and political forces of the country? It has sometimes been said in the past 25 years that the American population has poured into the West and the South, thereby pursuing the conquest in depth of their immense territory. What will be the situation fifty years from now, provided peace is maintained? True, the worldwide diffusion of American power is the reason why, for a long time, this nation has ceased to look exclusively toward Europe. It seems, however, that developing exchanges and even more the worldwide responsibilities of the United States in terms of assistance and stimulation will enhance continually the value and attractiveness of coastal areas. Can we imagine the stupendous perspectives of the northwest, liberated from the hydraulic servitudes of California, if normal relations were established with China? Meanwhile, to the benefit of Chicago and neighboring urban cities, the Seaway has already started powerful aeration of the Continental mass. Will the Mississippi in the year 2000 be as creative as the St. Lawrence? One is tempted to think so if a solution to the social and racial problems of the South permits it.

The question also arises whether the liberalization of political relations between nations will not incite the United States, an area of low democratic pressure and high economic pressure, to reopen rather broadly the doors of immigration. Modifications in the geopolitical balance of the states between themselves and even maybe of the federal state could result. Short of a foreseeable answer, the question is nevertheless worth asking.

Democracy is a fragile thing: Each one has the power to introduce in it as many factors of disorder as of progress. This power will grow inordinately in the next fifty years in proportion to the number of men and the considerable material means at their disposal.

HARVEY S. PERLOFF
Resources for the Future, Inc.

Just what is "national development"? In the case of the less developed poor countries, there is no difficulty in defining its meaning. It is the achievement of a rapid and self-sustaining growth in national product per capita; the policy problem is to bring about the changes necessary for this end. But what does "national development" cover in the case of a rich country, in fact, the richest in the world? Here the situation is necessarily more complex. There is no one agreed upon meaning or generally accepted goal. It involves a search.

Lyle Fitch attempts such a search. He seeks understanding by looking back into history (at the national development policies for the settlement of the West and the development of agriculture in an earlier period, and at the application of full employment policy in a more recent period), and by projecting into the future—if not for fifty years, at least to the year 2000. The building of something approaching a consensus around development goals is essential if development is to be consciously guided, as it is in the case of our full employment policy. Thus, he sees an urgent need to clarify our national goals and he makes some proposals toward that end. The complexity of the situation is reflected in the complexity of his goal structure; they are of different kinds and at somewhat different levels. I would interpret his goals to cover the following:

1. Rapid growth of national product, which is critical even for the richest country in the world. It is the key ingredient in the achievement of all other national goals. (For example, he calculates that a 3 percent annual growth of GNP between 1967 and 2000 would not be adequate to meet the "low goals" for a low population projection, while even a 4 percent growth rate would be inadequate for his "high goal" projections.)

2. Maintenance of a lower rather than a higher birth rate; this is complementary to achieving a high income per capita and the good life for all.

3. Improvement of the urban environment; making urban areas as efficient, convenient, and aesthetically pleasing as possible. (He includes rural areas at only one point, clearly as an afterthought, and does not refer to them again. This is an area that requires more thought in the context of "national development.")

4. Eradication of poverty and extension of education and health services; in other words, improvement in the human resources.

This is certainly a sensible and practical agenda and does give substance to the vague idea of national development in a mature nation.

The means for achieving such goals, he suggests, would include a marked improvement in planning, since planning is needed to guide innovational change. State and local governments must be greatly improved and modernized if we are not to lose the advantages of innovational variety which they can offer—at least potentially. And the federal government must provide incentives to stimulate these innovations.

It is hard to quarrel with any of this. It is eminently sensible as far as it goes. But I am sure that Fitch himself must recognize that the list is incomplete, that he has chosen the more formal, organizational, technologically oriented items for discussion. Also, and even more important, the key linkages between the goals and the means, and among the different means, are largely missing. Fitch, I know, could supply the links, and maybe he intends to do so in another paper. However, it might be worth raising some of the substantive issues, to put the subjects he does discuss into a somewhat broader and deeper context.

His main concern, and justifiably so, is with improvement of the urban environment. In fact, he argues that "the greatest national development task of the next few decades is getting accustomed to and raising the standards of urban life." I find it odd that in terms of substantive policy to achieve this end, he examines in any depth only two proposals—decentralized distribution of urban populations and new-city building—only to express his doubts that they can contribute anything significant to the basic goal or even that government policy can have much of an effect on urban settlement patterns.

I sense that Fitch is trying to head off the cry for decentralization and for the building of new cities as an escape from the tough and very real problems of improving the present metropolitan areas—which, under any circumstances, are likely to have to absorb by far the greatest part of future growth. But we do need a broad policy framework for urban development, and scholars and planners can, and should, contribute to the clarification of basic concepts and to the analysis of alternative possibilities.

In this light, it is important to distinguish between the type of decentralization that is involved in a more rapid growth of the presently less densely built-up multistate regions as against the type of deconcentration that is involved in the settlement pattern *within* a single metropolitan region, that is, within a single labor market area. Conceptually and practically, new towns and new cities could play a minor role, if any, in the first category and a major role in the second.

Interregional decentralization can take place on the basis of the confluence of many private decisions, but it can also be encouraged or discouraged through governmental policy. On the first score, there has been enough study to establish the fact that most industrial location decisions are made first in terms of the relative advantages and disadvantages of the various competing broad regions, and once the region has been chosen, for the decision then to focus on the specific city and finally the site within the city or metropolitan area. Thus, a great amount of decentralization can take place across the nation without any new towns being built, and that is exactly what has been happening over a long period of time. Furthermore, government policy is always having an important impact on the degree of interregional decentralization, whether this is conscious or not. Government policy can, and at times does, influence the relative degree of decentralization or centralization by the way in which roads are built, the nature of transport policy generally, relative emphasis in water resources expenditures, and the geographic location of defense, space, and other governmental contracts. The establishment of space centers at Huntsville, Cape Kennedy, and Houston was, in impact, a decentralization decision—without involving any new town decisions. Clearly, a case can be made for the notion that a concern for national development should logically involve, at a minimum, very careful study of the relative advantages and disadvantages of the current trends of differential regional growth and a probing of the consequences that could be expected to follow from alternative policies with regard to the geographic distribution of government expenditures and contracts.

This, however, is the less important part of the equation. While the question of the location and relative growth of cities and the degree of inter-regional decentralization deserves attention, the question of the *internal* substance or character of cities or metropolitan areas is certainly much more important. Because of his emphases on form, technological innovation, and governmental efficiency, Fitch gives practically no attention to the questions of race, class, segregation, ethnic politics, or similar matters which are likely to dominate the urban scene and the degree of urban improvement (his major goal concern) for a long time to come. It may be that he assumes these questions will not be important by the year 2000 or over the even longer period of fifty years, but he doesn't say so. I suspect that they will be important for a long time to come.

The key element is, of course, that if present trends continue, a substantial proportion of our major communities will have a majority of Negroes in the central cities by the year 2000 and beyond. What will it take to be elected mayor or a member of the city council in the larger cities? What kinds of goal will dominate? What kinds of innovation will be undertaken? It is hard to see the technologically and governmentally innovating city as a really great concern of big city politics under extremely segregated conditions. From the standpoint of the quality of urban life, the question is: What kind of politics will most probably provide the greatest improvements for the majority of residents? Will racial integration speed or retard the process of urban improvement? If one assumes that integration will speed the process—and there is a very powerful case to be made for this assumption—then the question arises: How is integration to be brought about? The rapid reduction of poverty would certainly be helpful. So would a really large investment in education. So would meaningful policies to help small businessmen.

But another kind of question arises. Could the process of racial integration be telescoped through the use of the new town idea? It is conceivable that substantial federal grants for new city construction could be geared specifically to this goal; not a technological goal, but a social goal. Such grants could be associated with the requirement of a sizeable proportion of low and moderate income housing in the new communities, as well as genuine open housing, while the federal subsidy might make possible really attractive services and facilities, including outstanding educational and recreational facilities. Thus, racial integration might be encouraged through the self-selection of families attracted by the superior facilities and, hopefully, good design. Such policy, at a minimum (even assuming a certain amount of segregation in the new towns), would serve to break up the kind of massive segregation in the central cities that essentially cuts off communication with the white community. All of this might be done in existing cities, but the limitation of the present facilities and ethnic politics could make it much harder, costlier, and much longer in coming. It is also quite possible that the new cities will encourage a certain amount of governmental innovation. The building of new cities cries out for innovation by its very nature.

I can only applaud Fitch's emphasis throughout his paper on the need for research and experimentation in our approach to improving the urban environment, and on federal government assistance for innovational programs. But surely technological experimentation is not the dominant issue. Our greatest lags are in the areas of social and human relations, as well as in government. These are areas in which innovation and experimentation are most urgently needed. In the past, Fitch has written perceptively about social and human relations problems so he certainly cannot be accused of lacking understanding of their relationship to national development. My main point here is that we should concern ourselves continuously with the linkages between form and substance. If we do so there will be little danger of overlooking substance when we talk about national policy as it applies to the form our cities might take in the future and to the kinds of urban improvements that should dominate national development policy.

JEROME P. PICKARD
Office of the Deputy Undersecretary
U.S. Department of Housing and Urban Development

There can be only minor disagreement in substance with a great deal of the content of Fitch's paper. My principal areas of constructive criticism must, therefore, center upon *emphasis* (including greater attention to the enormous importance of urban development in an urbanized nation) and on *treatment* of problems. I should call attention to what appear to be two deficiencies in this paper:

1. The author is "locked in" to a system of national economic accounts as a framework for measurement and evaluation. This does give substance to his discussion but has the disadvantage of creating too limited a focus in evaluation of future development.

2. There appears to be a lack of imagination in suggesting comprehensive approaches to deal with future problems at their enlarged scale.

If any clear point emerges from this paper, it is that the future promises to enlarge most existing problems. For example, the future family income distribution postulated implies a heightened future differential between the poor and the rest of society—the continuation of a long-term economic trend. To emphasize small "incremental" steps in dealing with national problems is to overlook the necessity to advance "great ideas" to attack large problems.

Daniel Burnham's oft-cited planning dictum warns:

> Make no little plans. They have no magic to stir men's blood and probably themselves will not be realized. Make big plans. Aim high in hope and work remembering that a noble, logical plan once recorded will never die but long after we are gone will be a living thing asserting itself with ever-growing insistency.

The portion directly relevant to our topic is the latter portion of the statement. Experience would indicate that there is basic truth to the Burnham concept that there is an insistency to "great ideas." It is both desirable and necessary to advance such ideas in discussing a fifty-year future.

The author's projections at two different population levels assume relatively little difference in gross national product (GNP). Since people produce, as well as consume, and since the impact of a larger young population will create demands for education and other services from the adult members of society, it is not reasonable to project such a small differential in GNP for a difference of 80 million in future population. People are producers as well as consumers, and with greater leisure time and shorter work weeks, there is a greater flexibility for the employed labor force to increase output in the face of greater demand. Assumptions made in the Fitch paper should be seriously challenged and carefully reexamined.

Furthermore, in the year 2017, or before, is it not possible that not GNP, but GSP (gross social product or gross satisfaction product) or GCP (gross computerized product) or some other G–P will be the best single measure of national well-being? Let us be extremely cautious not to limit the future in terms of the past. What is likely to be the most relevant unit of national accounting in future American society?

In any case, GNP has been treated as a basic measure of national well-being and affluence, but it is not so simply and purely that. Schechter analyzed costs of urban development[1] and concluded that slightly over 1 percent of the 1957 GNP was attributable to cost increases created by inefficiencies in the urban development pattern built during the preceding four years. Inefficiencies, inferior goods (which need more frequent replacement) and other subtleties may increase the GNP. It is desirable to use GNP as simply *one* measure of total social and economic progress and welfare.

The assumption encountered at one point in Fitch's paper, that the shape and location of development doesn't significantly affect some costs, is not supported by Schechter's analysis or by the majority of current opinion on this point. The issue of planned development needs, in any case, to encompass more than purely economic considerations. It is conceivable that the most imortant effects of the planned community would be the social effects of reducing the size of the community to the "human scale." For example, in Reston, Virginia, the average population for each of the seven villages is planned to be about 10,000.

Current middle-range projections of the U.S. population for 2000 indicate a population of 310 to 320 million. Allowing a 10 percent variation either way would yield a range from 285 to 345 million population. A different approach would be to "establish" a median value figure of about 315 million and vary the year, stating it as for 2000 ± 10 years. Middle-range population growth thus amounts to about 115 million in about 35 years; an increase of 58 percent above the present U.S. population or just under 200 million.

This enlarged population will in all likelihood have the same quantity of land, even though changing technology will alter man-land relationships. The basic Malthusian issue must continue to be faced: land is virtually fixed in supply. As human populations increase within fixed geographical areas, available land per capita shrinks; land becomes more scarce, and more valuable; land utilization must become more rational and more intensive. Fitch compares my urban region population projections with national densities of England and Wales, and of the Netherlands. But he does not add that the historical evolution of these densely settled nations has resulted in a much higher degree of land use regulation and of national economic planning than presently exists in the United States.

The total quantity of future population growth may prove *not* to be the most important element in the future quality of American life. The geographical location and distribution of the future population, and the character of physical and social planning for the expanded urban population may be of far greater moment. These will affect not only future levels of GNP, but also capital needs for both public and private investment, environmental pollution problems and public health, and the effectiveness of future land use and its planning.

Serious issues will need to be faced. The concentration of more population in large metropolises and megalopolises may entail very high "frictional" costs to provide utilities and services, and for the internal movement of people and goods. At the same time, capital stock in non-growth areas may be under used. On the other hand, as the paper suggests, the implementation of the alternative pattern of dispersed new urbanization would appear to make excessive demands upon the existing economic framework and would offer questionable potentials for success.

As a "great idea," let us suggest a middle-range solution. This, following the British experience, would entail the encouragement of new communities and attempt to channel growth into "new towns" but at *intermediate distances* from existing major metropolises (in the U.S. this might be at ranges of 50 to 200 miles). Resource and environmental planning could establish preferences for location based upon amenities and necessities (especially water supply) provided at competing sites. Remote rural regions and areas not provided with resources for the maintenance of large populations would remain sparsely populated.

There has been a good deal of discussion about population densities in planning, and also about the "ideal population size" for urban communities. As a second "great idea," let us propose that there be a deliberate concept of *diversity*, to offer choices in life styles. This would apply at all scales of future urban development: in the "neighborhood" or planned community unit, in the metropolis, in the megalopolis, and at the regional and national level.

This means that varied types of housing structure (some not yet designed or even conceived) which entail residential settlement at different densities and in different modes would be built into urban communities by deliberate plan. Non-residential land uses would be similarly treated, and, to a greater degree, integrated harmoniously with residential areas.

New communities might vary in population size from 5,000 to 10,000 to 1 million or more. Such growth could be accommodated by "expandable" planning which would have a built-in capacity to articulate a grouping of settlements of intermediate size into a "planned metropolis" or, at the other end of the scale, which could provide a neat structure for a single unit of small town population size.

In the very long-term future, urban ecology must be considered. Efficient land use should be encouraged so that urbanization would not unduly consume the very earth, which must be cultivated to nourish the human community. Economic forces alone will not preserve this land in productive use; where the supply is critical (as in certain climatic regions, e.g., parts of California) a higher level of planning and citizenship is called for to preserve really irreplaceable land resources for the national future. Issues of this nature are already built into the experience of some densely settled western European nations and we might learn from them. In the buoyant atmosphere of the American scene, ways and means of dealing with land use conflicts might be quite different from those used in Europe. However, it is now time to realize that the long view needs to prevail and that we must all take a hard look at present processes of planning and committing the use of land, especially in regions and areas of concentrated urbanization.

Notes

1. Opinions expressed herein are those of the individual author, not necessarily of the organization named.

2. Henry B. Schechter, "Cost-Push of Urban Growth," *Land Economics*, Vol. 37, No. 1 (February, 1961), pp. 18-31; quotation from p. 30.

Natural Resources—Wise Use of the World's Inheritance

The commission of this paper intended a comprehensive statement of just how important our air, water, and land resources are and how they can be used for the greatest long-range potential of our expanding urban society —the ecology of environment for the next fifty years.

Conservation balanced with utilization is involved, open space as a resource as well as minerals in the earth. (The sense of urgency that should be a part of all of these papers is especially important regarding open space.) This is not a treatise concerning the depletion of various resources. These studies have already been done better than can be attempted here. This issue is more a matter of a qualitative human consideration of our environmental resources and impacts. Much has been proposed in recent air pollution legislation, stream pollution control, and other measures. Are these adequate, or how are they to be effected? What quality of human environment should be sought?

Author: Joseph L. Fisher, Resources for the Future, Inc.

Chairman: Charles W. Eliot, AIP, Planning Consultant

Committee: Edward A. Ackerman, Executive Officer, Carnegie Institution of Washington; Gilbert F. White (Past President, Haverford College), Department of Geography, University of Chicago; Harold J. Barnett, Department of Economics, Washington University; Abel Wolman, Johns Hopkins University; Frank Gregg, Conservation Foundation; Rev. Benjamin F. Payton, Executive Director, Department of Social Justice, National Council of Churches; Ian McHarg, Institute for Environmental Studies, University of Pennsylvania

XI

Joseph L. Fisher

Resources for the Future, Inc.

Natural Resources—Wise Use of the World's Inheritance

One of the great concerns of people in all past ages, at the present time, and most surely for as far ahead as one can see is that the natural environment be occupied, used, and preserved for the future in such a way as to yield as satisfying a living as possible. The prehistoric cavemen undoubtedly pitted themselves against the resources-population-welfare problem. The ancient Egyptians dealt with the same basic situation and made major advances in irrigation agriculture as a part of their constructive response to it. The Romans of classical times made significant innovations in law, social organization, construction, and transportation in their mighty effort to find a satisfactory basis for living. In the Western countries of the modern era, breakthroughs in science and technology have led the way through the so-called agricultural and industrial revolutions to societies of relative affluence in which people generally have confidence that the future can be of their own making. Coexisting in the modern world with the economically more developed Western countries are the less developed places embracing two-thirds of the world's population, who daily are pressed against an inadequate supply of food and other materials.

But throughout this long sweep of history and extending today to every corner of the globe, the concern for resources and population continues paramount, however much the details of the different situations may vary. The Food and Agriculture Organization of the United Nations tells us that per capita food consumption is hardly increasing at all in most of the less developed countries. At the same time in the economically advanced countries most people are worried about eating too much. For these countries there is no Malthusian ghost, save for a small minority of desperately poor people; their challenge is to manage their natural resource environment so as to produce needed products and services with ever increasing efficiency and do what they can to assist their less fortunate brothers in other places.

In the United States, which exceeds all other countries and all other times in history in its material advancement, it is sometimes thought that natural resources are becoming less important. One farmer, it is pointed out, now feeds more than thirty persons, whereas a century ago he could take care of no more than four or five. The portion of total consumer expenditures going for food and other raw materials, if anything, has been falling while the total expenditure curve continues on up apace. But this should not deceive us into thinking that the natural environment of land, water, minerals, and air are not still supporting the entire pyramid; all we have done is to become more clever in the ways by which we refine, manufacture, distribute, and use the things that all began with the natural resources.

Fortunately the natural environment is no more static than is population or the ways in which individual persons behave. Many now living can remember seeing their first automobile and airplane, their first television set and orbiting satellite. The list of new products or new uses from old products that have come in during recent decades is a long one extending from hybrid corn to synthetic fibers and plastics to titanium and uranium. Those arithmeticians among us who are given to extrapolating birth and death rates to the ultimate situation in which the earth is swamped under with people should give equal attention to the extrapolation of technological trends by means of which more and more people can be fed, clothed, housed, educated, kept in good health, and entertained. And they should not overlook the critically important possibilities, of which all people are now becoming more aware, that science, technology, and human ingenuity and motivation can be directed toward the reduction in population growth itself. The most profound aspect of the modern birth control movement is not that by reducing births it can lead to improvements in the level of living of people, but that it opens up the possibility for *homo sapiens* to assert a rational and ordered influence over his own numbers. This, it seems to me, would be an immense stride forward toward civilization.

In our day the word "crisis" is used and overused with regard to almost everything. Not only is there a population crisis, but on the resources side there is an air pollution crisis in this country, a food crisis in India, a water crisis whenever and wherever there is flood or drought, a crisis in recreation and the use of leisure time, and so on. Although the word is useful in whipping up public enthusiasm, it is the enemy of careful planning and action. An early variant of the title for this paper was, "Natural Resources—Proper Use of a Chance-in-a-Lifetime Inheritance." This seems to say that if we don't do something right now, the one "chance in a lifetime" will be lost for all time. If this were true, then I suppose the word crisis would be accurate for describing our present situation with regard to clean air and water, enough open space, and the like.

Fortunately the world of nature offers many chances; even bad mistakes usually can be redeemed though at a cost in human effort. The constructive attitude in my judgment is not one associated with the word crisis and is not a "now or never" kind of thing. Much more needed is a hard and steady look at trends and emerging problems so that helpful policies and activities can be instituted well before crisis is upon us and tendencies toward destruction have become irreversible. It is well to keep in mind that between now and the end of this century capital expenditures embodying profound technological advances in this country may well exceed those made thus far in our entire national history, and that in a gross and overall sense we shall literally be remaking our environment. The opportunities for better planning are staggering to the imagination. Regarding the natural environment we need less talk of crisis and more hard work in planning in a deliberate and highly professional manner. With many more people expected in the decades ahead, with rapidly growing cities, with more intricate patterns of transportation and communication, with more leisure time, and with ever higher incomes, it becomes imperative that the natural environment be examined more intensely and imaginatively than we have done in the past if this aspect of our future is to make its maximum contribution to better living. We shall have to examine the natural environment and its several parts more comprehensively and systematically, looking further ahead, and paying more attention to the interrelations between that environment on the one hand and the cultural environment of research, technology, economic development, and human welfare on the other hand. Planners will have to be among the leaders in this examination.

I want now to return to the resource-population matter. The search for an optimum population in some sense continues. What is the most satisfactory level of population or trend of population increase, remembering the problems of sustaining the natural resource base and developing it so that the desired number of people can find the highest possible level of satisfaction? I want to deal with two aspects of this question: the quantitative in the sense of enough food and other resource products and services for people, and the qualitative in the sense of an aesthetically pleasing natural environment. Actually the two are interrelated in many ways, both competitive and complementary.

The Outlook for Demand and Supply: The Quantitative Picture for the U.S.

First, on the quantitative side, the outlook for several decades ahead in this country turns out to be quite favorable when examined in a systematic manner. The population may be expected to increase from its present 200 million persons to around 245 million in 1980 and 330 million in the year 2000. The labor force will double by the year 2000, with the labor force as far ahead as 1985 being quite predictable since most of the new entrants for that year have already been born. Productivity, that is production per worker, has been increasing at something approaching 3 percent per year during recent years—a higher rate than characterized the American economy for many decades prior to World War II. A reasonable estimate of productivity during the coming years points to a 1980 gross national product of well over a trillion dollars and more than double this amount between then and the year 2000. Personal consumption expenditures will increase in line with total national product, while per capita consumption expenditures will be scaled down from this as the number of people grows.[1]

Accompanying a U.S. economy growing in this general way will be increases in almost all of the sectors and industries. For example, the number of households will approximate 100 million by the year 2000, and this will be accompanied by the construction of an estimated 4.25 million new dwelling units which in turn will require a much larger amount of lumber, metal products, and many other things that probably will go into the house or apartment building of the future. And this in its turn will add to the requirement in future years for timber, iron and steel, electricity, and so on. The accompanying diagram, prepared several years ago at Resources for the Future, suggests not only the likely future requirements for a large number of resource materials, but also portrays the interrelatedness of a growing population and national economy with its raw materials requirements. The estimates need redoing in the light of what has happened recently, but the general magnitudes shown are still good enough for purposes of indicating relationships.

For this country a check on the availability of the resource base to furnish the raw materials that will be needed indicates that, with perhaps a few exceptions, supplies should be forthcoming at reasonable costs. This favorable outlook will hold true only with certain provisos: scientific work and technological development will have to continue forward at something like the pace of the recent past so that new sources and substitutes will be found for items becoming scarcer and more costly. The world's trading and investing system will have to be maintained so that this country can import increasing amounts of a large number of minerals and some other products. Conservation programs will have to be sustained so that the resource base will not be eroded. And resource policies, planning, and administration will have to continue to gain in coherence and effectiveness. In addition, of course, a large-scale war or a severe depression would considerably alter the outlook.

This general view for the United States will strike some as overoptimistic, even with the caveats held firmly in mind. They will say: this is all very well in general, but how about being sure of enough fresh water, or parks and open space in cities, or some other item. I would have to concede that there probably will be difficulties for particular items, at particular times and in particular places—for example, not enough water in the western desert areas, too few parks in large cities, or occasionally an insufficient supply of copper at a reasonable price. Furthermore a few of these problems will probably remain chronic, such as high quality water in streams and lakes near centers of population, adequate amounts of usable open space in metropolitan *facing:*

**Resources and Economic Growth: Some examples
of resource/output relationships, 1960, 1980, and 2000.**

The selected items in the chart illustrate how (1) the estimated future demand for various consumption items on the basis of population and general economic growth, (2) the demand for key materials, and (3) the demand for basic resources were derived in this study. The chart also indicates the numerous cross-relationships that must be investigated in a study of this sort, and how very different elements in the economy combine to create the level of demand for particular resources. It does not attempt to show all of the interrelationships investigated even for the items selected, nor the exact lines of derivation, which ordinarily involve many steps intermediate to those shown.

From Hans H. Landsberg, Leonard L. Fischman, and Joseph L. Fisher, *Resources in America's Future* (Baltimore: Johns Hopkins Press, 1963).

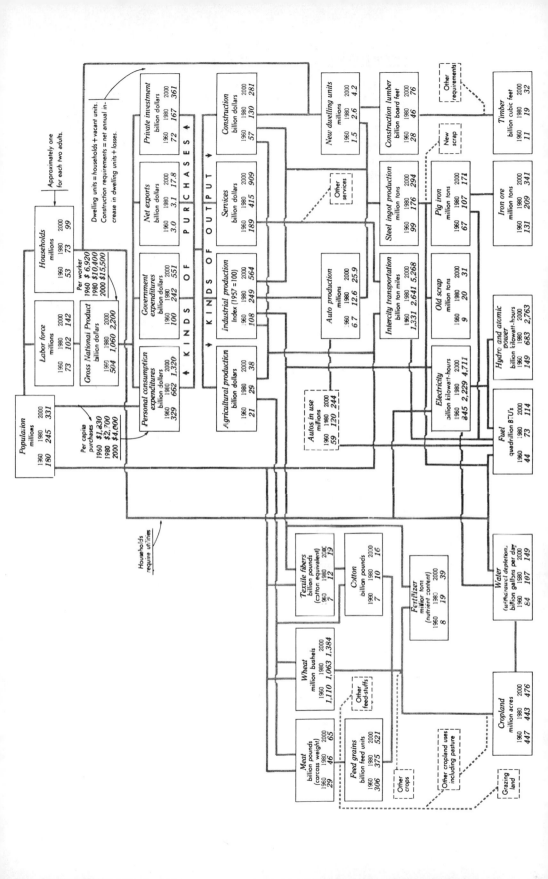

areas, and enough recreation areas for weekend and vacation use. National and even regional totals and averages of resource availability frequently cover up the sore spots that planners have to spend most of their time dealing with. The greatest challenges will be found precisely in correcting or alleviating these particular situations before they spread and infect the whole.

The World Picture

When one turns to the world as a whole, especially the less developed two-thirds, the outlook is much less certain. A continuation of recent trends of population and resource production and consumption indicates that, by the year 2000, the world as a whole will require a tripling of aggregate food output just to provide adequate calories, and considerably more to provide adequate proteins and vitamins. For energy the trends indicate a five-fold increase will be necessary in the year 2000 if the world as a whole is to reach the level of consumption achieved in western Europe in 1960. A similar increase in iron ore and ferroalloys is indicated, somewhat less for copper, but a much larger increase for bauxite-aluminum. Lumber requirements may quadruple.[2]

The most severe world resource problem will probably be food, for which recent trends have not been encouraging. It is true that if the yields now achieved in more advanced agricultural regions could be applied generally in less developed countries by the year 2000, then most or all of the shortage problem could be taken care of. This would be difficult, however, and would entail much more commercial fertilizer, better seeds, more irrigation, improvements in cultivation, more adequate credit, road building, the development of more efficient processing, transportation, and marketing systems, and so on. The problems essentially are those of investment, incentives, and social organization. In addition, there are considerable amounts of land in various less developed countries not now in agriculture which, with fairly heavy investments, could be brought under cultivation. Also some modest gains could probably be made in world diets from fish, especially fish protein concentrate for food additives. Other possibilities are further out, such as use of seaweed, algae, and some other sources for edible products. The future problem will be eased considerably if the masses of people in the less developed countries will continue to consume grains and other food products directly rather than converting them first into meat which is then used for consumption. Calories available for human consumption are cut to one-third or one-quarter if they are put through a meat cycle. But in the main, the world food problem is essentially a problem of increasing yields on existing acreage through more efficient use of labor and capital.

The outlook for energy, which is the other truly basic natural resource, is much more favorable. In the last ten or twenty years, per capita increases have gone up fastest where they are needed most, in the less developed countries. In a sense, energy is the key that unlocks the doors to resource plenty. Critical for the production of commercial fertilizers is electric energy and to some extent heat. Energy is needed to pump water. Low grade ores can be upgraded through the application of energy. Fresh water can even be extracted from the ocean if there is a sufficient supply of low cost power. Electricial energy on farms lightens human burdens and frees individuals for other tasks. Fortunately the outlook in the world is quite favorable for additional energy supplies. The Middle East, North Africa, and the Caribbean contain immense reserves of oil and natural gas. Pipelines and other means of transportation have improved so that these supplies can be made quite widely available. Coal exists in considerable abundance in many places, while large potentials of water power remain in Central Africa, Southeast Asia, numerous locations in Latin America, and elsewhere. Coming rapidly over the horizon is commercially available nuclear power already well on its way in this country and a few other places. In reserve are large amounts of oil shale in western United States, Brazil, and elsewhere, plus tar sands in Canada. For the next few decades at least, energy is probably the brightest part of the whole resource picture.

For metallic minerals the prospects are mixed. Basic reserves of iron ore, bauxite, and some others are plentiful, having in mind new discoveries in various parts of the world, new methods of upgrading low-grade ores, and the possibilities of substitutes such as plastics, glass, and ceramic materials. For some of the other metals the outlook is more precarious; these include copper, lead, zinc, tin, and many others. Reclamation of scrap, substitutes, rigorous conservation at all stages from mining to final use, and new discoveries will help.

The Qualitative Side

Turning now to the qualitative side of natural resources, and thinking primarily of the United States, one is immediately struck by the widespread and growing belief on the part of most people that things are going downhill—the air over our cities is becoming fouler, streams more polluted, landscape littered, urban design more monotonous and unimaginative, pesticides and radioactive fallout threatening humans and animals alike, and so on through a long dreary catalogue. If the natural environment generally is becoming dirtier and less attractive, there are, it must be noted, numerous encouraging exceptions. The corner seems to have been turned with regard to pollution in an increasing number of our streams, in the Ohio and the Potomac for example. The deterioration of quality of the air over a few of our cities has at least been slowed down. And there are numerous examples of tastefully designed highways, urban developments, and natural areas.

Unfortunately hard, factual indicators of air, water, and landscape quality are not easy to come by, and one must rely on scattered bits of information and subjective impressions. The effort now underway in the government and in other quarters to construct social and economic indicators of trends in environmental conditions is a worthy one. To date most of the indicators are physical: such as the dissolved oxygen content and coliform count of streams, the record of sulphur compounds and particulate matter in the atmosphere, the number of acres of parks and open space in urban areas, and so on. Ways need to be found to relate these trends of physical conditions to human satisfactions and social amenities.

For the future, great resource developments for water and land will have to be equally directed toward qualitative as well as quantitative results. In the Washington, D.C., metropolitan area, people are greatly concerned about the quality of the water in the Potomac River. This is not primarily a matter of the amount or even the purity of the drinking water supply; this latter can be handled at low cost by conventional forms of water treatment. The major issue is the quality of the water in the stream as it flows past Washington where more and more people are interested in swimming, boating, fishing, and clean scenery. Indeed, something approaching half of the several hundred million dollars now proposed by the Army Engineers for development of the Potomac finds its justification in recreation and scenic amenity. These, it should be noted, are classified as nonreimbursable; that is, the portion of the total cost of development ascribed to these purposes is paid for by the federal government. Thus local citizens and governmental units can encourage a maximum of recreational development without much restraint since the bill is footed elsewhere.

On the heels of growing public awareness of environmental quality problems has come a batch of notable federal enactments. The Water Quality Act of 1965 requires that each state establish water quality criteria by mid-1967 on penalty that otherwise the federal government will do it for them. The Clean Water Restoration Act of 1966 authorizes the appropriation of $450 million for the fiscal year 1967–68, with this rising to $1 billion two years later. Probably some $30 million of federal money is now going for research on water pollution, waste treatment, and related subjects. States and localities are mustering even larger sums for the actual construction of water quality control and treatment facilities. One quite readily comes by estimates of up to $100 billion over the next couple of decades of expenditures on water quality alone, and this probably does not include large expenditures made directly by industry in treating and recycling water. A similar story can be told shortly for air pollution, and the country is already making tentative though promising steps in the direction of improvement of urban and rural design through establishment of standards and through incentives of one sort or another. Pollution is truly becoming every man's concern. There is a growing skepticism about a very high and increasing GNP which includes large expenditures simply to prevent or clean up the mess that is being created.

A useful term for environmental quality management is the environmental problem "shed" which could be an air circulation area, a river basin, a metropolitan region, or a natural recreation area.[3] It is evident on the face of it that the typical political jurisdiction at the local level of government is not well suited by geography, financial capacity, or planning scope to deal with these environmental pollution problems. Therefore, progress toward solution is largely a problem of political decision and governmental organization. For this reason one must be especially concerned for the process by which anti-pollution plans and actions are worked out. The role of the planner and the technician is to identify the realistic policy alternatives; to fit together many forces and effects into designs, or plans, so that the parts can be seen in their functional context; to analyze each plan with respect to its benefits, costs, and other effects; and finally to present the alternatives in understandable form to those charged with deciding what to do.

The recent experience of the Delaware River Basin Commission in approaching this matter is instructive. In order to get on with quality management in the Delaware estuary the Commission has had prepared several of what it calls "objective sets" which delineate different water quality objectives. Alternative means are considered for achieving each of these objectives. Costs and benefits for the various engineering and other measures are presented. All of this is refined and sifted so that it can be made understandable to groups and individual citizens in the area as a basis for public discussion and ultimately for decision. The whole thing is done with the most advanced and sophisticated of data and analytical methods, yet comes forward in such terms that people can understand the issues involved and presumably make intelligent decisions which will be supported. This approach, which involves data, analysis, and public discussion, could probably be adapted to other environmental quality situations to good advantage. Whether this admirable approach can be made to work remains to be seen; the start at least is encouraging.

Although I have been talking first about the outlook for resource quantities and then about the quality problems separately, it should be understood that the two are closely interrelated. For example, one possible way of reducing water pollution in a metropolitan area is by building dams and storage reservoirs upstream from which the flow of the river can be augmented when necessary to dilute polluted water and carry pollutants downstream. Thus, added quantities of water may be used to deal with a quality problem. The web of interrelations includes the several resources as well as their quantitative and qualitative aspects. Thus the connections between air and water pollution are numerous. For example, pollutants going up an industrial smokestack may simply be discharged into the atmosphere, or to some extent they may be removed by various processes and then discharged into the sewer system and carried out into the nearby stream or lake. This latter, of course, contributes to water pollution. Or the particulate matter—the soot, grime, and fly ash—can be reduced to solid form and then burned or dumped, thereby contributing again to air pollution in the first instance or perhaps to land pollution from solid waste disposal in the second. And so it goes, around and around. There is something to be said for the multipurpose environmental problem shed as a means of looking at the full range of environmental quality problems and devising appropriate laws and programs.

Possibly the most useful geographic unit to deal with as an environmental problem shed is the large metropolitan region such as New York, Philadelphia, Chicago, or Los Angeles. In many of the country's metropolitan areas, particular kinds of pollution—air, water, or solid wastes—are already being approached on an areawide basis. The problems of obtaining agreements from the numerous units of local government in a single metropolitan area are formidable; tradition, local pride and prerogative, interjurisdictional jealousies, and sheer lack of imagination on the part of local officials all conspire to make a truly metropolitan environmental quality program difficult. One would like to see somewhere in the country a sturdy metropolitan council of governments undertake to experiment with an environmental quality program in which the several specific kinds of pollution would find their place and with adequate attention to the interrelations among them. If environmental conditions continue to get worse, it is predictable that considerations of public health and welfare will require some kind of special area wide authority to enter the picture in order to reverse the trend and begin to bring the situation under control. Voluntary locally oriented environmental control programs, which most people would prefer, may have their last chance during the next few years; thereafter, if this kind of response is not forthcoming, actions more centrally directed by the federal government would seem inevitable.

Improving Resource Plans and Policies

Having dealt at a little length with the resources outlook especially in this country, but to some extent elsewhere in the world, in terms of quantities and quality, I want now to turn directly to the subject of public policies and programs in the resources field. Especially I want to try to suggest a framework within which policy changes can be seen to better advantage. First I shall deal briefly with a few of the highlights of historical development of resource policies in the United States and what would seem to me to be the broad objective of these policies. Then I want to consider in more detail some of the ways, principally through research and analysis, of viewing resource problems to better advantage so that policies may be made more cohesive and responsive to the longer term trends and needs. And finally I shall make a few concluding suggestions for improving resource policies for the years ahead. Improving policies, I would argue, is basic to improving plans and programs and can give direction and purpose to them. If you like, better policy planning is necessary for better works or program planning.

Policy Objectives in Historical Perspective

Throughout United States history natural resources of land, water, and minerals have been matters of central concern for public policies and programs. Agricultural development was the principal concern of people during the colonial period. Difficulties between the American colonies and England leading to the Revolution revolved around the efforts of the mother country to continue to impose a colonial system and an agricultural regime upon the colonies. The story of American development during the nineteenth century in large measure is the story of the westward movement from the Appalachians to the Pacific coast and the opening up of new lands, new mines, and new waterways. America was loaded with resource potentialities; economics, politics, and the whole national psychology combined to place a rapid resource development at the top of the priority list of things to be done.

A few light and tentative notes were struck by those concerned with conservation of resources for the future, but not until toward the end of the nineteenth century did the conservation-minded individuals begin to be heard clearly. Drawing scientific guidance and a measure of inspiration from the writings of George Perkins Marsh and the work of a number of scientists in the federal government, and basing their program on the growing realization that the frontier days were over, the leaders of the first conservation movement during the administration of Theodore Roosevelt gathered their forces together and made a major impact on the country with their ideas about the interrelatedness of all natural resources and their programs for resources conservation, management, and a stronger governmental role. World War I and the last gasp of the nineteenth century which we know as the 1920's followed, during which time significant legislation was enacted at federal and state levels but the main attention of the country was directed to other matters.

Since then, through the Depression of the 1930's, the war and immediate postwar period of the 1940's, and so on through the fifties and into the sixties, natural resources policies and programs have occupied a significant place in national affairs—partly in their own right and partly because of their importance for anti-depression policy, win-the-war policy, aid-to-less-developed countries policy, and Great Society policies. Fear of running out of low-cost raw materials which characterized the war and immediate postwar years has given way in the United States to a deepening concern for the quality of resources and the natural environment. But the quantitative problem remains paramount for the less developed countries.

Objectives of Policy

Across this panorama of history the objectives of resource policies have remained the same at the most general level, but have shifted in more specific terms. At the most general level, the objective of resource policy has been to utilize, and in some cases to preserve or protect, natural resources so as to make the best contribution to national development and individual welfare over a fairly long but unspecified length of time. At different times the more specific interpretations of this general objective have shifted, and throughout this laudable objective has been subjected to the pulling and hauling of regional politics. For the present period I would factor the following somewhat more specific objectives out of the general one:

1. Economic growth and stability, both in nationwide and regional terms.

2. Social welfare, especially for disadvantaged persons and regions.

3. Improvement in the quality of the natural environment, especially for health, aesthetic satisfaction, outdoor recreation, and preservation of selected sites.

4. Contribution to the broader objectives of international policy, including raw material imports and exports, aid to development of resource industries in less developed regions of the world, and in other ways.

5. Contribution to national defense in terms of stockpiles of critical and strategic materials, assuring adequate supplies of oil and other materials, and some other matters.

It will be seen immediately that these objectives of resource policy do not stand on their own feet entirely; they depict resource policy as parts of economic policy, social welfare policy, international policy, defense policy. However, the connections among the several natural resources are sufficiently close in physical, biological, economic, and social terms that one has to aim toward integrated, or at least interrelated, policies for land, water, minerals, and the others. The lines of consistency have to run between the various resources and also between resources and other great areas of public policy. I doubt if there will ever be a single resources policy—or even a single water policy or energy policy. But ways can be found of blending more smoothly the policies that deal with the various resources.

The Meshing of Resource Policies

Probably the most effective way to secure a better formulation and coordination of policies is to come at the matter through the side door. Instead of a head-on assault the idea is to do some other things which will result in better policies as a kind of fallout effect. Here are a few activities of this kind that can contribute toward a better articulation of natural resource policies:

1. The comprehensive and systematic projection of demand for resources and resource products plus a careful analysis of supply alternatives can furnish a broad quantitative perspective within which policies can be visualized. The future estimates of demand have to fit within the overall growth and productivity of the economy. Despite many technical difficulties, the demand and supply look into the future can give guidance to present decisions about programs and investments with long-term consequences. If nothing else, the discipline of long-range and interrelated projections will restrain enthusiasts for any particular resource or raw material from trying to run away with the game. Efforts to stimulate or restrain production of basic farm crops, petroleum, metals, and many other things will have to be worked out in the light of the best picture of the future it is possible to obtain—even though one knows at the start unseen events will occur and alter the picture. All this means is that one must redraw the picture from time to time, taking the new factors into account. It is interesting to note that the Water Resources Planning Act, passed in 1965, calls for the long-range perspective that can only be furnished by systematic projections of demand and supply for water in the major river basins of the country.[4] Similarly the establishment of quotas on fuels or minerals has to be done with reference to a long-range perspective, and consideration of export and foreign aid policies in the agricultural field will hinge on the outlook for the several commodities involved.

2. Continual refinement of the various methods for analyzing resource projects and programs can contribute much to the coordination of them. At the individual project level, benefit-cost analysis is already required for water development projects and a strong effort is made through Budget Bureau circulars to see that this kind of analysis is applied in a uniform manner by the various agencies. Although there is some temptation to place more reliance on benefit-cost calculations than in common sense should be placed, I am of the opinion that such analysis is far more helpful than hurtful. Furthermore, I believe we have no other direction to go than to try to improve the analysis, point out clearly where it is appropriate and where not appropriate, and make certain that other forms of evidence as to the merits of projects are placed in the hands of those who must make the final decisions. Problems related to benefit-cost analysis abound. In addition to the well-known difficulties of the rate at which to discount the flow of future benefits and costs to obtain comparable present values and of the level of prices to use in future years, there is the even more important matter

of how to deal with intangible benefits and costs and with spill-over effects, many of which are registered on large groups of people difficult to get at. Efforts to grapple with this problem at the theoretical, methodological, and data levels can themselves lead to better understanding among agencies concerned with these matters.

Another form of analysis which recently has come to the center of the stage is systems analysis. This is a comprehensive way of looking at a set of factors in a problem so as to bring them together in such a way that stipulated objectives can be achieved most efficiently. The management of river systems, or portions of river systems such as the Potomac River estuary in the Washington area, provide an excellent opportunity for the application of the systems approach. In Resources for the Future, Inc., we have seen how the very attempt to deal with the Potomac estuary in this systematic way can bring together a variety of approaches, agencies, and individuals into a greater understanding of the alternative courses of action and of the conditions for a more integrated total program.[5] I suppose also that the present emphasis on PPB (Planning, Programing, and Budgeting) as a systematic technique for formulating and evaluating specific government activities will also lead to better articulation of projects and programs among the resources agencies.

3. Planners and public administrators have always been concerned with how things are organized, both in the big picture and in the many little pictures. No doubt the very way agencies and the flows of authority and responsibility are arranged can promote or inhibit not only the effective carrying out of policies, but the formulation of the policies themselves. Traditionally some have argued that one must begin with a good organizational set-up, while others have maintained that one should begin with the problem and the program and expect suitable organization somehow to follow automatically. Obviously this is a chicken-and-egg situation. Typically, problems and pressures build up for organizational change, leading to a change which frequently goes well beyond what could be explained simply as an outgrowth of the immediate problems and pressures. With a large going concern, such as the executive branch of the U.S. government, small organizational changes are much more likely than large ones, although a series of small changes can sometimes be more important than a large one. For example, I think the Department of the Interior has been significantly enlarged in scope and function over the last two or three years through a series of small changes. The establishment of the Bureau of Outdoor

Recreation, the Water Resources Planning Council and the river basin commissions that it is sponsoring, the Water Resources Research Program, and the Water Pollution Control Administration is propelling Interior onto the national stage. No longer will it be the department of the western region, although it may take a little time for the full awareness of this historic change to sink in. But in any case, efforts to reshape the organizational form of the resource part of government, whether on the executive or legislative sides, or whether at federal, state, or local levels, can lead to improved interrelations among various policies and programs.

4. A special word can be said here about regional planning, programing, and organization of resources activities. Natural resources obviously have a strong space and locational orientation; therefore the regional dimension has always been important. And since natural resource regions tend to be large, they typically embrace more than one state and a variety of local governmental units. Resources can be the testing ground for intergovernmental experiments and the creation of new governmental instruments. One can mention the Delaware River Basin Commission as an example of a new (or new adaptation of an old) federal-state design. The Water Resources Planning Act is being developed flexibly so that a variety of intergovernmental river basin organizations can qualify under the act to receive various aids. Metropolitan regions in many places are becoming so large that they merge with river basin and other kinds of natural resource regions. New organizations may be needed to embrace these two traditional types of region if, for example, water supply and quality programs are to be comprehensive enough in scale for economic and social efficiency, not to mention geographic integrity.

5. Of particular importance will be the joint planning of research and development by several governmental agencies. My belief is that nothing is more important for conservation than research and development. Any threat of running short on a particular raw material or deterioration in quality of the natural environment inevitably points to the need for some kind of research and development activity to deal with the problems. If a shortage of fresh water is imminent, then we must look to research on desalinization, on water conservation, on long distance transport, and even legal and economic research to facilitate shifts in water use as the principal means of dealing with the problem. Research and development regarding oil shale can open up one of the

great safety valves in case we begin to run short of conventional oil. Technical advances in mineral prospecting and in the handling of low-grade ores in the past have saved this country from considerable difficulty, and most likely will continue to do so in the future. Unfortunately, however, despite major efforts of research and development in a number of the resource areas—including some of the newer ones like desalinization, weather modification, and ocean resource development—the broad pattern of resources research and development in government and in the country generally leaves many gaps. Efforts to deal with resources research on a broad scale can lead to more effective use of research funds and of scarce personnel. This does not mean there is not room for overlap and even some duplication of research in different quarters, and certainly it does not mean that our research efforts should not continue to be rather flexible; it simply means that the research planners and the administrators in the various parts of the government should continue and intensify their efforts to keep the whole scene in view. The work of the Office of Science and Technology and various units of the National Academy of Sciences and the National Science Foundation in the natural resource fields are steps in the right direction. As an integrating and coordinating device joint planning is extremely important since research and development sets the general direction for future programs.

6. A final coordinating and policy improving device is worth a little attention: the use of federal government incentives to state and local governments and private agencies in a more interrelated way. In my own county the voters recently approved a million dollars in bonds for acquisition of parkland and open space land. The county elected officials, and administrative officers immediately set to work with a fine-tooth comb to figure out the best way to take advantage of a number of different federal matching programs, some of which operated directly and some of which operated through the state. We had a small operations research type problem, perhaps combined with a gaming problem, to figure out how to make the most out of our own million dollars. We had to appraise the various uncertainty factors; minimax principles were relevant; and alternative sequences of actions and reactions had to be considered. The same kind of story can be told with regard to other local government activities which the federal government aims to affect through various programs. The National Association of Counties has been strongly urging all of the more than three thousand counties in

the country to appoint someone to their staffs who will specialize in federal aid programs. All of this leads to a good deal of sympathy for the so-called Heller-Pechman plan of rebating a certain modest percentage of the federal personal income tax receipts to the states for use over wide ranges of programs at the discretion of the states. Perhaps a portion of any such rebate should automatically be passed on by the states to the cities and counties. I would argue that some preferential treatment might be accorded regional governmental agencies in river basin areas and in metropolitan areas since many of the resource problems, such as the pollution problems mentioned earlier, have to be dealt with on a regional scale. Perhaps it would be possible for the natural resource-related programs of the federal government, through whatever department they may be administered, insofar as they affect states and localities, to be more closely interrelated so that the states and localities will not have to play the games I have referred to. Perhaps the Departments of the Interior and Agriculture—or an agency in the Executive Office of the President, or one of a combination of committees of Congress—could take more initiative in introducing a greater degree of consistency and logic into the numerous federal programs and incentives which are meant to influence state and local governments. Recent recommendations of governmental task forces and committees have pointed the way. The experience of the National Resources Planning Board and its predecessor agencies in the period 1933 to 1943 should be reviewed in terms of the present situation.

A Few Suggestions for Improving Resource Policies

From all of this you will see that when I speak of a framework of public policies and program in the natural resources field I am not thinking in rigid or stereotyped terms. Such framework as can be erected will have to flow from the historical development of resource policies and programs and will have to recognize that resources are only one element in a framework for total governmental activity. I am sure it is good to review the broad objectives of resource policy at the several levels of government as a prelude to any consideration of specific issues of policy and program. And I am of the opinion that progress in improving resource policies and programs, especially progress in interrelating the various parts, is more likely to be made by dealing with a few fairly specific matters which, if successfully done, will inevitably lead to better policy frameworks and better program coordination.

Let me conclude by referring to the six items indicated in the preceding section through which, I believe, better resource planning and programing can be achieved, and for each one offer something specific. Long range problems will probably be met, not by means of some grand design of plans and actions, but through numerous discrete decisions which are thought at the time to be workable. Perhaps it is better this way.

Long range projections of demand supply of water in the twenty or so major river basins of the country are called for by the Water Resources Planning Act. I would propose that this be extended to cover all of the natural resources and that leadership be taken either in the Executive Office (through the Council of Economic Advisers or perhaps through the Office of Science and Technology) or more directly by the Departments of Agriculutre and the Interior. Much of the work is being done; but it needs to be brought together into one consistent framework. Other agencies could cooperate on special parts of the job, such as the Federal Power Commission for electric power and natural gas. Of course, such projections have to be based on assumptions about population growth, new technology, and other factors, each of which may be subject to increasing influence by social policy. The planner has to take care lest he glorify his particular projections and assumptions as prophesies to be fulfilled.

Regarding economic analysis of resource projects and programs I would suggest a planned program of experimentation with systems analysis as a basis for clarifying choices among different projects and clusters of projects in the various resource fields. As a part of this, benefit-cost analysis would be pushed to its outer limits of usefulness, but with care being taken not to promise too much. Also I would propose a program of post-audits for projects and programs already in being and for which we have had a number of years of administrative experience. It is possible that the General Accounting Office might undertake such a program. It never ceases to puzzle me how we all give lip service to history and the lessons of history, but seem unwilling to face the music of careful historical or post-audit examination of actions we have already taken.

Coming more directly to planning, programing, and budgeting for resource programs, we still have not established in clear-cut terms long-range development programs for water, power, forestry, energy, and the other major resources. We do have the six-year federal works programs, and the annual budget message has good material on the subject, but it does not seem to me that the federal government agencies, or the states either, have truly united in an effort to develop a capital programing system in the resources field, which is one of the most obvious candidates for this kind of treatment.

Regarding organization, planners and public administrators have always been interested in making big and little proposals. It seems to me that events of the last few years have led the Department of the Interior far along the road toward becoming a general natural resources department, with nationwide responsibilities. Sooner or later it may seem sensible to add the civil works functions of the Department of the Army so far as these pertain to water resources. Whether the Departments of Agriculture and the Interior will ever merge is an open question; I suppose it would not present obstacles more difficult than the merger of the three military service departments into the Department of Defense. However, I would not strain at this, but rather let events unfold and conditions change with the hope that consensus could precede any major reorganizations of this sort.

In the regional resource planning field I would hope the Department of the Interior would go as far as it can in encouraging a variety of designs and forms in the various river basins and other kinds of resource regions so that we may take full advantage of regional differences and talents. Particularly important will be the offering of federal incentives to resource developments in river basin and other natural resource areas and in metropolitan areas, so as to encourage units of local government to get together in their programs. Similarly, the Department of Health, Education, and Welfare for air pollution, the Department of Housing and Urban Development for open space, and the Bureau of Outdoor Recreation for land and water conservation areas should proceed along directions already taken to encourage with technical aid and support with funds the metropolitan and other local efforts.

For resources research and development, which I think is tremendously important, I have two suggestions. First, I would like to see an Undersecretary of the Interior for research and development, and the same thing in other departments concerned with natural resources. This would symbolize the importance of research and development as nothing else would and could lead to a much better organized overall program of research, better balance among the several parts, more attention to general objectives, and improved performance all along the line.

My second suggestion would be the establishment of a resources research and development fund to be used to supplement various programs in this area in the several departments and agencies at points where they are weak and where there are gaps. Such a fund might be used with particular effectiveness in opening up whole new approaches or areas of research. The allocation of the funds might be placed in the Office of Science and Technology or in a special Resources Research Board made up of representatives of the agencies chiefly concerned. Much of the research would be done by existing governmental units. Congress would specify the amount of money and the general criteria for its use. A strong advisory committee of non-governmental people could be of assistance in determining general directions. Grants from the fund might also be made to qualified state, regional, and local agencies, and to universities and research institutes. Ultimately there might emerge a National Institute for Resources Research and Development, perhaps modeled after the National Institutes of Health.

The foregoing suggestions apply to this country, but something like them may have relevance on an international scale, especially with regard to less developed countries. Thus, long range estimates of resources demand and supply, more rigorous analysis of benefits and costs of projects, better planning of resource development programs, more attention to research and development specifically for underdeveloped regions, financial and technical aid programs with more leverage—all of these open up avenues for international progress. As one example, I have advocated elsewhere the establishment of a World Institute for Resource Analysis and Planning made up of experts in the relevant branches of science and engineering, and in economics, planning, and administration.[6] The aim of such an Institute would be to improve the whole process of resource planning, including basic data, selection of projects, and integration of resource programs with regional and national development. In addition, work at the Institute would constitute a practical training for resource planners.

Conclusion

This paper carries the title, "Natural Resources—Wise Use of the World's Inheritance." The words are carefully chosen: use, not intact preservation; wise, not only economic or efficient; the world's inheritance, not the nation's inheritance. The terms, of course, defy precise definition, but the thrust of the meaning is clear. I have resisted the temptation to make grand pronouncements about the distant future of the twenty-first century; social scientists have not been particularly successful as prophets. I do not know if the world can hold 20 or 50 billion people, or if it will ever be called upon to do so. If I had to speculate on the outcome of the race between population and natural resources in any world that I can visualize, I would bet that neither would win, or lose, but that each would be brought progressively within the scope of deliberate planning and management. The capacity of human beings to cope with their problems through altered behavior and new institutions should never be underrated, especially if they understand what is at stake and are able to consider the alternatives. Perhaps this is primarily a matter of faith, but recent investigations into attitudes about resources suggest that the very way planners describe alternative plans may be decisive for the choices that are made. But lest an occasional planner conclude that his influence is greater than it will be, or should be, let me say that not all of tomorrow's problems can be foreseen and solved today. We can only try to create the knowledge, institutions, and processes that will give each succeeding generation a better chance to cope with its particular problems and opportunities as they emerge.

I have resisted also an urge to say that, although science, technology, and enterprise might furnish all of the electricity, building materials, machinery, water, and food people would require fifty years from now, the country or the world will be running out of space, especially land space in metropolitan areas. Some will say that in a pinch we can get lots of fresh water from the ocean, usable metals from ordinary earth and rock, energy from the atom, and food from the test tube; but space is strictly limited to the land area of the seven continents. I am not so sure. There is air space above our cities, also over-water and underwater space. Half the land in our metropolitan areas is presently unused; it could not even be regarded as useful open space. The carrying capacity of urban and other kinds of land space is elastic and can be stretched by the imagination of the planner and the enterprise of the developer.

As one tries to look into a misty future, he may conclude that the wise use of the world's natural inheritance involves several things chiefly: two have to do with fertility, one with vision about tomorrow's world, and one with the will and capacity for effective action. These four are interrelated. Fertility needs to be dealt with in two ways but in opposite directions; human fertility, especially in poorer regions, needs to be reduced; agricultural fertility needs to be increased. Vision of what the future can become, of where past trends are carrying us, of the possibilities for creating a better life for all, of how to express these possibilities in plans that people can act on—these are the magnets which can draw the world forward. Here is where the planners come into the picture; their role is a crucial one. Finally, there is the ultimate test: the will and capacity of people to act. In the natural resources field this means to press forward with research into new uses of raw materials; with conservation programs to prevent misuse; with education of resource planners, managers, and conservation officers; with the application of knowledge and technique in agriculture, forestry, water development, and energy and minerals. These are some of the ways that can lead to wiser use of the world's inheritance.

In making the foregoing suggestions for improving resource policies especially in the United States, I have tried to stay within the realm of the practical and still point to a few changes that over time could yield large returns by altering the way we look at our natural resources, make our plans, and proceed with our programs of action. The next year will be critical; the next ten years will be critical; and so will the next fifty years. Good policies will be ones that have been tested against the immediate, the intermediate, and the long range future. Similarly, each place is important: one's own city, region, and country as well as all the others in the world because all are linked. The natural environment is basic to a national consultation on the future environment of a democracy in whatever perspective of time or space.

Notes

1. These estimates are taken from Hans H. Landsberg, Leonard L. Fischman, and Joseph L. Fisher, *Resources in America's Future* (Baltimore: Johns Hopkins Press, 1963).

2. See Joseph L. Fisher and Neal Potter, *World Prospects for Natural Resources* (Baltimore: Johns Hopkins Press, 1964), for these and following estimates.

3. See various writings of Allen V. Kneese, especially *The Economics of Regional Water Quality Management* (Baltimore: Johns Hopkins Press, 1964).

4. Research now being done by Nathaniel Wollman at the University of New Mexico, with the aid of a grant from Resources for the Future, Inc., aims to produce a set of such projections through applying a fairly sophisticated estimating methodology. An early and tentative version was prepared for the Senate Select Committee on National Water Resources.

5. See the forthcoming Resources for the Future study by Robert K. Davis on water quality problems in the Potomac estuary.

6. Joseph L. Fisher and Roger Revelle, "Natural Resource Policies and Planning for Developing Countries," in *Natural Resources: Energy, Water, and River Basin Development*, Vol. I, U.S. papers prepared for the U.N. Conference on the Application of Science and Technology for the Benefit of Less Developed Areas (Washington, D.C.: U.S. Government Printing Office, 1963).

Comments on

Fisher

A . J . W . S C H E F F E Y
Center for Environmental Studies
Williams College

Joseph Fisher provides a lucid accounting of the place of resource management and policy within a larger planning and development context. He
describes the comprehensive web of opportunities and constraints that must
be understood as we proceed with the task of building a more liveable environment in the years ahead. His position is presented with equanimity and
restraint, in sharp contrast to the emotion that characterizes much current
discussion on the environment. Mr. Fisher is sensitive to the increasingly
compelling role of intangible factors and aesthetic demands, and he voices
these concerns within a broad perspective which helps to alleviate the now-or-
never type of ultimatum so frequently presented.

His balanced approach is welcome, but the essentially sanguine outlook
could be disquieting to the extent that it may contribute to complacency
instead of heightened citizen awareness and participation. Mr. Fisher makes
a strong plea for "more hard work in planning in a deliberate and highly
professional manner" in place of the more common crisis reaction to resource
issues. But emphasis upon greater professional expertise must not be allowed
to obscure the equally compelling need to promote more effective citizen
involvement in the identification of environmental needs and the determination of development goals. More adequate means for expressing and measuring
these individual values are required.

The generally optimistic tone of the paper rests upon the promise of science
and technology for ameliorating future resource shortages or imbalance. Without minimizing the profound technological advances that can be anticipated,
important reservations remain regarding the priorities for action that could be
assigned. An overriding reliance upon technical research and development
may tend to submerge more subtle questions of human needs and individuals'
motivations—ranging from the psychological effects of crowding to the visual
stimulation of highway design—as they influence resource decisions. The profit
motive and demands of national security will assure continued research
progress in the technological sphere, and few people today would question
the self-generating qualities of scientific advance. The same confidence, however, does not exist with respect to the capacities of our social institutions

and political processes for shaping the direction of this upward spiral. We can count on an increasingly abundant flow of energy, speed, and wealth but the same certainty does not exist in terms of individual satisfactions.

Mr. Fisher illuminates this underlying dichotomy. He observes that people in the affluent Western societies have a general confidence that the future can be of their own making, while later he notes the "widespread and growing belief on the part of most people that things are going downhill." A similar dichotomy is reflected in his discussion of world food and population: after twenty years of international development effort, human fertility still outpaces agricultural productivity in most parts of the world, primarily because of failures of human institutions rather than technological limitations.

It is imperative, therefore, that a significant portion of the proposed research effort be directed toward investigation of human and community values as they will ultimately determine resource development goals. Much research will be needed to assess the ways in which people perceive different aspects of the physical environment and the varying satisfactions they derive from it. Mr. Fisher has set forth an imaginative yet reasonable set of targets for improved "meshing of resource policies" on the part of government agencies and planning authorities. But in the final analysis it is the private citizen who must be moved to participate more fully in this process of policy formulation at all levels of jurisdiction. The citizen, as a consumer of the public landscape, must be able to press effectively for appropriate response from both the private and the public sectors.

The municipal Conservation Commission programs taking shape in many parts of New England today illustrate one type of response that is needed. In community after community overwhelming votes of confidence are being received for Commission proposals to purchase open land and to launch other forms of land use control. More significant than either the dollars appropriated or the land preserved is the process whereby citizens are being encouraged to think about environmental values, to undertake serious research and discussion, and to express themselves regarding qualities they consider important and costs they are willing to incur to see them maintained. In Massachusetts the movement is developing into an effective statewide lobby for resource action, and in the last ten years legislative acceptance has been realized for nearly every major conservation proposal. Without comparable political arrangements at the local level, this opportunity for determining the "public interest" in relation to the physical environment would not be so readily available.

Mr. Fisher recognizes the "territorial imperative" of bureaucracy and wisely advocates a series of incremental changes which could lead to better coordination of resource policies. Greater attention might have been directed to improved methods of ecological surveillance of resource trends as an additional means of bridging the coordination gap among agency programs. The proposals for a scheme of post-audits of existing programs and greater use of systems analysis in resource planning are particularly applicable to the whole process of international resource development. While quantitative problems remain paramount for most regions of the world, we are now in a position to avoid past mistakes by giving fuller consideration to questions of "environmental diseconomies" in a qualitative sense early in the design stage of development proposals. Incorporating the ecological point of view within a systems framework could further this objective by providing a clearer focus on the role of natural processes.

Mr. Fisher demonstrates his faith in the capacity of human beings to cope with new situations through altered behavior and new institutions when he suggests that the "race" between people and food will be brought progressively within the scope of deliberate planning and management. This raises fundamental issues concerning the new patterns of living and the degree of institutional innovation that will be required as the demands of an urban population are projected upon the resources of the natural environment. Kenneth Boulding has proposed that the "modest society" constitutes a more appropriate image of the future than the "great society," something more akin to a tea ceremony than a parade ground. Manifold cultural and economic ramifications would be involved in such a shift of orientation, but the need to limit certain forms of consumption in order to insure other environmental values is already apparent in many situations.

It is pointed out that the very way in which planners describe the alternatives can be instrumental in determining the choices that are made. In the past their choices have been largely within the realm of physical planning, but this has changed steadily in recent years. The present AIP consultation goes beyond anything formerly undertaken in the exploration of national goals and individual values as they relate to specific planning decisions. Perhaps what is needed as a practical follow-up measure is a continuing series of publicly sponsored forums of a similar nature, planned for sustained citizen participation and linked in some form to the platforms of political parties and candidates. These might be organized within defined resource regions of the country, and geared specicifically to exploring questions of individual values as they will ultimately determine the quality of the human environment.

S T A N L E Y   A .   C A I N
U.S. Department of the Interior

Such an expression as "wise use" often leaves much to be desired. In the case of Dr. Fisher's essay we do not find conventional wisdom or that of a limited understanding. Instead he has drawn on broad scholarship, deep humanism, penetrating studies by the organization he has headed since its inception, consultation that he has had with government, and personal experiences in the complexities of elected local office. There is much here that is frank and honest and that seems wise to me. I can do little more than call attention to certain points that might have been printed in bold-face type.

In discussion of the resources outlook for the United States he cautions us that national and even regional statistics cover up sore spots, and by implication that the same is true of aggregated world data. The high per capita use of resources in the U.S. does not tell the story of Appalachia, for example, nor do the comparatively meager averages for low-economy countries come close to describing the state of poverty of vast majorities of people. This is well known if frequently forgotten. The fresher point in this connection is that planners have to spend most of their time dealing with the sore spots of cities, nations, and the world.

In discussion of resource plans and policies, Dr. Fisher emphasizes that better policy planning is necessary for better works or program planning. The sequence, logically if not pragmatically, is longer. It moves from national purposes or goals to policies, programs, and projects. One may be skeptical that the first can be planned, but policies, programs, and projects do require integrated planning if we are to use natural resources wisely. When Dr. Fisher uses the term "planning" he means comprehensive planning, not single-purpose planning, whether or not the distinction is explicit at any one place in his statement. His position is quite clear when he gives five categories of policy objectives (national purposes or goals) and then says: "It will be seen immediately that these objectives of resource policy do not stand on their own feet entirely: they depict resource policy as parts of economic policy, social welfare policy, international policy, defense policy."

He doubts that there will ever be a single water policy or energy policy, for example, and might have added that if there were, it would work against planning as he conceives it, for it would work against allocation, zoning, flexible multiple-use choices, and the differing needs of contrasting regions.

The wisdom of what he says is most telling in the section on the meshing of resource policies in which he calls for: (1) comprehensive and systematic projections of supply and demand, (2) continual refinement of analytic methods, (3) improvement in the organization of institutions, (4) more attention to regional differences, (5) joint planning of research and development, and (6) a hard look at the carrot and stick of Federal incentives and restraints on other levels of government.

Finally, Dr. Fisher does not speak in rigid or stereotyped terms. He is not for the grand scheme. He seems to be uneasy with, perhaps suspicious of, panaceas, for he says that progress in improving resource policies and programs is more likely to be made by dealing with a few fairly specific matters. If, I would add, national goals are clear.

His plea for post-audits is very timely. We seem to have a habit of starting something, often worth doing, and then not checking up on the unexplored or unanticipated consequences of the action. The common expression "side effects" suggests a minimizing of consequences that certainly deserve analysis and evaluation and which should have been taken into consideration in the first place.

Following the logic of his argument, he speculates about the relations between the civil works functions of the Corps of Engineers and the Department of the Interior, and between Interior and the Department of Agriculture. He raises such questions and leaves them open, perhaps wisely, but I find cogency in the suggestion that Interior would benefit from having an Undersecretary (or Assistant Secretary) for research and development. He moves from this to the suggestion of a National Institute for Resources Research and Development (in the Department of the Interior?), perhaps modeled after the National Institutes of Health.

As to criticism, a small dog can chase a large train, and I do not wish to get caught on my own figure of speech; still I would suggest that several sentences must not be taken from the context of the paper as a whole. If one does this there are spots where Dr. Fisher would seem to overemphasize the roles of science, technology, engineering, economics, and public administration and minimize the difficulties of cultural change. The importance of human satisfactions and social amenities is given a nod, but it seems to me that it is possible to believe that he is not fully appreciative of the glacial slowness with which traditional thinking changes and old ways are given up.

His reluctance is most evident when he talks about the world picture. He cannot, I believe, quite bring himself to the state of pessimism that the facts seem to warrant. Part of the imbalance here may be due to looking at the world, as we all tend to do, from our own front yards. Can America, should America, plan for economic growth and the consumption of the world's natural resources at existing, much less augmented, rates? While the U.S. gets richer and most of the world poorer, both actually and relatively, nearly all international relations seem to be deteriorating at a frightening rate. And resource opportunities and needs are near the base of our pyramiding troubles.

To sum up, and to do so on the complimentary note that this paper deserves, we are reminded of much that we should not allow to escape our attention, and we are rewarded by numerous fresh and wise suggestions.

Research for Choice

This paper was commissioned to add a new dimension for decision-making concerned with the creation of the national, the urban, the total environment and through increased participation of the interested individual. It was concerned with proposing useful systems of data collection and retrieval, in closing gaps in knowledge, in establishing productive interdisciplinary research and in delimiting computer capacities and limitations regarding development toward an optimum environment.

What data is to be collected at what frequency, by whom, on what basis (keyed to latitude and longitude for worldwide application), when considered in the context of the next fifty years? Who will request this data, and how will it be presented?

Whole new research institutions, devices, and organizations to assure sound work toward an optimum environment are possible with electronic technology. How is this technology to be used to assure maximum interaction with leadership groups? Might such devices as a "socioeconomic cyclotron" be used to handle complex data and project graphically the consequences of alternative decisions so that leaders can take their appropriate part in making decisions in complex subject areas?

A coupling of socioeconomic-physical research concerning environment calls for the establishment of priorities and utilization of studies to build a framework to advance the "state of art," like those discussed at the AIP's Portland Conference and reported in *Environment for Man*. This sort of work leads to quantifying and qualifying research as to priority, cost, and skills needed for the next fifty years.

Author: Herbert A. Simon, Graduate School of Industrial Engineering, Carnegie Institute of Technology

Chairman: Barclay G. Jones, AIP, Associate Professor, Department of City and Regional Planning, Cornell University

Committee: Daniel Bell, Department of Sociology, Columbia University; John W. Dyckman, Chairman, Center for Planning and Development, University of California, Berkeley; John R. Hamburg, AIP, Director of Planning, Tranportation Planning Program, New York State Department of Public Works; Willard B. Hansen, AIP, Bureau of Community Planning, University of Illinois; Britton Harris, AIP, Department of City and Regional Planning, Graduate School of Fine Arts, University of Pennsylvania; Edward R. Hearle, Assistant Director, Office of Regional Economic Development, U.S. Department of Commerce; Edgar M. Horwood, AIP, Director, Urban Data Center, University of Washington; Richard Ruggles, Department of Economics, Yale University; Rev. Dr. Lauris B. Whitman, Executive Director, Bureau of Research and Survey, National Council of Churches; Rev. Dr. D. Campbell Wyckoff, Princeton Theological Seminary; Leo F. Schnore, Department of Sociology, University of Wisconsin

XII

Herbert A. Simon

Carnegie Institute of Technology

Research for Choice

Under its terms of reference, this paper is to be concerned with "proposing useful systems of data collection and retrieval, in closing gaps in knowledge, in establishing productive interdisciplinary research, and in delimiting computer capacities and limitations regarding development toward an optimum environment."[1] I have interpreted these terms to encompass (1) the nature of the knowledge and information about the *structure* of our social system that we need for planning, (2) the nature of the knowledge and information about the *state* (past, present, future) of the system that we need, and (3) the advances that we need in the technology of the choice and design process itself.

The discussion is arranged in six main sections followed by a summary and conclusions:

1. The main relevant kinds and uses of information and knowledge, with particular reference to the distinction between "structure" and "state" mentioned above.

2. Some of the critical gaps in the substantive knowledge and information now available.

3. The information needs for fundamental research, that is, for an understanding of structure.

4. The information needs for planning and design, over and above structural information.

5. Progress and prospects of research on the processes of decision and design.

6. The present and prospective information technology, in the light of the demands that are likely to be placed on it.

1. Uses and Kinds of Information

Considerable pains are taken to ascertain periodically the per capita gross national product in the United States. To what questions is this information addressed? First, it may be used to answer: "How well are we doing?" It serves as a crude scorecard of economic well-being.

Second, the per capita GNP may be used to call attention to problems when they arise. When GNP drops from last year's level, a nation looks to needed shifts in its economic policies.

Third, the GNP, along with other statistics, may become grist for the mill of research that is trying to understand the structure of an economic system—how the government's budget balance affects the level of economic activity, say. This use does not aim at immediate action, but at understanding systemic response, to make subsequent actions more intelligent.

Fourth, the GNP together with measures of productivity may be used to ascertain the present state of a system in order to plan for its future—to predict, for example, future levels of economic activity, in order to predict future consumption of electric power, thus to make plans for building generating stations.

Information has, at least potentially, these four broad classes of use: as scorecard, to direct attention, to analyze a system's structure, and to ascertain parameters of its state. As the example shows, a single statistic may serve, at different times, in all four uses. On the other hand, data of particular kinds may be especially appropriate to one of these uses. All four uses are important to planning and social choice, and they often lead to quite *different* demands on the processes and institutions that produce information.

Planners and policy makers tend to be most aware of their needs for data in the fourth category—for facts and figures that they can use for projecting trends and designing actions. Their projections and plans depend critically, however, on how the system operates—on its structure —hence, on the use that fundamental researchers have previously made of information in the third category.

Much of the significance for professional planners and policy makers of the first two kinds of information is also indirect. Scorecards and attention directors are the links between professional activity and the political process. The FBI index of major crimes is not used to manage law enforcement activities, but to call public attention to a problem and to marshal public resources to deal with it.[2] The same is generally true of auto death statistics, or an index of air purity for a city. These measures are less concerned with the administrative question of what to do than with the political question of what problems should be near the top of society's agenda and what it is worth—economically or socially— to solve them. The operation of this part of the information system may have a great deal to do with whether first things are put first.

There are some problems common to all four information categories, in particular, problems about what kinds of fact a society needs in order to enable it to deal with the important social goals. The next section discusses these common problems relating to substantive gaps in the information system.

2. The Substantive Information Gaps

Relatively speaking, we are best informed about demography, economics, and technology. However inadequate specialists may find them for particular purposes, our data in these areas are extensive, and improve continually in quantity and technical quality. Although we should not relax our efforts toward bettering these kinds of information, there are almost complete gaps in our information system that require even more vigorous efforts to fill them. We need to have much better information about the quality of life, and we need better data bases for making longitudinal comparisons of social indicators from one point in time to another.

The Quality of Life

The availability of any or all of the four kinds of information about a problem encourages social action to deal with that problem. The careful statistics we maintain on whooping cranes inform us whether we are succeeding in saving the population from extinction, warn us when we (or they) have had a setback, provide basic information that can be used to investigate the causes affecting birth and death rates of whooping cranes, and provide data for planning the nesting areas the birds will need.

Our relative wealth of information about economics, the industrial system, and our natural resources contrasts sharply with our lack of information about other dimensions of the quality of life. There is a sharp contrast, too—probably not coincidental—in the relative amount of effort we devote to solving problems of economics and the natural environment as compared with other social problems.

Yet economic problems are no longer the central problems of our society, and problems of our physical and biological environment, though troublesome, are well within the capacity of our existing scientific knowledge and resources to handle. Contemporary statements of national goals, while not ignoring these traditional areas, place increasing emphasis on more subtle and difficult aims: enhancing human dignity, realizing human potentials, widening the range of opportunities for choice.[3] A society that wishes to advance such goals must be prepared to measure or assess the qualities to which they refer.

Notwithstanding those who point with pride or view with alarm, we do not know whether public and private morality are declining or improving, whether human lives are fuller or emptier than they were a generation ago, whether there are more risk takers or more organization men, whether we are lonely or smothered in togetherness. The trends in our happiness, in the richness of our lives, in our morale, and in our morals must become matters of fact rather than opinion, just as the degree of our wealth and our hunger have become matters of fact.

There are now modest beginnings toward taking such measures. We have some data, very imperfect, about mental illness, crime, and delinquency. Improvement in their scope and comparability will develop them into useful instruments for social policy. The last thirty years have seen great progress in techniques for taking public opinion polls, and for measuring expectations and attitudes. We are technically equipped today for a continuing, large-scale undertaking that will generate the information we need about the quality of life. We should aim at launching such an undertaking in the immediate future. It will need to have several components, of which direct data-gathering will be one part, fundamental behavioral research (see section 3) another. An annual expenditure of $70 million (.01 percent of GNP) would be a not inappropriate initial scale for the data-gathering effort. Part of this sum might expand programs of the Census Bureau or other government information agencies, but a large part should be granted—in the spirit of long-term research and development grants—to non-governmental organizations that could adopt a highly experimental attitude in their approach.

To pursue social goals that involve the less tangible dimensions of the quality of life, we will need greatly expanded and improved information about the distribution of knowledge and skills among the population, and the distribution of values and attitudes. As time replaces money as the principal scarce resource in our society, we will need to know in considerable detail how various kinds of individuals in our society allocate their time.[4] Another crucial scarce resource is attention, particularly attention to political matters. We need sophisticated information about the allocation of attention.

Longitudinal Comparisons

Measures of achievement of social goals are always relative. Hence for all four data uses we have an especially great need for retrospective, longitudinal measures.

We do not really know, for example, whether leisure has increased or decreased over the past hundred years. We do not even know—the statistics are so poor—whether per capita crime rates are rising or falling. We are especially deficient in longitudinal studies where the identity of respondents is retained—Project TALENT being a rare contemporary example of the sorts of panel study we need.

Generating data for intertemporal and intercultural comparison poses well-known technical and conceptual problems. Economists have faced these problems in their realm with sufficient success so that meaningful (if not perfect) comparisons of economic well-being can be made between Japan and England, or between 1900 and today. A satisfactory technical level of comparability is also achievable for measures of the other dimensions of the quality of life.

Measures that have naturally defined units, e.g., hours per day as measures of time allocation, offer the simplest opportunities for longitudinal comparison. But we need not, and should not, limit ourselves to these. We need measures, for example, about how happy people are— how they feel about life and their well-being. We know a great deal about how to take measures even as intangible as these.[5] We know much less about how to interpret comparative differences in the measures from place to place or from time to time. Our interpretations will improve only as our theories of human behavior and attitudes improve, and our theories will improve only as we have better data for developing and testing them. We must view our task as a bootstrap operation, in which better data will improve theory, and better theory, data. This is the characteristic path of progress in all sciences.

3. Information for Fundamental Research

No amount of information about the social system, no amount of awareness of its problems, will enable us to improve it unless we understand *how* it works: its structures, mechanisms, processes. Improved information in increased volume about juvenile delinquency will contribute only indirectly to solutions of the problems. Unless we understand something about the relations of cause and effect, knowing the present state of the system, in whatever detail, will not help us change it. Change will become possible only with improved scientific knowledge.

Expansion of Research Activity

The main goal, therefore, in improving our social information system must be to provide the information that will be most useful for behavioral and social research aimed at broadening our understanding of social structure and process. It is through this indirect route that better information will make its main contribution to the achievement of social goals. A generation hence we may wish to shift emphasis, when better social science knowledge is available. Then engineering measures of the state of the system and managerial and political attention-directing measures may take first priority. But it a little futile to know what needs to be accomplished until we know better how to do it.

Parallel, then, with the expansion of activities aimed directly at gathering more and better data must go a great expansion of activities aimed at advancing basic behavioral sciences and our society's competence—qualitative and quantitative—to carry on basic behavioral and social research. A reasonable target for the next decade might be a production rate of 5,000 capable, well-trained Ph.D.'s per year and a national basic research budget in the behavioral and social sciences of $1 billion. The expenditure estimate assumes that the aspirations and imaginations of behavioral scientists will grow with their opportunities and competence—as has happened in the natural sciences since World War II.

Much of the new information needed for basic research will be generated within the research activity itself. Special information-gathering activities, of the sorts mentioned in the previous section, will account for only a small part of the growth in information—but an essential part. (Similarly, a small but important part of the information of natural science is generated in a "data bank" mode: astronomical and meteorological observations, exact determination of important physical and chemical constants and standards, taxonomic and ecological data in biology, and so on.)

Most information relevant to social planning, however, will continue to be *ad hoc* data—gathered as accessory to particular research inquiries. With the improvement of theories and the standardization of measuring instruments, such data will increasingly find uses beyond the particular inquiry that generated them. This is another—and important—aspect of comparability of information, which grows hand in hand with the progress of good basic theory.

Access to Operating Data

Vast amounts of data about social phenomena are gathered by governmental and other organizations in our society today as a byproduct of their regular administrative activities. Obvious examples that come to mind are the Social Security files and the records of the Internal Revenue Service. Relatively little of this information is now available either for social research or for social planning. When efforts have been made in the past few years to tap these data more effectively, two kinds of difficulties have been encountered, and only partly surmounted: technical problems of combining fragmentary information for different time periods and from different files; and problems of preventing invasion of privacy by misuse of the data. In many respects, the two problems are opposite sides of a coin—solutions to the technical problem generally increase the dangers to privacy.

The threats of invasion of privacy must be taken seriously, but in perspective with threats from other directions. The association with names and fingerprints of the kinds of information already collected in the files of the FBI and various security agencies constitutes a far greater threat to privacy than could conceivably be created by coordination of government operating statistics. Electronic eavesdropping is a much more serious threat (and more difficult to control) than any potential eavesdropping in computer-stored records.

The answer, of course, is not to ignore the threat to privacy, but to find the technical means for safeguarding privacy while making data available for the broadest possible research purposes. Storage and processing in electronic computers gives us the technical basis for combining data from various sources, while maintaining the identity of reporting units over time. The latter is essential, because many of the questions our research will need to ask require longitudinal panel data for their answers. Maintenance of identity of reporting units compounds the privacy problem, but does not make it insoluble. Privacy, like security, is relative, and is maintained by raising the costs of achieving successful violations. Development of the technology for providing research access to operating data, while protecting privacy, is an important item for the current action agenda. The problem can almost surely be solved by an expenditure not exceeding a few million dollars, and probably for much less.

Modeling Social Systems

One of the important new techniques that computers have contributed to social science research is the simulation of the behavior of social systems by constructing models of them. In this way, systems can be studied that are far too complex to be analyzed by classical verbal or mathematical means. Modeling may be used both in basic research, as a technique for computing the system behavior implied by hypothesized complex theories, and in planning, as a technique for predicting the behavior of a system characterized by a known set of mechanisms.

The use of modeling in planning requires that the important features of system structure be already known—that is, that the basic research job has already been done. For this reason, the most serious limits on the use of modeling in planning today are limits on our understanding of system *structure*, not limits on our data about the *state* of the system. We will say more about this point later. The experience with modeling reinforces our general conclusion, however, that the weakest link in our information system is information about structure and that strengthening this link requires the expansion of basic research activity.

4. Information for Planning

A case has already been made for emphasizing an indirect route, through basic research, to improving information for social decision. This does not mean that progress in our measurements of the state of our social system must stand still while this indirect route is being pursued. Progress in measurement does not necessarily mean *more* measurement than we carry on now. As a matter of fact, it might even be argued that public planning has, in general, been too much preoccupied with data collection and projection, and too little with design and decision. Progress will come, not through mere collection of information or assembly of impressive "data banks," but through thinking through the relation of data about the state of the system to the planning process. What are the guidelines for deciding what data will be important in planning?

Time Horizons

Prediction for its own sake is a costly and pointless game. The objective in making predictions and projections into the future is to provide a basis for the decisions that are to be taken today; tomorrow's decisions can and should be made on the basis of the information available tomorrow.[6] Some decisions are required today to provide lead time for tomorrow's actions.

The future is relevant to decisions taken today only to the extent that these decisions have consequences for the future that are in some sense irreversible—that cannot be undone. The main reason, for example, why forward planning is so closely associated with decisions about physical structures is the permanence of those structures, and the long future period during which the design decisions have consequences that cannot be altered without cost. We need to identify, therefore, the principal forms that permanence and irreversibility take.

Discounting consequences by distance in space or time has great pragmatic value, for it makes decisions manageable where otherwise we would become lost in tracing out an endless maze of consequences. Whatever its usefulness in matching the decision-making process to the cognitive limits of the decision makers, it also incorporates assumptions as to the relative value of the here-and-now as compared with the there-and-thereafter. The interest rate used in a highway cost study may decide whether or not the project will make a net positive contribution to welfare. The interest rates we assume in our planning reflect the relative importance we attach to our grandchildren's welfare and our own, and affect greatly which resources we will consume and which we will try to conserve.

The higher the interest rates we use in discounting remote consequences, the less sensitive are our decisions to predictions of the future, hence the less important it is to make such predictions. Thus sensitivity analysis should be employed in designing information systems for prediction, because it is uneconomical to predict the future so accurately and distantly that the predictions will have no influence on present decisions. This Occam's Razor should be applied systematically and consistently to existing as well as proposed data systems and predictive procedures.

Since the development and diffusion of innovations takes considerable time—years and decades—there is usually little need for "blue-sky" prediction in a decision system. For example, the possibility of central electricity from atomic reactors became generally known in 1945. The economics of atomic stations in relation to conventional stations and the potential effects of the new technology on the economy had already been estimated reasonably accurately by 1948. By that time, electric utilities and equipment manufacturers could obtain most of the information they needed to make sound decisions about the design of new stations or the probable profitability of manufacturing atomic facilities. (Not all firms made wise decisions, but where they failed their failure cannot be charged to the absence of sound predictions.)

Using an aggregate model of the system to predict from advances in science that have already occurred to their technical, economic, and social consequences can often be important means for improving the accuracy of those predictions that are really crucial to planning. At least as much attention needs to be given, in the planning field, to these possibilities as to the improvement of prediction by enlarging the data base. Some predictions have already been made of the probable consequences of the introduction of computers, extensions of automation, continued progress in medical science, and other technical advances. This kind of prediction technique needs systematic development.

Elements of Irreversibility

Four kinds of decision are especially likely to entail long-term irreversibilities: (1) decisions about physical structures, (2) decisions committing a system to a new technology, (3) decisions about education and training, and (4) interrelated sequences of non-simultaneous decisions. Decisions about physical structures have irreversible consequences for the obvious reason that we don't want to bear the cost of premature obsolescence.

Commitments to a new technology are often irreversible because they bring with them many decisions in the other three categories. A shift from freighting by railroad to freighting by truck leads to decisions to build highway facilities and not to build railway facilities, to train people for highway occupations and not for railroad operations, and to construct all sorts of facilities that *assume* the trucking operations (e.g., filling stations, factories on highways rather than sidings, and so on).

Decisions about education and training result in storing "programs" of useful knowledge and skill in humans. These programs may suffer from obsolescence just as physical structures do.

The fourth category cuts across the others, often taking the form of a "standardization" problem. A complex system—a railroad, say, or a city— once built is not renewed all at once, but in a piecemeal fashion. Thus, if the wrong track gauge is chosen for a railroad, it may never be economical at any subsequent moment to change it, for it may be more efficient to make each new partial replacement or extension compatible with the existing gauge. Similarly, the question of whether the United States should, at any given time, shift to the metric system is distinct from the question of whether it would have been better to have adopted it initially.

In public planning, "comprehensiveness" is not, in itself, an important or desirable planning goal. Many economic, technical, and social affairs are better regulated by the operation of the decentralized market than by attempts at central planning. Rather, public planning should focus its attention on the crucial "standardization" problems—including the problem of coordinating manpower and structures with technological commitments.

In urban planning, for example, the key standardization problems arise from interdependencies in land use. As all urban planners know, planning a new city in the middle of the jungle is quite different from planning for existing cities.

Planning focused on standardization problems must take as its first task identifying the technologies, and changes in technologies, that will operate as prime organizing factors and driving forces in the society. Its second task must be to discover varieties of economic, technical, legal, political, and administrative means for modifying these key factors. Its third task must be to assess the consequences for the rest of the system —including consequences mediated through markets—of changes in the key factors. Such analysis is usually best carried out with aggregate models that sacrifice detail to ability to trace main systems effects.

For example, an important contemporary planning concern should be to assess the relative roles that transportation (of employees) and communication (of messages) will play in white-collar work activities a few years hence. The shape of our cities (including the effectiveness of possible mass transportation systems) will depend crucially on the relative extents to which people or messages move. From the standpoint of both prediction and design, planning will need to focus on this feature of the technology.

Planning directed toward key factors will make quite different information demands from planning conceived as "comprehensive" prediction and control of the system. As already suggested, its greatest need will be for thorough understanding of system structure rather than masses of detailed data on the current state of the system. In this kind of planning, the most valuable sorts of model will be those that reflect the basic structural relations of the system (including, of course, those that determine its dynamic behavior).

Strengthening the Planning Capability

This kind of planning and data use described above will require, for implementation, large numbers of well-trained applied social scientists. In our social structure, a cadre of engineers stands ready to apply physical science knowledge, and a medical profession to apply biological knowledge. We are sadly lacking in social engineers. An immediate requirement, then, is to accompany actions to increase the number of research social scientists by actions to create a large number of professionals competent to participate in the design and implementation of social policy.

Some of this manpower can come from existing professions—law, architecture, social work—and some from the liberal arts, provided that large amounts of modern social science knowledge and skills can be introduced into their curricula. The numbers of students now enrolled in undergraduate social science, business, and architecture curricula might be almost enough to meet our needs if appropriate training could be provided. We should be taking steps to train 50,000 to 100,000 "social engineers" per year at the bachelor's degree level.

5. Research on the Choice Process

When design and planning are described as "arts," the main intended implication is a negative one: they are not sciences, hence do not rely solely on analytic methods, hence cannot be fully systematized but depend essentially on such indescribables as "judgment" and "intuition." As a historical statement, this is true; it is rapidly ceasing to be true about the present and prospective state of the art.

A Theory of Design

Great strides have been made in the past ten years toward learning how human beings solve problems, discover facts and theories, and design devices and systems. Much of the mystery has been stripped away from the processes we call "judgment" and "intuition." A number of computer programs have been written that imitate human problem solving or design processes closely (cognitive simulation), or that provide functional substitutes for them (artificial intelligence). Some of these schemes have already reached the stage of industrial application—to the designing of motors and generators, the locating and designing of highways, the scheduling of large civil engineering projects.

Esthetic processes and criteria have not been entirely neglected in this exploration of the processes of human thought and creation. Simulation has already made significant contributions to our understanding of music and musical composition. The general structure of planning processes has been investigated in such work as Christopher Alexander's *Notes on the Synthesis of Form*.

Synthesis of Form

Opinions can and do differ about the present state of the art. What seems eminently clear, however, is that we are about to have, if we do not already have, a clear, powerful, precise theory of the processes of planning and design. The existence of this theory will have the most momentous consequences for the activity of planning:

1. *We will be able to automate increasingly large aspects of the design and planning processes*—in many instances, perhaps the whole process. Typically, planning organizations will be systems with human and automated components working in intimate relation with each other.

2. *We will be able to teach planning and design skills.* There is a constant tendency, in professional schools, to encourage formal, intellectual analytic skills to drive out the "intuitive" skills of synthesis and design. The former meet the academic criteria that the modern university sets for "proper" subjects, while the latter do not. As a result, the stronger engineering schools have become schools of mathematics and physics, teaching precious little engineering, while the best medical schools have become schools of biology. (Schools of law and architecture have been less subject to this academic erosion.)

As we gain a scientific understanding of the design process itself, it becomes possible to restore design as a central subject in the professional school. But now the main emphasis will not be on *designing*, but on devising effective design *systems*. The design curricula will emphasize our scientific knowledge of intelligence, human and artificial, and the principles underlying the design of systems that exhibit intelligence.

This is not the place to describe the emerging theory of intelligent systems. Discussions can be found, for example, in the papers edited by

Feigenbaum and Feldman in *Computers and Thought* and in Alexander's book, mentioned earlier. Today the number of persons familiar with the emerging theory of design is not more than a few hundred. It needs to be increased rapidly to several thousands as part of the training programs proposed in previous sections.

6. The Information Technology

The task of this "Research for Choice" paper is itself a planning task—planning for decision-making systems. Hence, the earlier discussion of planning and prediction is quite relevant to this task also. Anyone who looks at what has happened to our information processing technology over the past twenty-five years will despair of predicting what that technology will look like twenty-five—much less, fifty—years hence. Almost no one in 1942, certainly no one in 1917, would have or could have predicted the computer revolution we have already had.

On the other hand, it is not clear that anyone would have been well advised to have behaved differently in 1917, even if he had known the exact shape and form of the coming computer revolution. The failures of planning that we observe are failures to plan five, three, or even one year in advance, not failures to plan twenty-five or ten years in advance.[7] These short-run failures generally involve failure to *credit* prospective changes that are entirely predictable and even predicted. The question of credibility will be mentioned again later.

If we accept the premise that the twenty-five-year future of information processing is at least as unpredictable now as it was in 1940, then we will look for techniques that allow us to get by with minimal predictions. One such technique is to consider a few basic paramters that characterize such systems, rather than the detail of hardware. Indeed, this is the basic strategy we have followed in our discussion so far. In this section, I should like to make more explicit some of the key assumptions about the future information-processing technology that underlie this whole analysis.

The Information Processing System

An information processing system comprises means for collecting (or "inputting") information, means for storing it, and means for retrieving it. At any stage of collection, storage, or retrieval, the information may be changed in form—usually to make subsequent processing steps more effective or economical. For example, information may be indexed when it is collected and before it is stored, to facilitate its later retrieval. Or existing files of information in storage may be "up-dated" by collating with them newly collected information.

Between the engineers of an information processing system and the users there stands not only the "hardware"—electronic machinery—but also the "software," which consists of programs stored more or less permanently in the system to facilitate the users' interacting with it. Software includes monitor programs which control and schedule the system and coordinate its activities, assembling and compiling programs which translate instructions written by the user into the language of the machine instructions, and various kinds of data banks. Increasingly, the software characteristics of information processing systems are becoming more significant than hardware characteristics in determining system performance and the range of tasks to which the systems can be adapted.

The following assumptions about the information processing technology of the near future (ten years, say) appear reasonable:

1. Substantially all information available to humans in the society in verbal or symbolic form will also exist in computer-available form. At present, it is costly to put the content of an existing book into a computing system. The book must be copied by a human teletypist or a photoscanning device. In the future, books will be stored in electronic memories at the same time that hard copy is produced for human use. The technology for doing this already exists, and is in considerable use.

Many data that are now recorded or transcribed by humans will be transmitted directly to automated information processing systems without human intervention. For example, if a counter is installed to record traffic density on a road, it will store its information directly in the computing system.

2. Memories in information processing systems will be of sizes comparable to the largest memories now used by humans—for example, the book collection of the Library of Congress.

3. It will be feasible and economical to use English or another natural (noncode) language in interrogating the memory of an information processing system. (This does *not* mean that all information in the store will be available to each inquiry independently of what preparation has been taken by way of indexing.)

4. Any program or information that has proved useful in one information processing system can be copied into another part of that same system or into another system at very low cost and without severe problems of standardization.

5. Even the most optimistic assumptions about the power and capacity of prospective information processing systems will remain puny in relation to the size of real-world planning problems. The chess board is a tiny microcosm compared with the macrocosm of real life. Nevertheless, there is absolutely no prospect of an increase in the power of information processing systems to the point where they will play chess by "considering all possibilities" (some 10^{120}!).

Therefore, the significant limits on the power of information processing systems for handling planning problems will be limits on (1) knowledge of the laws that govern the system being planned, (2) cleverness in discovering representations that handle salient characteristics of the situation unencumbered by a mass of detail, as well as (3) availability of the relevant real-world data. The first two limitations are likely to be even more important than the third, and ingenuity (human or computer) in devising powerful problem representations will remain crucial to effective planning.

6. Information processing systems will become increasingly capable of learning, in several senses of that term. In particular, they will be able to "grow" their own indexes as new information is added to their stores. Thus, the important contemporary bottleneck in human indexing and abstracting capability will become less significant.

What consequences crucial to our inquiry follow from these assumptions? The main import of the first three and the sixth assumption is that computers will become substitutable for men (within twenty years, say) with almost all the tasks performed by information processing, designing, and planning systems. Hence, the division of labor between man and machine in such systems will be determined by economic rather than technical considerations. Each will do the jobs he (or it) can do more cheaply. Because of the cheap copying capabilities of computers (item 4), they are likely to have a comparative advantage for tasks where many copies of information or programs that have been generated by the system are required.

The fifth item is of fundamental importance, for it implies that the basic logical structure of the design and planning processes will not be changed by partial or complete automation. Since most of the discussion of sections 3 and 4 rests on assumptions about the nature of that process, the validity of assumption 5 is critical.

If we are concerned that social planning is menaced by an information explosion, items 2, 3, and 6 should give us some comfort, while item 5 should help us recognize that human intelligence has never solved problems by searching enormous spaces (filled with information or anything else) exhaustively, but always by discovering ways of conducting the search in a highly selective manner. But the whole problem of information overload needs reexamination in the face of the changes in information processing technology. We turn to this topic next.

Who Needs to Know?

Decision making rests on knowledge about the present and beliefs about the future. In traditional information processing systems, we could say that a person "knew" something if the information was stored in his memory or in a book in his possession, and if it was "indexed" so that he could retrieve it. When information, or purported information, was communicated to a person, it was subject to an accrediting process before storage. If it passed the test, it was believed. The tests of believability could be applied to the information itself ("the world cannot be round, else people would fall off") or to the source ("he has no reason to deceive me").

Traditional notions of "who knows" and "who believes" were never entirely satisfactory when applied to entire organizations instead of individual persons, and they are still less satisfactory when applied to the new information technology. At what point did the City of New York "know" that it would have a serious smog problem in the 1960's? This belief may first have been stored inside the city government years ago in the mind of an engineer working in the Bureau of Smoke Control. Perhaps at some later time—when Los Angeles smog received widespread publicity—it migrated to other city administrators and was adjudged credible by them. At a still later time, perhaps, it became credible to the mayor and other leading politicians, and to some members of the public. The actual path may have been quite different, of course. The point is that an organization (and an information processing system) has many minds, some in its head, and some in its tails.

The design of a planning system must therefore handle the problems of (1) who needs to know—at any given time—and (2) how to establish credibility so that information can diffuse.

With a modern information processing system, we must take a systems approach, and avoid identifying "what is known" with "what is stored now in local memories." Generating information on demand or obtaining it from another part of the system are important alternatives to storing it, and alternatives that are becoming available on more and more favorable terms of time and cost. If I have access to a telephone, for example, I "know" the names of the best American experts on any subject you care to mention. For by a succession of three or four telephone calls (following a sort of "twenty questions" strategy), I can locate the experts' names. I could probably do no better if they were stored in my memory—with the usual defects of indexing ("I think it starts with S").

Any thorough application of the "who-needs-to-know" test to information storage practices in our society would almost certainly reveal an excessive preoccupation with multiple storage of information. The design of new information processing systems will call for more attention to the indexing and retrieval processes, including the processes for drawing inferences from information. Progress in planning will stem more from improving these processes than from securing larger and more complete stores of information.

The Focus of Attention

In systems that have access to very large stores of information, the question of what is *known* becomes less important than the question of what is *attended to*. The larger the store of information, the smaller part of it that can be in the focus of attention of particular processors and particular decision makers at any given moment.

Inference and indexing processes, of the sorts discussed in the previous section, become crucial in bringing to attention the most important information, and in summarizing information so that the ratio of amount of meaning to numbers of symbols, so to speak, will be high. When the information that is transmitted is highly processed, not raw, then it also becomes crucial to determine what credibility is to be attached to it by the parts of the system that receive it—to determine how seriously they should consider it and act on it.

Determining credibility requires the application of tests—which in itself consumes information processing capacity. A major factor in determining how rapidly new information can gain credibility is the presence or absence of bottlenecks of attention. There have been great lags, for example, in the credibility attached by high government administrators and business executives to technical forecasts of the role of computers in decision making. In this, as in other fields, changes are credible to top managers only some years after they were believed with a high degree of certainty by technicians. Often there is disagreement among the technicians themselves as to the directions and rates of change. This has been spectacularly true, for example, with respect to the economic effects of automation, and the whole field of "artificial intelligence"; less true in the case of atomic energy.

Information processing systems for decision making are quite as much systems for transmitting and accrediting inferences and beliefs as they are systems for gathering and analyzing data. Some research has already been done in recent years on the diffusion of knowledge about and acceptance of new technical practices (hybrid corn and antibiotics). This remains a promising and important area of behavioral science research for the immediate future.

Conclusions

I shall undertake to summarize this analysis only to the extent of recapitulating some of the major recommendations for action to which it has led:

1. Expand programs for gathering data systematically and periodically about the quality of life—say to a scale of about $70 million per year. These programs should produce information about the distribution of knowledge and skills among the population, the distribution of values and attitudes, and the allocation of time.

2. Through these information gathering programs, develop a rich set of measures of the quality of life that can be used for assessing important longitudinal trends in our society.

3. Set as the main goal in improving our social information system providing the information that will be most useful for behavioral and social research aimed at broadening our understanding of social structure and process.

4. To reach this goal, train research personnel at a rate of at least 5,000 Ph.D.'s per year, and support basic social research at a level of at least $1 billion per year.

5. Intensify current activities to solve the technical problems of giving effective social science access to the files of operating data that exist in our society, while protecting personal privacy. In particular, privacy can and must be protected without losing the information that would make longitudinal studies possible.

6. Support research to reduce the dependence of planning efforts on impracticable attempts at predictions by improving techniques for sensitivity analysis and by developing systems models for predicting from key technological factors to their social consequences.

7. Train 50,000 to 100,000 professional personnel per year with broad competence in applied social science.

8. Reintroduce research on the theory of design, and the teaching of design as core activities in the professional schools that will be concerned with social policy and social planning. As a means to this, give high

priority to exposing several thousand students and professionals to current knowledge and developments in the theory of design and intelligence.

9. Intensify the research effort devoted to understanding the processes of information diffusion, including the ways in which new information becomes credible.

Any list of priorities is attention-directing information, hence implies that items not mentioned do *not* deserve high priority. Among the items not mentioned here, hence not marked for high priority, are large-scale efforts to build up stores of detailed data about the state of various components of the social system. This is not to say that we should not be making imaginative experiments with the new technical equipment for data storage and retrieval. But the experiments are unlikely to be imaginative if they are conceived as experiments on data systems. They are more fruitfully conceived as byproducts of basic social science research programs and programs of research on the design of decision-making systems. Only within such frameworks will appropriate criteria emerge to guide the design of the data storage and data retrieval components.

In these recommendations, I have also said almost nothing about hardware systems. Hardware there will be, in vast quantities and increasingly possessing the operating characteristics postulated in Section 6. Whether the hardware, however impressive its electronic capabilities, will make major contributions to social planning and social choice will depend almost entirely on our success in deepening our understanding of changes in the quality of life, of the structure of society, and of the theory of the design process. In these latter three areas an acceleration of effort and an allocation of much larger human and financial resources are urgently required.

Notes

1. I have had valuable comments and assistance from members of my Committee of Correspondence and from my colleague, Igor Ansoff.

2. I am not concerned at this moment with the *quality* of these indicators, which are often unsatisfactory, but with the uses to which they are put.

3. All three of these aims are set forth in the opening paragraph of *Goals for Americans*, the report of the President's Commission on National Goals.

4. Some interesting international comparisons of time budgets are now being made under the U.N. auspices. They illustrate how much can be contributed by even simple beginnings.

5. McClelland's exciting, if controversial, intertemporal and intercultural comparisons

of achievement motivation provide an excellent example of the kind of exploration that should be going on on a large scale and on many fronts.

6. For this reason, I have ignored the term of reference instructing me to make specific recommendations for action in 1970 and various subsequent dates. I see no point in recommendations for actions that are not to start now, or very soon, unless they require preparatory actions—in which case the latter should be recommended. Hence, all the recommendations in this paper are for action now.

7. As our manpower discussions indicate, failure to plan manpower needs and to think through the implications of scientific discoveries ten or more years in advance may cause subsequent failures to plan five or three years in advance!

<hr />

Comments on

Simon

<hr />

BERTRAM M. GROSS
Maxwell College, Syracuse University

Herbert Simon's paper demonstrates the value of thoughtful understatment. He has unquestionably offered many valuable insights into what is needed to provide improved information for decision makers. But in so doing, he has *understated* the importance of the problem, the difficulties involved in coping with it, and the nature of the efforts that will be required in future years. In attempting to redress the balance without going to the other extreme of *overstatement*, I should like to suggest that (1) throughout the nation, and in our urban areas particularly, we face a serious *intelligence crisis*, and (2) one of the difficulties is the obsolescence of basic concepts we use in acquiring data. Furthermore, an intelligent approach to the intelligence gap, in my judgment, requires a multidimensional social systems approach.

The Intelligence Gap

Herbert Simon points out that "there are almost complete gaps in our information system." He then discusses the need for "better information about the quality of life." In very positive terms he refers to the need for specific measures to pin down the realities behind such grand abstractions as "enhancing human dignity, realizing human potentialities, and widening the range of opportunities for choice."

Obviously, these terms are broad enough to include the reverse also. If properly interpreted, they may include information on the escalation of offenses to human dignity and denials of human potentialities. In the light of rising aspirations, they may include the narrowing of the range of opportunities for choice among the millions of Negroes trapped in urban ghettos and the greater millions of middle class youngsters trapped in suburban emptiness and materialism.

Simon has brilliantly set forth "four broad classes of use" for information. Thus, a city planner or a mayor may obtain information on the urban plight or traffic tie-ups for any one of the following purposes, or for all of them together: (1) to attract attention to situations that might otherwise be ignored, (2) to ascertain the facts of a situation, (3) to analyze a situation, and (4) to evaluate—that is, prepare a scorecard.

As Simon points out, attention-attracting and appraisal are "the links between professional activity and the political process." But this seriously understates the social conflict aspects of all four uses. Historically, knowledge has always been *a* source of power. In the modern age, information is *the major source of power*. Indeed, it is the basis for exploiting all other sources of power. It is, therefore, sedulously sought and used by all wielders of power and seekers after more power. It is used by all parties, factions, and coalitions. Hence, economic or social indicators—to use the cogent terms invented by Albert D. Biderman—inevitably serve as vindicators or indictors.

With the growth of data gathering and dissemination by government, indeed, one may wonder whether we need not reconsider the nature of "the State." There was a time when political theorists regarded as a state's distinguishing characteristic its monopoly over the legitimate use of physical force as concretized in armed might. We may well be entering a world in which a centralized network of computerized data centers may become a distinguishing characteristic. Indeed, the governmental data network might well become the basis not only for directing armed services, but also for the manipulation of the currency, the control of fiscal policy and the managing of public attitudes. All of these potentialities for the use of information by government are visible in governmental activities within all highly industrialized societies.

Part of this visibility is provided by controversies over the "credibility gap." These controversies are taking place in many countries where people complain that their government is not giving them the basic facts on what is going on or is managing—or mismanaging—the news. Thus in the United States the criticism is continuously made that the administration has not been "leveling" with the American people on the nature of our involvements in Vietnam or on the true course of military operations.

However, there is a singular naïveté in most criticisms leveled at a "credibility gap." This naïveté flows from the implicit assumption that top policy makers in government *really know* what is happening and what is imminent in the future. It is assumed the root of the difficulty is, at best, a lack of candor or, at worst, a deliberate intent to deceive.

Let me suggest, however, that the credibility gap may not be nearly so dangerous as the "intelligence gap"—that is, the absence of reliable information that policy makers can choose to withhold or manipulate. The intelligence gap is "rooted in *one-sided, missing, distorted, misinterpreted, or unused information.* The initial impact of the intelligence gap is that national policy makers themselves are misled—or, to put it more mildly—are led into *oversimplified partial and outdated views of major policy problems.*"[1]

In a recent talk, the philosopher Anatol Rapoport has challenged the validity of the intelligence at the disposal of the men at the top of war-waging states:

> Like all of us, the men at the top have been insulated from the world by verbal screens. In their roles as members of ruling elites, they experience the world not as a place of sights and sounds, filled with people who have joys and sorrows, who would rather live than die. In the rarefied atmosphere of geopolitical calculations, human beings do not exist. Instead "reality" is pictured as a struggle for power among from two to half a dozen states which are accorded the title of a Power if they can wage autonomous war, i.e., if they are able to conduct a war without assistance from a stronger "power."[2]

But it is not only in foreign affairs that the men at the top are "insulated from the world by verbal screens." At home, our national leaders seem to be living in the past. They are largely people whose most important life experiences took place during the traumatic periods of the Great Depression and World War II. They are too little tuned in to the present and have little or no sense of the future. They have little or no realization of the fact that since World War II the United States and the world have entered a new era of system change. In a "tough guy" pose they may ask "What's the name of the game?" This is a pathetic posture at a time when the names remain the same, but all the games and all the rules thereof are changing. The new game is "post-industrialism"—a science-based, cybernetic, service society which is coming into being far more rapidly than the industrial revolution of the nineteenth century and is rendering obsolete old institutions, old values and old ways of life.

Concept Obsolescence

Simon is wise in pointing out that useful information for planning purposes depends upon "knowledgeable laws that govern the system being planned." As one who has contributed to the development of the new technology that is leading us into post-industrialism, Simon is more aware than most people of the fact that the system and the laws that govern it are themselves in a state of change.

Under these circumstances we cannot understand the system as a whole or the various subsystems with which most of us are involved without trying to re-create—or formulate *ab initio*—the concepts needed to ascertain, analyze and appraise the changing parameters of system structure and performance.

Probably our greatest challenge lies in creative designing of more useful concepts. One of the most exciting ideas in modern social science is the general system approach to society as a set of overlapping, crisscrossing people-resource systems in physical and social environments. From this point of view, our basic objects of observation (or, in the terminolgy of some statisticians, "the reporting units") are (1) individuals as they develop and behave "separately," (2) the groups—of families, informal groups and formal organizations—in which they interact, and (3) the territorial entities in which individuals and groups tend to congregate. At each point in the spectrum from the single individual to the state, the nation, and world society, people are linked with natural resources and with a rapidly changing array of man-made resources. One of the difficulties of understanding territorial entities—whether at the level of the metropolis or the megalopolis—is that they increasingly tend to be loose aggregates of organizations, families, and individuals that are losing their local roots and increasingly operating outside as well as inside the territorial boundaries.[3]

Improved information on these systems can scarcely be obtained by the utilization of existing concepts. GNP, which Simon seems to regard as a very useful measure, is increasingly inadequate to deal with the expanding areas of economic activity that do not fall squarely within price and market sectors. Population residence information—ideally suited to deal with a relatively non-mobile population many decades ago—cannot give us the multidimensional measurements of people-land ratios needed to chart the daily, weekly, annual tides of human movements across space. Additional information on wages tells us less and less about the material gains that people may get from an expanding array of fringe benefits. Our views on work week and leisure time are seriously beclouded by traditional information on working hours—a subject increasingly irrelevant to the expanding millions of professionals whose work week is rising and for whom indeed work cannot really be separated from leisure. In the field of basic information concerning security, insecurity and the feelings of belonging and alienation, we have little information on which to go. Our data on "mental health," for example, is nothing of the sort; it merely provides a count on the number of people who come into and leave certain institutions. In other words, unless remarkably vigorous steps are taken to improve our concepts, we run the risk of perverting our growing data processing capacities by feeding into the computers larger and larger arrays of irrelevant, useless, or misleading data.

Simon's fiscal proposals are firmly grounded on the warning that experiments with new data processing equipment are unlikely to be useful, unless conceived as "byproducts of basic social science research programs." Our task in coming years is to accept this challenge and design research programs capable of grappling with the complexities of a social system and world undergoing revolutionary system changes.

Notes

1. Bertram M. Gross and Michael Springer, "New Goals for Social Information," in *Social Goals and Indicators for American Society*, Vol. II, *The Annals*, September, 1967, p. 209.
2. From his address, "The Nature of Social Man," Maxwell Graduate School, Syracuse University, October 20, 1967.
3. This theme is developed at greater length in my article, "The City of Man: A Social Systems Reckoning," *Environment for Man*, William R. Ewald, Jr., ed. (Bloomington: Indiana University Press, 1967), pp. 136-56.

C. E. LINDBLOM
Professor of Political Science, Yale University

In this paper Herbert Simon has again displayed the sense of perspective, the breadth, the originality for which he is famous. One wishes the paper were longer; he obviously has even more to say on the subject than he has packed into this short paper. My comments fall under two headings.

1. The Research Design of the Next Fifty Years Project

Defining "research" broadly, we can say that the Next Fifty Years project is itself an exercise in research for choice. That is, it is an example of the kind of research regarding "development toward an optimum environment" that Simon was asked to discuss. Simon's ideas about appropriate research design for choice about future environment lead him to dissent on some important points from the design of the Next Fifty Years project.

His dissent is explicit when he says:

> I have ignored the term of reference instructing me to make specific recommendations for action in 1970 and various susbsequent dates. I see no point in recommendations for actions that are not to start now, or very soon, unless they require preparatory actions—in which case the latter should be recommended. Hence, all the recommendations in this paper are for action now.

The dissent rests on a principle.

> The objective in making predictions and projections into the future is to provide a basis for the decisions that are to be taken today; tomorrow's decisions can and should be made on the basis of information available tomorrow.

The principle, you will remember, leads him into a discussion of lead time, discounting the future, and the kinds of decision that are likely to entail long-term irreversibilities, decisions that he argues do indeed require attention today to the long-term future. An excellent discussion, it needs to be read not merely as an abstract comment on research for choice but as significant for those who are carrying through the present fifty year project.

2. Social Structure Process

You will remember that Simon discusses several kinds of knowledge that we need for choice. To one he gives special emphasis:

> The main goal, therefore, in improving our social information system must be to provide the information that will be most useful for behavioral and social research aimed at broadening our understanding of social structure and process.

I agree. But how to study structure and process? Simon proposes to put more people and more money into basic research on structure and process. He also argues for freer access of researchers to operating data like the Social Security files, and he proposes computer simulation of the behavior of social systems by constructing models of them. Although the proposals are useful, they do not add up to anything approaching a systematic analysis of the required strategy for basic research on structure and process.

By contrast, he has a great deal to say about the strategy for collecting and utilizing data about the *state* of social systems, and similarly he has a great deal to say about research on the choice process itself, under which heading he discusses the theory of design and information processing systems and raises as well his interesting question: Who or what needs to know and/or attend to what for purposes of decision making?

Are there no comparable strategic issues to raise with respect to research on structure and process? I suspect that it is not sufficient to reply that the general canons of scientific inquiry, continually refined as they are, give us all the guidance we need. It is just possible that we need the same kind of fresh thinking on this topic that Simon has brought to the other parts of his paper. Basic research into social structure and process is not, it can be suggested, making satisfactory progress. It cannot now generally perform the tasks to which Simon assigns it, nor do its prospects for doing so in the future appear encouraging.

On structure and process, I take it that Simon holds economics to be the most advanced social science. Economics still flounders badly in explaining how the Soviet economy works, how underdeveloped economies work, how economies grow, how economic activity molds the tastes and personalities of participants in economic life, how market relations do or do not "cause" such effects as impersonality in human relationships, personal anxiety, bureaucratization, and alienation. As systematic explanation or theory—the kind that I would agree with Simon we need—the success of economics is narrowly limited—primarily to a description of a narrow range of economic processes in the predominately private enterprise economies in advanced industrial nations. If its accomplishments in the next fifty years are an extrapolation of present trends in rates of discovery and theoretical growth, economics in the year 2020 will fall far short of providing the fundamental understanding of structure and process that Simon argues we need urgently for design, planning, and policy making in such problem areas as Simon's "quality of life" or in such less elusive areas as economic development.

In political science, a less well developed field, a new buoyancy among its practitioners reflects new gains in theoretical ambition, in accomplishment, in rigor, and in sophistication in employing empirical data. But important cause-and-effect relationships in political structure and process (and systems of them) still largely escape political scientists. There are, to be sure, scattered theories of varying degrees of verification about party competition in certain democratic systems, about voting behavior in them, or about some of the preconditions of democracy. But there is no general systematic theory about how the democratic process works, or even any established agreement in the profession as to what such a theory would attempt to encompass. Moreover, any general theory about the democratic process, it seems commonly to be thought, would either have to be fruitlessly abstract or would have to be limited to only one or a few of many possible kinds of democracy—to mid- or late-twentieth century American democracy, for example.

This is not to argue that the social sciences are not worth their keep, or against immensely heavier investment in them. It is only to suggest that our ambitions for basic research in structure and process ought to be reconsidered. If it is unlikely that in the next fifty years we can even roughly approximate the gains in basic research that Simon endorses, should we not consider carefully just what it is we most need to know about structure and process?

I do not know what we need to know. But I should like to see an inquiry made into a strategy for basic research on structure and process based on an assumption that our common ambitions for this kind of research are preposterous. To suggest something of the character of such an inquiry, one possibility is that basic research into structure and process could best be guided —not by law or any kind of formal control, but by the researcher's own choice—by the researcher's understanding of the theory of design and by the input requirements (or information and analysis) for selective decision making (selective, because, as Simon says, comprehensiveness is not to be desired). That is, one might explore the desirability that a large number of basic researchers in social structure and process might systematically subordinate their basic research to a new sophisticated perception of the needs of the choice process in the same way that Simon has proposed that information on the state of systems be subordinated to those needs.

I am not simply suggesting that basic research be practical or that it have a short-run payoff, or that it never respond to idle curiosity. I am suggesting that our growing understanding of design, planning and policy-making processes could be drawn on to give such guidance to basic research as would sharply reduce the possibility that in attempting comprehensive understanding of structure and process it forever falls short of an acceptable minimum level of competence.

In any case, if research on design processes is as important as Simon says it is (and I agree with him), so also is research on basic research processes.

New Incentives and Controls

The intention in commissioning this paper was that the paper be grounded on an understanding that present incentives and controls are inadequate to assure sensitive development and protection of the environment at the scales on which we will be building in the next fifty years. Yet there is a maximum limit to which it is desirable to control, as well as a minimum limit. For greatest achievement, definitions for both limits as they affect the individual and his society need to be sought and related to new incentives and controls.

Legal, moral, and economic issues are all concerned here. The question is raised, "How much of what man needs for his own self-development is determinable by the marketplace decision method?" Or what other method might be used?

This paper was expected to publicly recognize that improvements are possible in present urban reconstruction procedures and to propose them. It was to recognize that the means to assemble and build whole new communities in the numbers and quality needed are not now in hand and to define how they could be achieved, possibly through changed taxation policies.

Author: Daniel R. Mandelker, Professor of Law, Washington University, St. Louis

Chairman: Allen Fonoroff, AIP, Director of Planning, University Circle Development Foundation

Committee: Jacob H. Beuscher (deceased), Professor of Law, University of Wisconsin; Chester Rapkin, AIP, Professor of Urban Planning, Columbia University; Walter H. Blucher, AIP, Planning Consultant; David R. Levin, Deputy Director, Office of Right-of-Way and Location, U.S. Department of Commerce; S. J. Schulman, AIP, Commissioner of Planning, Westchester County Planning Department; Jack Noble, Smith, Hanes, Lundberg and Waehler, Puerto Rico; Dennis O'Harrow (deceased), Executive Director, American Society of Planning Officials; Richard S. Gordon, Director, Central Research Department, Monsanto Company; Clyde Fisher, Puerto Rico; Richard F. Babcock, AIP, Ross, Hardies, O'Keefe and Babcock

XIII

Daniel R. Mandelker

Professor of Law
Washington University, St. Louis

New Incentives and Controls

We begin with a focus on the legal institutions through which we intervene in the physical environment. They provide us with a complex and intricate set of legal techniques for dealing with the use of land and its development. Regulatory controls deal with such widely variant problems as the character of new residential development, the size and placement of billboards, and the maintenance of housing quality. Each of these techniques has a quite different and varying legal history which gives each a different legal setting. Rationalizing these techniques is one of the focal points of this paper, but space does not permit a full elaboration of all aspects of the problem. The focus is also on land and manmade increments to land in an urban context, omitting the related but different issues that arise out of social welfare programs, the conservation of natural resources, and planning for economic development.

Compulsory powers of land acquisition and assembly are used for such different purposes as the building of highways and the clearance of slums. Charting new directions in the face of this legal array is not easy. While it is almost a truism that existing legal institutions do not meet the objectives and expectations of a growing urban society, it is equally true that no satisfactory basis has yet been found for a new legal order. For this reason, a discussion of new incentives and controls must begin with the major influences that will have an impact on legal institutions in the next fifty years, their causes, and the tolerable limits within which the legal system can respond to meet these challenges.

Pressures for change in the legal system affecting the physical environment come from several directions. Population increases, however projected, will be substantial enough to intensify greatly the demand for land in metropolitan areas. The rate at which land can be expected to urbanize will continue to accelerate.[1] At the same time, demands for improved quality in the physical environment will continue to increase.[2] Both of these influences—an intensification in the use of urban land, a demand for higher quality—will intersect to prompt closer public control and more extensive public intervention in the management of our urban physical resources.

How these resources are deployed has serious consequences for large segments of the population, especially those who are underprivileged or who are not able to carry their own weight in the political arena. Partly for this reason, because racial and economic minorities can secure a better hearing at higher governmental levels, recent decades have seen a gradual but constant drift of power upward,[3] to state and especially to national levels of decision making. These changes have also been prompted by the financial necessities, by federal preemption of the income tax, and by the corresponding need for heavy fiscal outlays in developmental programs such as highways and urban renewal.

Shifts in the governmental balance of power are pervasive; they permeate all governmental programs that affect the urban environment, and are a critical focus in a reevaluation of the public role. Local autonomy, as a consequence, has been severely curtailed. Uncompensated regulatory controls, such as zoning and housing codes, are the most important areas of public power in which local autonomy is relatively unrestricted. Apart from the influence of the Workable Program in urban renewal, the absence of national standards for the control of land use and housing quality contrasts with the application of such standards in a long and growing list of developmental programs that range from highways to community parks. Increasing interdependence between local regulation and the effective provision of public services and facilities makes this disparity increasingly acute.

Shifts in the direction, movement, and organization of governmental power highlight yet another concern. As issues concerning the management of the physical environment become increasingly national in character, we are pushed to find an appropriate forum in which critical policies can be articulated, free of the narrow approach that generally marks the local community. Legal institutions can only be developed against a firm background in which issues, goals, and policies come to be explicitly stated. So far, a meaningful consensus on these questions has not been attained, and we accept, as a beginning, that consensus cannot be achieved in the fragmented governmental framework that is so typical of our metropolitan areas.

Consensus is equally inhibited by the failure to provide a meaningful role for the political process in decisions on policy questions. Political influence has a place in substantive policy-making, sometimes marginally, sometime critically, but unlike the English we have not been able to institutionalize the role of the political structure so that it has a direct impact on program content. We cannot make a cabinet decision on the redevelopment plan for a Piccadilly Circus! The marginality of political involvement results in part from federal encouragement of independent legal units for the execution of developmental programs like urban renewal, in part from the historic independence of the planning function, and in part from our dedication to the tradition of separation of powers.[4] Perhaps surprisingly, separation of power is weakest at the local level, where it has no formal legal recognition.[5] Here, especially through the involvement of elected political officials in regional planning agencies, we have the best opportunity to relate the political process more directly to policy-making. As changes in methods of political participation continue, as urban policies move increasingly into the political domain, we might find expanded opportunities for achieving a political consensus on the critical issues. Whether political leaders will face the hard issues, especially in the context of regional agencies heavily dependent on suburban direction, is in turn questioned by many. That they would do so without federal pressure is doubtful. Here and elsewhere the need for direction at the national level becomes increasingly obvious.

Rather than concentrate on specific areas of concern, such as central city or suburban problems, this paper will examine in more general fashion the possible directions that legal controls and incentives should

take in response to the increasing pressures for governmental intervention that have been described. The discussion will be divided into two
parts: (1) the need to improve the governmental framework within
which land-use and developmental decisions must be made; and (2)
the need to improve the conceptual framework within which the available legal mechanisms must be structured.

1. Limitations on Existing Incentives and Controls

Problems in Governmental Structure

We have noted an upward drift of power in governmental programs
that affect urban areas. Nevertheless, responsibility for administration
and implementation still resides at local levels, where the governmental
pattern is heavily fragmented and where obstacles to change have inhibited a realignment to units which are more appropriate in size. Unfortunately, the rigidities built into our present system are the product
of causes which are not easy to remedy. Lacking a tradition in which
change can rather easily be executed through superior legislative or
administrative intervention, reliance on electoral consent for governmental change means that the present structure of urban government
must be taken as given for some period of time.

What is not always recognized is that the inadequacies of our governmental framework, coupled with our tradition of local autonomy, seriously limit the effectiveness with which substantive legal powers will
be exercised. The problem is that important legal powers are split among
governmental units with radically different legal characteristics. Thus
municipalities possess a wide range of legislative powers but cannot
operate region-wide and have limited extraterritorial jurisdictions. Special districts can be utilized on a regional basis to provide essential
services and facilities, but are not readily adaptable to the exercise of
legislative functions. Responsibility is often spilt, as when urban renewal
agencies can plan and redevelop slum areas but cannot control the way
in which they are zoned. Other agencies are all too insulated from
external control, as in the case of independent special districts exercising
responsibility for the provision of schools and other important public
services. Different programs have widely different goals, often competitive if not conflicting, and reinforced at the federal level by governmental agencies backed by powerful constituencies.

Intergovernmental coordination of urban-oriented activities then becomes the central issue, for the upward drift of power has blurred the

lines of federal, state, and local influence. Adjustment of responsibility is complicated by a wide variety of program types. In some instances, as with highways, power lies with a state agency. Sometimes administration is local, as with urban renewal, and the significant contact is between federal and local levels. Elsewhere, as in public welfare and the construction of health, hospital, and airport facilities, responsibility for administration may be local but policy is set by state agencies subject to federal direction.

Against this background of divided governmental responsibility, lawyers have traditionally relied on the judicial process to give content to program policies. It is our only point of contact for the impartial consideration of major policy problems outside the working administrative framework. But judicial influence has variable success, due to the fact that public decisions affecting environmental patterns take many and different legal forms. Regulatory programs which rely on uncompensated controls usually affect legal rights and interests in such a way that judicial review can be obtained. Zoning provides the best example of this type of regulation, although tendencies for judicial withdrawal are noticeable even here.[6] Public programs which rely on powers of compulsory acquisition enjoy a high degree of judicial immunity once initial problems of public use in the exercise of the power of eminent domain are overcome. Thus questions relating to the priority, size, and location of urban renewal projects are generally unreviewable. Federal programs which rely on the spending power are in an equally insulated legal position.

Perhaps the courts can be encouraged to assume more responsibility for policy-making.[7] I doubt it, and I doubt whether increased judicial responsibilities along these lines would be desirable. Judicial review can be made available to ensure fairness in administration and in the application of substantive policies, and to provide marginal consideration of the relevance of program criteria to program objectives.[8] To set and give direction to the central content of urban policies, we must make more effective use of the potential to be found in the intergovernmental decision-making process.

Even today, federal leverage is often the only effective sanction. Sometimes we applaud the results, as when federal pressure is exerted for racial integration in public housing. Sometimes we find a need for countervailing pressures against federal influence, as in disputes over highway route locations, when federal and state agencies often disregard social and ethnic factors that other governmental agencies are forced to take into account. There are other limitations. Federal leverage is less effective in programs like urban renewal, which rely on one-time grants, than in programs like public housing and public welfare, to which the federal contribution is made annually. There is no magic in federal power, but the opportunities for a more comprehensive view of urban and metropolitan problems at the federal level press us to rely more extensively on the possibilities that are latent in federal direction.

Problems in Substantive Controls and Incentives

When we turn to an examination of the substantive programs and controls that have been developed so far, we find that much of what we try to accomplish wanders aimlessly, from failure to select the critical points at which consensus must be obtained and the right amount of leverage to be exercised. What is essential to realize is that meaningful decisions about the urban environment will influence patterns of land holding and development in critical ways, with implications for policy-making that we are not yet ready to accept. Most obviously—and the new breed of regional plans points clearly in this direction—we are going to have to be highly selective about those points in the environment at which development must be allowed if not encouraged, and those points at which development must be restricted if not prohibited. The result will increase both the advantages to be realized from the development of land with public consent and the burdens to be assumed from public restriction of a more intensive use of land. We must find a way to make either result equitable, to both the property owner and the public.

We are not assisted in making these adaptations by the present structure of our implementary programs, which so far have failed to develop as a rationally integrated system. While federal assistance plays an expanding role in financing critical urban endeavors, substantive regulatory and developmental powers reside in local units acting under state authority. These powers derive from an inherited legal framework, created at a time when the problems of an urban environment were more simply perceived. We have become increasingly aware of the need for greater sophistication in the range of choice required in the legal mechanisms governing urban development, and in the administrative techniques needed if legal intervention is to be effective. Land use controls, and direct programs of governmental intervention, operate in a complex matrix of human, social, and economic interactions in which the adjustments that are required for effective public involvement must be finely tuned if the consequences of public direction are to be the correct ones.

Awareness of these complexities creates difficult problems to which the legal system must respond.

Lawyers have not been as creative as they can be in responding to these challenges, because they have concentrated most on measures which rely on compulsion. What lies hidden are the hard choices between the proper and effective roles of public intervention and private initiative in what is becoming an increasingly mixed market for land use and land development. Urban renewal experience should at least have taught us that shifting land into the public domain does not solve the problem of securing the appropriate market reaction when land moves again into private hands. Unfortunately, the legal response often concentrates too closely on institutional forms, without considering the impact of a given technique on the adjustment between private and public roles. Institutional alternatives—public "pricing" vs. public regulation, for example— hide the important reality that increased public intervention of any kind will always limit private choice in some fashion. Conditions attached to FHA-insured or other types of governmentally sponsored credit can confine the developer's initiative as much as a tightly drawn zoning ordinance imposing restrictive site requirements.

Nevertheless, my own preference is for compulsory techniques, which have the advantage of directness but the disadvantage that pressures for change and modification build up as the use of public power grows in effectiveness. So far, our uses of compulsory power have been relatively crude. We have relied alternatively on compulsory powers of public acquisition and development or on uncompensated regulatory controls, forcing us to mutually exclusive choices which can be quite troublesome. These tendencies are evident in housing rehabilitation, where the alternatives lie between full compensation and clearance in urban renewal, and an inadequately subsidized program of rehabilitation under local housing and related codes. Difficulty of choice between regulation and full or partial acquisition in open space preservation provides another example. We need especially to find a bridge between controls such as zoning, in which no compensation is paid for the imposition of the regulatory burden, and programs based on the power of eminent domain, where compensation is paid in full.

We have only started to experiment with techniques calling for direct public intervention to achieve a developmental objective. So far, our gropings have been tentative. In highway programs, we have missed the opportunity presented by interchange construction to acquire excess land in order to regulate the growth that takes advantage of highway access.

Urban renewal is clouded by the absence of meaningful criteria for the sale of project land, and by difficulties in handling the byproducts of clearance and displacement. We are only beginning to realize the importance to housing rehabilitation and residential development of attractive governmental financing and other direct and indirect subsidies. Our approach to the provision of off-street parking facilities in the city core provides a more constructive model, ad hoc though it may be. Here we combine zoning which requires off-street parking spaces with public construction of parking garages, often using the leverage of public borrowing to provide a more attractive financial base for private investment. Possibilities for combining a range of complementary techniques should be explored in other contexts.

2. Proposals for New Incentives and Controls

An exploration of possible directions for new incentives and controls forms the basis for the rest of this paper, focusing first on problems of governmental structure and next on a reworking of the substantive legal framework. Two time periods will be adopted in each section. Stage I will consider possibilities for the next decade. Stage II will look as far into the future as it is reasonably possible to foresee.

Governmental Structure and Coordination: Stage I

As responsibility for policy has shifted upward in the governmental hierarchy, statutory and decision-making frameworks have been created in which locally oriented planning and developmental programs are checked against criteria determined with the needs of the larger community in mind. State and federal agencies participate in this decision-making process, interlocking with regional agencies through which the claims and interests of local communities can be heard. Strengthening the legal base of regional agencies continues to make sense, both for regional planning agencies in the traditional sense and for metropolitan councils of governments and their variants, which are becoming more widespread. Given the autonomy of local governmental units operating in fragmented metropolitan patterns, and the resistance of these units to structural change, the most promising short-run option is to build on the power of the regional agency as a mediator between national and local policy.[9]

Changes in this direction are impeded not so much by the formal structures that are available for making important policy decisions, but by attitudes toward the way in which this formal power is exercised. Most of the hard issues are ignored, such as meaningful standards for urban development, or adequate programs for low-cost and minority housing. For example, a regional agency, after thorough study and discussion, could formulate a policy for racial dispersion and the provision of housing for minority groups throughout its area. But political sensitivity to minority issues makes the explicit articulation of policy on minority problems difficult if not impossible. Federal agencies stand reluctant to impose sanctions or to use incentives which may antagonize large segments of the constituencies on which they depend for political support. A review of the program standards of federal agencies will make the point. Especially in defining the community planning function, these standards insist on evidence of policy-making without giving content to that policy or to its implementation.

In the face of these obstacles, a redefinition and expansion of the federal policy-making role is forced on us by the developing shape of urban America. Informed forecasters predict the emergence of several continuous urban regions, urban corridors akin to the east coast megalopolis. Except for a few free-standing urban areas and the urban centers in Florida and California (in the latter, the sheer magnitude of urban concentration suggests the need for a national policy), these regions cross state lines. In the sense in which interstate is used in the federal Constitution, urban problems will become interstate. What is needed at the federal level is conscious recognition of this change, acceptance of the implications of interstate urban regions, and a national urban policy which will take this fact into account.

We cannot shape new legal incentives and controls until we know what issues will receive attention at the national level. For the most part, those problems that require national attention are the hard problems that we have managed so far conveniently to ignore. Density standards for urban regions provide one critical issue for federal policy-making. Another is urban form—the size of urban centers, a developmental policy for "new" towns. Equally important are the shape of the urban transportation network and the relative roles of highways and public transit. The provision of low-cost housing is another. Finally, cutting through all of these, is a comprehensive program on racial integration. It is not intended to ignore resource pollution—water and air—which clearly needs a national policy and national controls, but this requires somewhat different methods of legal intervention. Our existing intergovernmental network should undergo continuous refinement to develop a policy-making process in which federal agencies increasingly share responsibility for major policies with regional, state, and local counterparts.

Because substantive power is exercised by state and local agencies acting under state authority, any system of sanctions and incentives to implement a nationally oriented program of policy-making will have to take this fact into account. Powerful sanctions do exist at the federal level, especially in the power to give, withhold, and condition the availability of federal financial assistance. For example, the potential of federal banking and lending policy for shaping developmental patterns has not yet been fully realized. Nevertheless, federal control must be indirect. For direct substantive controls we must continue to depend on state and local units.

We have assumed the continuance of fragmented patterns of local government at the same time that we have called for a national initiative in decision-making that recognizes the interdependence of urban regions. Within this framework, two significant initial steps at the state level should be taken as soon as possible to implement nationally determined development objectives. These suggestions are not original with the writer. They have been made by others, and taken alone they may seem marginal, but in a comprehensive framework they are critical. One step requires an important change in the character of state enabling legislation. Legislation should be amended to condition the exercise of substantive regulatory and developmental powers on compliance with policy directives set at higher governmental levels. Thus the acquisition of land for highways should be conditioned on regional and national directives affecting the development of a comprehensive transportation network. The exercise of local zoning should be conditioned on municipal compliance with state or regional plans affecting patterns of regional growth. While the courts should be relied upon to supervise the enforcement of this sanction, their role should be marginal once the critical planning decisions have been made. They should review for compliance, not content.

Opportunities for implementing developmental and planning objectives can also be greatly strengthened by giving land acquisition powers to planning agencies, especially to agencies at regional levels.[10] There is nothing radical about this suggestion. It was originally proposed as the principal method for implementing the urban renewal program. Comparable powers can also be conferred on state planning agencies. Not only would the responsibility for executing policy be placed with those agencies which participate in the policy-making process, an important step if planning objectives are to be fully realized, but a planning agency with a regional jurisdiction can implement policies which are unpalatable to local units, or beyond their capacities. One example is a program of housing for racial and economic minorities. Land acquired by regional agencies can then be conveyed to coordinate regional development authorities, which would assume the task of development or redevelopment. Within this framework, complementary powers of land assembly would be retained by locally centered planning and development agencies, which would in any event be subject to nationally and regionally determined policies, and which could also accept land acquired by regional agencies for use in local development programs.[11]

Governmental Structure and Coordination: Stage II

Ultimately, a decision must be made either to rework the existing local government structure to create governmental units of a more apppropriate size, or to continue to shift responsibility in critical areas of concern to higher governmental levels that enjoy a more appropriate jurisdiction. While pressures will undoubtedly mount for radical changes in the pattern of local government units, the obstacles to this process that have been detailed earlier will remain considerable. Existing governmental units with an inadequate fiscal and governmental base will probably find that their substantive functions atrophy as responsibility shifts elsewhere for the provision of important services and facilities, and for critical decisions over land use and development. But existing units that are inadequate in scale can be expected to persist for long periods, if only to exercise residual and relatively less important powers.

In view of these limitations on radical structural change, more promise is contained in rearranging the exercise of governmental functions that affect critical policies. In the first stage, policies were determined for urban regions subject to national directives, and compliance was obtained by enacting state statutes conditioning the exercise of local powers, and by conferring powers of land assembly on planning authorities. At this point, a shift in methods of control would occur, with regional plans subject to direct sanctions exercised at state and regional levels. One possibility is a state agency with regional counterparts. Part of its authority would come from the power of initiative, not only the power to initiate developmental projects along lines that have already been outlined, but in some instances to initiate and even to administer controls dealing with land use and land development. Precedent for this kind of action already exists in states which regulate new residential development that affects highways, lakes and rivers, or other resources which have statewide significance. In some instances, administration could be delegated to local units, subject to state standards, supervision, and review.

As an alternative, when responsibility for policy formation and administration is left at the local level, the state or regional agency would exercise supervisory powers of review. How such a system would operate can be illustrated by an application for a development as straightforward as a regional shopping center, to be located at a major highway interchange in a small suburban community. A local decision to allow or disallow the application could be appealed to the reviewing agency, which would have the power to affirm, reverse, or modify, depending on how the local decision fitted with regional and state policies.

Suggestions along this line are not new, but have usually been confined to such limited areas as state or regional review of local planning and zoning decisions.[12] What is proposed here is a more pervasive system, in which responsibility for the content of major urban policy decisions is shifted to state and regional agencies with widespread powers to determine standards, initiate programs, and review local actions. These proposals recognize the importance of the administrative process, both as a method for resolving conflicts and priorities in significant governmental programs, and for providing a forum with the continuing expertise and involvement to make the critical decisions on policy content and direction. As in other contexts in which administrative process is utilized, courts would exercise a marginal reviewing function.

If we are to proceed along the lines of restructuring responsibility for the exercise of major governmental functions, then we must ask ourselves what remains to be handled at the local governmental level, and what needs to be shifted upward to higher units. This is the hard question, but it need not be answered absolutely and for all time. My own impression is that those issues which have more than local dimensions are as much national in character as they are regional. For example, density levels need to be determined regionally, but if density is so important that it cannot be left to local policy-makers, then regional densities become a national issue as well, given the assumption that national policies will be worked out in a regional context. Much the same comment can be made about regional housing and transportation policies.

So a principal conclusion is that the major distinction lies between those policies that can be left to local determination, and those policies that need to be worked out above the local level. My contribution as a lawyer is to suggest that the line be drawn in terms of a process, not in terms of a distinction based either on a particular resource, such as the transportation network, or a particular program, such as the preservation of open space. If intergovernmental mechanisms of adjustment are used to resolve policy conflicts, then the important point is that the opportunity be available to remove *any* decision, whether in the use of regulatory controls or the provision of facilities and services, to higher governmental levels in any case in which the decision affects regional and national policies. Methods of creating such a process, preempting the local unit whenever necessary, should not be hard to devise. Thus decisions on land use, or even entire local programs, such as urban renewal, could be "called up" for regional and state administration as the necessity warrants.

What results may perhaps be a workable compromise. Local authority is severely diluted, but locally responsive decision-making can continue so long as it is consistent with overall policy. Policy implementation subject to regional and national policy-making demands nothing less.

Substantive Controls and Incentives: Stage I

Growing recognition of the differential impact that various legal techniques have on land use and development, and of the need for sensitively relating publicly made decisions to the desired developmental result, lead us to proposals for an expanded range of program options which call both for compensated and uncompensated methods of intervention. Suggestions for the protection of highway corridors provide a good example. Regulation to preserve scenic values can be joined to outright acquisition of land and development rights in land which is found to have a scenic interest.

While these tendencies should be encouraged, adjustments will have to be made in the use of public power to even out the impact of public intervention on private landholding, since in the short run the private ownership of land will continue to be the dominant mode. At one extreme, a method must be found to provide compensation for public decisions that restrict and limit private land uses. At the other extreme, when public decisions enhance the value of land which is privately held, a way must be found to recoup for the public the additional increment which public decision-making has created. Implementation of this objective will be greatly assisted by shifting land-use controls away from a system in which regulations are present, as in zoning, to an administrative system in which decisions are made on a case-by-case basis.[13] Presently scattered land-use controls would be unified, and run directly from state legislation without the need for intervening local ordinances which set the regulatory framework. Major policies, determined through regional plans, would be implemented by agencies at the local level which can settle local policies as the need arises.

This suggestion solves the problem surrounding the legal status of the comprehensive development plan by avoiding it. Doesn't this make sense? The plan becomes an advisory but presumptively controlling document which is given more specific content as developmental decisions arise. The use of individual cases to determine larger issues of policy is not unknown as an administrative technique. This change alone would help measurably to secure an integrated public policy over land use and development, for it would convert the act of the controlling agency into a subsidiary administrative rather than a legislative decision. Consistency in regulation would then be obtained through the review procedures at state and regional levels that were described earlier, with direct state or regional assumption of responsibility as another option.

Administering agencies should be given a wide range of choice which allows for full or partial compensation to restricted landowners when the burden of public intervention is unfairly or unconstitutionally excessive. This technique can work in a variety of settings. Protection of highway corridors again provides an example. Within these corridors, any application for development would need the approval of the controlling agency, which would have a range of options in passing on the application, from outright prohibition without compensation, to outright acquisition of the legal interest in the land on which application is made. While criteria would be needed to guide these choices, the importance of the alternative selected would diminish as the legal system adjusts to provide for comparability of compensation, no matter what technique is utilized.[14]

Powers of public land assembly should be made increasingly available to assist in programs of land development. The precise content of these programs is not as important as understanding the purposes for which extended powers of land assembly should be used. Present-day zoning often creates monopoly values in land which is zoned for major developments that are limited in number and strategically located. Getting these sites on the market at the right time is often difficult. Even if some of the necessary land is available, it may not be at a size which is optimal to achieve the desired planning results. Public acquisition of sites for which development is indicated can be used to overcome these obstacles.

While extended use of public powers of acquisition will create hard problems of administration which require careful resolution, the problems are not insuperable. What is most needed is careful guidance on the types of program in which land assembly powers will be used, on priorities in project selection, on project distribution, size, and scale, and in particular on the transfer of publicly acquired land back to the private sector. On the assumption that the development and redevelopment stage will be left largely in private hands, we need to do more than rely on modifications of the competitive bidding process to make our choices, as we so often do in urban renewal. Ideally, the use of land assembly powers for development or redevelopment should be related directly to objectives determined regionally and nationally through the planning process. Direct reliance on the planning process to justify development and redevelopment decisions will create new problems of legal acceptability relating to doctrines of public use in the exercise of powers of eminent domain. These issues can only be noted here.

Extended use of public land assembly powers should also be utilized to recoup from private developers the increment in land values that public land-use and developmental decisions often produce. The problems posed in seeking to do equity in this situation are complex, and attempts at comprehensive solutions have been difficult to achieve. These problems are best attacked pragmatically. In some contexts, as in urban renewal, land assembly techniques should be used to inject a subsidy into land and development costs. Elsewhere, especially in urbanizing areas on the fringe of urban regions, new development will enhance land values. In these areas, increments in value produced by public decision making can be recouped by the acquisition of undeveloped land at its existing use value, and its resale at the enhanced price. In the alternative, land can be leased for long terms, subject to a provision for periodic rent adjustments.

Substantive Controls and Incentives: Stage II

As our system of public controls matures, as we become accustomed to using public intervention to secure developmental results directly, we should shift to a system in which the right to use and develop land passes entirely into public hands. As we make this change, the need to distinguish between compensated and uncompensated controls will disappear entirely, for the public will own the right to impose whatever planning or developmental decision is thought to be in the public interest. I do not propose the wholesale nationalization of land and of rights in land, but the pragmatic extension of public ownership in those instances in which public control is critical.

In urbanizing areas, land earmarked for development would be subject to public ownership and control through a variety of measures. In some instances, as in the case of new towns and other large-scale developments, title to land should be acquired outright, and leased for development or sold subject to a residual interest in the public at the end of the life of the improvements. We also need intermediate devices, large development holding zones, in which public ownership and assembly for development are anticipated but postponed. Pending public acquisition, any private development in these zones would be closely controlled. In other sectors, in which land is nearing the development stage, the global appropriation of development rights over large areas is an alternative device. This method has the advantage of leaving title and the management of land in private hands, reserving to the public the ownership of its future use. At the appropriate time, publicly owned development rights can be sold to willing developers, who would either buy out the owner of the residual interest or pay him a ground rent. Holding public powers of acquisition in reserve can make the process move smoothly. For example, ground leases in the desired land can be condemned if necessary, and assigned to the developer along with his purchase of the developmental interest. England has just adopted a method of public land assembly along the lines discussed here.

In the city core, large-scale land assembly and clearance will still be needed in many badly blighted neighborhoods. In other sections, where substandard housing continues as a problem, a radical restructuring of ownership patterns will be required. As an equivalent to the public ownership of development rights in urbanizing areas, public agencies can acquire takeover easements of property maintenance. In effect, they would buy the right of dwelling occupancy as it is needed to secure an improvement in housing conditions. These rights would be written down, on their acquisition, to the fair value of the improvements, discounting any value imputed from illegal code and other violations. Powers possessed under takeover easements should be exercised whenever buildings fell below minimum standards. Substandard buildings would be physically repossessed and rehabilitated, and then returned to private control. Costs of rehabilitation would be written down with public subsidy, or subjected to long-term recoupment. Again, ground leases could be condemned from reluctant owners whenever necessary.

As development rights in land ready for development and takeover easements of property maintenance shift into the public sector, corresponding changes should occur in private forms of land holding and management. The danger of monopolistic institutions—public housing authorities owning the bulk of our core city housing, for example—

suggests that a diversification of both public and private forms of owner-ship and management is desirable. Changes in ownership and manage-ment patterns will reflect an expanding need for public subsidy. In many instances, of course, the market can be expected to support whatever development is desired in a given context, especially in developing areas on the urban periphery. Elsewhere, public subsidy will have to be used openly and frankly, for the cost of rehabilitatng slum housing will have to be written down directly, as well as the cost of housing for low-income and minority housing in new town and other settings. I accept the conclusion of most experienced observers, that direct subsidy is needed to bring the cost of acceptable housing down to price levels that disadvantaged groups can afford. What form public subsidy will take requires a fundamental choice between contrasting approaches. We can subsidize the institutions that we expect to bring about the desired result, such as slum clearance and new town agencies. Or we can try direct subsidies of consumers, who may be expected to purchase what they need. Direct housing payments to low-income families illus trate the second approach.[15]

So far, we have tended to choose the first alternative, an approach which enhances opportunities for public control but which carries other disadvantages. In housing programs, management demands and the demand for a reasonable economic return have created pressures which exclude the most disadvantaged groups from public benefits. The re-moval of "undesirables" from public housing projects provides one such example. Experimentation will have to include new forms of subsidy and incentive which will allow the most pressing needs to be taken into account. For example, shifting the property tax burden in core cities to state or federal levels would provide a better economic base for the provision of low-cost housing by relaxing economic pressures on costs.

What is equally important to realize is the effect that increasing involvement with public support will have on private institutions that participate in public programs. New methods of private accountability to public sponsorship will have to be created. We need a new form of private corporate entity, explicitly oriented to the achievement of social goals, and subject to external controls for lack of compliance with stipu-lated objectives. Privately directed agencies will increasingly become the beneficiaries of public subsidies, and through them increasingly subject to public direction. Ownership of rights in land will disappear in importance as we concentrate on the social implications implicit in the use and allocaton of physical resources in land and housing. We have returned to the point at which we began.

3. Conclusion

This paper has proposed a legal system in which enough initiative and power are shifted to the public sector to enable it to accomplish whatever community objectives will advance the public interest. Community goals will be set through an intergovernmental decision-making process in which important decisions are based on a larger perspective in which national and regional needs are carefully considered. These goals will be implemented through a combination of techniques. Government programs, especially federal programs of financial aid and assistance, will be used to set the framework in which the desired public and private developmental responses can be expected to occur. State and regional agencies will secure the implementation of objectives that are articulated in the larger planning process, through the direct exercise of regulatory and developmental powers, and through the review of local developmental and regulatory decisions. Substantive controls to implement these objectives will be predicated on the public ownership of land, development rights in land, and rights of occupancy, creating a legal base for public intervention which rests on acquired legal interests and not on the constant need to justify the use of uncompensated regulatory powers.

These changes will require an increasing sophistication in intellectual competence and public administration which presently we do not possess. For a corollary of heightened public power is the heightened if not critical importance of public decisions which, in the new framework, will have a decisive impact. Housing subsidies and related programs will have a crucial influence on housing patterns. Decisions on growth and development in urbanizing areas will require mutually exclusive choices in the use of land. Permitting development at one point in the physical environment will require restriction and prohibition elsewhere. Presently, we do not have this kind of leverage. If we are going to possess it, we must know what we are about. The challenge to planning and related professions is considerable.

Changes on this order will also demand extensive innovations in our political institutions. Shifting effective power to national, state, and regional levels, where the political constituency is diffused or nonexistent, will require a radical reorientation in methods of political control. As planning and related issues move increasingly into the public domain, we must find a way to reach a political consensus at broader governmental levels if truly effective developmental powers are to be made workable within the limits of our political order.[16]

Notes

1. Review comment by Fonoroff: How much?—double 1960 urbanized land? Astrid Monson thinks that is much too low, unless acreage zoning gives in widely.

2. What *real* demands has there been for improvement in the quality of the physical environment? Better architecture? aesthetics? transportation? elimination of pollution, noise, or congestion? billboard control? The problem seems to be that there has not been a demand. (Blucher)

3. This is more because of the scale of the problems and the need for a broader fiscal base. (Fonoroff)

4. Isn't there a confusion here between (a) the level of government that makes the decision (there is no federal leverage on many decisions), and (b) the lack of political control at any level? (Fonoroff)

5. However, this is also because there are not enough people to staff separate local power centers. (Fonoroff)

6. This is a major understatement in most states. (Fonoroff)

7. Some are doing it already to a considerable degree. (Blucher)

8. Fonoroff, in disagreeing, stated, "The major role is to enforce basic values, for example, in regard to integration."

9. They have not functioned in this manner! (Blucher)

10. This changes the character of the planning agency. (Blucher)

11. This should be spelled out. What are the implications of giving line functions to a staff agency? Why stop at land acquisition, why not include construction powers as well? (Blucher)

12. Regional planning in the U.S. is today very weak. It grows weaker as it proliferates and scrapes the bottom of the barrel to find directors. (Blucher)

13. Development control—by whom? Review of development control in Great Britain by the Ministry has not achieved "consistency." (Blucher)

14. This is a good example but the situation is quite different in the acreage zoning conflict on land use. (Fonoroff)

15. Subsidies are required also for middle income. —————— is one method (Blucher)

16. There are several basic problems and perhaps principles that are either created or left unanswered by this paper:

a. A lengthy discussion of governmental organization prior to a determination of land use and development policies appears at best to be an academic exercise. One should fix objectives and goals before choosing or creating the vehicle to achieve them.

b. The author does an excellent job of building a political structure to deal with land use and development decisions. This approach is appropriate since the paper is supposed to look fifty years ahead. However, there are serious questions about the interim period. For example, should government be given power beyond its present and future capacity to acquire technical competence? Will the ground rules for exercising such power insure rational decisions based upon policy principles rather than immediate economic pressures? Does the public (local) need additional assurances that rational decisions will be made by non-local administrators? In other words, regional and state decision-making machinery is probably more efficient and lends itself to accomplishing good results. However, the converse is also possible, as in this case the decision makers are removed from those affected. (Fonoroff)

Comments on

Mandelker

DESMOND HEAP
Comptroller and City Solicitor, London

All those who have the best interests of town and country planning at heart (and there is an increasing number of such people) will be grateful to Professor Mandelker for his article, "New Incentives and Controls." He has produced a thoughtful and thought-provoking paper. After sketching the limitations and inefficiencies of current town planning controls (demonstrating thereby that the present position is not only unsatisfactory but is not getting better), he turns attention to the future and looks ahead, first for ten years, and then "as far into the future as it is reasonably possible to foresee."

This self-imposed limitation in vision is wise, for it is no good having town planning controls which will function only in Heaven—they must be sufficiently realistic to function down here on Earth.

I have read and reread Professor Mandelker's paper with advantage and satisfaction. The comments which follow in this statement of mine derive from the stimulating expression of Professor Mandelker's own views.

Town planning control is, without doubt, a drastic interference with the liberty of the individual to do with his own exactly as he pleases. In the United Kingdom the common law of nuisance has long since prevented a man from doing *exactly* what he wants to do with his own property while over the last fifty years or thereabouts (the first town planning law in Britain was enacted in 1909) there has grown up an increasing public awareness that, in a crowded island such as the United Kingdom, there is a pervasive necessity for every man so to conduct himself that in the enjoyment of his own property he pays all proper regard to the right of other people also to enjoy their own property.

Indeed, so far from regarding town planning control as an interference with the freedom of the individual, the public in the United Kingdom is realizing more and more that *reasonably* conceived controls, *wisely* administered, do, in the long run, provide not for an erosion of liberty but for a positive furtherance of it to the greatest extent available in a land where people and the automobile (to mention only two things) continue to grow apace while the land mass itself remains constant.

This needful control over the use of land involves (to reduce the matter to basic essentials) two kinds of agency. The first may be called "the control-making agency" and the second "the control-administering agency."

The control-making agency should function over a much wider area than the control-administering agency. I would say (though I speak with reserve and subject to correction, coming as I do from the east side of the Atlantic) that in the United States the control-making agency might very well be the state, functioning through the state legislature of each individual state.

Thus in each state there would be a statewide basic format of patterns and standards, all emanating from the state capital. The application in any individual case of these state-created controls would be a matter for the control-administering agency of the particular locality concerned. Such a control-administering agency could be any one of the many and varied existing agencies which today are responsible for the governance of towns, cities, and so on.

I must not allow myself to get bogged down in the intricacies of American local government but I think my basic thesis will be understood, for it is simply that while control-making is a matter for a state as a whole, control-administering is a matter for a variety of individual agencies up and down the length and breadth of each state.

It seems to me that this arrangement is a good one because while the controls themselves remain (as I believe they should remain) basically uniform throughout each state, the actual application of such controls is in the hands of a variety of agencies each one of whom can bring to the administration their own individual line of approach.

This will produce variety in the local pictures which are to be contained within the basic state framework of control. Variety is the spice of life and a variegated coalescence is the thing to be achieved if it possibly can be. In regard to town planning, it is certainly "a consummation devoutly to be wished."

What form should these state-conceived but locally administered controls take? Are they to be nothing more in the next fifty years than the current, well known type of zoning control? Zoning control seems to be town planning through the business of saying "No." It is a negative form of control constantly waiting, like an inverted Micawber, for something to turn *down!*

If experience during the last twenty years in the United Kingdom is anything to go by (and maybe it is not), then it would seem that town planning control will, in the future, make its effective impact more and more by the reduction of demarcated areas of land into public ownership so that the public agency which owns the land will be able to control its future development not only through the argumentative procedures of town planning control but also through the far more incisive procedure of landlord-and-tenant control. For the landowning agency, having obtained possession of the land, will be able to dispose of the land by way of leasehold interests to the private sector leaving it to private sector developers to develop the land subject not only to town planning control but also to the more detailed control available under the leasehold principle.

It would appear that in areas of bad layout and obsolete development (sometimes referred to as areas of blight and often to be found in the run-down, worn-out centers of older towns) the only real way in which to get things moving is to get the whole of the land in such blighted areas reduced into one ownership. It is a matter for argument as to who should be that one owner. It is submitted that it should be a public agency. But the public agency, having got the land, should then arrange for individual development, here and there all over the face of the land, to be carried out by individual people functioning in the private sector. Thereby the spice of variety will again be cultivated. All the development will not look as if it had all been done by the same person however good (or bad) he may be.

This business of land being acquired by a public agency in order to further the best interests of town planning control is, admittedly, a matter of contention and disputation. It is also a matter which has some distinguished precedents. Research discloses that the most seemly, orderly, efficiently, conveniently and beautifully laid-out cities on the continent of Europe have usually had behind them a strong town planning control born of the fact that large tracts of land were held by some single land-owning agency whose main intent was to function in the public interest.

Piecemeal development on a higgledy-piggledy basis is all very well in small communities, especially when it has become overgrown with ivy or roses and tends to look what the picture postcards call "quaint." But this sort of development, when done on a large scale, merely leads to inefficiency of one kind or another. The essence of the whole thing is to get controlled development which does *not* appear to have been controlled at all. This, of course, is the old case of art concealing art. It is not easy to achieve but it can be done if the medium of control reposes in enlightened hands. It is, however, a form of control which does require that large areas of land be held by some public land-owning agency.

It seems to me that more and more of this sort of thing will be seen at the root of all sound and effective town planning control as it continues to develop throughout the next fifty years.

Controversial though some of these points may be, there need be no hesitancy in mentioning them. After all, in a democracy the people get only the town planning control they want. If they do not want town planning control at all they are not obliged to have it, in which event they must be prepared to put up with the consequences and not complain about increasing congestion, expanding traffic jams, shortages of water, failures in electricity supply, and all the other well known features of thoroughly inconvenient and inefficient towns.

Town planning is, and always has been, a controversial subject. In the last analysis the whole thing is, of course, neither more nor less than a matter of education. As time marches on and society becomes more sophisticated, the need for control, within limits clearly circumscribed by law, becomes more and more evident.

But it must be repeated (for it is important) that it is for the people to say what amount of this control they want. How much is it worth to them? How much are they prepared *to pay*, in money or in discipline, order and decorum, in order to have it? Good town planning does not grow on trees and well-designed towns and cities and interstate highways do not drop like the gentle rain from heaven upon the place beneath. They have to be thought about, talked about, argued about, and (finally) planned about.

If the people want these things, they can be got and, under the more sophisticated town planning controls of the next fifty years, one is bound to say they are likely to be got more easily than they have been in the past. The simple question is: do the people want them at all?

How much do the people really want them? How much are they prepared to pay for them? How deeply, if at all, do the people care?

NORMAN WILLIAMS, JR.

Visiting Professor of Law
Rutgers Law School

American planning and American land use controls have brought some modest and some substantial achievements—plus a few spectacular ones, and many more necessarily unpublicized. As a result of such public intervention into the "normal" operations of the real estate market, much of the American scene is now more pleasant and convenient, and safer as well, and investment in public facilities has often been made more wisely. Yet, in an essay of this type, primary emphasis is naturally and inevitably concentrated upon the critical approach—so much so, in the prevailing mood of most such discussions, that anyone whose information derived wholly from these would conclude that everything was in terrible shape.[1] No doubt there is an element of the intellectual smart-aleck in such things; yet the critical approach is based upon reality too, for much of our environment is shabby, and not a little is horrendous—and, in a period of rapid growth, we are missing a lot of opportunities which will not recur.

Major Reservations

In approaching this topic, two major reservations must be noted at the start. First, I always feel uncomfortable in talking about control devices and

administrative machinery, without any clear definition of what these are supposed to do. Any serious inquiry into what sorts of incentive and control are
appropriate should start with a choice as to various possible regional development policies; there is no such thing as an all-purpose set of incentives and
controls, equally adaptable to such varying policies as suburban sprawl, recen-
tralization, the development of major subcenters of employment, radial corridors, new towns, or whatnot.[2] As on any other major problem, the really
difficult job is to define clearly what you want to do; once this is done, the
choice of legal tools is (relatively) easy. Moreover, in the present period of
dynamic expansion, what is needed above all is widespread experimentation,
on policy, on incentives and controls, and on administrative machinery; for
no one really knows all the answers, or even very many of them. We should
therefore look forward to a period of continuing change and creative flux in
the entire planning field—and so of continuing review and evaluation of the
effectiveness of land use controls in actual operation.

To state the same point in a different way—the types of incentives and
controls which are needed are likely to vary considerably, not only from
region to region, but also between five types of problems and areas.

1. The urbanization of new land at the suburban fringe.

2. Private redevelopment on relatively small lots—primarily in central
business districts, in rehabilitation areas, and in other older areas undergoing
redevelopment for multiple dwellings.

3. Large areas appropriate for slum clearance. (They still exist, unhappily.)

4. The protection of conservation areas.

5. Those large areas of the country where population and economy are
stable or declining.

Second, despite all the lively discussion about reforming the system, we
know very little about how it really works. The literature thickens by the
minute, but most of it is written in law-school libraries, with an occasional
glance out the window. Except for Beuscher and his colleagues in Wisconsin,
almost no one has taken the trouble to do field studies to see how our present
controls are working in actual practice; rather absurdly, at this late date,
law-in-action studies would be a revolutionary new concept. This is no small
oversight, for the factual basis for reform is largely lacking; each of us simply
(and necessarily) generalizes from his own experience.

In addition, I had better indicate right away dissent from a prime theme in
current discussions; for some of the better current analyses have gone off on
a tangent which is vague, irrelevant for many areas,[3] and at best a side issue—
the primary emphasis upon the question of "flexibility." These critiques fall
into two different groups. According to one, the rigidity of our principal
existing land use controls is to blame for many of our environmental difficulties, and so an escape to flexibility is the great need of the hour.[4] According
to the other, the existing controls have been administered so over-flexibly
that these have broken down widely, from the excessive use of variances,

special permits, and rezoning. Clearly this notion of "flexibility" needs some sharper definition. Most current discussions have not bothered much with details of that kind; and this is not the place to fill the gap, particularly since I believe that the really important problems are elsewhere. Suffice it to say that the main question involved in all this is the appropriate extent of administrative discretion; and the answer to this depends in turn upon one's assumptions about the sociology of local government.[5] Under present conditions, it seems to me quite out of the question to turn over a more complex and sophisticated set of controls, with broad discretion, to local governments which (particularly at and just beyond the critical suburban fringe) characteristically have trouble keeping track of a copy of the local zoning map; precisely the opposite approach, to provide a few simpler rules, would often be more appropriate. The strange thing is that such advocates of greater flexibility are often more or less on the Left; apparently they are operating on the odd assumption that, if local governments misuse their present powers for antisocial purposes, all that is necessary is to give them a broader range of discretion, and this will inspire them to work for the opposite goals. Now, according to one school of thought, the solution for this dilemma is to bring increased professionalism to bear upon the local decision-making process. I read the signs differently, and believe the problems run much deeper. For, under present arrangements, the problem is not merely that those who hold the instruments of control in the critical areas are inefficient; the worst thing is that they are so thoroughly unrepresentative. Moreover, the local tax system provides (or at least is thought to provide) substantial financial rewards for pursuing an exclusionary social policy, reactionary in the extreme. I see no reason to be surprised that these present arrangements do not work in precisely the opposite direction.

Major Planning Problems

In view of the wide variety of current experience in planning affairs, it is entirely possible that several different people approaching this subject would end up talking about quite different things, perhaps even with relatively little overlap. It therefore seems appropriate to start by indicating what types of problem[6] we are talking about. Some of these are obvious enough: the rapid scale of growth, involving major difficulties merely to keep up, and the need for rapid expansion of investment in the public sector. Beyond these, along with the traditional planning dilemmas, I suggest we should be thinking about such matters as the following:[7]

1. Open country has been the historic setting for American settlements. For a lot of people, it disappeared in the last century; now, as metropolitan areas extend their sprawl, it is rapidly disappearing for practically everybody.

2. The sharp contrasts between conditions in the older central cities and in the newer suburbs, particularly in income levels, in ethnic backgrounds, in housing, and in educational facilities—and, above all, the implications of

these trends for the democratic spirit. Will our future environment tend to breed friendliness, equality of opportunity, and other such traditional American values? (I am assuming that there is an interrelationship.)

3. The conflict, potential and/or real, between (a) a realistic program for satisfying mass needs, particularly in housing, education, and transportation, and (b) the preservation of a high-quality environment in the limited areas where this now exists. Assume, for example, that the use of land use controls in a growing suburb should be made conditional upon providing employment and housing (and space therefor) for some reasonable number of the urban poor, or perhaps of the middle class; if so, how much land would be needed, and to what extent would this affect the rest of the environment? Moreover, if the quality of public education were to be maintained, precisely what would this involve?

4. In general, planning should emphasize a range of choice—in housing, in employment, in recreation, etc.

5. The conflict between the popular preference for low-density living and the increasing need to provide more efficient transportation (particularly travel to work) into and around the central parts of metropolitan areas.

6. The inherent conflict between attempts to improve the environment, and the increasing demands of automobile traffic.

7. The appallingly impersonal character associated with the most characteristic types of current development. Again and again, the worst thing about the efficient modern type of development—whether it be mass-produced, single family housing, high-rise multiple housing projects, glass-box office buildings, suburban shopping centers, or limited-access superhighways —is that there is no sense of the human scale, and that it is all excruciatingly dull.

8. Most growth is (and will be) concentrated at the suburban fringe of metropolitan areas; and sudden rapid growth in semirural townships there creates serious problems for local government—sharply rising costs, overcrowded facilities, etc. Heavy burdens are thus dumped upon municipalities quite unprepared to deal with them, all quite unnecessarily—simply because we have not managed to develop legal techniques to regulate the rate (and sequence) of growth in such areas in relation to the practical possibilities of providing public facilities.[8] The most common technique adopted by rural townships to deal with these problems of sudden, rapid growth is to enforce artificially low-density zoning, and thus "suburban sprawl," as each township tries to avoid being in the position of having the smallest lot-area requirement.

A Major Reorganization?

In considering how to deal with all these problems, two guiding principles should be regarded as basic. First, the really critical decisions on the future environment[9] should be made by officials whose responsibility is to broad groups in the population, so that democratic pressures may catch up with them eventually. Second, in evaluating related systems of control, and particularly the tax system, a major criterion should be that these should help implement good development policy, or at least should not work against it.

Suppose that there were a possibility of a really drastic reorganization of the present system; if we were to set up a new system, designed to do what we want, what would it be like, and how would it differ from the present set-up? While this may seem irresponsible or academic from the viewpoint of those responsible for immediate decisions today, a brief consideration of this is worthwhile, if only to give some perspective—and the logic of events is moving faster than we sometimes think. Such an approach would involve consideration of at least three basic changes, each of which would run squarely counter to major political forces. These are:

1. A shift to higher levels of government for the financing of the major public services, so that this will no longer be dependent primarily upon local real property taxation.

2. A shift from the local level to the regional, for most planning and for some land use controls, to an extent as yet undefined.

3. A shift to large-scale public land ownership, especially outside the suburban fringe, as the primary basis for control over the development and use of land in such areas.

Another major shift is equally important—the increasing coordination of physical planning with social and economic factors. So far, the latter factors have been taken into account, all right, but primarily in two major distortions of planning policy—i.e., in planning decisions taken for fiscal reasons and for snobbish reasons. However, more creative approaches are in order, with the increasing use of physical construction as one element in implementing social and economic programs and goals, and with the increasing attention to the culture of poverty generally, as in the "war on poverty" and "demonstration cities." It still remains an open question whether incentives and controls on land use are as adaptable to a socially creative purpose as to an obstructive one.

Fiscal Factors. Under the existing system, several of the most important (and most expensive) public services are financed largely by local government, which in turn is heavily dependent upon local real property taxation. Even considered just as a tax, this system has few real advantages,[10] except the one obvious one: by definition, real property cannot run away. However, the secondary effects of this tax system are devastating, particularly on planning policy. The revenue produced is hopelessly inadequate for modern urban needs. As a result, the system is constantly breeding heavy financial pressures, which normally work against good physical planning policy. Specifically, in any given land use conflict, the pressure is always for the more intensive type of land use,[11] simply because this will bring in more revenue. More generally, local governments are under strong pressure to go into active competition to attract those land uses which bring in a lot of taxes; a location which is appropriate under normal planning criteria may or may not be available, but that is not particularly relevant. Conversely, and even more important, there is the constant temptation to discourage those land uses which require expensive services, particularly improved housing for the lower income groups who need it most—and also to chisel on land needs for public services. Now much of the standard talk about the relative tax consequences of various local planning decisions is nonsense;[12] but, to a harassed public official, an unwise planning decision, bowing to a powerful speculator, may seem more like a realistic and necessary move to enable the community to pay for needed new services.[13]

This system is breaking down from its own weight, and the time is ripe to start working out new solutions. First, the financial base for many services has already and necessarily been shifting to higher levels of government, primarily state and federal.[14] Second, there are all sorts of opportunities, mostly as yet unexplored, to work out various kinds of arrangement for a more equitable redistribution of both costs and benefits at the regional or subregional level. To take one obvious example, a small community which resists the admission of a large tax-exempt regional private high school does have something of a point, albeit a rather minor one;[15] there really is no reason why one community should bear all the costs (tax-exemption, police and traffic, etc.) for developments whose benefits are primarily for other communities.

Finally, a shift to a broader tax base may have another incidental advantage, for this will tend to give a broader and more representative group a sense of responsibility and a share in control.

Regional Planning and Regional Land Use Controls. Many major problems and pressures in a metropolitan area are now on a regional scale; and obviously both planning and land use controls could be more effective, if these could be handled on the same levels as the problems. In some cases, such as air pollution, action on the larger scale is necessary for any effective solution; in others, handling at a regional scale is simply far more efficient. Equally (in fact, more) important, most regions include a broad range of activities and groups of people; and so a shift of the principal control instruments to the regional scale will also give them a more representative base— so that, at least to some extent, the pressure will be to take into account the interests of all major groups in the population. For these reasons, Professor Mandelker has placed primary emphasis upon this area.[16] My only regret is that he has not undertaken the difficult task of sorting out what should be planned, managed, and controlled at the local or regional or national level.[17]

Even more interesting is his suggestion for a further step of developing national policies on metropolitan development and making local controls conform to national and regional policies reflecting broader interests. Again, one would like to have more details and examples.

Public Land Reserve

Finally, if public agencies could acquire large areas of land around existing communities and metropolitan areas, in the continental European tradition, we would obviously have the basis for a far more effective system of land use controls for the suburban fringe. For once the main legal base is shifted from the police power to ordinary contract law, public control could encompass broader objectives (as for example various aesthetic controls), and could also regulate development in more detail. Moreover, in such a situation, the difficult problems normally involved in regulating the rate of development and the sequence of development at the suburban fringe could be resolved rather easily; and the public could, at least in part, get the benefit of the rise in land values which accompanies development—which in turn would help to finance necessary services instead of merely enriching speculators.

If all the above could be done, obviously we could cope more effectively with many major problems; and if the perspective is set at the next fifty years, we should certainly see progress along some of these lines.[18] If we are serious in wanting a major reorganization of land use controls, all three changes are essential; my impression is that any one, alone, would be inadequate, and might set up a new set of distortions. And I must confess that the one on which I have some reservations is the one emphasized by Dan Mandelker—the shift to the regional scale. By now everybody knows all the arguments in its favor[19]—and yet there remains a nagging doubt. Local government is one of the few areas where the citizen can retain some meaningful participation in public affairs at first hand; and there remains a sense of uneasiness at shifting almost all power over the use of land to vast anonymous bureaucracies, where often you can't even find out who decides anything—if, indeed, such a character really exists. The real problem here is in defining, in terms of specific land uses and public facilities, the appropriate role for local and for regional agencies, in planning, in financing, and in administration.

Yet if our concern is action in the real world, and not just generating bright ideas, there is no point in kidding ourselves; very powerful countervailing political forces are likely to be in opposition to each of the above. In particular, now that reapportionment is strengthening the political position of suburban areas, there is grave doubt whether these areas can be persuaded to give up local autonomy on land use, no matter how logical the arguments, and no matter how convincing the case in terms of their own self-interest.[20] It is not necessarily the highest wisdom to put all our eggs into these baskets.

An Interim Program

It is not difficult to visualize the possibility that progress along the above lines may prove politically impossible, or painfully slow; and there are still plenty of important and useful things that can be done to improve American land use controls, if only during an intervening first stage. As guiding principles, I suggest: (a) a relaxed acceptance of the increasing role of direct public action, along the lines evident in recent federal legislation; (b) a clear recognition that land use incentives and controls cannot be considered separately from the planning of public facilities; (c) in the regulation of private activities, a shift toward fewer and more stringent controls, focused on strategic spots; and (d) a general recognition that many problems are best attacked indirectly. The most important points are summarized below:

1. Under the existing system, the developer normally fares pretty well, for all his loud protests—for essentially the system is stacked in his favor. (In contrast, the small property owner may sometimes be the victim of arbitrary restrictions.) However, when neighbors want to protest against some relaxation of zoning or other restrictions, the legal weapons available to them are relatively feeble, and in some states almost nonexistent. A third point is far more important. In some critical instances, land use controls have their maximum impact upon the interests of those not directly involved; the obvious example is the effect, in the typical snob-zoning situation, upon those potential future residents who are effectively precluded from access to good residential areas. What is needed above all is some institutional expression for the interests of such third-party non-beneficiaries, who are wholly unrepresented under the existing system.[21]

2. All legal controls over land use should be tied to a requirement for a "master plan" and for continuous planning, with a suitable grace period to allow communities to conform.

3. Existing controls often forbid what is really harmless, or even actively prevent something good, and so are inefficient or genuinely arbitrary. The key to progress here is the recent shift toward more direct controls, phrased in terms of measuring what is actually wanted. Current examples include performance standards in industrial zoning, modern density controls, and residential bulk regulations phrased directly in terms of access to light and air and requirements for open space. The difficult problem here comes in what is the most complex part of most zoning ordinances: can the long commercial use lists be rephrased in performance terms?

4. As indicated above, the widespread trend toward using land use controls to exclude certain groups of people—particularly poor people, or those with different ethnic backgrounds—from access to good residential areas (and to good public services)[22] is heavily reinforced by other pressures under the present system. Obviously counterpressure is growing, and must be main-

tained at all times. During the interim period, a major role may be played by the judiciary in reasserting the supremacy of basic democratic values, for its function should be far broader than merely checking for compliance with planning requirements and enforcing procedural due process.[23]

5. American land use controls have traditionally relied too heavily on police power, originally because American cities could not afford to do anything else. As a result, normally the only choice available is between (a) taking a number of property rights, without any compensation, and (b) acquiring the whole fee in public ownership. We have barely made a start on developing intermediate arrangements and incentives, as a supplement to police-power controls. As Professor Mandelker has indicated, all sorts of intermediate possibilities should be explored;[24] and I suggest a beginning should be made in three areas—aesthetic controls, open space, and more rapid termination of those nonconforming uses which are located in substantial buildings designed for that purpose.[25]

6. The possibilities of using public facilities to influence the pattern of private growth should be recognized more overtly, and exploited to the hilt.

7. American zoning litigation has been concerned almost exclusively with constitutional issues; and various devices can be worked out to shift at least a large part of this to the more prosaic question of conformity with the enabling legislation.

8. Finally, the traditional concept of a "master plan" should be recast, so that the formulation of such a plan becomes primarily a periodic summary of thinking in a continuous planning process, constantly readjusting to changing conditions.[26]

Notes

1. Those whose experience has been primarily at first hand have usually been much too busy to write; these critics tend therefore to be a different group. It is perhaps natural that they should concentrate on the large gap between the American potential and current performance; but one would never know, from reading this literature, that housing standards for the majority of the population are now probably at their highest point in history.

2. Nor is there any reason to assume that the same administrative machinery would necessarily be equally appropriate for all of these.

3. As I understand it, the concern here is wholly with the problem of urbanization at the suburban fringe.

4. The point is brilliantly argued, with great intellectual honesty and some overstatement, in John W. Reps, "Requiem for Zoning," in *Planning 1964*, p. 56.

5. How should local decisions be regarded—(a) as motivated genuinely by consideration of the general welfare, (b) as expressing the interests of one group of local taxpayers, often directed against another group, (c) as probably involving political favoritism, or maybe even corruption, or (d) merely confused?

6. My experience has been in the northeast ("megalopolis"); I am implicitly assuming that the problems there are typical of those which are important nationally.

7. The more specific parts of the statement of purposes in the standard enabling acts

has been of great value, particularly in legal tests upholding new and different devices to accomplish those purposes. On the technical level, a major need to redraft these statutes to provide for broader purposes, such as those suggested herein. For one attempt along these lines, in a specialized context, see the proposed Vermont Planning and Development Act (House Bill 205, 1967 Session), section 4302.

8. But see Josephs v. Clarkstown, 24 New York Miscellaneous 2d 366, 198 New York Supplement 2d 695 (1960).

9. One major task is to define exactly what these are.

10. A recent discussion is in Dick Netzer, *Economics of the Property Tax* (Washington, D.C.: Brookings Institution, 1965).

11. The obvious exception is the protection of strongly established, homogeneous single-family areas. But note the characteristic jargon, soon learned by anyone working in the field, that a "favorable" influence on land values means something which pushes land values up, i.e., which makes everything more expensive before you can even start to build—and incidentally, gives more unearned increment to somebody.

12. My impression is that the concern so often expressed is genuine, albeit obviously exaggerated. There is always the possibility that this may be a cover-up for something else, usually some antisocial attitude. If so, merely to bring that out in the open will be a major gain.

13. Or, perhaps, to make a tax cut.

14. To the extent that special-purpose authorities take over, the resulting problems of coordination may be more difficult, rather than easier; for these may turn out to be the crassest kind of profit-making organizations, whose outlook on the world would make a caucus of the average suburban local government sound like a convention of left-wing social workers.

15. See Roman Catholic Diocese of Newark v. Ho-Ho-Kus, 42 New Jersey 556, 202 Atlantic 2d 161 (1964), and 47 New Jersey 11, 220 Atlantic 2d 97 (1966).

16. The prerequisites here are, of course, first some sort of regional consensus, and then a regional plan.

17. A simple (even crude) but fairly effective mechanism along these lines already exists in Westchester County, with county review of certain major developments along all state and county highways, which, after all, represent the main framework of development.

18. It would then be appropriate to turn major attention to the question of "flexibility" —although I seriously question whether great advantages would come, without first professionalizing the relevant governmental services and raising the level of public taste.

19. Along with everybody else, I have set forth the shortcomings of local government myself: see *Development Controls and Planning Controls: The View from 1964*, 19 Rutgers Law Review 86, 99 ff (1964), where a lot of these issues are spelled out in more detail.

20. One can hardly blame those who can afford (and who have) a pleasant physical environment for wanting to keep it; and there are quite a lot of them. And so a prerequisite for success here is an analysis of what impact a genuine program for satisfying mass needs would have upon that environment, and upon its public services—along the lines indicated above.

21. But compare *Barrows v. Jackson*, 346 U.S. 249 (1953), where the Supreme Court refused to sanction enforcement of a racial (anti-Negro) restrictive covenant by means of a suit for damages, brought by neighbors against the white vendor—over a dissent by Chief Justice Vinson, who argued that the latter had no standing in court to raise the question of Negro rights in this situation.

22. One of the really remarkable developments, in the recent case law, has been the blind enthusiasm with which courts have interpreted "the general welfare" to cover what are really parochial advantages for small groups.

23. The point has been superbly stated by Justice Frederick Hall, dissenting in *Vickers v. Gloucester Township*, 37 New Jersey 232, 252, 181 Atlantic 2d 129, 140 (1962).

24. As, for example, acquisition and sale subject to covenants, acquisition and lease-back, acquisition subject to a right of occupancy, direct acquisition of less-than-fee rights, etc. Several states already have a rudimentary approach, in "scenic-easement" statutes; for a more comprehensive approach, see *Vermont Scenery Preservation* (Montpelier, 1966), c. 2.

25. But if developers are often compensated for a major taking, should they not also make payments for major benefits, e.g., a rezoning to commercial. Obviously this would raise plenty of problems; in effect, a bastardized version of this has already developed, in the form of bribes for rezoning or variances.

26. See Mitchell, "The New Frontier in Metropolitan Planning," *Journal of the American Institute of Planners*, Vol. 27, 1961, p. 169.

New Institutions to Serve the Individual

This paper was commissioned to propose new institutional forms within the framework of a democratic society and an open society to enable both private enterprise and government to make more constructive contributions toward the creation of optimum environment for the individual. Excepting for the most basic precepts, it is assumed that in the next fifty years, fundamental institutional changes will be necessary to cope with and direct the changes ahead to their most creative use for the development of the individual and mankind as a whole.

This will mean exploration of new quasi-public private forms, new Comsats, governmental organization reforms and improved interrelationships, new Appalachias, private contracting of public services, the growth of problem-solving institutes versus universities or government or profit-making organizations, new representative regional bodies, basic public and private charter changes, and so forth.

Both public and private institutional changes are to be considered to assure that their complementary roles as well as their "apartness" is understood when making final recommendations. Financing, representation, profit making, professional standards, areawide issues such as land planning and pollution control are all interrelated pieces of this whole study.

Also, there may be reason to question whether goal formulation is exclusively the province of public decision making or whether private and nonprofit entities should not have more active roles in this important process through newly established representation and/or organization.

Author: Alan Altshuler, Associate Professor, Department of Political Science, Massachusetts Institute of Technology

Chairman: William R. Ewald, Jr., AIP, Development Consultant

Committee: Clarence H. Danhof, Program of Policy Studies in Science and Technology, The George Washington University; Robert S. Herman, Executive Director, Temporary State Commission on the Constitutional Convention, New York; Rev. George Todd, Assistant for Urban and Industrial Ministries, Board of National Missions, National Council of Churches, Thomas Reiner, Department of Regional Sciences, Wharton School, University of Pennsylvania; Robert Theobald, Socioeconomic Consultant; Seymour Mellman, Professor, Department of Industrial Engineering, Columbia University; John Bailey, General Manager, Southeastern Pennsylvania Transportation Authority

XIV

Alan Altshuler

Department of Political Science
Massachusetts Institute of Technology

New Institutions to Serve the Individual

What should the comprehensive planner leave unplanned? More generally, what should a society which has shed its inhibitions about public intervention leave unregulated? Planners—along, I hasten to add, with most other liberals, and most other public officials—have never denied the relevance of these questions, but they have congenitally neglected them. Until recently this neglect was probably justified, given the weakness and fragmentation of the public sector. It certainly is not any longer, and we may expect it to become progressively less so over the next fifty years.

My focus, consequently, will be on ways of reducing the trade-off prices between two sets of fundamental political variables. On the one hand, we appear quite rapidly to be tending, in accord with the devout wish of most planners, toward (a) more effective regulation of the "neighborhood effects" of private activities, (b) increasing the extent to which the nation's resources are allocated in accord with politically determined priorities, (c) improved coordination of public programs with one another and with allied non-governmental activities, and (d) a greater role for planning staffs that are organized to bring broad perspectives and disciplined analyses to bear on policy problems.

Reinforcing these trends are the most striking phenomena of the age: the dizzying, and still accelerating, rate of technological progress; the gigantic scale of numerous machines, productive processes, and other endeavors rendered possible by modern technology; concomitantly, the enormity of their byproducts; the virtual death of fatalism about social misfortunes and inequities; the galloping concentration of humanity into huge urban settlements; the decline of the family as a welfare institution and carrier of culture; increasing specialization and consequent interdependence; and the breakneck expansion of *knowledge* about interrelationships among apparently disparate activities.

On the other hand, we desire: (a) to encourage citizen participation in community affairs, (b) to enhance the individual's sense of political efficacy, (c) genuinely to diffuse power widely throughout American society, (d) to increase the variety and accessibility of options available to members of the society, (e) to economize rigorously on the use of compulsion, and (f) more generally, to minimize the need for citizens to think consciously about governmental constraints upon their behavior.

These two sets are by no means comparable. The first is of means whose use we may expect to grow inexorably over the foreseeable future, though not at a constant or predictable rate. The second is of high priority national values that are particularly easy to ignore in everyday planning (which focuses, quite naturally, on the kinds of problem that seem to call for *increased* regulation and coordination), but that are also particularly prone to being smothered by the items on the first. In the past it has been left to opponents of planning and the welfare state to worry about this conflict. Now it is high time for planning theorists to deal explicitly, and as a central theme, with the social costs of public control. Such, at least, is the central assumption which informs this paper.

What specific adaptations of planning doctrine and governmental practice are called for? Many more, unfortunately, than can usefully be reviewed in a brief essay. I shall confine myself, therefore, to two pressing needs in the sections which follow: debureaucratization and decentralization.[1] I shall also confine the discussion to governmental institutions, though its essential argument, I believe, applies to large private organizations fully as well.

Before proceeding, two explanations and a disclaimer are in order.

First, let it be noted that my concern is with policy planning for the public sector as a whole. I recognize that most professional planners espouse a far more modest conception of comprehensive planning. It seems clear, however, that planning for such limited sectors of public policy as land use and transportation will increasingly be viewed as specialized components of a broader planning function and must be conceived within the broad framework assumed—and partially outlined —in this paper if they are to have a plausible claim to the prefix "comprehensive."[2]

Second, I shall be using the term "institution" in two senses, to refer to formal organizational arrangements and procedures, and to customary, but well entrenched, modes of thought and practice.

Third, I make no claim to personal originality. Both theory and practice are already moving in the directions here charted. I hope that what follows may prove a useful distillation of some of the most promising ideas currently in the air, but I certainly would not pretend that it is more.

1. Debureaucratization

My purpose here is to present some thoughts about ways of facilitating the phase-out of obsolescent programs and of reducing the bureaucratic, command, and red-tape components of those that are still functional at any time. Unfortunately, I have no neat or fully developed solutions. The following are some of the central themes that I think will have to be emphasized, however, if planning theory and practice are to deal adequately with the threat of bureaucratic giantism.

For a start, it will be necessary to encourage planners to think more systematically about the virtues of disaggregation vs. integration, pluralism vs. coordination, and the free market vs. regulation in social life. A complete strategy of encouragement would involve the whole spectrum of influences upon planners, from the content of professional education to the general political climate. In the present essay, however, I shall focus more narrowly, on the formal structure of planning institutions and assignments.

The tendency of planning until now has been to favor the proliferation and centralization of bureaucracy. Planners as individuals, however, are as devoted to the values of liberty, diversity, and pluralism as the members of any other professional group. Nor do they fail to sense the basic tension between these values on the one hand, as against bureaucratization and centralization on the other. My central assumption, therefore, is that the biases of planning in practice have been functions of planning responsibilities as they have been conceived till now, rather than of any basic alienation between the values of planners and those of other Americans. To be more precise: (a) the main function of planning has traditionally been the rather narrow one of conceiving ways to offset the dysfunctional byproducts of free market activity in land; (b) the second function, rapidly increasing in relative importance over the past decade, has been to call attention to the problems posed by inadequate coordination of public programs; and (c) more generally, public issues arise in our society when nonpublic forms of social control are perceived to have failed.

I do not expect the collective impact of these factors to decline rapidly. The serious question, then, is how they can be offset. In other words, how can the value of implementing collective goals in non-bureaucratic ways be structured more effectively into the policy-making process?

One vital component of the answer may prove to be carefully structured disaggregation of the planning function. In a political system whose central features are the separation of powers, checks and balances, the two-party system, the protection of individual liberties by an independent judiciary, and federalism, this basic concept should be simple enough to grasp. Theorists of administration today stress the frequent utilities—in terms of total organizational ends—of decentralization, of subunit competition, and of separating "weak" but important functions from large units in which they are likely to be ignored. What I am suggesting is that just as long-range planning tends to be neglected in operating agencies, planning for debureaucratization is unlikely to flourish in general planning agencies.[3]

I would urge that planning for debureaucratization should be the central responsibility of a special planning staff. The personnel of this staff should be few and high-powered, and it should have status as one of the key staff arms of the chief executive. (It is irrelevant at this point whether we are speaking of President, governor, or mayor.) There is no reason why many of its special studies could not be contracted out, but the precise balance between internal staff capacities and the use of consultants would presumably vary from place to place and time to time. In any event, this is just one among many variables that would determine the effectiveness of planning for debureaucratization in any specific jurisdiction.

The crucial point to keep in mind is that we must not overestimate the degree of comprehensiveness that is actually attainable by any single agency. Reorganizations of the future may be based on more sophisticated "program package" concepts than those which have prevailed in the past—one hopes so!—but no chief executive is going to consolidate his government's whole administrative apparatus into a single department, or assume that he needs only a single set of staff advisors. What better systems of organization can do is to structure subunit assignments so that top officials are more likely to be presented with the most important issues to decide and the most relevant arguments to ponder. So-called comprehensive planning staffs will continue to be limited by the capabilities of the human intellect. Chief executives of the future will (in all probability) pay increased attention to comprehensive planning staffs; but the increase will reflect changing priorities, not any absolute view that the preoccupations of comprehensive planning staffs should always take precedence over those of other agencies.

Let us turn now from form to substance. The first theme that I would expect a staff charged with planning for debureaucratization to stress is that, wherever possible, public regulation should be *probabilistic* rather than strictly deterministic. By this I mean that it should operate by affecting the structure of incentives, with an eye toward achieving certain aggregate results, while leaving those subject to regulatory constraint as many options as possible.

The most obvious way to plan probabilistically is to work on the structure of prices. In a strikingly high proportion of cases this approach should prove most compatible with efficiency as well as with liberty. To illustrate, policy makers in a given region might well decide that the public interest required cutting sulphur dioxide emissions into the atmosphere by 80 percent. One way to accomplish this result would be to set up an elaborate, highly judicialized regulatory system, whose outputs would be limited permits on the one hand, prohibitions on the other. Alternatively, the mechanisms of regulation might be metering and charges. The measurement of sulphur dioxide emissions would involve little or no bureaucratic discretion, meat for political controversy, litigation expenses, or red tape. The level of charges would be controversial, but it would be fairly easy to see whether the charges were adequate to control emissions in the desired degree. The risk that regulation would bog down in the case-by-case approach, with each regulated enterprise obtaining a partial waiver on the basis of its own tragic circumstances, and with permits becoming permanent free licenses to pollute, would be substantially reduced. Each enterprise would remain free to decide whether, and in what degree, to pay or change its ways. Presumably it would be better able to evaluate the economies involved —for it—than any regulatory agency. If particular enterprises were thought worthy of special consideration, because of the social value of their activities, open dollar grants to bring down the prices of their finished products would almost surely be preferable to hidden subsidies —i.e., regulatory permits—which induced them to economize by polluting the atmosphere. I do not have to be reminded that there are formidable political obstacles to widespread adoption of this approach. This is simply another way of saying that the "natural" way for government to grow is by increasing the direct command component in our social system. The critical question, however, is whether a different intellectual climate can be established, and offsetting forces can be institutionalized, with the result that this tendency will be substantially reduced.

If space were not so rationed, I would develop numerous other illustrations, because I am persuaded that this model is very widely applicable. One of my particular favorites is automotive safety regulation, with insurance pricing as the lever (on top, admittedly, of a system of minimum standards).

I think it essential to dwell for a moment, however, on the issue of how much quantitative precision should be expected from the cost-benefit analyses that must underlie regulatory pricing decisions. There is no question but that data processing and related conceptual advances have greatly increased the feasibility of measuring the external costs and benefits of vast multitudes of activities. These advances have been far outrun by the claims of many cost-benefit analysis enthusiasts, however. Among the crucial components of regulatory pricing choice that we may expect to remain "political" (as opposed to "scientific") for a long time to come are the following: What dollar values should be assigned to social costs and benefits that do not, in the most fundamental sense, have monetary equivalents? What external costs and benefits are sufficiently important that public power should be invoked to influence them? What level of control (e.g., of sulphur dioxide emissions, of deaths from automobile accidents) should be sought? When is government by command preferable to government by pricing incentives (see the current official arguments—with which I disagree, parenthetically— against substituting pay incentives for the draft)? Should the price per "unit" of social cost take any account of ability to pay? If so, by what method? And so on.

Thus regulation by pricing by no means promises an end to politics. What it does offer is a way of substantially debureaucratizing the implementation of some political decisions, of increasing the visibility of these decisions, of concentrating responsibility for them, of equalizing and rendering more predictable their impact on the parties subject to them, and (perhaps! this is the point on which my views are most tentative) of increasing the likelihood that regulatory officials will take a broad view of their responsibilities.

If working on the structure of prices were the only technique of probabilistic planning, of course, the concept would hardly warrant a special label. Let us take a quick look at several other approaches that appear both to fall within its rubric and to warrant careful attention.

1. Even where it is deemed that government must act via direct permits and prohibitions, it will often prove possible to establish options. Contemporary land use planners recognize this with respect to zoning and building codes, to cite just two examples. The aim in both cases is to permit the greatest amount of architectural and engineering freedom compatible with the public's interest in maintaining health, safety, and environmental attractiveness. Needless to say, the private and public interests are not invariably, or even normally, a conflict. The hand of regulation can be kept light if its reach is confined to the relatively few *aspects* of the typical regulated activity that genuinely warrant regula- tion, if the public interest in these aspects is defined in terms of func- tional performance standards, and if it is kept in mind that the public interest is in excluding a range of possible outcomes, not specifying just what should be done.

2. Another way to plan probabilistically is to influence the structure of competition for consumer patronage. In the form of antitrust policy, this is one of the most venerable regulatory techniques in the American tradition. On the level of positive planning, it led the government to encourage labor union organization in the 1930's, to sell off its aluminum plants after World War II in such a way as to create two strong com- petitors for Alcoa, and—most recently, and controversially—to take a few tentative steps toward encouraging the political organization of the poor. Less explosively, it suggests that, if the public is dissatisfied with

the range of consumer options provided by commercial television, the most promising path to improvement would be to subsidize one or several nonprofit networks.[4] This would certainly seem far preferable to regulation of the content of commercial programming, or to the European alternative of governmental monopoly.

Moving back to explosive ground, it suggests to me that Milton Friedman's call for the perfection of competition between schools in the public and private sectors deserves—with appropriate adaptations—the most serious consideration. Suppose that we moved to a system in which: (a) the government gave parents tuition vouchers for use in approved schools, public or private, and (b) the government confined its regulation of private schools to such *key aspects* of their operation as academic quality, racial balance, and (perhaps) religious and social class balance. Diversity, innovation, and parental participation would be far more likely to flourish than they are in the present institutional framework. It is hard to doubt that the public school systems, at least in our largest cities, would be shaken up in extremely healthy ways by the competition. If taxes for education were distributed to children in private as well as public schools, political support for school taxation would probably be far greater than it now is. As parents would be free to supplement the tuition vouchers, total spending on education would certainly be much greater than at present.

It is often argued that such a system would increase racial and class segregation. This argument is hard to credit. The present system of neighborhood schools and independent suburban systems produces near-total segregation insofar as most children are concerned. In a competitive system, some standards of racial and class balance could quite easily (speaking now of administrative, not political, feasibility) be imposed as standards of aid. If the standards were sufficiently rigorous and the aid sufficiently generous, this system might produce a far higher degree of integration than prevails at present. Many private schools even now give scholarships to disadvantaged students, and their spokesmen frequently claim that the key limiting factor is money, not their willingness to accept more. Every scholarship student is extraordinarily expensive when the school must pick up the whole cost of his education. (Parenthetically, the tuition vouchers might be on a graduated scale, based inversely on family taxable income.) Similarly, there are probably a great many middle-class white parents who would send their children to mixed schools if the choices were less drastic—both financially and in terms of the mixes—and more varied than they are at present.[5]

A policy of treating public and private school systems alike might also lead to the more effective regulation of local *public* school practices that violate high-priority national values. For example, it would highlight the following question: if a lily-white private school should not qualify for federal or state aid, should a lily-white suburban school system? Similarly, by divorcing school taxation from school administration, it would reduce the force of arguments against broadening (and thus equalizing) the base of public educational support from the local school district to the region, state, and nation.

3. In our attempts to alleviate poverty, the probabilistic planning approach would suggest emphasizing the provision of opportunities for the motivated poor rather than force-feeding of the pathological poor. It might even suggest that the poor should be given cash or vouchers to spend on social services, and that the various social service agencies (hopefully, public and approved private alike) should be left on their own to compete freely for patronage—and support themselves from the revenues earned thereby. I would not claim that this model is applicable to all social services, or to all of the poor. Nor would I deny that social services should be aggressively "sold" to the poor, just as television sets and deodorants now are. What I do maintain is that the model is applicable across quite a wide range, that most of the poor do respond to incentives, and that what the apathetic poor need above all is to see substantial numbers of their neighbors succeed as a result of grasping opportunities thrown down by the larger society. It will be pointed out that success examples exist today, if the poor want to see them. This is surely true, and many of the poor *are* influenced by them. At the same time, there are probably contagion thresholds that have not yet been approached. One must hope so, because unless chain reactions of high motivation can be triggered, social service spending is more likely to increase dependency than stimulate self-sufficiency.[6]

Let us turn now from probabilistic methods of governance to a brief consideration of other themes that one might expect a staff charged with planning for debureaucratization to stress.

1. It would probably home in quickly on the potential for accomplishing public purposes by the application of technology rather than the application of more manpower and regulation. This is hardly a new idea, of course, but it has scarcely begun to be applied systematically in the domestic policy arena.[7] Areas in which this strategy would seem particularly appropriate are crime prevention, housing, transportation, and waste disposal. No doubt its promise is equally great in other areas with which I happen to be less familiar. As government organizes to

exploit this potential systematically, one would expect the recognition to become widely diffused. The wise application of technology to social problems is a complex "systems" assignment, not a narrow technological one. It generally involves a wide variety of political, social, and economic ramifications that are unlikely all to occur, or to receive adequate emphasis, from any single group of specialists.

The institutional problem, then, is to ensure that planning for technological innovation in the domestic policy arena be: (a) given sufficient emphasis, (b) entrusted to "mixed" teams of technologists, social scientists, and humanists (the latter concerned with history, aesthetics, the analysis of value implications, etc.) rather than to the former alone, and (c) tied into the political and social systems in ways conducive to breadth of perspective, intellectual vitality, and active education of the attentive public.

I am not an enthusiast for precise organizational blueprints, but I would suggest that the research and development function here under discussion is not likely to flourish within the government as well as outside of it, under most circumstances. This is also true, by the way, of a good deal of the fundamental thinking about administrative structure and procedure called for above. It suggests that the administrative planning staffs should be largely concerned with contracting out the development and analysis of ideas that look promising, and with evaluating, transmitting, and (where appropriate) lobbying for implementation of the products of these studies. The serious question is: who should conduct the studies?

In part, of course, the answer is private consulting firms, industrial corporations, and universities. It seems doubtful that these will suffice, however. The truly competent consulting firms are too few, and under too severe pressure to produce "quickie" results. (This may change, however, as the market grows and clients become more sophisticated.) The industrial corporations are too secretive. And the academics have too many other obligations, in particular, teaching and basic research. Perhaps even more important, I believe that we should be thinking about how to reduce rather than to increase the extent to which the universities are "for hire."

All the above will have roles to play, but they will require supplementation—unless the private consulting firms come along much faster than seems likely. Perhaps what we need is a substantial number of institutions set up on the Rand and Stanford Research Institute models, free from civil service restrictions on pay and hiring procedures, receiving annual retainers from one or a number of "regular" clients, but also free to bid on study contracts let by other public authorities. I do not have strong views at present on how many of these institutions we ought to look toward. Some of the largest metropolitan areas could very likely support their own; one would hope that at least several would operate nationally; some might serve multistate regions.[8] The serious limiting factors will be the shortage of first-rate talent to staff them, and the need for each to achieve critical thresholds of staff size and diversity, not the number that the country might support.

Opinion will differ on whether these institutions should be firmly tied to a single government, on whether they should perform mid-career training as well as research and development functions, on how heavily *they* should rely on consultants by comparison with in-house staff, on what proportions of their staffs should be on loan (or leave without pay) from other organizations, and so on. I assume that experimentation and diversity should flourish with respect to these variables.

On a related issue, however, freedom to publish, I feel most strongly. Left to themselves, many public officials will treat policy studies as a form of weaponry, to be kept under guard until needed in battle and then released selectively to further tactical objectives. Society's larger need, however, is for the widest possible diffusion, discussion, and criticism of policy studies. Fortunately, talented people are already reluctant to work on studies that will not be published, because publication is the key to professional prestige and mobility. One must hope that the professions as organized communities will increasingly reinforce this reluctance by articulating its social value in an open society, by campaigning actively against secrecy in government, and by intensifying the social pressures upon members not to work for their immediate paymasters alone.

2. A second focus of the debureaucratization program would be on building "ease of phase-out" into new programs from the start, before the hardening of vested interests around them. One illustration of a technique must suffice. On a number of occasions in recent decades, the government has cooperated with private industry on a research and development effort, the understanding being that the government's contribution would cease when the new technology became economically competitive. The development of saline water conversion and nuclear electric power are examples. As a matter of fact, the whole American tradition of spurring development in which the public interest is strong—e.g., of railroad and air transportation—by temporary subsidies

to infant industries, is worthy of the closest attention. On the whole, liberals have been hostile to this technique, emphasizing the potential for commercial enterprises to grow rich at the public trough. The public does have a vital interest in development priorities, however. And the alternative techniques of permanent partnership (e.g., on the Comsat model) and public enterprise seem far less attractive. One would like to know whether "ease of phase-out" can be built into regulatory as well as development programs. I am not sure, but it is clear that programs of development (for example, of new industries, and of new competitors in old ones) are often substitutable for programs of regulation.

3. A third line of development might be a new look at the "filter down" theory of social welfare. I have already touched on this in connection with the choice between focusing social services on the highly motivated versus the pathological poor. The more general point is that tax revenues are chronically short, and that in consequence we should be looking for ways to harness private resources to the service of collective needs. I mention the "filter down" theory for illustrative purposes, because it frequently provides a means of benefiting the poor without having to fight appropriations battles explicitly on their behalf. Consider the field of housing. In it, the political obstacles to aiding the poor directly are particularly intense. On the other hand, the various mortgage and savings deposit insurance programs that have spurred private housing construction since World War II have had an enormous favorable impact on the housing conditions of the poor. Today Section 221 (d) (3) (of the Housing Act of 1965) housing for moderate income people seems to be attracting a high degree of political support and investor interest.

These and a variety of other points too numerous to list here suggest that the focus of planning for improved housing should be on: (a) research and development to bring down costs, (b) development of a national, model, performance standard building code, (c) national grading of new building materials with respect to the criteria employed in the model code, (d) subsidies for demonstration projects, (e) the development of new institutions able to provide scale markets for new materials and processes, (f) preservation from the bulldozer of the better housing vacated by those who move up, and (g) tax incentives and credit innovations to stimulate the improvement of older properties and discourage their neglect.[9] I would have no objection to a large rent subsidy program on top of all this, but Congress almost certainly will, so I would not pin my hopes upon it. The advantage of the "filter down" approach in this case is that it might make quite a substantial acceleration in the rate of improvement of the national housing stock politically feasible—because its cost in direct appropriations would be low, because the vast middle and working classes would have a stake in it, because a great many businesses would stand to profit from it, and because it would look like private enterprise rather than socialism.

4. A fourth theme worthy of extensive exploration is how to obtain continuous feedback with respect to the consequences of ongoing programs. Virtually all institutions resist the idea of supporting research which might tell them that their efforts are counter-productive. Business organizations cannot help noticing, however, when they fail to make profits. In government, evaluation is far more difficult, not only because the profit criterion is absent but also because the government acknowledges responsibility for external costs and benefits. Consequently, the need for explicit program evaluation on a regular basis is particularly important in government. As one of my colleagues, Leonard J. Fein, has remarked, "Only with such feedback can we hope to turn our failures into investments." Perhaps even more important, only with it can we hope to prevent resources being thrown down ratholes indefinitely, or until political explosions occur which discredit harmful, wasteful, and valuable program concepts indiscriminately.

The most plausible argument against this idea is that candor about program failures will sap support for governmental activities—at least where the activities are themselves controversial, as in the antipoverty field. (The qualifying clause dismisses the space program's experience as beside the point. It bears recollection, however, that numerous Cassandras counseled a policy of secrecy about launchings in the early years of the space program.) Even if the argument were empirically valid, it would hardly, by itself, support a judgment that candor should be forgone. Over the short run, "costs"—e.g., a few worthwhile programs stillborn, reduced appropriations for some others—would have to be set against gains in the form of program improvements. Over the long run, as the public caught on to the new level of discourse, one might expect the benefit side of the ledger to increase in relative importance. The case is essentially the same as that for the open society itself.

It seems doubtful that the argument *is* valid, however, even over the short run. The public is scarcely in a state of euphoria today as regards the effectiveness of antipoverty programs. Enough bad news had, inevitably, leaked out so that rosy official pronouncements have little credibility. I would hypothesize: (a) that the irreconcilable opponents of redistributive programs will always manage to secure plenty of ammunition, (b) that the key to building public support for antipoverty efforts lies in persuading a rather intelligent "swing group" of politicians and attentive citizens that such programs have high pay-offs, and (c) that the most promising path to persuading them is genuinely to adopt a strategy of rigorous and open program evaluation, followed by corrective action, including major shifts of resources from low to high pay-off programs.

How should the evaluative function be organized? In the first instance, it will have to be confided to the executive departments themselves. There is no substitute for infusing the top echelons of the executive with a sense that adaptation and innovation, rather than static defense, are their central political responsibilities and the decisive criteria of their professional achievement. The studies themselves may be carried out by in-house staffs or by outsiders on contract.

The more difficult challenge, however, will be to keep pressure on the departments to perform this function well. To meet it, the capacity of outsiders to conduct independent evaluative studies will have to be beefed up substantially. In part, this suggests that the development of improved reporting requirements (including a system of social accounts) should be pressed, so that independent analysts can have more useful data with which to work. Even more important, however—because private support for program evaluative research is quite inadequate, and because one often needs political muscle to extract damaging information from executive agencies—it suggests a need for strengthened legislative staffing. Daniel P. Moynihan has recently urged that Congress establish an Office of Legislative Evaluation in, and on the model of, the General Accounting Office.[10] I would differ from Moynihan on a few specifics: for example, my preference would be for a new agency well-insulated from the narrow accounting mentality of the GAO, and I would place more emphasis on the role of watchdog legislative committees. The direction in which he points, however, is clearly right. Congress should require the executive departments to engage in systematic program evaluation; it should institutionalize its review of executive performance of this assignment; and it should greatly strengthen its capacity to conduct independent program analysis. In their essence, quite clearly, these recommendations are as applicable to state and local legislatures as to Congress.

2. Decentralization

Must the local community wither away in the age of comprehensive planning and coordination? Perhaps events will demonstrate that it must. On the other hand, it is nothing short of terrifying to imagine an

America in which half or more of the nation's resources are allocated by public decision;[11] in which political involvement for all but a miniscule elite is confined to periodic voting for candidates known only through the mass media; and in which the typical citizen feels that his political options are confined to resignation, civil disobedience, and rioting. I do not for a moment consider this vision implausible. In certain areas of policy—most notably, national security—its latter two clauses essentially describe current reality. In some jurisdictions (e.g., New York City) and in the lowest social strata, they are probably descriptive across the board and for nearly everyone.

There are no simple or ultimately satisfying solutions. The effort to alleviate the tension between coordination and pluralism promises to be eternal, unless it is given up. This is no excuse for neglecting it, however.

I have set out my basic approach to change in the previous section. From here on, therefore, I shall confine my remarks to local urban institutions, and I shall state my judgments baldly.

Taking off from the status quo, I would expect and hope that the long term trend will be toward building up metropolitan and neighborhood institutions at the expense (at least relatively) of today's local jurisdictions. The definition of neighborhoods, of course, will depend more on popular perceptions than technical standards, so that many of today's suburbs will no doubt flourish in the role of neighborhood. I would expect the central cities and largest suburbs, however, increasingly to decline relative to subdivisions within them and metropolitan governments above them. In view of the thrust toward comprehensive planning and coordination discussed previously, I would also expect today's special districts to be gradually incorporated into, or subjected to more effective control by, general purpose governments.

The major ideas that I would expect to infuse this process of change are the following:

1. In any time period, power tends to flow to those institutions which are perceived as competent to perform the functions that society accords highest priority. Increasingly, the collective needs on which attention is focusing are those which exceed the capacities of existing local governments and special districts. The consequence has been a flow of power and responsibility to higher levels of government, primarily the federal. It follows that increased centralization and competence at the state and local levels are the keys to national decentralization. The states have tradition on their side, but they do not (on

the whole) constitute "regions" that have much meaning in today's world. By no means do I write them off, but neither do I think they can prove adequate substitutes for metropolitan government.

Over the short run, what is most obvious about the metropolitan government concept is its apparent political unfeasibility. Over the long run, however, I expect that the need for institutions below the national level which are also well suited to deal with the highest priority domestic problems will prove decisive in its favor. Its competence would extend to taxation as well as problem-solving. A great many individuals and enterprises have a high degree of locational freedom to move within any metropolitan area. Extremely few are likely to select their metropolitan region on the basis of tax comparisons.

Regional government should prove interesting enough to draw top-flight talent into urban politics and administration, to warrant extensive coverage in the mass media, and to attract the close attention of a large segment of the public. It should also be large enough to sustain a fairly high degree of party balance. Not for a moment, of course, should it be supposed that reorganization can render difficult social policy decisions—particularly those involving race and redistribution—easy. At best with respect to these issues, it may bring certain inequities into clearer focus and make their alleviation a bit more probable. The main justification of the reform, however, is that it may provide a way of keeping important aspects of governance closer to home than Washington, and better adapted to local needs, without any significant *loss* of competence or *sacrifice* of equity.

2. The main virtue of the neighborhood is that ordinary people—including those with very little education—can identify with it, understand its issues, and know its leaders personally. I would expect demand to grow, so that the larger local jurisdictions would deal with neighborhoods more or less as I am about to urge that the federal government deal with metropolitan regions.

3. It has always been recognized, at least in principle, that the nation has two sets of objectives with respect to state and local government. On the one hand, it wishes to ensure that public functions are performed competently and that certain national values (e.g., nondiscrimination) are respected locally. On the other, it genuinely values the grass roots democratic ideal. It believes that for many purposes national uniformity is far less important than (a) having local decisions adapted to local desires, (b) having local government flourish as a school of democracy, and (c) giving ordinary citizens the pleasurable experiences of local communion and political efficacy.

By comparative world standards, the American grant-in-aid system pays remarkable attention to the latter set of objectives. The conviction has been growing for some time, however—and with excellent reason—that it does not pay nearly enough. One proposed solution that has attracted a good deal of support is the so-called "Heller" plan of block grants to the states.[12] As will be clear, I oppose it as it stands, but it clearly points out the direction in which I think we should be moving.

My own view is that the block grant should be held out as an incentive to states and metropolitan regions to put their governmental houses in order. Increasingly there are federal programs that provide bonuses to grantees who link the program's implementation to statewide or metropolitan planning processes. It would be no more than an extension of this concept—though a rather giant one, I admit—to provide large bonuses in the coin of increased *discretion* to local areas whose governmental systems met specified criteria. Any precise scheme would be highly controversial, but the arguments against block grants without state and local government reform are quite overwhelming.

The core of my argument is that the federal government should conceptualize its interest in terms of a relatively few key variables. These might include the following: racial nondiscrimination; some standards of racial and class integration in education and housing, minimum budget proportions spent on such broad "program package" categories as education, transportation, and environmental purity; and so on. For the rest, it should concern itself with shifting resources from rich to poor metropolitan areas, and with ensuring that local government meet high standards of representativeness and competence. Needless to say, these points apply with equal force to federal policy vis-à-vis the states. I would be very much opposed, however, to any federal block grant policy which focused solely on the states. Practical political considerations, of course, also militate in favor of dissociating the block grant idea from that of enhancing state (versus local) power.

4. Just as the federal interest in local policy can be defined quite adequately in such a way as to permit a very high degree of local discretion, the metropolitan region's stake in developments within any particular neighborhood is quite limited. This is especially true if one believes, as I do, that a high priority aim of regional policy should be to strengthen neighborhood institutions.

There are at least two senses in which regional planning and neighborhood power are compatible. First, there are many subjects in which the regional interest is negligible. From a comprehensive planning standpoint, the balance sheet on these would show grass roots democracy values on the one side outweighing the potential benefits of centralized decision on the other. Second, there are numerous subjects in which the regional interest can be defined in aggregate terms, so that the techniques appropriate for influencing neighborhood decisions are probabilistic. Let us suppose that the region decides to build a "magnet" school. The school's planners will probably be able to find quite a few more or less equally suitable sites if they try. There is little reason why they should not have to negotiate with neighborhood leaders before selecting any one of them.

5. Block grants, or authorizations to tax, might be provided the neighborhood institutions as well. A bill has recently been drafted in Pennsylvania that would authorize the formation of neighborhood redevelopment corporations. The bill specifies criteria for establishing neighborhood boundaries and procedures for neighborhood decision making. A neighborhood redevelopment corporation would have no power to exercise eminent domain or to violate the regulations of higher jurisdictions (e.g., zoning). It would be able, within specified limits, however, to tax; to borrow; to buy, sell, improve, and operate property; to receive grants-in-aid from higher levels of government; to enter into binding contracts; and to employ a staff.[13] Going a step beyond this model, one can imagine neighborhoods being authorized to purchase additional police, sanitation, and street repair services from the appropriate regional agencies as part of their improvement programs.

6. The in-house staff capabilities of neighborhood institutions will be quite meager, of course. This suggests a need for consultants to be available when they require technical studies or management services. I have no strong views on just how the consultant function should be organized. One model would be for the region to establish one or several agencies to act as neighborhood consultants. (A related question would be whether the region or the neighborhoods, the latter perhaps on a fee-for-service basis, should support these agencies financially.) Another would be for the neighborhoods to rely on private consulting firms. If a region selected a model which required the neighborhoods to pay for services received, one would expect it to combine the model with a system of equalization grants.

7. The implicit assumption of the previous two paragraphs is that the neighborhoods will have middle-class problems and resources. In the urban ghettoes, however, the scale of demand will be radically greater. Among the vital needs to which neighborhood institutions

might address themselves (in concert with higher levels of government) are employment, credit, housing, medical care, legal and consumer protection services, youth group and child-care centers, etc. The corollaries of this overwhelming burden of need will normally be a meager resource base and substantial citizen fatalism. Thus, far more ambitious and ingenious efforts will be required to infuse neighborhood institutions with vitality and competence.

One possible solution may be to develop new forms of neighborhood enterprise which combine the best of the public and private sectors. The most ambitious experiment along these lines to date is currently getting under way in the Bedford-Stuyvesant section of Brooklyn. Hopefully, it will mobilize the resources of a wide variety of federal, state, and city agencies in concert with those of major corporations, local businesses, universities, labor unions, churches, civil rights organizations, and philanthropic institutions; and essential policy making control will reside with representative neighborhood institutions. One must hope that this effort will "succeed," i.e., achieve substantial and favorable results. Even if it does, however, there will be grounds for doubting that it is widely applicable as a model. For one thing, Bedford-Stuyvesant is about as untypical as a project can be. As a national pioneer effort, it has attracted degrees of talent, attention, and financial support that will not be available to many which follow. Not least, Senator Robert Kennedy has invested a great deal of energy in it and staked a good deal of prestige on its success. Furthermore, it is difficult to imagine representative neighborhood institutions finding much room to grow or control in a forest of such well-established, well-endowed, and professionally led organizations. Neighborhood participation could easily become a façade for manipulation of the residents by outside institutions, perhaps united to aid them but, even if so, probably interpreting that mission in terms of charity and riot control rather than fundamental social change.

This is not to disparage the Bedford-Stuyvesant effort. It is to emphasize, rather, that we remain far from having an adequate model for the organization of partnership between neighborhood and other institutions in the big city ghettoes. (Indeed, we do not even have reliable techniques for developing broadly representative neighborhood institutions, or for keeping them so.) The urgent need is for experimentation with a wide variety of modes, guided by the aims of mobilizing vast resources to deal with ghetto problems *and* of giving ghetto residents some real sense of mastery over the process. As the enthusiastic reports on these experiments come in, we should keep in mind that many ideas which prove ultimately deficient do work for a time—in the hands of their enthusiastic creators. Insofar as possible, though, this potential should be exploited, not viewed with disdain. More generally, it should be kept in mind that human abilities, attitudes, and relationships matter more than formal organization, that wisdom often lies in adapting organization to personnel rather than attempting the reverse, and that poor neighborhoods (not to mention their institutional environments) differ greatly from one another. Thus, solutions of genius in one set of circumstances may have virtually no potential for transference.

I would have enjoyed proposing more organizational blueprints in this paper, fewer approaches to thinking about organizational options. (Even the few blueprints have to do mainly with structuring the government's collective cerebration about options.) As a conscientious vendor, however, I have judged that precious few of the former which are available deserve to be sold—particularly in a study in which the time scale is measured in decades. This is not surprising. Organizational forms are much like house designs: a wide variety are desirable to suit individual tastes and circumstances, style changes are unpredictable, and within broad categories the main features of social (family) life are not greatly influenced by them. I come away from this intellectual exercise more than ever persuaded that a society's most basic institutions are its characteristic values and ways of thinking. These change slowly—in response to the truly massive currents of history—but as they do, the range of socially acceptable modes of formal organization tends to shift with them. Such, at least, appears to be the case in pluralistic societies, and so I hope against hope ours may remain these next fifty years.

Notes

1. A full presentation of my views would require at least two additional sections, entitled respectively: protecting the individual and reorienting the professions.

In the first, I would deal with such themes as the following: (a) compensating the victims of rapid change in general, and of government programs in particular; (b) developing the ombudsman and public defender concepts; (c) providing one-stop social service centers, and expediters to help citizens find their way in the remaining bureaucratic maze; (d) securing withdrawal of the law from concern about most "crimes without victims"; (e) utilizing computers to eliminate red tape and arbitrariness at the lower levels of public bureaucracies; (f) developing judicialized institutions to protect (and publicly articulate) the needs of individual privacy as against those of "society" in the distribution of central data bank information; (g) securing the political rights and enhancing the privacy of public employees in nonsensitive positions; and (h) improving consumer information, most notably by official grading of goods.

In the second, I would focus on the potential for imbuing social service professionals with far more of a "service"—as opposed to "police" orientation than they now typically have. Some of the more promising possibilities appear to lie: (a) in restructuring assignments to relieve those whose primary function is service for policing responsibilities; (b) in developing improved "service indicators" of job performance; (c) in devising relatively painless ways—on the order of today's employer reporting of employee income—of collecting and retrieving data required to establish benefit eligibility; (d) in simplifying the requirements themselves; (e) in training and employing clients for social service professional and subprofessional work, so that roles in the service processes may be less sharply and permanently defined.

2. The argument for the second point is set out fully in my book, *The City Planning Process: A Political Analysis* (Ithaca: Cornell University Press, 1965), pp. 1-4, 299-332.

3. Within the past two years numerous planners have reacted enthusiastically to another proposal for disaggregation of the planning function: the concept of "advocacy" planning. See Paul Davidoff, "Advocacy and Pluralism in Planning," *Journal of the American Institute of Planners*, Vol. 31, No. 4 (November, 1965), pp. 331-38.

4. The most constructive thinking along these lines to date, I believe, has been done by the Carnegie Foundation's Commission on Educational Television. Its report, entitled *Public Television: A Program for Action*, was issued in January, 1967, and has since been published by Harper & Row in hard cover and Bantam Books in paperback.

The Commission proposed that Congress establish a nonprofit corporation for public television, charged with developing a comprehensive system of noncommercial television, and authorized to receive both governmental support and private contributions. The corporation would be directed by an independent board, appointed for staggered six year terms by the President with the consent of the Senate. Its main financial base would be a federal trust fund into which would be channeled the proceeds from a manufacturers' excise tax on television sets. The latter would begin at 2 percent and rise to 5 percent. The higher figure would produce $100 million annually, about 5 percent of commercial television's advertising revenue. By comparison, the national Educational Television network has an $8 million budget, 75 percent supported by the Ford Foundation.

Needless to say, Congress would remain free to alter or terminate the arrangement at any time. The working assumption would be permanence without political interference, however, and no annual appropriations would be required.

Would Congress in fact leave the corporation alone? Only time and many political battles would tell. But wisdom in politics is generally the choice of "least bad" risks.

5. It is likewise charged that permitting public money to be spent on the education of parochial school students would increase religious segregation. On the other hand, the system could very well be structured so as to lure them into religiously mixed schools for much of each day, while permitting them an unsubsidized parochial school component.

6. These are essentially the judgments that underlie the "war" on poverty. It is important that these judgments not become discredited, however, on the basis of the record the program has made with the paltry sums appropriated for it to date.

7. The major exceptions to this generalization, of course, have been medicine and agriculture. Numerous lesser exceptions might also be cited. The question at issue, however, is the rate at which we should be moving on a spectrum, not whether any movement at all has taken place before now.

8. The most carefully elaborated proposal that has been made along these lines to date, I believe, is William Ewald, "Appalachian [Development] Institute: Prospectus, Budget, Funding," a report to the Appalachian Regional Commission, September 30, 1966, 84 pp. The Commission did not act upon it.

9. Current policies, of course, tend to do just the reverse.

10. Daniel P. Moynihan, "Comment: A Crisis of Confidence?" *The Public Interest*, Spring, 1967, pp. 3-10; see especially p. 9.

11. Over the past forty years, the proportion (federal, state, and local expenditures combined) has risen from one-ninth to nearly one-third of GNP.

12. For a clear and authoritative exposition, see Walter Heller, *New Dimensions of Political Economy* (Cambridge: Harvard University Press, 1966), chapter 3.

13. I am indebted to John Bailey for bringing this bill to my attention.

Comments on

Altshuler

PAUL N. YLVISAKER
Commissioner, Department of Community Affairs
New Jersey

A lot of us these days, in our more honest moods, are wondering whether we've built a more complicated civilization than we are able to plan, direct, or reform—or, for that matter, even to understand. Altshuler is a member of the clan—and his paper has a refreshing quality born of that willingness to wonder. But, if honest, he is not a pessimist or a cynic—and he should be commended for this. He is still ready to climb mountains, still of a mood to affirm.

There is no reason, I think, for doubting his diagnosis of our befuddling complexity. We have all wrestled enough with the imponderables and elusives to accept his judgment that we cannot control every writhing variable or anticipate every wriggling event. In fact, you are a genius if you can even discern what and who it is you are struggling with—or remember why it was you started the battle in the first place. Altshuler does not forget—and he has not quit.

What he is out to prove is that we can still be captains of our soul and masters of our fate, while cutting out a lot of bureaucratic nonsense and increasing individual freedom as well as a sense of community. Once or twice I winced at his contortions—as when he began to twist into being the bureaucracy that would plan the annihilation of bureaucracies which plan. But his heart is in the right place. Even his logic got the better of him. I boggled a bit, too, as he romanticized the "metropolitan region" and "the neighborhood." Somehow, jurisdictions that do not exist always look better than those that do.

But Altshuler should not be judged by his lapses, rather by his instincts. And his instincts are good. He does not want our society to drift into demise

—and that is precisely what it is capable of doing. He does not want men who have achieved free choice to trade their birthright for a mess of bureaucratic pottage. And there is enough uncertainty among free men, enough false starts among those who would govern, to invite the stalemate citizen Altshuler describes, of waiting interminably upon bureaucratic Gastons.

What of Altshuler's prescription? It is a fascinating variation upon Adam Smith, and I say so with much sympathy. He would, in effect, strive in the public sector for the same revolution wrought by benevolent capitalism in the private sector: by using the price system; by relying on competition; by emphasizing enterprise; and by stressing incentives, consumer complaint mechanisms, the discipline of the market, the rigor of evaluated performance, and the stimulation of research and development.

Why not? These have brought about vast changes and progress in the private sector. Isn't it about time we released some of the same surging power into a public sector long stifled by the authoritarianism and monopolistic legacies of the medieval state? Even when overlaid by nineteenth century Fabianism, or twentieth century public administration?

We have come to a pass in the development of our industrial civilization where we are becoming publicly immobilized. Despite the bulk and bulging muscles of laws, regulations, appropriations and bureaucracies, our governmental Gulliver has been pinioned by the littler beings surrounding him— free to think and speak but not to act. We all are the little people who have tethered Gulliver—and most of us are ambivalent about what we have done. We tremble when we think of Gulliver loose—knowing that his one false step could trample us. We grieve when we see him tied, wistful for the miracles he could accomplish beyond our strength and vision. Now the social engineers among us are pondering anew how to free the giant without enslaving ourselves.

It is obvious we need towering perspectives and an equivalent capacity to act. We are leading history, by our technology and kinetic energy, if not by guided intent. As a matter of fact, the more I penetrate the veil of power in the United States, the more I have the uneasy feeling no one is in charge. In charge of small sections, yes, but not in full command.

In more than one respect, we are on a collision course; the summer of 1967 should have convinced us of that. Annually, our Negro ghettos are growing by another half million and bursting with hostile determination to break free. Nothing in our national policy or in our local capacities points toward a resolution of these tensions or a solution of the problems that arouse them. Like the pre-Keynesian depressions, they will not disappear merely because Providence historically has seemed willing to rescue us. Quite the contrary: the problem of the ghetto grows worse as the nation generally fares better.

We should also be convinced by the accumulating devastation of industrial and urban wastes. Only a four-hour jet ride from the clean air of Colorado Springs to the grime and grit of Newark can give the measure of what some of us have passively become accustomed to. And still the nation, suffocating in its wastes, wonders whether it should release Gulliver.

We do release him to make war on the stars and on other people's territories. How are we to release him at home? Partly by domesticating Gulliver —but mostly by civilizing ourselves.

WILLIAM R. EWALD, JR.
Consultant to the AIP Project on the Next Fifty Years

Plan for freedom. Plan what not to plan. To do so, Alan Altshuler would have us nurture the individual, as we move into the next fifty years, by decentralizing and debureaucratizing government. Although he has concentrated his paper on public institutions, he suspects, quite properly, that the term "government" applies just as well to any large institution, public or private.

As far as Mr. Altshuler's statements go, excepting the sort of difference Parkinson would have with him, there seems little reason to disagree. Vigilance within undoubtedly will be required to preserve and serve the individual in our many-headed, technological future. The manner in which he circumscribes his subject of New Institutions to Serve the Individual is appropriate and inventive, but the general context into which his proposals will fall has been left unstated. A look at this context might be worthwhile here, both to clarify any assumptions as to the necessity of his proposals and to provide the basis for emphasizing an additional proposal.

If the term government can be properly applied to any large-scale decision-making institution, public or private, perhaps we should begin by looking first at them. What do we find? With very few exceptions American institutions reward and discipline their members on the basis of short-term, successful performance. Contrary to the myth, corporations do not make long-range plans ahead. Corporate chairmen of major corporations have been known to warn their top executives not to waste their valuable decision-making time on long-range considerations, meaning five years or often only beyond 18 months. And politicians are probably in agreement with the statement Ben West made when he was Mayor of Nashville, that "a good politician is one who gives the illusion of being out in front of the crowd while following closely behind."

Now it is fair to point out that the businessman must make money every year or he goes out of business and that the politician must be a hero every year or he is not reelected. That is the way we have established our two basic institutions. It keeps them responsive to our democratic "votes": in the marketplace and in the ballot box. In one sense this short-term, responsive outlook is good, and it is practical. In view of long-term consequences, however, such a short-term view may be incompetent, impractical, immoral, exhorbitantly expensive, or all of these (in social and physical as well as economic terms).

In considering New Institutions to Serve the Individual we should put more emphasis than Alan Altshuler has on *how* his proposals can be implemented. Can they, in fact, be implemented through our institutions as they now are? Only marginally, would be my estimate, because neither of our two great institutions now thinks this way. In the fast-moving times into which we are now heading, even partial implementation through our existing short-term oriented institutions is in doubt. First of all, public and private executives will be preoccupied with short-term reactions to accommodate change. There is no comprehensive or accurate recognition of how fast the rate of change is actually picking up speed or of some of its ultimate consequences. That is a flat assertion on which attack might be mounted from two standpoints. One is that there is nothing fundamentally new or different about present or foreseeable rates of change. Without being dire about its necessary effects, there is no way for this reviewer to believe that the impact of present technology, symbolized by the computer and atomic energy, can be mastered and humanely directed in the terms of "business or politics as usual." Whereas it may be true that the foreseeable future portends a rate of change that has been known before, I would contend with Herman Kahn that this has heretofore happened only two or three times[1] in the history of man. Calling this a second revolution or an extension of present industrial growth does not diminish the impact or an awareness that we are fast building an environment that is more than the body, the mind, or the spirit can bear.

The second rejoinder might be that present institutions are already planning for the long range. There is a test to apply to see if this is so. In any institution, public or private, university, industry, or government—isn't it true that the man in charge of a two-year project is a big shot? This, generally, is the maximum workframe for an institution's respected thinker-doer. In the greatest of institutions that span of time might stretch perspective, within its special task force or study group, to ten or at the most fifteen years. Resource-oriented industries, possibly utilities, may be the exception. But neither really considers the future in truly comprehensive social and economic *and* technical terms.

When a large corporation puts money down for pure research, it is generally pledging a small percent of its profits to hedge its bet on the future. If it takes a ten to fifteen year look ahead at all, it is fundamentally a market study—as if the corporation is insulated from the other vital forces of change, particularly those created by society.[2]

Big government gives its one-time task forces a matter of months to pull together long-range complex perspectives. The National Resources Planning Board, the only continuous body we ever had that took studying the long-range future of this nation seriously, was abolished in 1943 after only four years of work performed in a climate hostile to gathering knowledge.[3]

Little corporations and little governments take a still shorter look ahead. Seldom do they spare the time for their key men to take their eyes off the ball. They fear they'll lose it altogether. Meanwhile the private citizen as an individual is even more rigidly confined in his useful time perspective. He is comforted in this by homely advice "to live each day to its fullest and let tomorrow take care of itself," and maxims like "don't borrow trouble," or "eat, drink, and be merry, for tomorrow we may die." The hippies exemplify a recent trend toward not planning ahead, not sacrificing anything of today for something in the future. Their motto, "tune in, turn on, drop out," may be a personal right, but it may also be applicable to middle-class civic leaders who think they are performing civic duty but do not grope with issues of the longer range future.

University people, as individuals, may create a stir from time to time about the future, but few communicate this and their institutions have somehow avoided learning how to do research on the future of the human species and environment, much less to teach it. The ring of truth is much louder and easier to follow in the hard sciences, where it is also more easily coupled with technology to find its way into the marketplace or weaponry and is more easily financed.

Perhaps the time is now for the people to know that World's Fair Futuramas are no more than the best idea of the future that public relations departments could come up with, that the federal government has no policy for national development, that there exists no feasible mechanism to handle the rebuilding of our cities, and not even a workable concept adequate for creating the human environment on open land that must be created for 100 million people within this generation.[4] The list could continue with dozens of other critical issues.

Along with our present urgent need to provide the poor with reason for hope, some of us need to be considering *now* how to prepare for what as a nation we haven't yet thought much about: the real meaning of our unspoken concern for the creative development of the individual and of our society in terms durable enough to have meaning in the future in which our children will live.

At our present pace it may take two or three generations[5] of top management to develop a private enterprise that really plans for a long range and unashamedly places serving the public need alongside profit motive. Our present evolution of government may require another twenty to thirty years to adopt and implement generally what we have learned from isolated experiments. It used to be said that it takes seventeen years from an invention to its marketing (radar took six years); twice to six times that length of time is needed to implement social and political inventions.[6]

This present "way of going" appears inadequate to foreseeable needs. Passions have stirred needs that *are* urgent. Expectations are high. And it is becoming clear that while we may overestimate change in the short range (five to ten years), invariably we have underestimated it in the long range (twenty to fifty years and beyond). If the discussion thus far is basically valid, that our present institutions are responsive to and *bound* to the short term, that only slowly will they evolve from their present perspective—too slowly to meet foreseeable human needs—what is the answer? Attempting a partial response to the future through existing institutions as they are is clearly one way we must begin, as Alan Altshuler has proposed.

An additional response would be an accelerated modification of the present institutions and motivations (rewards and disciplines). Key participants in government planning and decision-making processes (public and private) would decide differently if long-range future benefits were taken into account. This can be hoped for. Greater and greater reliance is being placed all the time on skilled, well educated professionals in critical positions—David Bazelon's "new class."[7] There is hope, too, that the moral issues (beyond sex) identified by the hippies can reach some of the middle-aged executives and bureaucrats about to go into command positions. Perhaps more potent than all of these will be the impact of the dedicated young militants working with the oldest continuous human institution of man, the church. The church may well become the means to motivate key individuals within public and private governments in such a way as to temper their decisions usually measured exclusively in short-term dollars or votes. As for universities, they have yet to create status respectable enough to attract the great minds they need to work on the practical impact the long-range future should have on current decision making, and besides, they have not yet perfected their major teaching mission. These are the existing institutions that it might have been hoped would lead the way into the future in their hoped-for evolution and their potential impact one upon the other.

What about new institutions? If we assume the desired future must evolve under the exclusive direction of existing institutions, however modified, haven't we already confined ourselves to one basic group of alternative futures? How, if we are to qualify as rational our efforts to grope with the future, can we begin with any such assumption? In fact, wouldn't it be wiser to assume the opposite—that the dramatic pressures of great change, besides reshaping existing institutions, will cause the creation of totally new ones, especially if they are more responsive to the needs of the individual?

The fundamental new strength needed to cope with change and realize the greatest human opportunities of the future might well come from a third force, separate from but responsive to private enterprise and government. A whole array of institutions might well be encouraged into existence by private enterprise, government, labor, the church, and the university. For the moment we might call this the third force, the nonprofit force, or the professional force.

The motivation for the individuals creating and serving these institutions would be challenging original work, good pay, high morale, non-bureaucratic surroundings, public service, stimulating colleague exchange of great scope, a greater opportunity to see one's work influence basic decisions of real importance to the circumstances of man and the satisfaction of a "clear channel" for communication. That present government, private enterprise, or university institutions cannot satisfy such a list of lusts must be clear. And it is unlikely they will soon modify their present operations substantially. Each already has a practiced, successful style for realizing the sort of future it has envisioned for itself, however short term a future that may be. Being successful at this, for the moment, it is unlikely these instititutions can determine basic reasons for any basic modifications. And that is perhaps as it should be.

Private enterprise should not be pilloried for everything the public sector is not doing, and the public sector should not be expected to operate like a private corporation. Though both have much to learn from each other, there is no fundamental reason to assume the whole answer to the future is confined to these, the short-term thinkers. Has any society in history developed into greatness with such a view? Alfred North Whitehead said, "Vigorous societies harbor certain extravagance of objections so that men wander beyond the safe surfeit of personal satisfaction."

Desite improvements that we know are badly needed and should be constantly pressed for in both the public and private sector, there would seem to be no reason to believe that such actions, if taken, would thereby realize the desired future. Perhaps a third force is necessary to accelerate those needed improvements, both directly by its influence on institutions and indirectly by its influence with key individuals in those institutions. It could perform what cannot be performed as well either by the public or the private sector about decisions made now that will determine the long-range future. Further, such a third force is consistent with American history, growing directly from our prolific penchant to form associations.[8]

The Rand Corporation is an up-to-date model for the sort of nonprofit instrument that comes to mind as a means by which institutions or individuals could understand the consequences of various choices in their technological future. The Air Force created Rand for independent policy research on issues too important to leave to the mercy of any one institution, however perfect such an organization might be, since it is constructed of imperfect people. Rand, also constructed with imperfect people, was insulated from direct Air Force control and in a sense asked to argue its own case. This separate but responsive stance is the most critical ingredient of Rand's contribution.[9] Certainly there are peaceful issues concerning future man and his environment too important, too technical, to be left solely to the decision maker who is rewarded and disciplined by short-term dollars and votes and without an adequate public airing of the long as well as short range consequences.

We can envision every major corporation ultimately realizing that it needs access to an independent "think-and-do tank" continuously responsive to its needs but not intimidated by it. Both in-house staff and the sporadic use of consultants have their place, but they cannot fill the third force definition.

There is a similar policy research and development need for the thin, overworked staffs of the U.S. Congress. A "consumers report" analysis on alternative legislative proposals is more and more a necessity as the human meaning of the application of certain technologies becomes more vital. Each area of the federal government, perhaps each agency, each major metropolitan region, the states, all need clear, professionally competent examinations of the consequences of their various choices. Responsive but not dominated by its client(s), these third force institutions must be multidisciplinary, proficient with systems analysis and the computer, but slavish to neither. The comprehensive mission they would be attempting to relate to the onrushing future demands the focus and continuity of work of many different professional, sensibly integrated skills. Fundamentally each such institute would be striving to make science and technology responsive to the will and needs of the individuals it is intended to serve. A major order of communication to those citizens interested would become a critical part of its work, a substantial percentage of the total cost of our public education system.

Many such institutes would be needed also to work for specific geographically definable settlements and, very important, to provide competing knowledge centers. No one institute could be given total responsibility. In the time ahead, even more obviously than now or in the past, knowledge will be power. "Knowledge power" in competition may be the only way to be certain knowledge will serve man without dominating him.

The church itself, insofar as it engages in the great issues of life, would be of this third force.

Two questions remain to answer how such possibilities become third forces. How will they be financed? How will their force be felt? The two are tied to each other.

In financing, the National Science Foundation and National Endowment for the Humanities as well as Rand are examples of the third force. The Public Television Corporation and the Urban Development Institute fathered by the 90th Congress are the two most recent examples. All these were funded by the federal government but in ways insulated from politics. The private foundations are another source of funding. What else have they as important to do? With the greater per capita incomes predicted and greater public communications, individuals will be able to provide effective funding. (The Sierra Club might be cited here.) But let us not forget the private corporations. At this writing a modestly potent ($25 million) foundation to do research into the future is being promoted among the "blue chip" industries. Of much greater significance is the report that U.S. private corporations are using only one eightieth of the 5 percent tax deduction the federal government encourages them to contribute to charitable and nonprofit institutions. Here is a source of funding in the order of billions annually. Wisely used, it could block the spread of government concentrated power into areas where it cannot perform with adequate freedom to be creative—funded 52 percent by the federal government without the usual Congressional appropriations restrictions.[10]

Suppose the third forces are financed, who will feel their force? There is a certain leverage at work in the answer to this question. Besides the institutions to whose decision-making processes the third forces would be most directly related and especially responsive there would be interested, not always innocent, bystanders. In the private enterprise system these bystanders would be the competitors, in government they would be the opposition, in nonprofit and professional circles they would be the "peers."

As in the case of the exceptional foundation-inspired research and action the third force could create and prove out pilot projects as "congenial threats" to existing private and public governments, hoping to be taken over by them.

If the function of the third force is to competently define and communicate basic choices and the alternative consequences, we believe the term *force* would be appropriately used. Already associations attempt this, but too few are free of a pure lobbying function and too many demand that their members be "true believers" of the current party line. Too few are objective, multidisciplinary, or concerned with the long-range as well as immediate effects of their recommendations.

Without the impact of a professional, skilled third force it does not appear that present public and private institutions can be "trusted" to evolve rapidly enough or that current associations are prepared for the technical task ahead. At present "institution breakdown" is evident in the society-saving resolution of social conflicts forced on the Supreme Court that in other days would have come through Congress. There are now, and will be, more complex and more technical issues that cannot appropriately be left to either our present sort of public or private sector, and would be equally inappropriately left to the Supreme Court.

To accomplish new functions, to realize Alan Altshuler's modifications of existing institutions, and to accelerate other modification of short-term marketplace or ballot decision-making, an array of potent new institutions, nonprofit institutions capable of considering the impacts today of the long-range future, should be included when we discuss "New Institutions to Serve the Individual"—the third force.

Notes

1. Herman Kahn states in his paper in *Environment and Change* (Bloomington: Indiana University Press, 1968) that after examining the past one million years "carefully" he could cite only two times comparable to now in the history of man: the agricultural revolution and the industrial revolution. He adds that religious men might cite a third.

2. IBM has put $10 million into the study of the relationship of future technology and society and the future values of society. Even if there is not a vested interest here or a new sort of patron-of-the-arts role, the intended scope in regard to the future is enough to consider this research the exception that proves the rule.

3. Secretary Gardner's HEW Task Force on the Environment, looking fifty years ahead, began November, 1966, and ended June 12, 1967. The Paley Commission, examining our nation's future natural resources, met from January, 1951, to June, 1952. Laurance Rockefeller's Outdoor Recreation Resources Review Commission surveyed national statistics and commissioned papers concerning future recreation needs from 1959 to 1961.

4. (Using the term generation to mean thirty-three years.) At the recent Cities of Tomorrow conference (December 10-11, 1967), at which six U.S. cabinet officers were host, Secretary of Agriculture Orville Freeman raised the question of a national policy for development of this nation that took into account the other 95 percent of the nation, which is the open land, but the conference speakers did not focus on this potential for solution to future urban problems.

5. (Using the term to mean 5 to 7 years.) The average time major corporation chief executives are in their top job has been estimated at six years by a 1956 Fortune study of 900 executives from large firms; NICB study of 191 chairmen and presidents in 1966 found 75 percent had been in their present position for seven years or less.

6. TVA was initiated May 18, 1933. Its closest version, the basically different federal-state region, began with the definition of the Appalachian Regional Commission that was authorized in 1965.

7. See this article, "The New Factor in American Society," *Environment and Change* (Bloomington: Indiana University Press, 1968), and his recent book, *Power in America: The Politics of the New Class* (New York: New American Library, 1967). See also J. Kenneth Galbraith's technostructure in *The New Industrial State* (Boston: Houghton Mifflin, 1967).

8. "The Americans of all ages, all conditions and all dispositions constantly form associations. They have not only commercial and manufacturing companies in which all take part but associations of a thousand other kinds, religious, moral, serious, futile, restricted, enormous, or diminutive. The Americans make associations to give entertainments, to found establishments for education, to send missionaries to the antipodes. Wherever at the head of some new undertaking you see the government of France or a man of rank in England, in the United States you will be sure to find an association." (Alexis de Tocqueville)

9. Back in the 1930's, Alfred Sloan built into General Motors at the vice president level semi-independent, forward-looking staffs to advise corporate level decision makers. The semi-independence grew mainly from Sloan's concept of giving a man enough rope to either hang himself or grow into a resourceful executive. This advisory staff is a significant part of the fly-wheel system that has kept GM on its course to world dominance, but who would say that society's needs have been adequately represented in their advice?

10. *The New York Times Magazine*, November 12, 1967.

Program of the Washington Conference

Appendix: Program of Washington Conference

MONDAY

Opening Presentation
Creating the Future Environment—The Next Fifty Years

Host's Welcome, HARLAND BARTHOLOMEW, AIP
Why It Makes Sense to Look Fifty Years Ahead, BERTRAND DE JOUVENEL
The Role of Art, Spirit, Science, and Technology in Creating the Future
Environment, HAROLD TAYLOR, JOSEPH SITTLER, JOHN R. PLATT, RALPH
G. H. SIU, CHARLES A. BLESSING, AIP, presiding

457

Afternoon Presentation
Prologue to the Future

The Culture of American Cities; The History of American Physical Planning; The Development of Administrative and Political Planning in America, JOHN E. BURCHARD, CARL FEISS, AIP, ROBERT C. WOOD, in discussion with JOHN A. KOUWENHOVEN, LEON N. WEINER, VICTOR GRUEN, Affiliate AIP, GRADY CLAY, FREDERICK H. BAIR, JR., AIP, presiding

Evening Presentation
A Future Filled with Change

Technology; Population Concentrations; The Expectations of American Youth, HERMAN KAHN, EMMANUEL G. MESTHENE, CARL OGLESBY, CLAUDE BROWN, in discussion with MAX LERNER, ROBERT THEOBALD, STANLEY B. TANKEL, AIP, presiding

TUESDAY

Morning Presentation
The Future American Society

The Necessity and Difficulty of Planning the Future Society; The New Factor in American Society, GUNNAR MYRDAL, DAVID T. BAZELON, in discussion with J. V. LANGMEAD CASSERLEY, RICHARD L. CUTLER, JAMES W. ROUSE, JOHN T. HOWARD, AIP, presiding

Afternoon Presentation
The Future Role of the Individual

The Individual, Not the Mass; The Renaissance Man of the Future, AUGUST HECKSCHER, SIR GEOFFREY VICKERS, in discussion with BARNABY C. KEENEY, RICHARD E. FARSON, ROBERT JUNGK, C. DAVID LOEKS, AIP, presiding

WEDNESDAY

Morning Special Event
New Towns Tour

A bus and walking tour to examine the plans, designs, progress, and potential of Reston, Virginia, and Columbia, Maryland.

Evening Banquet
The American Institute of Planners' Fiftieth-Year Citations Banquet

The Future Man, PIERRE BERTAUX
Citations presented by JOHN T. HOWARD, AIP, STEPHEN A. KAUFMAN, AIP, presiding

THURSDAY

Morning Presentation
The Urgent and the Important

Policy Recommendations Concerning the Great Social Issues—Minorities, Leisure, Education, Health, BAYARD RUSTIN, SEBASTIAN DE GRAZIA, ROBERT M. HUTCHINS, WILLIAM H. STEWART, in discussion with GERHARD COIM, JACQUELINE GRENNAN, BERTRAND DE JOUVENAL, MARTIN MEYERSON, AIP, presiding

Afternoon Presentations
Creating a New Standard of Life, with Man as the Measure

The contribution to be made through housing, CHARLES ABRAMS, AIP, GEORGE CANDILIS, in discussion with HEIKKI VON HERTZEN, JACK MELTZER, AIP, WILLIAM L. SLAYTON, P. I. PRENTICE, presiding
The contribution to be made through transportation, MAX L. FELDMAN, CHARLES M. HAAR, in discussion with HARMER DAVIS, ALAN ALTSHULER, ALAN VOORHEES, AIP, COLIN D. BUCHANAN, presiding
The contribution to be made through urban form, KEVIN LYNCH, AIP, JACOB BAKEMA, in discussion with CALVIN S. HAMILTON, AIP, DANIEL R. MANDELKER, GIBSON WINTER, GERD ALBERS, presiding

FRIDAY

Morning Presentation
A Nation's Policy for Its Future

A Statement by the President of the American Institute of Planners, IRVING HAND
National Development Policy; Research for Choice; Natural Resources; New Incentives and Controls; New Institutions to Serve the Individual, LYLE C. FITCH, HERBERT A. SIMON, JOSEPH L. FISHER, in discussion with KERMIT GORDON, DESMOND HEAP, ORVILLE L. FREEMAN, HENRY FAGIN, AIP, presiding

Concluding Presentation
Context of the Future—Youth, Technology, and the World

Technology and the Underdeveloped World; The People Build with Their Hands; The Hope There Is in People, RENATO SEVERINO, JOHN TURNER, ANN SCHRAND, concluding statement and discussion with BUCKMINSTER FULLER, WILLIAM L. C. WHEATON, AIP, presiding

Epilogue—Mood for Development, WILLIAM L. C. WHEATON